Stochastic Optimal Control, International Finance, and Debt Crises

Stochastic Optimal Control, International Finance, and Debt Crises

Jerome L. Stein

OXFORD

UNIVERSITY PRESS

OXFORD

UNIVERSITY PRESS

Great Clarendon Street, Oxford OX2 6DP

Oxford University Press is a department of the University of Oxford.
It furthers the University's objective of excellence in research, scholarship,
and education by publishing worldwide in

Oxford New York

Auckland Cape Town Dar es Salaam Hong Kong Karachi
Kuala Lumpur Madrid Melbourne Mexico City Nairobi
New Delhi Shanghai Taipei Toronto

With offices in

Argentina Austria Brazil Chile Czech Republic France Greece
Guatemala Hungary Italy Japan Poland Portugal Singapore
South Korea Switzerland Thailand Turkey Ukraine Vietnam

Oxford is a registered trade mark of Oxford University Press
in the UK and in certain other countries

Published in the United States
by Oxford University Press Inc., New York

© Jerome L. Stein, 2006

British Library Cataloguing in Publication Data

Data available

Library of Congress Cataloging in Publication Data

Data available

Typeset by Newgen Imaging Systems (P) Ltd., Chennai, India
Printed in Great Britain
on acid-free paper by
Biddles Ltd., King's Lynn, Norfolk

ISBN 0–19–928057–6   978–0–19–928057–5

10 9 8 7 6 5 4 3 2 1

Preface

This book focuses on the interaction between equilibrium real exchange rates, optimal debt, endogenous optimal growth and current account balances, in a world of uncertainty. The theoretical parts result from interdisciplinary research between economics and applied mathematics. The *raison d'être* of this research is to develop analytical tools that can explain and evaluate trends in real exchange rates, and provide theoretically based warning signals of currency and debt crises.

There is great concern about the current account deficits that the United States has been running for nearly a quarter of a century, and which have been increasing as a fraction of the GDP. Controversial subjects are: what is an "optimal" ratio of external debt/GDP and are the current account deficits/GDP causes for concern? What are the effects – upon the value of the dollar and vulnerability of the United States economy to external shocks – of debt ratios and current account deficit ratios that exceed the "optimum" levels? Although the current account deficit/GDP ratio has been large and growing, so far the real value of the dollar has not appeared to suffer significant ill effects, despite recurrent dire warnings of a catastrophe.

These are difficult and controversial subjects because a rational discussion of what is "sustainable" or optimal must recognize that there is uncertainty concerning the future rates of return on capital, interest rates, and exchange rates. The current analytical techniques based upon perfect foresight or certainty equivalence have led to false predictions. The only way to answer these questions objectively is to have an analytical framework that explicitly takes the uncertainty into account, and can be applied to available data. This is why the techniques of stochastic optimal control and dynamic programming developed by mathematicians must be integral parts of the theoretical framework. Explicit operational equations are thereby obtained for optimal values, against which we compare the observed values of the external debt and current account. The *stochastic optimal control* analysis is applied to evaluate the United States current account deficits and to explain the default crises in the emerging market countries.

The advent of the euro, the enlargement of the euro area to include the transition economies of Eastern Europe and the currency and debt crises in South-East Asia and Latin America have also posed challenges to economists. What analytical tools can explain trends in real exchange rates and evaluate whether existing exchange rates are "equilibrium" or sustainable?

How should one read this book?

This book is organized into four parts. The first section consists of Chapter 1, which is an overview of the entire book. It is a non-technical, self-contained presentation that effectively is a "review article". The rest is organized into three parts, and the reader can either proceed systematically or selectively.

Part II presents the theoretical and mathematical framework used throughout the book. Chapters 2 and 3 develop stochastic optimal control techniques needed to derive equations for optimal external debt, endogenous growth, consumption, and capital. The challenge arises because the key variables (the rate of return on capital, interest rate, and exchange rates) are stochastic and hence unpredictable. Chapter 4 presents the underlying economic framework of the natural real exchange rate (or NATREX) model.

The remaining sections contain a series of empirical applications of the theories developed in Part II. These chapters can be read independently of the material in Part II, as the required theoretical material developed in Part II is summarized and presented graphically in each of these chapters.

The first of the applied parts, Part III, provides a couple of examples of how the NATREX model has been used to evaluate trends in real exchange rates. Chapter 5 uses the NATREX model to evaluate trends in the euro exchange rate. The focus in Chapter 6 is to use the NATREX model to evaluate trends in the exchange rates of the transition countries – primarily Hungary and the Czech Republic.

Finally, Part IV provides a series of applications of a model which look at external debt issues and exchange rate crises. Chapter 7 is an application of stochastic optimal control to explain and provide theoretically based early warning signals of default risk for the emerging market countries. Chapter 8 applies both the NATREX theory of equilibrium exchange rates and stochastic optimal control to explain the Asian crises of 1997–8.

It asks, to what extent were the crises in the different countries due to misaligned exchange rates – where the real exchange rate deviated from the NATREX – and to what extent were they due to external debts that exceeded the optimum levels? Finally, Chapter 9 uses the stochastic optimal control analysis developed in Chapter 3 to evaluate the optimality and sustainability of the United States' external debt and current account deficits.

What led to the writing of this book?

This book represents an amalgamation of several strands of my research and the history of this research effort is relevant for understanding the approaches taken in the book and how they differ from the literature. The first area of research is *equilibrium real exchange rates*. In about 1990, Polly R. Allen (University of Connecticut) and I realized that the standard theories of exchange rates featured in the journals and graduate textbooks were unable to explain the trends in exchange rates since 1973. The dominant theories in the literature were based upon purchasing power parity (PPP) and short-run monetary models. At that time James Boughton at the International Monetary Fund wrote: "What do we know about the determinants of exchange rates? 'Precious little' would be a common and not unjustified answer among economists in this field."

We developed a different approach focusing upon trends in "equilibrium" real exchange rates, when there are neither deflationary nor inflationary pressures, rather than upon their short-run variations. Liliane Crouhy-Veyrac (HEC, France) realized that our "equilibrium" real exchange rate is analogous to Wicksell's "natural rate of interest" and named our theory NATREX. The NATREX is a central tendency where the actual rate is heading, when there are neither deflationary nor inflationary pressures, no changes in reserves and when there is external portfolio balance. The difference between the actual real exchange rate and the NATREX is due to speculative capital movements based upon anticipations or to cyclical phenomena. They average out to zero but have considerable variance. We explain the trends of the real exchange rate in this dynamic stock-flow model by real fundamental determinants. They are relative productivity and thrift/time preference. Our book, *Fundamental Determinants of Exchange Rates*, Oxford, 1995, launched NATREX.

In 1994, John Williamson edited a book '*Estimating Equilibrium Exchange Rates*' which brought both his Fundamental Equilibrium Real Exchange Rate (FEER) and our NATREX to the attention of a wider audience. Neither of us accepts the PPP hypothesis because it is unduly restrictive and lacks explanatory power. Although our approaches are different, we both follow a theme of Ragnar Nurske that concentrates upon moving equilibrium real exchange rates, which are associated with both internal and external balance[1]. Williamson's approach is normative whereas the NATREX is positive economics in a dynamic context.

Europeans realized very quickly that the NATREX is an operational model with considerable potential. At the time, there was an active discussion of the French Franc/Deutsche Mark exchange rate and causes of the European exchange rate crises. Moreover, the establishment of the euro as a European currency was seen on the horizon. There was considerable interest in understanding what are the determinants of equilibrium real exchange rates, and what factors will determine the "strength" of the currency in the medium to longer run? Liliane Crouhy-Veyrac (HEC, France) and Michèle Saint Marc (Banque de France) organized a conference jointly with the Bundesbank, whose chief economist at the time was Otmar Issing. The theme of the conference was the explanatory power of the NATREX model for the major European economies. The French and the Germans were the first groups attracted to NATREX. Just before the advent of the euro, the European Central Bank (ECB) invited me to talk about applications of the NATREX model. Otmar Issing became the chief economist of the ECB. The euro exchange rate was the key topic of discussion. I was asked: "If you were Director of Research at the ECB, what research agenda would you propose?" My response was that I would divide my group into teams/subgroups where each would have the same objective: what theories can explain the history from 1973 to 1999 of a "synthetic" euro, which is a weighted average of the currencies that will constitute the euro? Each group would use the same data but different economic theories, derived from the literature in journals and graduate textbooks. One would then compare the explanatory power of the theories. On that basis, one would decide which is the most useful theory to explain what determines medium to longer term trends in the euro.

A year or so later, the ECB sent me a series of papers that did exactly what I had suggested. Among other methods, the researchers applied an eclectic-econometric approach and the NATREX model. The former was not based upon an explicit theory, nor did it contain an economic transmission mechanism that could explain how real determinants

---

[1] See Driver and Westaway, "Concepts of equilibrium exchange rates", in Driver et al. (ed.) *Exchange Rates, Capital Flows and Policy*, Routledge, 2005, for an analytic survey of the literature.

operate in the medium to long run to produce the observed trends. It was an eclectic search for a cointegrating equation. The NATREX model, however, comes with a story – a dynamic stock-flow analysis, which explains medium to longer term trends in the real exchange rate in terms of real, objectively measured fundamentals.

Carsten Detken, Carmen Marin, Alistair Dieppe, Jérôme Henry, and Frank Smets, at the ECB and Romain Duval (Université Paris, Panthéon-Sorbonne) applied the NATREX model to explain the synthetic euro. Their research was published in 2002. With the enlargement of the euro area, the Eastern European countries were concerned with what is an equilibrium real exchange rate for their countries. The Central Banks wanted to avoid the problems that economic unification produced for eastern Germany, whose real exchange rate was overvalued. Economists at the central bank of the Czech Republic and Hungary were attracted to the NATREX model because it was important to evaluate what are the fundamental determinants of their equilibrium exchange rates and to understand the transmission mechanism. They realized that standard models based upon PPP or monetary models lacked explanatory power, as noted by Boughton above. These two Eastern European central banks published papers showing to what extent the NATREX model could explain the trends in the real exchange rates in their countries and could provide a basis for the effects of policies upon the equilibrium real exchange rate.

Economists at central banks and academic economists in Western and Eastern Europe, Asia and Latin American were attracted to the NATREX model, because it is a *theoretically based dynamic stock-flow model that is operational*: it is directly applicable to publicly available data.

My second area of research started upon my retirement from the economics department, when I was invited by the Division of Applied Mathematics (DAM) in 1997 to become a long-term visiting professor/research. My relation with the DAM has a long history. During the period 1968–80, Ettore (Jim) Infante of the DAM and I worked together using dynamic programming and related mathematical techniques to derive optimal growth in a system where there was not perfect knowledge of the basic relations. The existing literature on optimal growth was based upon the Maximum Principle, which requires perfect knowledge and foresight. Using dynamic programming, we developed a suboptimal feedback control that just used current measurements of observable variables and which would lead the economy to the unknown and possibly changing optimal steady state. We also wrote papers concerning fiscal policy in a growing economy and the government budget constraint. Jim was my mentor for many years. Our long collaboration was fruitful and stimulating interdisciplinary research.

When I migrated to the DAM, Wendell Fleming and I started a collaboration concerning the application of stochastic optimal control/ dynamic programming (SOC/DP) to international finance. The rationale for this research is that in international finance the return on investment, the rate of interest, and the exchange rate are all stochastic variables. Sensible optimization cannot be done on the basis of models that assume perfect foresight or certainty equivalence[2].

In addition to his many contributions to pure mathematics, Wendell is one of the key figures in stochastic optimal control, dynamic programming, and mathematical finance. The techniques of SOC/DP are basic tools used by mathematicians who publish in journals devoted to mathematical finance; however these techniques are not well known to economists, even though Robert Merton's book uses them extensively.

After many years of hard work where we learned from each other, we published several articles using the techniques of SOC/DP to explain optimal growth, debt, current account deficits, and debt crises in the stochastic environment. The key variables: the return on capital, interest rate, and exchange rates, have both deterministic and stochastic, unpredictable, components.

There were two reactions to our work: one from mathematicians and the other from economists. Mathematicians are eager to see applications of their elegant mathematics. I was therefore invited to give papers at conferences of mathematicians concerned with stochastic processes and optimization. These led to my first two published papers in mathematics (American Mathematical Society and the World Congress of Nonlinear Analysis).

The reaction of economists to our published article in the *Journal of Banking and Finance* (2004) was that it is "very high tech" and daunting. Our challenge was to show how it relates directly to economic policy. This was a challenge that had to be met.

In an article written in 2001 with Giovanna Paladino (San Paolo/IMI, Rome), we applied the SOC approach to explain country default risk in the emerging market countries. This is the substance of Chapter 7. The Bank for International Settlements and the Banque de France invited me to

---

[2] See the discussion of the literature presented in the excellent graduate textbook by Giancarlo Gandolfo, *International Finance and Open Economy Macro-economics*, Springer, 2001.

speak on that paper, since these institutions are directly involved in evaluating country default risk.

The second response was in an article written with Guay Lim (University of Melbourne) on the Asian crises, which was published in 2004. We synthesized the NATREX model of equilibrium exchange rates and the SOC/DP model of optimal and excessive external debt to derive early warning signals of crises. This is the substance of Chapter 8.

The third response to the economists' challenge is the last chapter. The literature could not arrive at any logically compelling, quantitative, and objective evaluation of whether the United States' current account deficits are sustainable and whether they are leading the US to a serious crisis. In Chapter 3, we derive an equation for the optimum debt ratio and explain how the deviation of the actual debt from the optimal debt increases the vulnerability of the economy to shocks. In the last chapter, we apply the equations derived from the SOC/DP analysis of Chapter 3 to provide quantitative estimates of the deviation of the actual from the optimal current account deficit. These equations permit one to see the sensitivity of the results to alternative estimation of the parameters.

Theoretical chapters in Part II and the application Parts III and IV are integrated and synergistic. The rationale for the theory and mathematics is the fruitfulness of the applications; and the way to evaluate the logic of the applications is to understand the theoretical foundations.

Many people have read and criticized earlier drafts of the chapters in this book. I thank the following for their excellent advice and suggestions: Peter Clark, TEAM-CNRS Université Paris I Panthéon-Sorbonne, Jérôme Hericourt, Karlhans Sauernheimer, Christoph Fischer Jan Frait, Peter Karadi Kirsten Lommatzsch, Rebecca Driver, Balázs Égert, Palle Andersen, Barry Goss, John Williamson, Ettore Infante, Otmar Issing, Catherine Mann, George Borts and Giancarlo Gandolfo. Foremost, I thank Wendell Fleming for leading me into a world that I never knew existed until we started our collaboration. Much of this book is based upon our joint work, and many of the insights in this book come from him. Finally, I thank the faculty and secretaries in the Division of Applied Mathematics for their hospitality and encouragement. I am dedicating this book to Hadassah, my wife and best friend.

Jerome L. Stein
Division of Applied Mathematics
Brown University
Providence, Summer 2005

Contents

List of Figures

List of Tables

Part I

Overview

1

Optimal debt and equilibrium exchange rates in a stochastic environment: an overview

This overview chapter explains in general terms the relevance and the contributions of this book to economic theory and policy. The economic theory and mathematics developed in Chapters 2 and 3 derive *benchmarks* for the optimal debt in an environment where both the return on capital and the real rate of interest are stochastic variables. The equilibrium real exchange rate, the subject of Chapter 4, is where the real exchange rate is heading. These benchmarks are applied in Chapters 5 through 9 to answer the following questions.

- What is a theoretically based empirical measure of a "misaligned" exchange rate that increases the probability of a significant depreciation a currency crisis?
- What is a theoretically based empirical measure of an "excess" debt that increases the probability of a debt crisis?
- What is the interaction between an excess debt and a misaligned exchange rate?

Several historical examples indicate the significance of these questions. Then we sketch how the analytical tools developed in Part II are applied in Parts III and IV to answer these questions in a stochastic environment, where the return on capital and real interest rate are not predictable.

In July 1997, the economies of East Asia became embroiled in one of the worst financial crises of the postwar period. Yet, prior to the crisis, these economies were seen as models of economic growth experiencing sustained growth rates that exceeded those earlier thought unattainable. Similarly, in 1998, the financial markets, the economics profession, and the International Monetary Fund viewed Argentina as a model of stability and growth. In 2001–2 the Argentine economy defaulted on its huge debt.

Why did the financial markets, the International Monetary Fund, the World Bank and the bond rating agencies fail to anticipate the crises? In 2004, the International Monetary Fund Independent Evaluation Office IEO published a report that reviewed why and how, despite the Fund's extensive involvement with Argentina, the Fund was not able to help Argentina prevent and better manage the crisis. The primary purpose of the (IEO) evaluation is to draw lessons for the Fund in its future operational work.

The IEO report stated (pp. 22–3) that there is a general agreement that a combination of several external and internal factors contributed to the crisis: a weak fiscal policy, a rigid exchange rate regime, and vulnerability to adverse external shocks. The IEO could not isolate the relative importance of these factors. "In the absence of the underlying vulnerability... the same adverse developments would not have had the catastrophic effects that were associated with the crisis, though they may well have produced some negative effects."

The factors underlying vulnerability must be given precise theoretical meaning with associated operational measures, to evaluate their explanatory power. The objective is to arrive at theoretically justified early warning signals, based upon available information. The main reasons for the failures to anticipate balance of payments and debt crises were that the theories were based upon deterministic models, which ignored uncertainty, or that the theoretical tools were unduly limited in scope. For example, the most frequently used method to evaluate whether an exchange rate was misaligned was to compare the exchange rate with its Purchasing Power Parity (PPP) value. The PPP hypothesis assumes that the "equilibrium" real exchange rate is constant, but it does not provide a theory to explain what is the equilibrium real exchange rate. Moreover, this hypothesis lacks explanatory power[1]. Empirical measures to estimate overvaluation compared the real exchange rate to its trend value[2]. These eclectic empirical measures just add a trend to the PPP but cannot explain if an appreciation of the real exchange rate is a sign of strength or weakness in the balance of payments.

The most widely used measures of excess debt, which may lead to a debt crisis, focus upon two variables: (i) the ratio of debt/GDP that would result

---

[1] See Breuer (1994), MacDonald and Stein (1999), and Duval (2002).
[2] See Kaminsky and Reinhart (1999).

if current policies continued into the future; (ii) the trade balance/GDP that would keep the debt/GDP ratio equal to its current ratio. It is hypothesized that the higher the number, the more likely it is that there would be a debt problem. Empirical researchers concluded that these measures lacked explanatory power.

Since both measures of overvalued exchange rates and excess debt or debt burden were inadequate, the implied early warning signals were unreliable. A question that is relevant for policy is: what are theoretically based, operational early warning signals that have explanatory power? One motive in writing this book is to answer this question.

Two theoretical tools are developed in this book. The analytical tool to estimate and explain the "equilibrium" real exchange rate is the NATREX model, an acronym for the **nat**ural **r**eal **ex**change rate. This is positive economics. The analytical tool to derive the optimal external debt/net worth and expected growth rate in an environment where both the productivity of capital and the real interest rate are unpredictable is stochastic optimal control dynamic programming (SOC/DP). This is normative economics. Both are benchmarks of performance. We then explain the interaction between misaligned exchange rates and excess debt that increases the probability of crises.

Equilibrium exchange rates and sustainable debts are not only relevant to the emerging markets, but also to the United States, the euro area and to enlargement of the euro area. The United States current account has been deeply in deficit in recent years. The growing negative net investment position leads to the question: how sustainable is the US current account deficit and associated inflow of capital? Is the US debt ratio excessive relative to the derived optimal debt ratio? What is the dynamic interaction between the real value of the dollar and current account deficits?

The real value of the euro relative to the US dollar has fluctuated drastically since its inception. A frequently discussed question is whether the value of the US dollar/euro has been "misaligned", and what are the effects of policies in the US or in Europe upon the exchange rate? A benchmark, the "equilibrium" real exchange rate, is required to answer this question.

The Central and Eastern European Countries (CEEC) are planning to join the European Monetary Union. These countries must establish the nominal values of their currencies upon entering the Exchange Rate Mechanism (ERM II). How should one evaluate the appropriateness of their nominal and real exchange rates? In the last 10 years, the real values of their currencies measured in terms of *tradable goods* have been appreciating relative to the euro. A correctly chosen exchange rate is a prerequisite for avoiding the depressing effects that occurred with German reunification. An overvalued exchange rate hinders real growth, leads to sustained current account deficits and a large external debt. These factors could lead to either a debt crisis or a currency crisis. If the CEEC run into financial difficulties then, unlike the Eastern part of Germany which has been supported by the Western part, their debts will not be forgiven by the other members. There is an explicit "no bail-out" clause in the Maastricht treaty (article 104b) that the CEEC signed when entering the EU. Moreover, if the exchange rate "disequilibrium" is sufficiently great, these countries may be forced to exit from the peg. An undervalued exchange rate would generate inflationary pressures that would violate the Maastricht criteria for entry into ERM II. We use the NATREX model developed in chapter four to evaluate what is an equilibrium exchange rate and to explain the appreciation of the real exchange rates of the CEEC: do they reflect strengths or are they Warning Signals of currency or debt crises? This question cannot be answered if "misalignment" is measured as the deviation of the real exchange rate from its trend.

The optimality analysis is based upon state of the art techniques of stochastic optimal control/dynamic programming (SOC/DP). The reasons for using these techniques are that optimization involves intertemporal decisions. Current decisions not only affect current welfare, but they also have consequences for future welfare. The future is unpredictable, so that the optimal controls or decisions made at any instant should enter as feedback functions of the currently observable state.

The dynamic programming/stochastic optimal control techniques are widely used in the mathematical finance literature published in applied mathematics journals[3], but are not widely used by economists. The stochastic optimal control techniques that we use to derive the optimal debt are quite technical. An attractive feature of our analysis of the optimal long-term debt and expected endogenous growth is that we are able to show how the SOC/DP equations can be understood in terms of the Tobin–Markowitz mean variance (M–V) approach to portfolio selection[4]. Thereby a relatively intuitive and graphic explanation – based upon the M-V techniques known to economists – can be given for the mathematical results.

---

[3] See American Mathematical Society, Contemporary Mathematics, Mathematics of Finance (2004). Merton's book on continuous time finance uses these techniques extensively.

[4] Tobin developed the M-V analysis in 1952, several years before its publication, when I was a student in his graduate class in macroeconomics. That is why I dedicated the Fleming–Stein (2004) paper in his memory.

1.1. Summary of the theme and contributions

The subject of this book is equilibrium real exchange rates, optimal external debt and their interaction. Our contributions can be summarized.

An explicit growth model is specified that explains how the real exchange rate and the external debt are affected by the exogenous and control/policy variables. A "story"/scenario is an integral part of the analysis.

Our equilibrium exchange rate, which is associated with internal and external balance, is called the natural real exchange rate (NATREX), because it is in the spirit of Wicksell's natural rate of interest. The medium-run NATREX is a flow equilibrium, which is similar to the equilibrium concept used by Ragnar Nurske and John Williamson[5]. The NATREX extends their work by developing the dynamics of capital and external debt. There is a trajectory from the medium-run to the long-run NATREX, where there are both flow equilibrium and stock equilibrium.

The equilibrium real exchange rate can be written as $R[Z(t)]$, where a rise is an appreciation and $Z(t)$ is a vector of measurable exogenous and control/policy real fundamentals that may vary over time. Misalignment $\phi(t) = R(t) - R[Z(t)]$ is the difference between the actual real exchange rate $R(t)$ and the NATREX. Explicit empirical measures of "misalignment" and "excessive debt" are derived from the theory.

The actual exchange rate differs from the NATREX because of speculative, cyclical, and other ephemeral influences with zero expectations, but considerable variance. The real exchange rate converges to a band that contains the NATREX. Specifically, the trends in the NATREX explain the trends in the real exchange rate. This tells us which way the exchange rate is going. If measured misalignment overvaluation $\Phi(t) > 0$ is "sufficiently" large and sustained, a significant depreciation or a currency crisis is likely to occur. Similarly, if there is a significant undervaluation $\Phi(t) < 0$ and a pegged nominal exchange rate, then there will be significant inflationary pressure.

Currency and debt crises occur because actual behavior is not optimal. The subject of *optimal* debt, current account, and endogenous growth concerns intertemporal decision making. The theoretical literature uses the Maximum Principle of Pontryagin or the Intertemporal Budget Constraint (IBC) to derive intertemporal optimality conditions[6]. The

---

[5] See Driver and Westaway (2005) on concepts of equilibrium exchange rates.

[6] Gandolfo (2001) and Turnovsky (2000) review the literature. Infante and Stein (1973) showed that this literature requires perfect knowledge and certainty, and showed that dynamic programming is a very much better method to derive intertemporal optimality conditions.

Maximum Principle is based upon perfect certainty. The trajectory to the steady state is unique, so that there is saddle-point instability if there are any errors, however slight. The IBC constrains the present value of consumption to equal the present value of GDP over an infinite horizon[7]. This literature is based upon certainty equivalence. Because the future GDP and interest rates are unpredictable, the present value of GDP over an infinite horizon, the IBC, is unknowable. The IBC is not operational and not enforceable. There is no feedback control mechanism to correct errors, which are certain to occur.

Instead, the techniques of stochastic optimal control/dynamic programming SOC/DP are used in this book to derive "intertemporal optimization". We derive the optimal external debt/net worth, capital/net worth, consumption/net worth and the optimal endogenous expected growth rate in a stochastic environment.

The optimal debt/net worth f^* or capital/net worth, derived from the SOC/DP analysis, is measurable for any arbitrary risk aversion. An excessive debt $\Psi_t = f_t - f^*_t$ is the deviation of the actual debt ratio f_t from f^*_t the optimal ratio. Generally the excess debt is produced by government budget deficits.

The greater the measured excessive debt Ψ_t the lower the expected growth rate of consumption and the higher its variance. It is therefore the more likely that random external shocks will lead to a debt default, rather than to a drastic decline in consumption.

The two types of crises are interrelated. A depreciation of the currency increases the real external debt burden, which raises the probability of a debt crisis. A debt burden adversely affects the current account and capital flows, which exert pressure on the exchange rate. We give precision to the concept of "vulnerability" to adverse developments on the basis of two theoretically based measures:

Excess debt $\Psi_t = f_t - f^*_t > 0 \Rightarrow$ probability of debt crisis increases;

Misalignment $\Phi_t = R_t - R[Z_t] > 0 \Rightarrow$ probability of currency crisis increases;

Interaction Probability of currency crisis $\Leftrightarrow$ Probability of debt crisis.

1.2. A guided tour

A "guided tour" highlights some of our contributions with specific examples. It starts with the NATREX model of equilibrium exchange rates. A measure of misalignment is Φ_t derived based upon this model. The

---

[7] The work of Obstfeld and Rogoff (1996) is based upon the IBC.

relation between the Purchasing Power Parity hypothesis and the NATREX is explained. An example shows how the NATREX model explains the medium to longer run movements in the real exchange rate of the dollar-synthetic Euro.

The second part of the guided tour is the analyses of both optimal short-term and long-term external debt. A measure of excess debt Ψ_t is derived in each case. Early warning signals of a debt crisis, derived from the theoretical analyses, are given for emerging markets and Latin America. The discussion of the United States' external debt and current account deficits, which is the subject of the last chapter, is not included in this guided tour.

1.3. Equilibrium exchange rates and misalignment

An equilibrium[8] exchange rate is where the exchange rate is heading. The concept and measure of the equilibrium exchange rate depends upon the time horizon and the underlying model. Several reasons have been cited in the literature[9], why it is important to estimate equilibrium exchange rates. First, there are significant and sustained movements in exchange rates. For example, see Figure 5.1 that graphs the US dollar/euro exchange rate. These movements affect the competitiveness of the economies and their macroeconomic stability. One wants to know whether these movements are ephemeral or whether they are responding to "real fundamentals"[10]. This information is important because the answer has implications for rational macroeconomic policy and for rational investment decisions. If the depreciation of an exchange rate is due to a depreciation of its equilibrium value, then exchange market intervention or a restrictive monetary policy designed to offset the depreciation is counterproductive.

Second, in the case of monetary unions such as the euro area, it is important to know how a potential entrant should select its exchange rate. An "overvalued" rate will depress growth and produce problems such as beset the eastern part of Germany. An "undervalued" rate will generate

---

[8] It is not edifying to say that at every moment of time the exchange rate is determined by supply and demand, unless one can explicitly explain in terms of measurable variables what are their determinants and their evolution over time.

[9] See, for example, the analytical survey article by Driver and Westaway (2005).

[10] The current controversy about the Chinese exchange rate revolves around the questions: what will be the effects of floating or a revaluation? What is the equilibrium exchange rate for China?

inflationary pressures. The measure of "overvaluation" and "undervaluation" must contain an explicit measure of an "equilibrium" real exchange rate.

Our emphasis is upon the equilibrium *real* exchange rate. It is defined as the nominal exchange rate times relative prices. In an adjustable peg regime, the nominal exchange rate is fixed and the actual real exchange rate varies due to changes in relative prices. In a floating exchange rate regime, both the nominal exchange rate and relative prices can lead to adjustments in the actual real rate. The only difference from our point of view is that the adjustment of the actual real exchange rate to the equilibrium will be faster when the exchange rate floats, because the nominal exchange rate is more flexible than relative prices.

A widely used approach in the literature is to "explain" the exchange rate by the uncovered interest rate parity theory (UIRP)[11]. It states that the anticipated appreciation of the exchange rate is equal to the anticipated interest rate differentials over a period of a given length. There are several limitations of this approach. First: the UIRP equation concerns the change in the exchange rate but does not contain any information concerning where the exchange rate is heading. As Driver and Westaway (2005) state, the exchange rate at any given time t will jump around to adjust to any change in either the anticipated exchange rate at some future date $t + h$ or to any change in anticipated interest rate differentials over the interval $(t, t + h)$. The UIRP theory *per se* has no anchor.

Second: for the theory to have significance one must tie down the anchors. One anchor must be the "equilibrium" exchange rate and the second must be the path of the interest rates. This is not done in the UIRP theory.

Third: the theory states that the interest rate differential at time t is a good and unbiased predictor of the subsequent change in the exchange rate. The "tests" of the theory generally relate ex-post changes in the exchange rate to the previous interest rate differentials. In general, the results of these tests are not encouraging. The interest rate differential has the incorrect sign and is unsuccessful in predicting exchange rate movements[12].

For these reasons, authors who are interested in explaining exchange rates focus upon the anchor, the equilibrium exchange rate – where the exchange rate is heading. Then the theory of UIRP has structure. The

[11] See MacDonald (1999, pp. 36–8) and Driver and Westaway (2005 Section 4.1) for critiques of this theory. See Stein and Paladino (1997) for a critique of the literature.

[12] A large literature is devoted to "rationalizing" the failure of the UIRP theory but does not test their conjectures in an objective manner.

actual exchange rate at time t is equal to the present value of the equilibrium exchange rate, where the discount factor is the interest rate differential. There are two types of candidates for the equilibrium exchange rate. One is Purchasing Power Parity (PPP), which assumes that the equilibrium real exchange rate is a constant. As mentioned above, this hypothesis is unimpressive as an explanation of the anchor[13].

The other candidate is an equilibrium real exchange rate that depends upon time-varying real, measurable "fundamentals"[14]. This has led to the literature of "equilibrium exchange rates", which was given great impetus by John Williamson's influential book (1994). The logic of this approach goes back to Ragnar Nurske's article. The "equilibrium" exchange rate is the exchange rate that is associated with both external and internal balance. Anticipations, speculative capital movements, and changes in reserves are excluded from the concept of an *equilibrium* exchange rate, which is where the exchange rate is heading. The NATREX model of equilibrium exchange rates generalizes the work of Williamson and Nurske. It is a neoclassical growth model, whose underlying equations are based upon intertemporal optimization by the private sector, but not the government whose decisions are political.

The NATREX explains the fundamental determinants of the medium-run equilibrium and the dynamic trajectory to the long-run equilibrium. In the medium-run equilibrium there are both internal and external balances. In both the medium run and longer run the NATREX equilibrium real exchange rate satisfies equation (1.1) below, subject to constraints. The *constraints* are that there is *internal balance*, where the rate of capacity utilization is at its longer term mean, and *external balance* where the real rates of interest at home and abroad are equal, there are neither changes in reserves, nor speculative capital flows based upon anticipations. The equilibrium real exchange rate is the mean of a distribution, which is based upon real fundamentals. The mean will vary over time due to endogenous changes in capital and external debt, as well as changes in the exogenous real fundamentals. Deviations from this mean are produced by speculative factors involving anticipations, by cyclical factors, lags in adjustment, and interest rate differentials. These disequilibrium elements average out to zero. These deviations produce considerable variation but their effects are ephemeral.

The terms in square brackets are that investment less saving $(I_t - S_t)$ plus the current account is equal to zero. Investment less saving is the non-speculative capital inflow. The current account $(B_t - r_t F_t)$ is the trade

1. Optimal debt and equilibrium exchange rates

balance B_t less transfers of interest and dividends $r_t F_t$. The net external debt is F_t and r_t is the "interest/dividend" rate. The international investment position consists of equity, portfolio investment, and direct investment. The debt F_t is the negative of the net international investment position. Measure investment, saving, and the debt as fractions of the GDP.

$$[(I_t - S_t) + (B_t - r_t F_t)] = 0. \tag{1.1}$$

All of the authors who take the equilibrium real exchange rate approach use equation (1.1) to determine the exchange rate. The main differences among them concern their treatment of the two terms. Some work with a concept of what is a "sustainable" current account such that the debt does not "explode". As is discussed in the chapter on the United States' current account deficits, their estimates are subjective, so their equilibrium exchange rate is a "normative" concept. The NATREX approach is quite different in several respects, primarily because the endogenous current account generates an evolving external debt, which feeds back into the medium-run equation (1.1). A trajectory to longer run equilibrium is generated. The other difference is that the underlying equations are derived from intertemporal optimization by the private sector.

The dynamics of the debt/GDP ratio F_t is equation (1.2) below, where g is the growth rate. The current account deficit is the change in the external debt. The real exchange rate affects the trade balance B in equation (1.1), and the trade balance affects the evolution of the actual debt ratio in equation (1.2). There is a dynamic interaction between the endogenous real exchange rate and debt ratio.

$$\frac{dF_t}{dF} = (I_t - S_t) - g_t F_t = (r_t F_t - B_t) - g_t F_t = (r_t - g_t)F_t - B_t. \tag{1.2}$$

In *longer run equilibrium*, the debt ratio stabilizes at a value that satisfies equation (1.3). The trade balance B_t is sufficient to finance the interest plus dividend transfer on the debt net of growth $(r_t - g_t)F_t$. A negative debt is net foreign assets.

$$(r_t - g_t)F_t - B_t = 0. \tag{1.3}$$

The *longer-run equilibrium* real exchange rate R_t^* and debt/GDP ratio F_t^* are endogenous variables that satisfy both equations (1.1) and (1.3). They are written as (1.4) and (1.5) to indicate that they both depend upon the real fundamentals Z_t.

$$R_t^* = R(Z_t) \tag{1.4}$$

$$F_t^* = F(Z_t). \tag{1.5}$$

We call the dynamic stock-flow model equations (1.1)–(1.3) the NATREX model, which is an acronym for the **nat**ural **re**al **ex**change Rate[15]. This is a model of *positive economics*. The literature associated with Williamson's FEER uses equation (1.1) and does not contain the dynamic interactions, equations (1.2) and (1.3). The NATREX model derives the *private* saving, *private* investment, and trade balance equations from optimization criteria. There is no presumption that the *government* saving and investment decisions are optimal, since they are based upon political considerations not upon social welfare.

1.4. Populist and growth scenarios

The NATREX model is a technique of analysis[16]. The purpose of the model is to understand the effects of policies and external disturbances upon the trajectories of the equilibrium real exchange rate R_t and equilibrium debt ratio F_t which depend upon the vector of fundamentals Z_t. Insofar as the fundamentals vary over time, the equilibrium real exchange rate and debt ratio will vary over time, as indicated in equations (1.4) and (1.5). The logic and insights of the NATREX model can be summarized in two scenarios. Each scenario concerns different elements in the vector Z_t of the fundamentals, and has different effects upon the *equilibrium* trajectories of the real exchange rate NATREX and of the external debt. NATREX analysis concerns the *equilibrium* real exchange rate and it is neither the *actual* real exchange rate nor the *optimal* exchange rate that would lead to the *optimal* debt ratio.

The first scenario, called the *populist scenario*, involves a decline in the ratio of social saving/GDP. This could occur when the government incurs high-employment budget deficits, lowers tax rates that raise consumption, or offers loan guarantees/subsidies for projects with low social returns. This represents a rise in the consumption ratio/a decline in the saving ratio, a shift in the S function in equations (1.1) and (1.2). These populist expenditures are designed to raise the standards of consumption/quality of life for the present generation.

The second scenario, called the *growth scenario*, involves policies designed to raise the productivity of capital. Policies that come to mind involve the liberalization of the economy, increased competition, wage

---

[15] The NATREX appellation was suggested by Liliane Crouhy-Veyrac who compared the model to Wicksell's "natural" rate of interest.
[16] Allen (1997) explains the flexibility of this method of analysis.

and price flexibility, the deregulation of financial markets, improved intermediation process between savers and investors, and an honest and objective judicial system that enforces contracts. *Growth policies improve the allocation of resources and bring the economy closer to the boundary of an expanding production possibility curve.*

Table 1.1 summarizes the differences between the two scenarios in the medium and the long run. The stories behind the dynamics are as follows.

The populist scenario involves increases in social (public plus private) consumption relative to the GDP. External borrowing must finance the difference between investment and saving. The capital inflow appreciates the real exchange rate from initial level $R(0)$ to medium-run equilibrium $R(1)$, where $T = 1$ denotes *medium-run equilibrium*. The current account deficit is balanced by the capital inflow. The debt rises, since the current account deficit is the rate of change of the debt – equation (1.2). Current account deficits lead to growing transfer payments $r_t F_t$. This populist scenario is potentially dynamically unstable because the increased debt raises the current account deficit, which then increases the debt further. The exchange rate depreciates, and the debt rises, *steadily*.

Stability can only occur if the rise in the debt, which lowers net worth equal to capital less debt, reduces social consumption/raises social saving. For example, the growing debt and depreciating exchange rate force the government to decrease the high-employment budget deficit. Thereby, saving less investment rises. *Long-run equilibrium* (denoted by $T = 2$) is reached at a higher debt $F(2) > F(0)$ and a depreciated real exchange rate $R(2) < R(0)$. The longer run depreciation of the exchange rate $R(2) < R(0)$ can be understood from equation (1.3). The debt is higher than initially.

Table 1.1. NATREX dynamics of exchange rate and external debt: Two basic scenarios.

Scenarios R = real exchange rate (rise is appreciation), F = external debt/GDP; initial period $T = 0$, medium run $T = 1$, long run $T = 2$.	Medium- run, $T = 1$	Longer-run $T = 2$
Populist: Rise in social consumption (discount rate, time preference), rise in high-employment government budget deficit, decline in social saving	appreciation $R(1) > R(0)$ Debt rises $F(1) > F(0)$	depreciation $R(2) < R(0) < R(1)$ Debt rises $F(2) > F(1) > F(0)$
Growth oriented: Rise in productivity of investment, expansion of production possibility set, rise in growth, rise in competitiveness	appreciation $R(1) > R(0)$ Debt rises $F(1) > F(0)$	appreciation $R(2) > R(1) > R(0)$ Debt declines $F(2) < F(0) < F(1)$

Therefore, the trade balance $B(2)$ must be higher than initially to generate the foreign exchange to service the higher transfers[17] $r_t F(2)$. The real exchange rate must depreciate to $R(2) < R(0)$ in order to raise the trade balance to $B(2)$.

The *growth scenario* is summarized in the lower half of Table 1.1. The perturbation is a rise in the productivity of investment and an expansion of the production possibility set. Investment rises because of the rise in the rate of return. The difference between investment and saving is financed by a capital inflow. The exchange rate appreciates to $R(1) > R(0)$ which reduces the trade balance and produces a current account deficit. The initial current account deficit equal to $[I(0) - S(0)]$ raises the debt. The trade deficit provides the resources to finance capital formation, which raises the growth rate and the competitiveness of the economy.

It does not matter much where the rise in the return on investment occurred or what factors led to an expansion of the production possibility set. If they are in the traditional export or import competing sectors, the trade balance function $B = B(R;Z)$ increases. The B function, which relates the real value of the trade balance to the real exchange rate R, increases with a rise in the overall productivity, Z, of the economy. For example, the real-location of resources leads to the production of higher quality/value goods that can compete in the world market. If the rate of return on investment and productivity increase in the sectors that are not highly involved in international trade, resources can then be released for use in the more traditional "tradable" sectors. Again, the B function supply curve increases.

The trajectory to longer run equilibrium differs from that in the populist scenario. The crucial aspect implied by the growth scenario is that, at medium-run equilibrium exchange rate R(1), *the trade balance function increases*. The real exchange rate appreciates and there are now current account *surpluses*, excess of saving over investment. As a result, the debt then declines to a new equilibrium $F(2) < F(0)$. The trajectory of the debt is not monotonic. The net effect in the longer-run can be understood from equation (1.3). The debt is lower, the growth rate is higher and the trade balance function B has shifted to the right. *The long-run equilibrium exchange rate must appreciate to reduce B to equal the lower value of $(r-g)F^*$.*

The dynamic process in the growth scenario is summarized in the lower half of Table 1.1. The *real exchange rate* appreciates steadily to a higher level $R(2) > R(1) > R(0)$. The *external debt* reaches a maximum and then declines to $F(2) < F(0) < F(1)$.

---

[17] The interest rate must exceed the growth rate if the expected present value of future income is finite.

1.5. The nominal exchange rate: PPP and the equilibrium exchange rate models

The most frequently used estimate of the equilibrium *nominal* exchange rate is based upon the Purchasing Power Parity (PPP) hypothesis. The PPP arbitrarily assumes that the equilibrium *real* exchange rate is a constant. PPP cannot and does not purport to explain what determines the equilibrium exchange rate, what are the effects of policy/control variables and exogenous variables upon the equilibrium real exchange rate. Hence it is not particularly useful for policy questions. For example, PPP is unable to answer the following significant questions: At what exchange rate should the CEEC enter the euro area, to avoid the problems that occurred with the integration of East Germany? What policies will be consistent or inconsistent with the established exchange rates to avoid deflationary or inflationary pressures? How can one explain the trends in the values of the euro and the US dollar?

The "equilibrium exchange rate" literature[18] takes a very different point of view. The NATREX model implies that one would observe PPP in the long-run only if $R(Z_t)$ in equation (1.4), a linear combination of the fundamentals, is mean reverting in the longer run. The PPP model is a special case of the NATREX model. The relation between the PPP and the equilibrium exchange rate models can be understood from Figure 1.1 and equation (1.6). The logarithm of the equilibrium nominal exchange rate,[19] denoted $\log N^e_t$, has two components: the logarithm of the equilibrium real exchange rate, $\log R[Z_t]$ which is the NATREX, and the logarithm of the ratio of relative domestic/foreign "prices"[20], denoted $\log [p_t/p^*_t]$. The PPP ignores the $R(Z_t)$ term by assuming that it is a constant, and focuses exclusively upon the relative price term. The NATREX is not a constant, but varies with the vector of fundamentals Z_t that underlie the saving, investment, and trade balance functions.

$$\log N^e_t = \log R[Z_t] - \log [p_t/p^*_t]. \qquad (1.6)$$

Figure 1.1 describes three values of $R(Z)$, where $R(1)$ is the most appreciated NATREX, $R(2)$ is the most depreciated value, and $R(0)$ is the mean NATREX. Suppose that $Z = 0$ and the corresponding *equilibrium real* exchange rate NATREX is $R(0)$. Then the equilibrium *nominal* exchange

---

[18] This is the approach taken by Williamson (1994) and Clark and MacDonald (1999), among others. NATREX is in the set of these models.

[19] A rise in the nominal or real exchange rate is an appreciation of the currency.

[20] The best choices are either relative GDP deflators or relative labor costs.

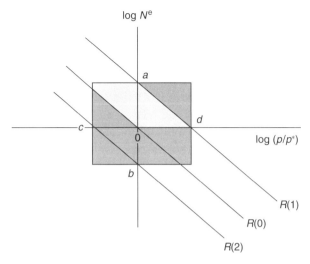

Figure 1.1. Relation between the equilibrium nominal exchange rate, the NATREX, and relative prices. If the NATREX varies between $R(1)$ and $R(2)$, and relative prices vary between c and d, and the equilibrium nominal exchange rate will be contained in the rectangle.

rate is a set of points along line $R(0)$. The PPP relation would hold as long as the NATREX remained constant. If the nominal exchange rate were above the line $R(0)$, the currency is overvalued. There cannot be internal and external equilibrium. The country would have difficulty competing in international markets. It would either lose reserves and the external debt/GDP ratio would rise, or there would be depressed economic conditions, particularly if the monetary/fiscal authorities attempt to stem the excess demand for foreign exchange. Similarly, if the nominal exchange rate were below the line, then reserves would rise or there would be inflationary pressures. Nominal exchange rates either above or below the line are unsustainable. Either the nominal exchange rate or relative prices must adjust, if both internal and external equilibrium are to prevail.

The NATREX changes with the fundamentals vector Z_t, as described in the two scenarios summarized in Table 1.1. As the NATREX varies between $R(1)$ and $R(2)$ and relative prices vary between c and d, the equilibrium nominal exchange rate will be contained in the rectangle. A regression of the nominal exchange rate upon relative prices would be based upon the scatter of points in the rectangle. If the relative prices are constant at log $[p_t/p^*_t] = 0$, then the equilibrium nominal exchange rate varies from a to b.

If the nominal exchange rate is fixed at log $N_t = 0$, then relative prices must vary between c and d.

Example: The euro – United States dollar exchange rate

With the introduction of the euro in 1999, there was a multitude of predictions concerning its future value relative to the US dollar. Most of the predictions were that the euro would appreciate – be a "strong currency" – as institutions diversified their portfolios away from the dollar. However, the euro depreciated from $1.16 in January 1999 to $0.87 in February 2002. Then the predictions switched towards pessimism about the value of the euro. However, the euro appreciated to $1.34 in December 2004. This appreciation caused consternation because it adversely affected the competitiveness of the European economies. Pressures were exerted upon the European Central Bank to offset the appreciation with an expansionary monetary policy. In June 2005, the euro was trading at around $1.20.

The standard theories were not able to explain these trends. As explained in the Preface, researchers in Europe examined to what extent the NATREX model could explain the movements in the euro. In particular, the staff of the European Central Bank had to decide whether the euro was "misaligned". The strategy of the researchers was to construct a "synthetic euro", which is a weighted average of the currencies of the countries in the euro area, from the beginning of floating in the 1970s to the advent of the euro. Chapter 5 is devoted to an evaluation of research concerning the euro exchange rate, and compares the NATREX explanation with other approaches.

The NATREX model states that the fundamental determinants of the real exchange rate $R(Z_t)$ and the debt ratio F_t are the variables Z_t in Table 1.1: relative social consumption ratio, relative productivity of investment, and relative productivity of labor in the pair of countries considered. The economic explanation of how these fundamentals affect the NATREX is the two scenarios. The signs of their medium-run and long-run effects are specified in Table 1.1.

The model in equations (1.1) – (1.5) has been tested and applied in several ways. The *structural equation* approach estimates the components, saving, investment, and trade balance equations to obtain the medium-run equilibrium NATREX from equation (1.1). Then, that solution is used in the dynamic equation (1.2) to obtain the long-run NATREX from equation (1.3). The *reduced form* approach just concentrates upon the dynamics of the real exchange rate. There is an excellent correspondence between the implied dynamic process and the vector error correction econometric approach. The long-run NATREX equation (1.4) is the hypothesized cointegrating equation.

Using the fundamentals Z_t for the euro area relative to the US, one obtains an estimate of the NATREX labeled $R(Z)$. The coefficients have the signs specified in the model, Table 1.1. Thus we have an estimate of the *equilibrium real exchange rate*. Adding the relative price variable, we obtain an estimate of equation (1.6)/Figure 1.1 for the *equilibrium nominal value* of the euro. A rise is an appreciation of the euro or a depreciation of the United States dollar.

Figure 1.2 graphs the *actual nominal* value of the synthetic euro (EUUSNERMA = $US/euro) and the estimate of the *equilibrium nominal* value (NOMNAT), based upon the NATREX model. The NATREX is a model of the equilibrium exchange rate, not the actual exchange rate. The actual exchange rate is hypothesized to converge to a distribution whose mean is the equilibrium exchange rate. The equilibrium rate varies according to Figure 1.1/equation (1.6) – because there are both shifts in the $R(Z)$ curve as well as movements along the curves due to relative prices. Since the equilibrium nominal exchange rate varies with both the vector Z_t and relative prices (p_t / p_t^*), price stability alone is not a sufficient condition for exchange rate sustainability.

Figure 1.2 shows the undervaluation of the synthetic euro (the over-valuation of the $US) in the first half of the 1980s, and in the period after 1996. Estimates of the equilibrium value of the euro from 1999 to 2001

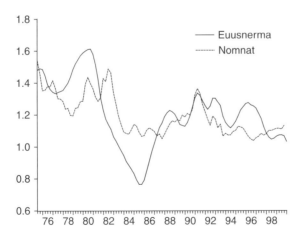

Figure 1.2. Nominal value of synthetic euro (4 Q MA), $US/Euro = EUUSNERMA; NATREX estimate, equation (1.6), is NOMNAT, 1970–2000.

indicated that it was undervalued relative to the $US. This estimate is consistent with the significant appreciation of the euro since 2001. The euro appreciated from $0.85 in 2001 to $1.29 in November 2004.

The NATREX model is a useful guide to policy. Insofar as the fundamentals Z – relative social consumption ratios, relative productivity, and relative returns on capital – have not changed drastically, the NATREX real exchange rate should be relatively constant. Insofar as relative prices also have not changed much, the NATREX nominal exchange rate should be relatively constant at about $1.20 in Figure 1.2. This is an equilibrium exchange rate. Speculative forces based upon anticipations, political events such as referenda, cyclical effects, and monetary policies will produce deviations from the equilibrium. However, these are transitory effects, that should wash out. Exchange market intervention, which attempts to drive the exchange rate from the NATREX, will be ineffective for the reasons given above.

This explanation of the euro rate is the subject of Chapter 5, and a similar analysis is developed in Chapter 6 for the exchange rates of the transition economies in Eastern Europe.

1.6. Optimal debt models

Many studies conclude that external borrowings, particularly by commercial banks and firms, were among the key factors responsible for the severity of the East Asian crises in the late 1990s. In particular, the authors argue that short-term capital flows are volatile and hence the size of foreign currency denominated debt contributes significantly to the occurrence of currency and debt crises. The volatility of exchange rates is strongly affected by the stock of external debt.

Countries have both short-term and long-term debt. The intertemporal optimization problem arises because the debt incurred to finance consumption and investment at one time affects the consumption possibilities at a later date. This choice is seen in balance equations (1.7) and (1.8). The optimal amounts of debt differ according to whether it is short-term or long-term.

In the case of short-term investment if the borrowing is at time t then it must be repaid with interest at later date $s = t + \Delta t$. In the case of long-term investment, the debt does not have to be repaid at any terminal date, but must be serviced regularly. Equation (1.7) describes the change in the debt dL_t. External debt L_t rises because consumption C_t plus investment I_t plus the debt service $r_t L_t$ exceeds Y_t the GDP. Alternatively, the change in the debt is $(I_t - S_t)dt$, investment I_t less saving $S_t = Y_t - r_t L_t - C_t$ over the period of length dt.

$$dL_t = (I_t - S_t)dt = (C_t + I_t + r_t L_t - Y_t)dt$$
$$= \text{current account deficit.} \tag{1.7}$$

The actual debt is generated by the decisions of the government and the private sectors. Fiscal and monetary policies are important determinants of investment and social saving by the private plus public sectors. In the Latin American countries the debt has risen due to high consumption and/or low social saving by the public plus the private sectors. In the Asian countries industrial policy stimulated private investment. The excess of investment less saving led to a capital inflow and an increase in the external foreign currency denominated debt. There is no presumption that these decisions – which produced the capital inflow dL_t – have been optimal, as is clear from the recurrence of debt and balance of payments crises in South-East Asia and Latin America.

The external debt has to be serviced and that would clearly affect future consumption. We can see this by writing consumption at some later time $s = t + dt$, in equation (1.8) below. It is another way of writing equation (1.7), but at a later date. Consumption is equal to the GNP, which is equal to the GDP less the debt service $Y_s - r_s L_s$, less investment I_s plus new borrowing dL_s. The new borrowing is the net capital inflow in the form of either direct investment, portfolio investment or short-term bank flows.

$$C_s \, ds = (Y_s - r_s L_s - I_s)ds + dL_s. \tag{1.8}$$

It is important to have a benchmark, what is the optimal debt, so that we can compare the actual to the optimal debt. Thereby we would obtain an early warning signal, $\Psi_t = f_t - f^*_t$ above, of a crisis. Three elements must be specified to solve the intertemporal optimization problem. Different models involve different specifications of these three elements:

- the constraints and controls/policy decisions;
- the dynamic stochastic process;
- the optimality criterion.

In Chapter 2, the debt is modeled as short-term corresponding to bank loans. In the model discussed in Chapter 3, the debt is long term, which would correspond to direct investment or long-term portfolio investment. The major theoretical difference concerns the *constraints*, so that the mathematical analysis is very different in each case. *They must be modeled differently*, and one case cannot be modeled as a special case of the other, for the following reason.

1. Optimal debt and equilibrium exchange rates

In the *short-term debt model* sketched below, debt is incurred in period $t=1$ which has a maturity at period $t=2$. It is a repeating two-period model. There are several constraints. First: at maturity, the debt must be repaid with interest. Second: the capital at the beginning of period $t=3$ must be the same as it was at the beginning of $t=1$, so the process is repeated. Third: consumption in period $t=2$, when the debt is repaid, must exceed a certain minimum, regardless of the state of nature. This is a "no bankruptcy" constraint. The argument is that, if the attempt to service the debt would reduce consumption below the minimum – which we arbitrarily set at zero – then the country would default. Faced with a choice: (a) repay debt and drastically reduce the standard of living, or (b) default but do not drastically reduce the standard of living, the economy would select the second option. The controls/policies are the consumption, investment, and resulting debt in period $t=1$, subject to the constraints.

In the *long-term model* of Chapter 3, sketched below, there is no maturity to the debt but it must always be serviced. It is an infinite horizon model in continuous time. The controls – debt, capital, and consumption – are *constantly* adjusted to keep these control/policy variables at their derived optimum levels. The constraints are that: consumption always be positive, regardless of the state of nature, and that net worth is always positive. The latter avoids Ponzi schemes, where new borrowing is used to service a growing debt. Intertemporal optimization in the long-term model involves the use of dynamic programming.

In both cases, a debt crisis is produced when the actual debt significantly exceeds the constrained optimal debt. The actual debt is generated by saving and investment decisions by the private and public sectors, which may be far from optimal. The economy is more vulnerable to external shocks when the actual debt significantly exceeds the constrained optimal debt.

The second specification concerns the stochastic process. We model the two sources of uncertainty that ultimately affect consumption. The first source of uncertainty is the ratio of GDP per unit of capital Y_t/K_t and the second source is the real rate of interest r_t. Two stochastic variables, real GDP and real interest rate, which will affect consumption at the later date, are written in bold letters in equation (1.8). Each one is highly variable. If bad shocks reduce the GDP and raise real interest rates, and investment falls to a minimum level then consumption in equation (1.8) may have to be reduced, unless there is new borrowing to offset the decline.

The output/capital ratio $Y_t/K_t = b_t$ has a deterministic component b, which is the *mean* return on capital, and a stochastic component with a zero mean and a significantly positive variance. The deterministic component b corresponds to the slope of a regression of the growth of GDP on the ratio of investment/GDP, and the stochastic part corresponds to the standard error of estimate. This stochastic part contains the "Solow residual", variations in the rate of capacity utilization resulting from fiscal and monetary policies, variations in the terms of trade, and the composition and quality of the investments.

The second source of uncertainty concerns the real interest rate r_t required to service the external debt L_t. For countries other than the US – such as emerging market countries – the real interest rate in terms of consumer goods r_t has three components. The first is the interest rate on US Treasury long-term debt. The second is the premium on dollar denominated debt charged to sovereign borrowers. The third is the anticipated exchange rate depreciation of the currency. A currency depreciation increases the amount of consumer goods that must be sacrificed to service/repay the foreign currency denominated debt. The equation for the real interest rate contains two terms: the first term is deterministic with a *mean* real rate of interest r and the second term is stochastic with a positive variance.

The expectations of the stochastic terms are equal to zero, but the productivity of capital and real rate of interest may be correlated. In developed countries such as the United States and Europe, the correlation is generally positive. In periods of rapid growth, there is a rise in investment demand and demand for money; and interest rates rise. When there are financial crises, such as occurred in Asia or Latin America, the growth of GDP and real interest rate are negatively correlated, for the following reason. A decline in GDP may occur because of a decline in the terms of trade and/or the anticipated return on investment turns out to be an illusion and the asset bubble collapses. The stochastic term in the productivity of capital equation is negative. Since firms borrow primarily from the banks to finance real investment and the banks in turn primarily finance their loans by borrowing US dollars in the international capital market, a domino effect is created in the event of a financial panic. When debtors are unable to repay their loans to the banks, the banks in turn are unable to repay their loans to international creditors. Financial panic leads to a short-term capital flight. The government may try to stem the outflow by using the dollar reserves, but that is only a stopgap measure. Sooner or later the monetary authorities will raise interest rates and, when that fails to stem the outflow, the currency will depreciate. The depreciation of the currency implies that the real rate of interest to repay a debt denominated in foreign currency rises. In that event, the stochastic term in the real interest rate equation is positive. The situation is exacerbated when banks also denominate their loans to the domestic firms in US dollars. Firms would find it very difficult to service debts denominated in foreign currency because they are faced with both a rising nominal rate of interest and a depreciating currency. A negative correlation between the productivity of capital b_t and the real rate of interest r_t makes an external debt very risky.

Faced with these sources of uncertainty, how then should a country select its optimal debt and level of consumption? The third specification concerns the optimality criterion. One criterion is that the controls are selected to maximize the expectation of the discounted value of a concave utility of consumption over the appropriate horizon. A second criterion is that the debt and capital are selected to maximize the expected value of the growth rate of consumption over a horizon, subject to the constraint that the ratio of consumption/net worth is a positive constant. A third criterion is a very conservative one. The controls are selected to maximize the minimum expected value of the utility of consumption[21]. Only the first two criteria are used in this book.

1.7. Short-debt model in discrete-time finite horizon

For many countries, short-term capital flows are important in financing investment less saving and have been associated with crises, such as in South East Asia 1997–8. In this part, we sketch the derivation of the *optimal* investment, consumption, and debt in the short-term capital movements model, which is the subject of Chapter 2. Explicit equations for excess debt Ψ_t and early warning signals of a debt crisis are stated. We provide specific examples of how this analysis can explain the default risk in emerging market countries and Latin America. Detailed empirical application of the *short-debt model* is the subject of Chapter 7.

The model assumes two repeating discrete time periods. In period one, the country has a stock of capital K_1 and a gross domestic product Y_1. The *controls* are consumption C_1 and investment I_1. If consumption plus investment is greater than the GDP, the country incurs an external debt L_1 to finance the difference. If consumption plus investment is less than the GDP the country is an international creditor, and the debt L_1 is negative.

---

[21] See Fleming (2005).

The debt, or net foreign assets, bears a known real rate of interest.[22] At the second period, the debt plus interest must be repaid. We consider a repeating two-period model, so that the capital at the beginning of period three must be the same as it was at the beginning of period one. This constraint means that the sum of investment over the two periods must be zero.

The productivity of capital $Y_t/K_t = b_t$ is a stochastic variable. When the investment decision I_1 is made in period one, the productivity of capital in period two, $b_2 = Y_2/K_2$, is unknown. Capital in period two is the capital at the beginning of period one plus the investment made in period one. Two possibilities are considered. Either the productivity of capital in period two, b^+, exceeds the interest rate r, with probability $1 > p > 0$, or the productivity of capital, b^-, is less than the rate of interest with probability $(1 - p)$.

The debt in period one, L_1, finances investment I less saving S. The stochastic variable b_2 is written in bold letters. Consumption in period two, C_2, is equal to the GDP in period two, $Y_2 = \mathbf{b_2}K_2 = b_2(K_1 + I_1)$, less the repayment of the debt plus interest $(1 + r)L_1$ plus the disinvestment to make capital at the beginning of period three equal to the initial capital K_1. Equation (1.9) describes consumption C_2 in period two. Since the return on capital can assume two values: $b^+ > r$ in the good case, and $b^- < r$ in the bad case, consumption in period two can assume either C_2^+ in the good case or C_2^- in the bad case.

$$C_2 = \mathbf{b_2}K_1 + [(1 + r)(b_1K_1 - C_1)] + (\mathbf{b_2} - r)I_1. \tag{1.9}$$

There are three components to consumption in period two, equation (1.9). If there is neither saving $(S_1 = b_1K_1 - C_1)$ nor investment in period one – if consumption is equal to GDP in the first period – then consumption in period two would just be the GDP in period two, $Y_2 = \mathbf{b_2}K_1$.

If there is saving but no investment in period one, then consumption in period two is the sum of the first two terms. The saving is invested abroad at the known rate of interest, and permits the economy to consume $[(1 + r)(b_1K_1 - C_1)]$. This term is not stochastic.

If there is investment in period one, then the additional consumption available in period two is the stochastic net return times the investment – the third term $(\mathbf{b_2} - r)I_1$.

If the bad state of nature occurs $b_2 = b_2^- < r$ then the burden of the debt resulting from $(b^- - r)I_1$ could depress consumption C_2 to an intolerable level. In that case, the country would default rather than accept the required reduced standard of living.

---

[22] This assumption is relaxed in the long-term optimal debt model.

1. Optimal debt and equilibrium exchange rates

The constrained optimization decision is to select the *controls*: consumption $C_1 > 0$ and investment $I_1 \geq 0$ during period one to maximize the expectation over the *stochastic* variable b_2 of the discounted value of utility over the two periods. We assume a HARA (hyperbolic absolute risk aversion) utility function, $U(C) = (1/\gamma)C^\gamma$, with positive risk aversion $(1 - \gamma) > 0$. A special case that we use frequently is $\gamma = 0$, so that the utility function is logarithmic $U(C) = \log C$. The great advantage of using the HARA function, particularly in the long-term model in Chapter 3, is that one can solve for the optimal controls analytically. Otherwise, the optimal controls are solved numerically by using a computer.

An important *constraint* is that there should be no default. This means that consumption in period two, in the bad case, should exceed a minimum tolerable level $C_2^- > C_{\min} \geq 0$.

The solution of the *short-debt model* is the subject of Chapter 2. The conclusions are described in Figure 1.3 for the optimal debt/capital $f = L_1/K_1$. Concentrate upon the logarithmic case, with risk aversion equal to unity, where the results are clear.

Optimal saving/capital is a constant independent of the expected net return $x = E(b - r)$. Optimal investment/capital is zero for expected net return $x < a$ in Figure 1.3. Risk premium a is related to the ratio of the possible loss from investment in capital relative to the return if all wealth were invested abroad at the safe return. This means that, for $x < a$, the country will be a creditor and will invest all of its saving abroad earning

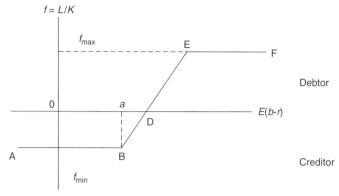

Optimal debt/capital $f = L/K$

Figure 1.3. Optimal debt/capital $f = L_1/K_1$ is curve ABDEF. Expected net return $x = E(b - r) = [pb^+ + (1 - p)b^-] - r$. Along ABD the country is a creditor. Along DEF the country is a debtor. If debt/capital exceeds $f_{\max}$, the probability of default is $(1 - p) > 0$.

the safe rate of return $r > 0$. The debt/capital will be $f_{min} < 0$, where the country is a creditor.

When the expected net return rises above a, investment will be positive, thereby reducing the capital outflow. When the expected net return $x = D$, investment will equal saving and the country will neither be a creditor or a debtor. When $x > D$, then investment will exceed saving. There will be a short-term capital inflow and a positive optimal ratio $f = \text{debt/capital} > 0$. The constraint that there be no default means that there is a maximal debt, f_{max}, such that in the event of a bad state of nature $b_2 = b^-$ the level of consumption would exceed C_{min}.

1.8. Summary of short-debt model

Curve ABDEF is the constrained optimal ratio debt/capital, in the short-term capital flow model. Expected utility is maximized along this curve. Insofar as the debt deviates from the curve, expected utility is reduced. The optimal debt is a benchmark of performance. *Debt crises result because the actual debt deviates from the optimal debt.* If the debt exceeds f_{max}, due to non-optimal behavior of the public and private sectors, then with probability $(1 - p) > 0$ consumption will be less than C_{min} and there will be a default. Alternatively, the likelihood of default rises continuously as the utility of consumption C_2 declines.

Example: Emerging markets

In Chapter 7, emerging market countries during the period 1979–2001 were divided into two groups: those that defaulted/renegotiated their debts with either official or private creditors[23] and those that did not. The relation between the debt/GDP ratio and the expected net return did not accord with the optimal ratio in Figure 1.3 in either set of countries examined (renegotiate/no-default). The main difference between the two groups concerned the excess debt, $\omega = (f - f_{max})$, the deviation between the actual debt/GDP ratio from the maximal debt/GDP ratio. The f_{max} is calculated in Chapter 7, based upon the short-term stochastic optimal control model in Chapter 2.

When there is an excess debt – the debt ratio f_t above the line f_{max} in Figure 1.3 – the economy is vulnerable. In the event of a bad shock,

---

[23] Define default/renegotiation as a condition where the scheduled debt service is not paid on the due date under the original contracted conditions.

Table 1.2. Mexico and Tunisia 1979–2001.

Variable	Mexico – default	Tunisia – no default
Debt/GDP f	0.45	0.61
Mean net return (b-r)	0.057	0.107
Variance of net return σ^2	$(0.16)^2$	$(0.09)^2$
$z = (b - r)/\sigma^2$	2.23	13.21
$\omega = f - (f_{max})$	0.322	−0.116

the level of consumption would fall below the minimum and would default. The bad shock will occur with probability $(1 - p)$. In the empirical applications of the short-term capital model to emerging markets, a warning signal $\omega = (f - f_{max})$ is equation (1.10). A *"flashing red" warning signal of a debt crisis occurs when $\omega > 0$.*

$$\omega_t = (f_t - f_{max}). \qquad (1.10)$$

Default is often a political decision, where international organizations and foreign countries are directly involved in bailouts and debt forgiveness. In the absence of bailouts, the excess debt is a sufficient condition for default. Our results based upon panel data were that:

In the cases where the debt was rescheduled/defaulted, the excess debt was positive in 84% of the cases. In the cases where there was no excess debt, default occurred in 17% of the cases.

A specific example concerns *Mexico and Tunisia*. Mexico defaulted to official and to private creditors during the period 1983–96, whereas Tunisia did not. Table 1.2 describes the relevant data from which one can infer that Mexico was more likely to default than Tunisia.

Compare Table 1.2 with the summary above. *First*: Tunisia, which did not default, had a higher debt ratio than did Mexico, which defaulted. *Second*: the risk adjusted net return z was very much higher in Tunisia. *Third*: the Mexican debt ratio was above the maximal debt f_{max} in Figure 1.3. The excess debt, which leads to a probability of default in the bad case, is ω in the last row. It is very large and positive. By contrast, Tunisia did not have an excess debt. The ω for Tunisia was negative; the debt ratio was below the debt-max level.

1.9. Dynamic programming optimization in long-term debt models

For many countries the main obligations to foreigners arise from direct investment and portfolio long-term debt and equity investment. These forms of "debt" have no maturity date, but must be serviced regularly with interest and dividend payments. The modeling of optimal long-term debt in continuous time over an infinite horizon is very different from the modeling of short-term debt in discrete time described above. In the long-term debt model, there is no maturity date. Bankruptcy can only occur if net worth, to be defined below, is negative. The *optimal* controls will prevent that from occurring, but the actual behavior may be non-optimal.

Consumption and the growth of the debt are described by equations (1.7) and (1.8) above. The two sources of uncertainty are the productivity of capital and the real interest rate, which may be correlated. First, the optimality criteria are discussed. Second, we describe two models with alternative stochastic processes concerning the sources of uncertainty: the *prototype model* and the *ergodic mean reversion model*. Third, we indicate why the literature that uses the "intertemporal budget constraint" (IBC) is inadequate. Fourth, we explain why and how we use the dynamic programming (DP) analysis. Fifth, the conclusions concerning the optimal debt/net worth ratio, capital/net worth ratio, and consumption/net worth are stated. Sixth, we give an example of the implications of the DP analysis by providing an early warning signal of the Argentine crisis of 2000–1. In Chapter 8, we give an example of the interaction of an overvalued currency and excess debt in producing the Asian crises of 1997–8.

1.10. Optimality criteria

Several reasonable optimality criteria are used in the mathematical finance literature. Usually the criterion is to select the *control/decision variables*, consumption, debt or capital subject to constraints, to maximize the expectation (E) of the discounted value of a concave utility of consumption $U(C_t)$ over a horizon $(0,T)$, where T may be infinite or finite. These are equations (1.11a) or (1.11b). In the infinite-horizon case, the discount rate is $\delta > 0$. The expectation is taken over the stochastic variables: the productivity of capital and real rate of interest.

Analytic solutions of the dynamic programming equation can be obtained if the utility function is HARA[24] described in equations (1.11a) and (1.11b). The coefficient of risk aversion is $(1 - \gamma) > 0$. The lower is γ, the greater is the risk aversion. Negative and zero values of γ imply considerable aversion to risk. In the case where $\gamma \leq 0$, the utility of a

---

[24] That is the reason that Merton (1990) used HARA. Otherwise, the DP equation must be solved numerically using a computer.

zero consumption is minus infinity. When $\gamma = 0$, the utility function is logarithmic.

$$J_1 = E \int^T C_t^\gamma / \gamma e^{-\delta t} \, dt \quad \gamma \neq 0 \qquad T > t > 0 \tag{1.11a}$$

$$J_2 = E \int^T \ln C_t \, e^{-\delta t} \, dt \quad \gamma = 0 \quad T > t > 0. \tag{1.11b}$$

Two *constraints* are imposed. Consumption is always positive. Net worth must always be positive. Define net worth $X_t > 0$ as "capital" less debt. A negative debt is a financial asset. Unless constraint $X > 0$ is imposed, Ponzi schemes are possible: borrow to finance consumption and borrow more to service the debt. In that case, capital does not grow. As the debt continues to grow exponentially, net worth will be driven to negative values. The constraint that net worth is always positive precludes Ponzi schemes.

There are two *subjective* variables, the discount rate and risk aversion. The discount rate is just another way of specifying the length of the horizon. A high discount rate places the emphasis upon what occurs in the near future, and essentially disregards the far future. A discount rate $\delta > 0$ is necessary to derive a finite optimum over an *infinite* horizon if $\gamma \geq 0$, whereas if $\gamma < 0$, then a discount rate is not necessary to derive a finite optimum over an *infinite* horizon.

Whenever the utility function is logarithmic, the optimal ratio of consumption/net worth equals the "discount rate". Consumption is social consumption, government plus private consumption expenditure. Low taxes and high government expenditures raise social consumption. Since the discount rate is arbitrary, this quantity can rationalize any social consumption policy. If populist policies lead to a high rate of social consumption/GDP, it can be "rationalized" as optimal policy with a high discount rate. Weight the present highly relative to the future. If the dictator, a Chairman Mao, follows policies that depress social consumption, it can be "rationalized" as optimal policy with a low discount rate. Weight the future highly relative to the present.

Criterion J_3 in equation (1.12) does not involve the arbitrary discount rate. Quantity J_3 is the expected growth rate of net worth over a horizon of length T, given any constant ratio c of consumption to net worth, $C_t / X_t = c > 0$. Since consumption is a constant fraction of net worth the maximization of J_3 is the same as the maximization of the growth rate of consumption from an arbitrary initial level.

$$\begin{aligned} J_3 &= (1/T)E \left[\ln X_T / X | C_t / X_t = c > 0 \right] \\ &= (1/T)E \left[\ln C_t / C | C_t / X_t = c > 0 \right], \qquad X = (0), \quad C = C(0). \end{aligned} \tag{1.12}$$

Criteria J_1 and J_2 allow us to solve for both the optimum debt/net worth ratio, capital/net worth, and the optimum consumption/net worth, whereas criterion J_3 only allows us to solve for the optimal debt/net worth and capital/net worth. We explain in Chapter 3 that the same optimal ratios of debt/net worth and capital/net worth are obtained whether we use criterion J_2 or J_3.

There is another criterion, which reflects extreme aversion to risk. The consumption in any period depends upon both the controls/decision variables – consumption, capital, or debt – and the stochastic productivity of capital. Suppose that there is a finite set of productivities of capital and a corresponding likelihood function. The *max-min* criterion of optimality is to select the controls that *maximize* the *minimum* expected values of consumption for very large values of risk aversion. Fleming (2005) analyzes this very conservative case.

1.11. Stochastic processes

The sources of uncertainty are modeled as stochastic processes in continuous time. The *prototype* model assumes that both the productivity of capital b_t and the world real rate of interest r_t can be described by statistical functions such as Brownian motion[25] with drift. The mean return on investment is b, but there is no mean reversion. The change in the return to investment from one "period" to the next is purely random with a zero expectation, Brownian motion. Similarly, there is a world real rate of interest at which the country can borrow or lend. The mean is r, but there is no mean reversion. The change in the real rate of interest from one "period" to the next is just the Brownian motion.

An alternative stochastic process is that the productivity of capital is still Brownian motion with drift but that the world real interest rate, dependent upon a large vector of factors, is described by *ergodic mean reversion*. This stochastic process is described by the *Ornstein–Uhlenbeck* equation, which states that the change in the real rate of interest from one "period" to the next is not completely random. One part is a reversion to the mean, and the second part is Brownian motion. The net result is that the real rate of interest is normally distributed and converges to a distribution whose mean is r with a positive variance. Mathematically, it is easy to reverse which variable is described by Brownian motion with drift, and

---

[25] A Brownian motion process has independent increments that are normally distributed. The expectation is zero and the variance is directly related to the length of the period.

which is described by ergodic mean reversion. The stochastic processes in the two models are summarized:

	Return on investment b_t	real interest rate r_t
Prototype model	Brownian motion with drift	Brownian motion with drift
Ergodic mean reversion	Brownian motion with drift	Ornstein–Uhlenbeck

In Chapter 3, we derive the optimal debt ratio and consumption ratio in the prototype model. In Chapter 9, where we evaluate the United States current account deficits and debt ratio, we explain how the equations for the optimum differ in the two cases: prototype model, ergodic mean reversion.

1.12. Intertemporal optimization: Stochastic optimal control, dynamic programming

The standard approach in the economics literature concerning inter-temporal optimization is to maximize the expectation of the discounted value of the utility of consumption subject to an "Intertemporal Budget Constraint" (IBC). The intertemporal case is treated as the analog of the standard deterministic case of consumer choice. In the timeless case, the consumer has a utility function over a vector of goods, leisure, and services whose prices are given and the consumer has a fixed amount of resources, money, and time. The constraint is that the choice is restricted to the amount of resources available. *The budget constraint is known with certainty* since prices and resources available are known when the choice is made. The IBC is of an entirely different nature. The object of an "intertemporal budget constraint" is to prevent a "free lunch", or engage in a Ponzi scheme where debts are never repaid. The IBC imposed is a terminal condition. At finite date $T > 0$ the debts are cleared, debt $L_T = 0$. We now explain why the IBC is inappropriate in a stochastic environment or a world of uncertainty. Instead, one must use the techniques of stochastic optimal control/dynamic programming.

From equation (1.7), the debt L_T at time T is the initial debt $L(0)$ plus the sum of the excess of expenditures for consumption C_t plus investment I_t plus interest on the debt $r_t L_t$ less gross domestic product Y_t. The IBC is that the debt is paid off at the terminal date. The condition that $L_T = 0$ implies the IBC, the sum of absorption $(C_t + I_t)$ is equal to the sum of the gross national product $(Y_t - r_t L_t)$.

The stochastic variables (in bold letters) are Y_t the real GDP, and r_t, the real interest rate. Given the uncertainty concerning the productivity of capital and real interest rate, the future is unpredictable. At any time $s < T$ when the debt is L_s, how can anyone know if any country will or will not be violating the IBC?

The IBC is unknowable, unenforceable, and is a non-operational concept. If a country has a debt L(0) at the present, how can one know if the IBC will be satisfied *even if a given policy – a sequence of investment and consumption – is followed*? The reason is that Y_t, r_t, the real GDP and interest rate, are stochastic variables with Brownian motion components. For example, when the price of oil (during the oil crises periods) was high the oil pro-ducing countries and the oil importing countries expected it to continue. In the former huge investment and consumption projects were under-taken in the expectation that the real GDP would remain high. In the oil consuming countries, costly energy-saving policies were imposed. These anticipations did not materialize and the oil producing countries were saddled with large debts.

This profound deficiency of the IBC approach led Fleming and Stein[26] to use a dynamic a programming DP approach,[27] which features promin-ently in this book.

1.13. The dynamic programming (DP)/stochastic optimal control (SOC) approach[28]

Our underlying models are Markov diffusion processes where the future evolution of the system depends upon the present state and not at all upon the paths leading up to the present state. The system is stoch-astic, unpredictable. Even if one specified the controls/decisions[29] from the present to any future date, the future is unpredictable because there are many paths that the system can take due to the stochastic processes describing the real GDP and the real interest rate. At each instant of

---

[26] Fleming and Stein (2004), Fleming (2004), and Stein (2004).

[27] The seminal work was by Bellman (1971). The DP approach is generally used in the mathematical finance literature, starting from the work of Robert Merton.

[28] This section is an intuitive discussion of Chapter 3, which is based upon techniques used in the mathematical finance literature.

[29] Controls and decisions are used interchangeably.

time the "controller/decision maker" knows the state of the system, and *only has information up to the present*. Since the controller cannot anticipate the future, the DP approach involves a multistage decision process. The *principle of optimality* of DP is that: whatever the initial state and the initial decisions are, the remaining decisions must constitute an optimal policy with regard to the state resulting from the first decision. *In a stochastic system, the optimal controls selected at any time depend upon the current information available and enter as feedback functions of the currently observable state. This is very different from the IBC approach.*

The state variable in the stochastic systems discussed in this book is net worth X_t defined as "capital" K_t less debt L_t. The change in capital is investment over the period, and the change in the debt is equation (1.7). The latter involves the stochastic variables, the productivity of capital, and the real rate of interest.

The DP solutions of the optimization of the expected discounted value of utility (J_1, J_2 in equations 1.11a, b), given the stochastic processes, involve the Hamilton–Jacobi–Bellman (HJB) equation discussed in Chapter 3. The DP analysis of intertemporal optimization is quite technical, however the optimal debt/net worth f in the HJB equation can be explained in terms of the well-known Tobin mean variance (M-V) model.

The optimal debt/net worth f_t in the HJB equation is chosen to maximize component W, equation (1.13)

$$W = \max_f \ [\text{Mean} - (\text{risk aversion}) \ \text{Risk}]. \qquad (1.13)$$

The *mean* term $M(f_t, c_t)$ is a *linear* function of the debt ratio and the consumption ratio. It is the percentage change in net worth[30] if there were no uncertainty. *Risk* is $R(f_t)$ and $(1-\gamma)$ is risk aversion. The risk term concerns the variance of the percentage change in net worth. In the logarithmic cases ($\gamma = 0$), risk aversion is unity. The term $R(f_t)$ contains the variances of the productivity of capital, the interest rate, and their correlation. The stochastic term $R(f_t)$ is a *quadratic* function of the debt ratio. A unique optimal ratio of debt/net worth is derived that maximizes J_1 or J_2 in equations (1.11a) and (1.11b). This maximization involves the maximization of W, which can be interpreted as M-V, expected utility. A graphical explanation of equation (1.13) presented in Chapter 3 provides the intuition behind the DP results.

---

[30] This is dX/X but it is not the growth rate, which is the percentage change per unit of time.

1.14. Implications of the DP solution of the long-term debt model

The stochastic optimal control/dynamic programming analysis is used to derive the intertemporal optimal conditions. The debt/net worth ratio $f_t = L_t/X_t = f^*$ that maximizes performance criterion J_1, equation (1.11a) is the one that maximizes equation W in (1.13). The derived optimal debt in equation (1.14) is a benchmark measure of performance in a stochastic environment. Net worth is capital less debt. Therefore, the optimal ratio k^* of capital/net worth is $k^* = f^* + 1$. In the logarithmic case, J_2, equation (1.11b), where risk aversion $(1 - \gamma) = 1$, the *optimum debt/net worth* is:

$$f^* = (b - r)/\sigma^2 + f(0), \quad \sigma^2 = \text{var } (b_t - r_t). \tag{1.14}$$

Several crucial variables are in this equation. First, variable b is the *mean productivity* of capital or return on investment, r is the *mean* real interest rate. In the logarithmic cases J_2 and J_3, risk aversion $(1 - \gamma) = 1$. Variable σ^2 is the variance of the quantity $(b_t - r_t)$, the current productivity of capital less the current interest rate, so that it also contains a covariance term. The intercept $f(0)$ is the optimal ratio of debt/net worth that minimizes risk. When the correlation coefficient between the growth rate and interest rate is less than the ratio of the standard deviation of the productivity of capital/ standard deviation of the interest rate, the intercept $f(0)$ is negative. The optimum debt ratio f^* in the prototype model is equation (1.14), which is our benchmark of performance. Equation (1.14) is graphed in Figure 1.4 as line the *U-S*. The debt ratio $f = L/X$ is plotted on the ordinate and the risk adjusted mean net rate of return $z = (b - r)/\sigma^2$ is plotted on the abscissa.

1.15. Summary and implications of the DP analysis[31]

Consider two countries, which differ greatly in terms of wealth and income. There is no necessary relation between per capita wealth and the risk adjusted mean net return $z = (b - r)/\sigma^2$. In a rich/developed country I, the risk adjusted mean net return $z = z_1$ and in a poor/emerging market country II, the risk adjusted mean net return $z = z_2$. *In the situation described in Figure 1.4, it is optimal that the poor country should be a creditor of the rich country because the mean return per unit of risk $z = (b - r)/\sigma^2$ is higher in the rich country. Either the mean net return $(b - r)$ is higher or the risk σ^2 is lower in rich country I than in poor country II.*

---

[31] These propositions refer to the case where risk aversion $(1 - \gamma)$ is unity, the logarithmic case.

1. Optimal debt and equilibrium exchange rates

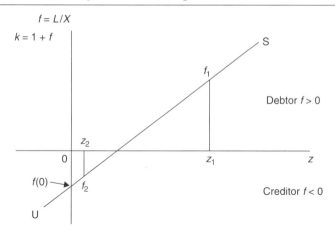

z = mean risk adjusted net return = $(b-r)$/variance

Figure 1.4. Optimal ratio debt/net worth f^* is line U-S, when risk aversion is unity. In the prototype model, the risk adjusted net return is $z=(b-r)/\sigma^2$, $\sigma^2=\text{var }(b_t-r_t)$. Optimal capital/net worth $k^* = 1+f^*$.

The expected growth of net worth and consumption is maximal, for any consumption ratio, when the debt/net worth ratio[32] is optimal at f^*. As the debt ratio rises above the line U-S which describes the optimum f^*, the expected growth rate declines, and the risk – the variance of the growth rate – increases.

Objective measures of vulnerability to external shocks are implied by the analysis. Vulnerability is taken as a situation where, if the debt is to be serviced, consumption must be reduced when there are external shocks. Say that consumption is a constant proportion of net worth. This proportion may or may not be "optimal". As the actual debt ratio rises above the optimum, say because non-optimal policies are undertaken by the public sector, the expected growth rates of net worth and consumption decline and their variances rise. The probability of a decline in consumption rises and the probability of a debt crisis increases continuously as the debt ratio exceeds the optimum. Therefore, the vulnerability to shocks increases continuously as f rises relative to f^*.

The *level* of the ratio[33] of debt/GDP *per se* is not a relevant variable in producing a crisis. Instead it is the *excess* of the actual debt ratio over

---

[32] The ratio of capital/net worth is equal to 1 plus the debt ratio.

[33] The ratio of $h=$ debt/GDP is positively related to the ratio $f^*=$ debt/net worth. The equation is: $h=(1/b)f/(1+f)$, where b is the mean productivity of investment. Therefore, one can speak of the ratios f and h interchangeably.

the optimal f^* that raises the probability of a crisis. A warning signal $\Psi_t = (f_t - f^*)$, based upon available information, is that the debt ratio is rising above line U-S in Figure 1.4. When the mean net return per unit of risk $z = (b - r)/\sigma^2$ is falling, the optimal debt ratio should be declining. If, however, the debt/GDP ratio is rising because non-optimal policies are followed, it is more probable that the debt ratio lies in the region above the curve *U-S*.

Example: Argentina: From triumph to defaults

Severe crises result from an interaction between an excess debt and a misaligned exchange rate. The interaction between them is the subject of the Asian crises, Chapter 8. In the present section, we give an example of how we apply the SOC/DP analysis of excessive debt to Argentina that went from triumph in the early 1990s to tragedy in 2001. Warning signals are based upon estimates of excess debt $\Psi_t = f_t - f^*{}_t$ using available information.

Michael Mussa's (2002) retrospective description[34], and the International Monetary Fund's Independent Evaluation Office Report (2004), of the Argentine crisis can be integrated with the SOC/DP analysis above. A new economic policy – the convertibility plan – was instituted in the spring of 1991 to deal with the hyperinflation that existed at the beginnings of the 1990s. The currency was pegged to the $US and a currency board arrangement limited domestic money creation. This plan was successful. During the period 1993–8, the inflation rate was below 3% and the growth rate was about 4% per annum. Whereas most of the miracle Asian economies collapsed into crisis from mid-1997 to early 1998, Argentina became the darling of the world credit market. It was able to float large issues of medium to long-term debt on the world credit markets at comparatively modest spreads over the US Treasuries.

Not only did the world credit markets and the International Monetary Fund applaud the Argentine policies, but also several academic economists viewed Argentina as a model of growth. Dornbusch (Lecture II: 1998) wrote: "A currency Board arrangement, a fixed exchange rate and a central bank that has no discretionary power over the money supply...is a very good system...One spectacularly successful case...is Argentina...the Argentine experience is the one that deserves most attention because, one, it has lasted, and two, it has been extremely successful as a cornerstone

---

[34] The description of the Argentine experience in this section often paraphrases Mussa's (2002) monograph.

of reform in an economy, and three, it has produced an average growth of six per cent".

Barely a few years later in 2001, Argentina's decade-long experiment ended in tragedy. The banking system was effectively closed at the beginning of December 2001, the exchange peg was gone, and the peso was trading at substantially depreciated rate against the $US. Argentina defaulted on its sovereign debt and was transformed within barely two years from the darling of the emerging market finance to "the world's leading deadbeat".

The reason why the financial markets, the International Monetary Fund, and academic economists failed to anticipate the crisis was that their attention was focused upon the monetary sphere – since inflation is a monetary phenomenon – and not upon the external debt. The debt did not alarm them because the debt did not seem to be high relative to that prevailing in many industrial countries. A benchmark of an excessive debt was lacking. Our analysis implies that debt crises are not produced by the *level* of the debt/GDP but by the *excess* of the actual debt over the optimum debt ratio.

The fundamental causes of the disaster were the growth in social (public plus private) consumption and a fixed nominal exchange rate pegged to the $US. The various levels of the Argentine governments succumbed to political pressures to spend significantly more than was raised by taxes. Much of the fiscal problems arose because the provinces retained the initiative for public spending, but the central government was ultimately responsible for raising revenues and servicing the debt. Since Argentina was thought of so highly by the financial markets, it was able to finance the excess spending by borrowing US dollars in the international markets at favorable interest rates.

An excess debt means that the debt ratio rises above the curve U-S in Figure 1.4. In the prototype model, the optimal debt ratio is equation (1.14). A relatively general way of taking all of these factors into account is to graph the normalized variables. The normalized return to investment is $b^*_t = [b_t - E(b)]/\sigma_b$, labeled B1_AR in Figure 1.5. It is the deviation of the return from its longer-term mean per unit of risk[35]. The external $US denominated debt/GDP, labeled DBTGDP_AR in Figure 1.5, is also normalized. It is equal to the (debt/GDP - mean)/standard deviation. The debt ratio rose by two standard deviations from 1992 to 2001. However, the return on investment b_t was declining from 1997 to 2001.

[35] In general, in the equation for optimal debt the variance is multiplied by risk aversion. In the logarithmic case it is unity, as in equation (1.14). There is also a constant $f(0)$ in equation (1.14). By using normalized variables, we are evaluating excess debt relative to its average value over a long period, where risk aversion and $f(0)$ are given.

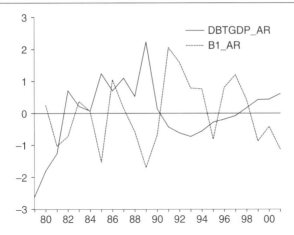

Figure 1.5. Debt/GDP (DBTGDP_AR) normalized, return on investment per unit of risk (B1_AR) = $(b_t - \text{mean})$/st. dev.

The rise in the actual debt ratio and the decline in b_t, the return/risk in Figure 1.5, corresponds to a rise in the debt ratio above the curve U-S for the optimal debt ratio in Figure 1.4. An "excess debt" is generated. Insofar as there is an excess debt, the expected growth rate of GDP declines and its variance rises. The variance comes from the external shocks, which are disturbances to the productivity of capital (GDP/capital), the real rate of interest, and their correlation. *Because of the non-optimal government policies, the Argentine economy became more vulnerable to shocks of the net return from its longer term mean.*

The major shock was the collapse of Brazil's crawling peg early in 1999, which led to a negative shock to the Argentine productivity of capital. When Argentina was forced to depreciate its currency – abandon the peg – the real rate of interest was positively shocked, because the debt was denominated in $US. Consumption would have to be reduced, if Argentina was to service her debts. Confronted with this choice, Argentina defaulted.

Our conclusion is that there was an early warning signal (EWS) of a sustained excessive debt, based upon available information. The debt ratio *per se* is not an EWS, whereas the excess debt $\Psi = f - f^*$ is an EWS of a debt problem/crisis/default/renegotiation. *Theoretically* this is the movement of the debt ratio above the curve U-S, and *empirically* it is that $b^*_t = (b_t - \text{mean})$/st. dev is falling significantly but the debt/GDP ratio is rising significantly for a period of years. This approach allows for gradual structural change in the productivity of capital.

1.16. Conclusion

The contribution of this book has been to answer the following questions.

• What is a theoretically based empirical measure of a "misaligned" exchange rate that increases the probability of a significant depreciation or a currency crisis?
• What is a theoretically based empirical measure of an "excess" debt that increases the probability of a debt crisis?
• What is the interaction between an excess debt and a misaligned exchange rate?

In this overview chapter we sketched the theoretical framework and gave several examples of how the theoretical analysis is applied. This book reflects interdisciplinary work that has been undertaken with coauthors. The NATREX model was developed and applied with coauthors who are economists. The use of stochastic optimal control and dynamic programming to explain optimal debt and endogenous growth was developed with coauthors who are mathematicians.

Chapters 2–4 are theoretical and Chapters 5–9 are applications of the theoretical material. A detailed application of stochastic optimal control/ dynamic programming for long-term debt in continuous time is in Chapter 9 concerning the United States current account deficits. The Argentine example above just gives a flavor of the approach. The short-term debt model is applied to the emerging market countries in Chapter 7. The interaction between misaligned exchange rates and excess debt is applied to the East Asian crises. The application of the NATREX model to the euro–US dollar exchange rate is presented Chapter 5, and the real exchange rate of the transition economies in Chapter 6.

Now that the reader has had a guided tour of some of the highlights, he can read the rest of the book either systematically or selectively by choosing the chapter that is closest to his interests.

References

Allen, Polly R. (1997), The Economic and Policy Implications of the NATREX Approach, in Jerome L. Stein, Polly Reynolds Allen, Michael Connolly, Liliane Crouhy-Veyrac, John Devereux, Guay C. Lim and Michèle Saint Marc. (1997) *Fundamental Determinants of Exchange Rates*, Oxford University Press, chapter 1

American Mathematical Society (2004), Providence, RI Mathematics of Finance, Contemporary Mathematics, 351 (ed.) George Yin and Qing Zhang

Bellman, Richard (1971), Introduction to the Mathematical Theory of Control Processes, Academic Press, New York

Breuer, Janice Boucher (1994) Assessing the Evidence on Purchasing Power Parity, in John Williamson (ed.) Estimating Equilibrium Exchange Rates, Institute for International Economics, Washington, DC

Clark, Peter and Ronald MacDonald (1999), Exchange Rates and Economic Fundamentals: A Methodological Comparison of BEERs and FEERs in Ronald MacDonald and Jerome L. Stein (1999), Equilibrium Exchange Rates, Kluwer Academic, Dordrecht

Detken, Carsten, Alistair Dieppe, Jérôme Henry, Carmen Marin and Frank Smets (2002), Determinants of the Effective Real Exchange Rate of the Synthetic Euro: Alternative Methodological Approaches, *Australian Economic Papers*, Special Issue on: Exchange Rates in Europe and in Australasia, December

Detken, Carsten and Carmen Marin (2001), The Effective Euro Equilibrium Exchange Rate Since the 1970's: A Structural Natrex Estimation, European Central Bank, Working paper, available at < webdeptos.uma.es >

Dornbusch, Rudiger (2003), International Financial Crises, CESifo Working Paper #206

Driver, Rebecca and Peter F. Westaway (2005), "Concepts of equilibrium exchange rates", in Rebecca Driver, P. Sinclair and C. Thoenissen (ed.) Exchange Rates, Capital Flows and Policy", Routledge, London

Duval, Romain (2002), What do we know about the long-run equilibrium real exchange rates? PPP vs. macroeconomic balance approach, *Australian Economic Papers* (2002) Special Issue on: Exchange Rates in Europe and in Australasia, December

Fleming,Wendell H. and Jerome L. Stein (2004), *Stochastic Optimal Control, International Finance and Debt*, Journal of Banking and Finance, 28, 979–996

Fleming,Wendell H. and Jerome L. Stein (2001), *Stochastic Inter-temporal Optimization in Discrete Time*, in Negishi,Takashi, Rama Ramachandran and Kazuo Mino (ed.) Economic Theory, Dynamics and Markets: Essays in Honor of Ryuzo Sato, Kluwer, Boston

Fleming,Wendell H. (2004), Some Optimal Investment, Production and Consumption Models, American Mathematical Society (2004) Providence, RI Mathematics of Finance, Contemporary Mathematics, 351 (ed.) George Yin and Qing Zhang

Fleming, Wendell H. (2005), Optimal Investment and Consumption Models with Minimum Consumption Criteria, Australian Economic Papers, Volume 44, December 2005

Gandolfo, Giancarlo (2001), International Finance and Open-Economy Macroeconomics, Springer, Heidelberg

Infante, E. F. and Jerome L. Stein (1973), Optimal Growth with Robust Feedback Control, Reviews of Economic Studies 40 (1), 47–60

1. Optimal debt and equilibrium exchange rates

International Monetary Fund (2004), Independent Evaluation Office (IEO), Report on the Evaluation of the Role of the IMF in Argentina, 1991–2001

Kaminsky, G. and C. Reinhart (1999), The Twin Crises: The Causes of Banking and Balance of Payments Problems, American Economic Review 89 (3), 473–500

MacDonald, Ronald and Jerome L. Stein (1999), Equilibrium Exchange Rates, Kluwer, Dordrecht

MacDonald, Ronald (1999), What do we really know about real exchange rates? in MacDonald, Ronald and Jerome L. Stein (ed.), Equilibrium Exchange Rates, Kluwer, Dordrecht

Merton, Robert (1990), Continuous Time Finance, Blackwell, Oxford

Mussa, Michael (2002), Argentina and the Fund: From Triumph to Tragedy, Institute for International Economics, Washington, DC

Obstfeld, M. and K. Rogoff (1996), Foundations of International Economics, MIT Press, Cambridge MA

Stein, Jerome L. and Giovanna Paladino (2001), *Country Default Risk: An Empirical Assessment*, Australian Economic Papers, 40, (2), December 417–436

Jerome L. Stein, Polly Reynolds Allen, Michael Connolly, Liliane Crouhy-Veyrac, John Devereux, Guay C. Lim and Michèle Saint Marc (1995, 1997), Fundamental Determinants of Exchange Rates, Oxford University Press

Stein, Jerome L. (2002), The Equilibrium Real Exchange Rate of the Euro: An Evaluation of Research, ifo Studien, 3/2002

Stein, Jerome L. and Giovanna Paladino (1997), Recent Developments in International Finance: A Guide to Research, Journal of Banking and Finance, vol. 21, December, 1685–1720

Stein, Jerome L. and Guay C. Lim (2002), Introduction to Exchange Rates in Europe and Australasia: Fundamental Determinants, Adjustments and Policy Implications, Australian Economic Papers, 41 (4), December 329–341

Stein, Jerome L. and Guay C. Lim (2004), Asian Crises: Theory, Evidence and Warning Signals, Invited Eminent Paper Series, Singapore Economic Review, **49** 135–161

Stein, Jerome L. (2004), *Stochastic Optimal Control Modeling of Debt Crises*, American Mathematical Society, Contemporary Mathematics

Turnovsky, S. (2000), Methods of Macrodynamics , MIT Press, Cambridge MA

Williamson, John (1994), Estimating Equilibrium Exchange Rates, Institute for International Economics, Washington, DC

Part II

Theoretical framework

2

Stochastic optimal control model of short-term debt[1]

2.1. The need for a paradigm of risk management of short-term foreign currency denominated debt

Data on the credit rating of bonds issued in the first half of the 1990s suggest that investors in emerging market securities paid little attention to credit risk, or that they were comfortable with the high level of credit risk that they were incurring.[2] The compression of the interest rate yield spread prior to[3] and the subsequent turmoil in emerging markets have raised doubts about the ability of investors to appropriately assess and price risk. After the 1997 crises, Moody's credit rating agency wrote that there was a need for a "paradigm shift" that involves greater analytic emphasis on the risks associated with the reliance on short-term debt for otherwise creditworthy borrowers.

The literature in international finance concerning intertemporal optimization in discrete time makes assumptions that imply certainty equivalence. A major implication is that investment should be increased as long as the expectation of the marginal product of capital exceeds the interest rate. If the marginal product of capital does not vary much as the

---

[1] This chapter is based upon Fleming and Stein (2001).

[2] See the International Monetary Fund, International Capital Markets, Washington DC (1999), and International Monetary Fund, Anticipating Balance of Payments Crises, Occasional Paper #186, (1999).

[3] The market expectations as embodied in interest rates did not widen significantly prior to the Mexican crisis. In the Asian crises, spreads hardly increased in the months prior to the floatation of the baht. The credit rating agencies and the market analysts all failed to signal the Asian crises in advance. They downgraded these countries only after the crises.

2. Stochastic optimal control model

Table 2.1. Capital flows, developing countries 1994–2001.

Billion $US	1994	1995	1996	1997	1998	1999	2000	2001
1. Total, net	159.9	186.3	189.9	161.9	108.1	75.1	26.7	46.4
2. Net official	20.7	33.4	2.1	31.7	42.9	25.4	10.7	38
3. Net private	139.2	150.1	187.8	130.2	65.2	49.7	16.1	8.3
3.1 Direct investment	74.5	82.4	104.3	128.6	129.8	131.8	129.9	147.3
3.2 Portfolio investment	93.5	16.7	64.4	36.8	1.8	12.8	−17.9	−51.5
3.3 Other private investment	−28.8	51.1	19.1	−35.3	−66.4	−94.9	−96	−87.5

Source: International Monetary Fund, World Economic Outlook, September 2002, Appendix Table 33.

rate of investment rises, then investment would greatly exceed saving, and an extremely high foreign debt would be incurred. The certainty equivalence assumptions ignore the risks inherent in such a high level of investment and foreign debt. The standard approach fails to address the questions of how should one optimize under uncertainty, or how to evaluate what debt is likely to lead to default.

The International Monetary Fund wrote that experience suggests that countries with high levels of short-term debt, variable interest rate debt, foreign currency denominated debt are likely to be particularly vulnerable to internal and external shocks and thus vulnerable to financial crises (IMF 1998: 83). This chapter develops a paradigm for intertemporal optimization under uncertainty in a finite horizon discrete time context, with the constraint that there be no default on *short-term foreign currency denominated debt*.

The dichotomy between models of short-term and long-term debt can be seen from Table 2.1 of capital flows of developing countries. The total net capital flows are divided between official flows which reflect political decisions and net private flows that reflect market-based decisions. The private flows consist of direct investment and portfolio investment, which may be considered as long-term investment, and "other capital flows",[4] which may be considered as short-term investment.

This chapter focuses upon short-term investment and capital flows, which would correspond to item (3.3) in Table 2.1. The inadequacy of the theoretical literature is discussed in section 2.2 2. Section 2.3 develops the short-term investment model and then provides an intuitive and graphic exposition of some of our results concerning *optimal* debt and investment. The object is to select consumption, investment, and the resulting short-term debt in the first period to maximize the expected present value of the utility of consumption over both periods. The constraint is that, regardless

---

[4] They are transactions in currency and deposits, bank loans, and trade credits.

of the state of nature in the second period, there will be no default on the debt. The general mathematical solution is in section 2.4. This two-period model can be solved by calculus, whereas the long-term debt infinite horizon case discussed in Chapter 3 uses the dynamic programming method with the technical mathematical difficulties encountered in the theory of continuous-time stochastic control. Chapter 7 is an empirical application of the short-term debt model to explain default risk in emerging market countries. A sufficient condition for a debt crisis is that the attempt to service the external debt would reduce consumption below a "tolerable" level. When the *actual* debt exceeds the *optimal* debt, expected utility of consumption is reduced. Moreover, we derive a measure of the "maximum debt". When the actual debt exceeds the "maximum debt", then a debt crisis is quite probable.

2.2. The solvency–sustainability criterion[5]

The literature has used a "solvency–sustainability" approach to monitor foreign debt. An economy is considered *solvent* if the ratio of external liabilities/GDP will remain bounded, and the debt service payments/GDP will not explode. The *sustainability* of the current account deficit relies on projecting into the future the current policy stance of the government and/or of the private sector. Sustainability is ensured if the resulting path of the foreign debt is consistent with "intertemporal solvency". We explain why the solvency–sustainability approach is not capable of revealing vulnerability.

Denote by $h(t) = L(t)/Y(t)$ the ratio of the foreign debt $L(t)$ measured in US dollars to $Y(t)$, the real GDP also measured in \$US. The rate of change of the foreign debt/GDP in equation (A) below is the sum of two elements. The first is the interest rate (r) less the growth rate (g) times the debt ratio $h(t)$. The second is the ratio $m(t)$ of the trade deficit/GDP. Solve (A) for the debt/GDP h(t) and derive equation (B).

$$dh(t)/dt = [r(t) - g(t)]h(t) + m(t) = a(t)h(t) + m(t), \quad a(r - g) \quad \text{(A)}$$

$$h(t) = h(0)e^{A(t)} + \int e^{(A(t)-A(v))}m(v)dv, \quad t>v>0, \quad A(t) = \int a(v)dv,$$
$$t>v>0. \quad \text{(B)}$$

Think of $A(t)/t$ as the average interest rate less the growth rate over the interval $(0,t)$, and $A(v)/v$ as the average interest rate less the growth rate

⁵ See, for example, International Monetary Fund, WEO, May 1998, Box 8, pp. 86–7.

2. Stochastic optimal control model

over the interval $(0, v < t)$. The debt/GDP can be attributable statistically to the components of (B): sustained trade deficits, $m(v) > 0$, equal to sustained excess of investment minus saving, and interest rates in excess of growth rate $a(v) > 0$.

The solvency–sustainability literature defines the "debt burden" $Z(t)$ as a measure of "vulnerability". The 'debt burden' $Z(t)$ is defined in equation (C) as the trade surplus $[-m(t)]$ required to keep the ratio of the debt/GDP ratio constant at its *current* level $h(t)$. The solvency–sustainability argument assumes that current $[r(t) - g(t)]$ is given. Solve equation (A) when $dh_t/dt = 0$ and derive (C). Then the higher is $Z(t)$ the more burdensome is the debt, and the greater the likelihood of default.

$$Z(t) = [r(t) - g(t)]h(t). \qquad (C)$$

This approach does not allow one to evaluate whether a debt is excessive and whether it will lead to vulnerability. The trade deficit, saving rate, investment ratio, and growth rate are interrelated. The trade deficit is equal to investment less saving. The growth rate $g(t)$ is equal to the product of the productivity of capital $b(t)$ times $j(t)$ the investment/GDP ratio. There are three reasons why the solvency–sustainability approach is not particularly useful.

First: it is impossible to know the future value of the debt $h(T)$ for $T > t$, because the future growth rates and interest rates are unknown. This means that quantities $A(.)$ in equation (B) are unknown. The debt in equation (B) will explode if interest rates exceed the growth rates. If $A(t)$, $h(0)$ and $A'(t) > 0$, then $\lim h(t) \to \infty$ as $t \to \infty$. Second: the trade deficit $m(t)$ and the growth rate $g(t)$ are not independent. A trade deficit that finances investment will lead to a higher growth rate in the future, since the growth rate is the product of the productivity of capital and the investment rate. Third: a trade deficit in the present does not imply a high debt in the future. For example, a high rate of return on investment $b(t)$ relative to the world interest rate stimulates capital formation $j(t)$. The latter raises investment less saving, generates a capital inflow, which appreciates the real exchange rate. The appreciation of the exchange rate leads to a trade deficit, which accomplishes the transfer of resources, and the debt rises. The higher investment ratio times the productivity of capital will eventually raise the growth rate. In other words, the higher productivity of capital $b(t)$ will eventually raise GDP and saving, and generate a trade balance to repay the debt. The debt may go through a cycle: it first may rise and then decline below its initial level. Consequently, it is misleading to look at the debt burden $Z(t) = [r(t) - g(t)]h(t)$

based upon the *current* values, and infer whether or not there will be a debt crisis. Nor is it useful to look at the current trade deficit $[-m(t)] = [j(t) - s(t)]$ to infer vulnerability.

The above argument explains why the empirical researchers who have used the solvency–sustainability approach have doubted its usefulness. The International Monetary Fund WEO Report (May 1998, Box 1, p. 87) wrote: "...these simple solvency tests would clearly have failed to signal problems ahead for the fast-growing Asian economies, including Indonesia and Korea".

2.3. A discrete-time finite-horizon model, risk and risk aversion

In modeling *optimal short-term debt*, we consider a series of repeating two-period cycles. In the first period, the GDP is denoted by $Y(1) = b(1)K(1)$, where $K(1)$ is the capital stock and $b(1)$ is the current productivity of capital. The country selects consumption and investment in period $t = 1$. The current account deficit, equal to consumption plus investment less the GDP, is financed through short-term foreign debt denominated in the currency of the creditor. The creditor country here is the United States, and the debtor is an emerging market country. The given interest rate is r_1. The balance equation in $t = 1$ is equation (2.1). The variables are real. The left-hand side consists of resources available, the GDP $Y(1)$ plus $L(1)/N(1)$, where $L(1)$ is the external borrowing in US dollars and $N(1) = 1$ is the initial exchange rate, \$US/domestic currency. A rise (decline) in N is an appreciation (depreciation) of the domestic currency. The right-hand side is consumption $C(1)$ plus investment $I(1)$. Alternatively, the capital inflow $L(1)$, or trade deficit, is absorption $C(1) + I(1)$ less $Y(1)$, the GDP at period $t = 1$.

$$Y(1) + L(1) = C(1) + I(1). \tag{2.1}$$

In period $t = 2$, the debt plus interest must be repaid. The balance equation at $t = 2$ is equation (2.2), written with consumption $C(2)$ on the left-hand side. Consumption is equal to the real GDP less the repayment of the debt plus interest less investment. The debt and its servicing is $(1 + r_1)L(1)/N(2)$ measured in local currency. The exchange rate is $N(2) = N(1)(1 + n) = (1 + n)$, where a positive n is the rate of appreciation of the local currency. Denote the effective interest rate as $(1 + r) = [(1 + r_1)/(1 + n)]$, which is the dollar interest rate adjusted for the change in the exchange rate.

$$C(2) = Y(2) - \left[\frac{1+r_1}{1+n}\right]L(1) - I(2) = Y(2) - (1+r)L(1) - I(2). \quad (2.2)$$

The optimization concerns the sum of the utility of consumption in the first period plus the expectation of utility of consumption in the second period. The consumption in the second period is equation (2.3). It is equal to the stochastic GDP less the repayment of debt and interest $(1+r)L(1)$ less investment $I(2)$. Default/rescheduling of debt will occur if consumption in period two falls below a certain minimum tolerable level, which we shall call $C(t)_{min} = 0$. The "no-default" constraint is that $C(2)$ in equation (2.3) be positive.

$$C(2) = b(2)[K(1) + I(1)] - (1+r)L(1) - I(2) > 0. \quad (2.3)$$

The debt carried into the second period $L(1)$ is consumption plus investment less GDP in the first period, the trade deficit. In a series of repeating cycles, let the terminal capital equal the initial capital $K(3) = K(1)$, or the sum of investment over the entire two periods $I(1) + I(2) = 0$. Then the consumption in the second period is equation (2.4), using the no-default constraint that consumption $C(2)$ be positive.

$$C(2) = b(2)K(1) + [b(2) - r]I(1) + (1+r)[b(1)K(1) - C(1)] > 0. \quad (2.4)$$

The risk/uncertainty concerns the productivity of capital $b(2)$ and the effective rate of interest $(1+r) = [(1+r_1)/(1+n)]$. The risk associated with investment is contained in the net return on investment $[b(2) - r]I(1)$, the stochastic productivity of capital $b(2)$ less r, the interest rate. The productivity of investment $b(2)$ is stochastic for the following reason. External debt is incurred to purchase capital and produce an output, which is sold in the world market. The value of output depends upon the terms of trade, the exchange rate and basic productivity of the investment. If the terms of trade deteriorate, the foreign currency earned from exports depreciates or the investment is ill advised, the GDP measured in domestic currency will decline.

Since the effective interest rate $(1+r)$ contains the exchange rate, it too is stochastic. Moreover, it may be correlated with the productivity of capital. In the long-term debt case considered in Chapter 3, we consider the case where both variables are stochastic and correlated. However, in this Chapter , we assume that the interest rate is known and that all of the uncertainty comes from $b(2)$, the productivity of capital. It can be seen

---

BOX 2.1. UNCERTAINTY CONCERNING THE NET RETURN $X = [B(2) - R]$

$b(2)$	$Pr(b)$	
$b^+(2) = r + a/2$	$1 > p > 0$	good case
$b^-(2) = r - a/2$	$(1 - p) > 0$	bad case

Productivity of capital in the second period is $b(2) = Y(2)/K(2)$. The interest rate is r. The net return is $x = b(2) - r$. The expected net return $E(x) = E[b(2) - r] = a(p - 1/2)$; range $[b(2) - r] = a > 0$. Risk concerns the realization of the "bad" case. $Var(x) = a^2 p(1 - p)$.

---

from equation (2.4) that this assumption is not very restrictive, and will simplify the exposition and analysis.

Box 2.1 describes the uncertainty. The range of $b(2)$ is $r \pm a/2$, $a > 0$. The values of the net return $x = [b(2) - r]$ are symmetrical around zero with a range $a > 0$, with probabilities $(p, 1 - p)$, $1 > p > 0$, in the good and bad case, respectively. This is a simple and general formulation that makes minimal assumptions about the distribution function.

The net return on investment $x = [b(2) - r]$ is $a/2$ in the good case with probability p, and $x = -a/2$ in the bad case with probability $(1 - p)$. The consumption in the good case is $C^+(2)$, and is C^-2 in the bad case. The debt carried into the second period $L(1)$ is investment $I(1)$ less saving $S(1) = b(1)K(1) - C(1)$.

The no-default constraint for the maximum debt, $L(1)_{max}$, is derived from equation (2.3), when $I(2) = -I(1)$. It is expressed as (2.5a) in terms of investment $I(1)$ and (2.5b) in terms of saving.

$$L(1)_{max} = b^-(2)K(1) + (1 + b^-(2))I(1)]/(1 + r) \qquad (2.5a)$$

$$L(1)_{max} = b^-(2)K(1) + (1 + b^-(2))S(1)]/(a/2). \qquad (2.5b)$$

If the actual debt exceeds the maximal, then with probability $(1 - p) > 0$ the value $C^-(2) < 0$ and there will be a default. Equation (2.5) is independent of any optimization, and just depends upon the chosen values for investment $I(1)$ in period $t = 1$, and the bad value $b^-(2)$ realized in period $t = 2$.

The criterion function is equation (2.6), the maximization, over the set of controls and the constraints, of the expectation (E) of J, the present value of the utility of consumption. The utility is a HARA[6] function $U(C(t)) = (1/\gamma)C(t)^\gamma$, where $\gamma < 1$. Risk aversion is $(1 - \gamma) > 0$. The $\gamma = 0$ case is $U(C) = \ln C(t)$, the logarithmic utility function. Controls $C(1)$ and $I(1)$ are selected in period $t = 1$ to maximize the sum of the expected utility of

---

[6] This is a constant relative risk aversion $d(\ln U'(C))/d(\ln C) = (\gamma - 1) < 0$.

consumption over the two periods, subject to the no-default constraint. This is equation (2.6), using equation (2.4) for $C(2)$.

$$J = \max \ (1/\gamma)C(1)^\gamma + (1/\gamma)[pC^+(2)^\gamma + (1-p)C^-(2)^\gamma]. \qquad (2.6)$$

Two cases are considered. The first assumes that $(1-\gamma) > 0$ is finite but not unity, and the second case is the logarithmic case $U(C) = \ln C$, when $\gamma = 0$. Simple equations are obtained in the logarithmic case. Another attractive feature of the logarithmic function is that the utility of zero consumption is minus infinity; therefore, the optimization will avoid that situation.

In Section 2.4 we present an intuitive and graphic description of the solution for the constrained optimal investment, debt, and consumption in the case where the utility function is logarithmic $\gamma = 0$. The solution of the model is sketched in section 5 and derived mathematically in the appendix. This mathematical analysis may not be familiar to economists, even though it only involves calculus.

2.4. Optimal consumption, investment and debt: Logarithmic case

The optimal debt, investment, consumption, and saving are described in the equations in BOX 2.2, derived in the appendix. All variables are measured as fractions of initial capital K_1.

Optimal consumption/capital $c = C_1/K_1$ is proportional to W, the present value of safe wealth per unit of capital. This is the value that would be obtained if all of the initial capital and GDP were invested in the safe asset yielding an interest rate of r. There is no uncertainty involved in W. In the repeating two-period short-term model, where the utility of each period is weighted equally and the utility function is logarithmic, consumption is one-half of the present value of safe wealth, equation (2.7). This is consumption smoothing.

Saving/capital s is GDP/capital b_1 less c consumption/capital, equation (2.8). In the logarithmic case, it is independent of the expected return.

In the standard literature that makes the certainty equivalence assumptions, the optimal stock of capital is adjusted until the expected marginal productivity is equal to the interest rate. If the expected productivity of capital is independent of the stock of capital and exceeds the interest rate, $E(b_2 - r) = E(x) > 0$, then investment would be maximal. A maximal amount would be borrowed at rate r to finance the maximal investment, and a maximal amount of risk is assumed.

BOX 2.2. SOLUTION OF OPTIMAL SHORT-TERM DEBT MODEL $\gamma = 0$ CASE

$$c = W/2 \tag{2.7}$$

$$s = b_1 - c = b_1 - W/2 \tag{2.8}$$

$$i = [1/\rho] [(E(b_2 - r) - \rho] \geq 0 \tag{2.9}$$

$$f = i - s, \quad \text{subject to} \quad i_{max} \geq i \geq -1 \tag{2.10}$$

$$f_{max} = [b^-_2 + (1 + b^-_2)s]/(a/2) \tag{2.11}$$

$$i_{max} = s + f_{max}. \tag{2.12}$$

Assumptions: Logarithmic utility $\gamma = 0$. Risk $(b^+ - r) = (r - b^-) = a/2 > 0$.
$$E(b_2 - r) = a(p - 1/2).$$

Definitions: Period $t = 1$: $c = C_1/K_1 = $ optimal consumption/capital > 0, $s = S_1/K_1 = $ optimal saving/capital, $i = I_1/K_1 = $ optimal investment/capital ≥ 0, and f $= L_1/K_1 = $ optimal debt/capital carried into period t $= 2$. Present value of safe wealth per unit of captial $W = [(1 + b_1)R - 1]/R$, interest factor $R = (1 + r)$; $Y_1/K_1 = b_1$ productivity of capital in period $t = 1$; loss in bad case $(r - b^-) = a/2 > 0$; risk premium $\rho = (a/2)^2 R(W/2)$.

In our model where risk is explicitly taken into account and there is a no-default/rescheduling constraint, we obtain a very different result. Even though there are no diminishing returns to capital, optimal investment/capital denoted i is equation (2.9). Constrain investment in period $t = 1$ to be non-negative. Optimal investment is zero, for values of the expected net return $E(x) = E[b(2) - r]$ less than ρ, where the risk premium $\rho > 0$ depends upon the downside risk divided by the return on safe wealth. When $E(x) > \rho$, the rate of optimal investment is proportional to the positive difference between the expected net return and the risk premium until we reach the maximum i_{max}, defined below.

The optimal debt/capital carried into period two, denoted as $f = L(1)/K(1)$, is equation (2.10), the difference between optimal investment $i = I(1)/K(1)$ less optimal saving $s = S(1)/K(1)$. The maximum debt/capital, f_{max} equation (2.11), is derived from equation (2.5b). Therefore, the maximum investment/capital i_{max}, given saving/capital, is equation (2.12).

Figure 2.1, based upon the equations in Box 2.2, describes the optimal values of investment i, saving s, and debt f, per unit of initial capital, associated with the expected return $E(x) = E(b_2 - r)$. Optimal investment/capital is the dark broken line, corresponding to equations (2.1) and (2.12).

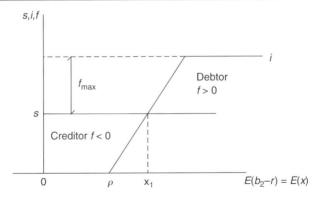

Figure 2.1. Optimal values of investment i, saving s, and debt $f = (i - s)$, per unit of initial capital, associated with the expected return $E(x) = E(b_2 - r)$. Investment $i = I(1)/K(1)$ is constrained to be non-negative.

The country should be a net creditor $f < 0$ as long as the expected net return on investment $E(x) = E[b(2) - r] = a(p - 1/2)$ is below $x_1 > 0$. It should be a debtor $f > 0$ when $E(x)$ exceeds $x_1 > 0$. The maximum debt/capital f_{max} is the debt/capital that produces zero consumption when the bad case occurs. Then default/debt rescheduling will occur with probability $(1 - p)$.

2.5. A sketch of the mathematical solution

The mathematical solution is sketched in this section. Technical details are fully explained in the appendix. We solve for the optimal debt ratio by taking explicit account of the uncertainty and the "no-default" constraint, rather than by using the certainty–equivalence approach in the literature. Consumption $C(2)$ in equation (2.4) is a stochastic variable in the repeating two-period model where the terminal capital is equal to the initial capital, $K(1) = K(3)$, so that $I(1) + I(2) = 0$. When the productivity of capital takes on the good value $b^+(2) = r + a/2$ with probability p, then consumption $C^+(2)$ is equation (2.13). Similarly, when the productivity of capital takes on the bad value $b^-(2) = r - a/2$ with probability $(1 - p)$, consumption is $C^+(2)$ in equation (2.14).

$$C^+(2) = (1 + r)[b(1)K(1) - C(1)] + (a/2)I(1) + (r + a/2)K(1) \quad (2.13)$$

$$C^-(2) = (1 + r)[b(1)K(1) - C(1)] - (a/2)I(1) + (r - a/2)K(1). \quad (2.14)$$

If there is optimal risk management in period $t = 1$, the country would select the controls $C(1) > 0$, $I(1) \geq 0$ to maximize the expectation of the

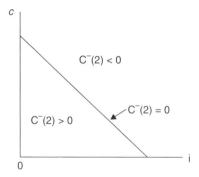

Figure 2.2. Constraint $C^-(2) > 0$ implies that $c = C(1)/K(1)$ and $i = I(1)/K(1)$ lie inside the triangle. For $c > 0$ and $i \geq 0$, the constraint is $(1 + r)c + (a/2)i \leq (r - a/2) + (1 + r)b(1)$, where $b^-(2) = (r - a/2)$.

discounted value of a strictly concave utility of consumption in equation (2.6), subject to the no-default constraint. Using (2.14), the constraint[7] that $C^-(2)/K(1) = c^-(2) > 0$, and $i(1) = I(1)/K(1) \geq 0$ imply that the values of c and i must lie within a triangle bounded by the coordinate axes and the negatively sloped line $C^-(2) = 0$ graphed in Figure 2.2.

If consumption and investment in $t = 1$ lie outside of the triangle, then default will occur in the "bad" state of nature, which occurs with probability $(1 - p) > 0$.

Since J is strictly concave subject to the constraint $C^-(2) > 0$, the maximum is at a unique $C^*(1)$, $I^*(1)$, which is either interior to the triangle in Figure 2.2 or on the boundary $I(1) = 0$. When the maximization is in the interior, it is found by setting the partial derivatives of J with respect to $C(1)$ and $I(1)$ equal to zero. The maximization equations are (2.15) for $\delta J / \delta C(1) = 0$ and (2.16) for $\delta J / \delta I(1) = 0$.

$$\frac{\delta J}{\delta C(1)} = 0 \qquad (2.15)$$

$$\frac{\delta J}{\delta I(1)} = 0. \qquad (2.16)$$

The model contains five unknowns: $C(1)$, $I(1)$, $C^+(2)$, $C^-(2)$ and $L(1)$. There are five independent equations. Variables $C^+(2)$ and $C^-(2)$ are defined in (2.13) and (2.14), the two maximization equations are (2.15) and (2.16) and equation (21) is the debt. The optimal controls in Box 2.2 refer to the logarithmic case when $\gamma = 0$. The general case $(1 - \gamma) > 0$ is contained in Box 2.3 in the appendix.

---

[7] If $c(2) > 0$ in the bad case, then it must be positive in the good case.

2. Stochastic optimal control model

We can now answer the questions in the logarithmic case: What is the optimal external debt/capital in the short-term capital flow model? How should we evaluate the risk involved with holding or issuing short-term debt? The optimal foreign debt per unit of capital $f = L(1)/K(1)$ incurred during the first period is simply the trade deficit. It is equal to optimal investment i less optimal saving s, all per unit of capital, subject to the constraints.

$$f_{max} > f = i - s > -1. \qquad (2.17)$$

The optimal debt/capital is equation (2.18) graphed as Figure 2.3. Using equations (2.8) for saving $s = [b_1 - W/2]$ and (2.9) for investment i derive equation (2.18). The indicator function ζ is unity for $E(x - \rho) > 0$ and zero otherwise.

$$f = [(1/\rho)\zeta E(x - \rho)] - [b_1 - W/2] \qquad (2.18)$$
$$E(x) = E(b(2) - r), \rho = (a/2)^2/(1 + r)(W/2).$$

The country should be a short-term debtor, $f > 0$, if the expected net return $E(x)$ exceeds quantity $E(x^*) > \rho > 0$ in Figure 2.3, and should be a short-term lender, $f < 0$, if the expected net return is less than $E(x^*)$ defined in equation (2.19).

$$E(x^*) = \rho(1 + s). \qquad (2.19)$$

Default will occur with probability $(1 - p)$ if the debt per unit of capital f exceeds the maximal debt per unit of capital $f_{max} = L(1)_{max}/K(1)$ in equation (2.5a) or (2.5b) above.

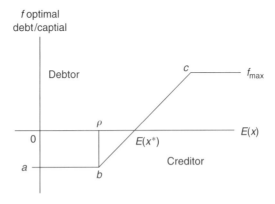

Figure 2.3. Optimal debt/capital f is equation (19), curve $a - b - E(x^*) - c - f_{max}$

2.6. Conclusion

The optimal short-term debt is graphed as the broken line $a - b - E(x^*) - c - f_{max}$ in Figure 2.3 in the repeating two-period model, equation (2.18) subject to constraint (2.17). Then the expected logarithmic utility of consumption over the entire two-period horizon – subject to a "no-default" constraint – is maximal[8]. A rise in the debt ratio above the optimum continuously lowers the expected utility of consumption. If the debt ratio exceeds f_{max}, then consumption in period $t = 2$ will be reduced below the minimum tolerable level if the "bad" state of nature occurs. The "bad" state where $b^- (2) < r$ occurs with probability $(1 - p) > 0$. Therefore, when the debt ratio f exceeds f_{max}, the probability of a debt crisis/default/renegotiation is $(1 - p) > 0$. This is a sufficient condition for a debt crisis. A crisis could occur as the debt ratio rises above the curve and the utility of consumption in period $t = 2$ is reduced but is above the minimum tolerable level for other reasons, such as a regime change.

In Chapter 7 we apply this analysis to explain the experience of emerging market countries: those that renegotiated their debts and those that did not. We do that by comparing their actual debt ratios to both the optimal and also relative to f_{max} the maximum debt. In that chapter, we do not ask why the countries had excessive debts. This is done in Chapter 8 concerning the Asian crises, where we synthesize the theoretical material in Chapters 3 and 4. Chapter 3 is concerned with the optimal long-term debt and Chapter 4 is concerned with equilibrium exchange rates.

Mathematical appendix

The method of solution is as follows. Start with maximization equations (2.15) and (2.16) which contain three unknowns: $C(1)$, $C^+(2)$, $C^-(2)$. These conditions are (2.15a) and (2.16a) respectively. Define $R = (1 + r)$, and crucial partial derivatives are (a)–(d).

Probability $p > 0$	Probability $(1 - p) > 0$
(a) $dC^+(2)/dC(1) = -R = -(1 + r)$;	(c) $dC^-(2)/dC(1) = -(1 + r)$
(b) $dC^+(2)/dI(1) = +a/2$;	(d) $dC^-(2)/dI(1) = -a/2$

---

[8] There are other optimization criteria. Fleming (2005) analyzes an alternative to the stochastic control formulation. He takes a max-min approach. Here the criterion of control performance is the minimum consumption over time, weighted by a coefficient that indicates

2. Stochastic optimal control model

Maximization equations

$$C^{\gamma-1}(1) = R\{p[C^+(2)]^{\gamma-1} + (1-p)[C^-(2)]^{\gamma-1}\} \quad \text{when}$$
$$\delta J/\delta C(1) = 0 \quad (2.15a)$$

$$\{p[C^+(2)]^{\gamma-1} (a/2) - (1-p)[C^-(2)]^{\gamma-1} (a/2)\} = 0 \quad \text{when}$$
$$\delta J/\delta I(1) = 0. \quad (2.16a)$$

The expression $C^{\gamma-1}(t)$ is the marginal utility of consumption in period t. Define variables A^+ and A^- as the ratio of marginal utilities of consumption in period $t=2$, in the good and bad cases respectively, relative to the marginal utility of consumption in period $t=1$. Due to the HARA utility function, these are equations (A1) and (A2) respectively. The consumption in the second period is a proportion of that in the first period.

$$[C^+(2)]^{\gamma-1} = A^+[C(1)]^{\gamma-1} \quad (A1)$$

$$[C^-(2)]^{\gamma-1} = A^-[C(1)]^{\gamma-1}. \quad (A2)$$

Determine the values of A^+ and A^- by substituting (A1) and (A2) into the maximizing equations (2.15a) and (2.16a), and obtain (A3) and (A4). The latter two equations concern the *maximization* with respect to control variables $C(1) > 0$ and $I(1) > 0$, and we solve for the values of A^+ and A^-. Consider the case where $I(1) > 0$, and equation (A4) is an equality.

The maximization equations, using HARA utility, involve two unknowns A^+ and A^-, the ratios of the marginal utility of $C^+(2)$, and of $C^-(2)$, relative to the marginal utility of $C(1)$.

$$pA^+ + (1-p)A^- = 1/R \quad (A3)$$
$$pA^+ - (1-p)A^- = 0. \quad (A4)$$

The resulting values of the ratios of marginal utility A^+ and A^-, are equations (A5) and (A6). These imply the ratios of consumption $C^+(2)/C(1)$ and $C^-(2)/C(1)$. They depend upon the probability $(1 > p > 0, 1-p)$ in the good and bad cases and $R = 1+r$, one plus the interest rate r.

$$A^+ = 1/2pR \quad (A5)$$
$$A^- = 1/2(1-p)R. \quad (A6)$$

Using (A5) and (A6) in (A1) and (A2), we obtain the values of consumption $C^+(2)$ and $C^-(2)$ in period two relative to the optimal control $C(1)$, equations (A7) and (A8).

$$C^+(2) = (2pR)^{1/1-\gamma} C(1) \quad (A7)$$

$$C^-(2) = (2(1-p)R)^{1/1-\gamma} C(1). \quad (A8)$$

the likelihood of any possible disturbance sequence. His analysis involves totally risk averse expectations.

Let us summarize what we have so far. Originally we had four unknowns: $C(1)$, $I(1)$, $C^+(2)$, $C^-(2)$. Equation (A4) implies that the expected relative marginal utility in the good case $pU'[C^+(2)]/U'[C(1)]$ should equal the expected relative marginal utility in the bad case $(1-p)U'[C^-(2)]/U'[C(1)]$. Equation (A3) states that the sum of the expected relative marginal utilities should equal $1/R = 1/(1+r)$. *Equations (A7) and (A8), derived from the maximization, give us $C^+(2)$ and $C^-(2)$ as a proportion of $C(1)$.* Since we know $C^+(2)$ and $C^-(2)$ as proportions of $C(1)$, we now need only solve for $C(1)$ and $I(1)$. We do this by using (A7) and (A8) in (14) and (15).

Substitute equation (A7), the relative consumption that results in the good case, in equation (14) to obtain equation (A9). Similarly substitute equation (A8), the relative consumption that results in the bad case, in equation (15), to obtain equation (A10). *These two equations permit us to solve for the optimal controls, c and i,* where $c = C(1)/K(1) > 0$ and $i = I(1)/K(1) \geq 0$, as a fraction of the initial capital $K(1)$, when there is uncertainty about the future productivity of capital.

$$B_1 c - (a/2) i = N \tag{A9}$$

$$B_2 c + (a/2) i = N - a. \tag{A10}$$

These equations are graphed in Figure 2.4. The crucial parameters B_1, B_2, and N are defined in Table 2.2. The general solution for optimal[9] consumption c, optimal investment i and optimal debt f, is in Box 2.3 for $1 > \gamma > 0$, and in Box 2.1 above for the logarithmic case $\gamma = 0$.

The two curves in Figure 2.4 have clear economic interpretations. Equation (A9) is consumption C^+_2 in the good case, which is proportional A^+ to the initial

---

Box 2.3

Optimal controls general case $1 > \gamma > 0$: consumption/capital, $c = C(1)/K(1)$, saving/capital $s = S(1)/K(1)$, investment/capital $i = I(1)/K(1)$, and the debt/capital $f = L(1)/K(1)$.

$$c = (2N - a)/(B_1 + B_2) \tag{A11}$$

$$s = b(1) - c \tag{A12}$$

$$i = \zeta(a/2)[(N - a)B_1 - NB_2]/[(B_1 + B_2)] < i_{max} \tag{A13}$$

$$\zeta = 1 \text{ when } [(N - a)B_1 - NB_2] > 0, \text{ and } \zeta = 0 \text{ otherwise} \tag{A14a}$$

$$\zeta = 1 \text{ when } (2p + 1)/2(1 - p) + 1 > (RW + a/2)/(RW - a/2) > 1 \tag{A14b}$$

$$f = [C(1) + I(1) - Y(1)]/K(1) = i - s = c + I - b(1). \tag{A15}$$

See Table 2.2 for definitions of N, B_1, B_2; equation (2.5a) gives the value of i_{max}.

---

[9] Variables are measured per unit of capital in period $t = 1$.

2. Stochastic optimal control model

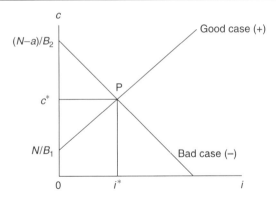

Figure 2.4. Optimal consumption and investment per unit of capital, equations (A9) and (A10).

Table 2.2. Definitions of crucial terms: two cases

	CASE I $\infty < \gamma < 1$	CASE II $\gamma = 0$
B_1 weight on good case	$(2pR)^{1/1-\gamma} + R$	$R(2p+1)$
B_2 weight on bad case	$(2(1-p)R)^{1/1-\gamma} + R$	$R(2(1-p)+1)$
$B_1 - B_2$	$(2pR)^{1/1-\gamma} - (2(1-p)R)^{1/1-\gamma}$	$2R(2p-1)$
$B_1 + B_2$	$2R + (2R)^{1/1-\gamma}[p^{1/1-\gamma} + (1-p)^{1/1-\gamma}]$	$4R$
N	$(1+b(1))R + (a/2) - 1 = RW + (a/2)$	$RW + (a/2)$
$(N-a)$	$(1+b(1))R - (a/2) - 1 = RW - (a/2)$	$RW - (a/2)$

Note: The values of the net return $b(2) - r$ are symmetrical around zero with a range $a > 0$, and probabilities $(p, 1-p)$. Expected net return $x = E[b(2) - r] = a(p - 1/2)$, $p = (x/a) + (1/2)$. The interest rate is r and define $R = 1 + r$. "Safe wealth" per unit of capital is defined as $W = [(1 + b(1))R - 1]/R$, and the risk premium in case II is defined as $\rho = (a/2)^2/[(1/2)RW]$.

period consumption. Since the net return $(b^+{}_2 - r) > 0$, both the initial period consumption c and investment i can rise without reducing consumption in the second period. Therefore, the slope is positive. Equation (A10) is consumption $C^-{}_2$ in the bad case, which is proportional A^- to the initial period consumption. Since the net return $(b^-{}_2 - r) < 0$, the initial period investment can only rise if consumption in the initial period declines. Therefore, the slope is negative.

The *optimal* controls must be selected in the first period before we know whether there will be a good or a bad outcome for the return on capital. Consequently, the optimal controls (c^*, i^*) are given by the intersection of the two curves, which is the solution of equations (A9) and (A10).

The condition for an interior maximum is that the solution to (A9), (A10) satisfy $C(1)/K(1) = c > 0$, $I(1)/K(1) = i > 0$. Optimal investment per unit of capital i will only be positive if the intercept of the curve "bad case" is higher than the intercept of the curve "good case"; that is the meaning of the condition that $[(N-a)B_1 - NB_2$ $] > 0$. A necessary condition for this to occur is that the probability of the good case $p > 1/2$. This is the meaning of equations (A14a) and (A14b) in Box 2.3 for positive investment in the logarithmic case.

References

Fleming, Wendell H. and Jerome L. Stein (2001), *Stochastic Inter-temporal Optimization in Discrete Time*, in Negishi, Takashi, Rama Ramachandran and Kazuo Mino (ed.) Economic Theory, Dynamics and Markets: Essays in Honor of Ryuzo Sato, Kluwer, Boston

Fleming, Wendell H. (2005), Optimal Investment Models with Minimum Consumption Criteria, *Australian Economic Papers*, Special Issue on Mathematical Finance Volume 44 December

International Monetary Fund (1999), International Capital Markets, September

—— (1999), World Economic Outlook, May

—— (1998), World Economic Outlook, Financial Crises, May

—— (2002), World Economic Outlook, Financial Crises, September

—— (1999) Anticipating Balance of Payments Crises: The role of early warning signals, Occasional Paper 186

3

Stochastic intertemporal optimization: Long-term debt continuous time

For many countries such as the United States, much of the external debt consists of long-term debt, portfolio investment, and direct investment. The model of short-term debt in Chapter 2 is not particularly relevant in that case. Instead in this chapter we consider long-term debt in continuous time in a stochastic environment. In order to motivate the mathematical analysis, consider the following questions. The United States[1] has been incurring trade and current account deficits since the beginning of the 1980s. The current account deficit has been rising strongly since 1991 and exceeded 5% of GDP in 2005. This phenomenon has led economists and the financial community to ask: Has the US borrowed "too much"? What is "too much"? Does a continuing external deficit mean that the country is living beyond its means? Are the trade deficits non-problematic, in the sense that they have within them the means to finance the repayment of borrowed funds or make good on expectations of return to equity value?

A country, like a household, is said to be living beyond its means – has borrowed "too much" – if its level of consumption is "unsustainable". A sufficient, but not necessary, condition for an unsustainable consumption is one that would lead to a negative net worth, where the debt exceeds its capital. Lenders would be reluctant to continue lending under those circumstances, interest rates would rise, stock prices would fall, the exchange rate would depreciate, and there would be a drastic decline in consumption.

Economies like the United States borrow to finance investment and growth as well as public plus private consumption. Long-term debt to

[1] The United States external debt and current account deficits are the subject of Chapter 9.

finance capital formation involves two risks. One is the return on domestic investment. The second is the real interest rate on debt. The variables of interest discussed in this chapter are the *optimal debt and capital, current account, growth rate*, and *consumption*. These benchmarks are used to evaluate to what extent the debt deviates from its optimal value, and what are the consequences of such deviations.

Optimality conditions should satisfy several criteria: (a) they involve observable and measurable variables, (b) if followed, would maximize the value of sensible criteria and (c) do not produce very bad results if there is imperfect knowledge or errors of measurement. Several approaches have been used to derive optimality conditions in open economies. The dominant ones use either "an intertemporal budget constraint" (IBC) or the Maximum Principle of Pontryagin. It is recognized that these approaches are deficient[2] in satisfying criteria (a)–(c) above.

As a rule, economists have used the Maximum Principle of Pontryagin to derive optimal control laws. This is an "open loop" type of optimization method that yields an entire sequence of controls to be followed from initial conditions. Half of the initial conditions must be obtained from transversality conditions, which imply the solution of differential equations. Given the likelihood of unpredictable disturbances, errors of measurement, formulation, and implementation, the overall system will not be stable unless converted into a feedback form. This is to be expected since the optimal path to the desired target is unique. It is clearly advantageous in economics to derive policies in feedback form, where the next move depends upon the current state, since these types of policies are self-correcting and robust to perturbations.[3]

When the economic system is deterministic, the controller can predict the future state of the system knowing the initial conditions and the controls used in the past. In a stochastic system – such as our case where both the productivity of investment and the real interest rate are stochastic and hence unpredictable – the controller cannot predict the future, because there are many paths that the system states may follow given the initial conditions and the past controls. *Since the controller cannot predict the future, the dynamic programming (DP) approach is generally used, where the optimal controls are based upon the observed state.*

---

[2] The deficiencies of the intertemporal budget constraint (IBC) approach in the economics literature have been discussed in the overview Chapter 1. We explained why the IBC is unknowable, unenforceable, and is a non-operational concept. See Gandolfo (2001, Ch. 1, 18) and Stein and Paladino (1997).

[3] This was the contribution of Infante and Stein (1973).

The aim of this chapter is to answer the following technical questions. In a *stochastic environment*, what is an *optimal* (1) long-term debt, (2) expected current account, (3) consumption, and (4) expected growth rate. The mathematical techniques necessary to answer these questions, concerning intertemporal optimization in continuous time, generally involve dynamic programming.

3.1. The intertemporal optimal decision process

Questions (1)–(4) above, concerning the optimal debt and expected growth rate, involve intertemporal optimization for the following reasons. Equation (3.1) describes the change in the debt dL_t, which is the current account deficit over a period. A positive change in the debt is a capital inflow or current account deficit. A negative change in the debt is a capital outflow or current account surplus. The current account deficit dL_t is the sum of consumption C_t, investment I_t, the servicing of the long-term debt r_tL_t at interest rate r_t less the GDP denoted, Y_t. Equivalently, the change in the debt is investment less private plus public saving $(I\text{-}S)dt$ over the period. In the Latin American countries the debt has grown because of low saving due to high government consumption, and in Asia it has grown because of high private investment. In the US it has been a combination of the two that varied by period. A government budget deficit is negative public saving. Monetary and fiscal policies are important determinants of social saving and investment, and hence of the external debt.

$$dL_t = (C_t + I_t + r_tL_t - Y_t)dt = (I_t - S_t)dt. \tag{3.1}$$

The intertemporal aspect is seen by putting consumption on the left-hand side in equation (3.2). At some later period $s = t + \Delta t$ when the debt is L_s, consumption is equation (3.2). The resources available are the GDP less servicing of the debt $(\mathbf{Y}_s - \mathbf{r}_sL_s)$ less investment I_s plus any new borrowing dL_s.

$$C_sds = (Y_s - r_sL_s - I_s)ds + dL_s. \tag{3.2}$$

There are two stochastic variables (written in bold letters here): the level of GDP and the real rate of interest $(\mathbf{Y},\mathbf{r})$. The long-term debt is serviced at a variable interest rate. If the external debt is denominated in foreign currency, then the change in the exchange rate is subsumed under the real rate of interest[4]. When the investment and saving decisions are made and

---

[4] This is discussed in Chapter 9 concerning US current account deficits.

the debt changes by dL_t over the period, the economic units do not know what will be the future levels of (Y,r). Therefore the economic units do not know the resources that will be available for future consumption. Moreover future borrowing (dL_s) is not guaranteed. Consequently the optimal consumption and investment decisions made at time t are intimately related to the processes that affect future GDP and interest rates. This is the reason why the dynamic programming approach is very important for intertemporal optimization.

The models discussed in the rest of this chapter are distinguished according to several criteria. (A) What are the stochastic processes? (B) What are the controls and constraints? (C) What are the optimization criteria? Thereby, our answers to questions (1)–(4) above differ according to the specifications in (A)–(C).

In the *prototype model* analyzed in this chapter, both stochastic processes – the productivity of capital and the real interest rate – are described by Brownian motion with drift. These stochastic process can be regarded as a continuous time limit of a random walk, with constant drift towards the left or the right. An alternative not discussed in this chapter is the *ergodic mean reversion* model. In the latter model, which has been studied by Stein (2006) as an alternative to the prototype model, one stochastic process is Brownian motion with drift but the second process is an *Ornstein–Uhlenbeck* mean reverting process. This is a mathematically more complicated model, whose solution is explained in the paper by Fleming and Pang (2004).

The stochastic optimal control/dynamic programming (SOC/DP) approach is widely used in the mathematical finance literature, but is not widely known by economists. We explain, and show graphically, how the SOC/DP solution of an inter-temporal optimization can be understood in terms of the Tobin–Markowitz mean variance (M-V) analysis. In this manner, the economists will understand the great advantages of using stochastic optimal control for intertemporal optimization.

3.2. Prototype model: Infinite horizon, continuous time[5]

The endogenous growth model summarized in Box 3.1 is a generalization of the models in the economics literature. The main differences are that (1) the production function is stochastic AK, and the interest rate on loans

---

[5] This is the model analyzed by Fleming and Stein (2004) and Stein (2003).

is also stochastic. There is a correlation of these two sources of uncertainty, which differs among economies. (2) The model is in real terms and is formulated in terms of the stochastic calculus. To formulate a stochastic control problem associated with the model, we must specify the *state* and *control* variables, the *constraints*, the *dynamics* of the state process and the *criterion* to be optimized.

Several optimization criteria are considered. The object may be to maximize the expectation (E) of the discounted value ($\delta > 0$) of the utility of consumption generally over an infinite horizon, equations (3.3) and (3.4). The choice of utility function $U(C_t)$ is very important. Assume that utility is HARA (hyperbolic absolute risk aversion), as stated in equations (3.3) and (3.4). Risk aversion ($1 - \gamma$) is positive[6]. When $\gamma = 0$, the utility function is logarithmic and the criterion is equation (3.4). There are several advantages to the use of the HARA function. First, it reduces the dimension of the problem and allows us to solve the model analytically. Second, it is scale independent. It is valid regardless of the size of the economy.

The *controls* are the vector $u = (c_t > 0, f_t)$, the positive consumption ratio $c_t > 0$, and the debt ratio f_t which can be positive, zero, or negative.

$$V(X) = \max_u E \int^\infty (1/\gamma) C_t^\gamma e^{-\delta t} dt, \quad 0 < t < \infty \quad 1 > \gamma, \gamma \neq 0 \tag{3.3}$$

$$V(X) = \max_u E \int^\infty e^{-\delta t} \ln C_t dt, \quad 0 < t < \infty. \tag{3.4}$$

An alternative, which has considerable advantages for empirical work and for policy analysis, is equation (3.5):

$$V(X) = \max_f E[(1/T) \ln C_T/C \,|\, c = C/X > 0], \\ C = C(0) \text{ and } c_{\max} > c > 0. \tag{3.5}$$

Solve for the debt ratio f_t that maximizes the expected growth rate of consumption over a finite horizon $(0, T)$, given an arbitrary ratio $c = C/X$ of consumption to net worth. The constraint is that the ratio $c > 0$ should be less than $c_{\max} > c > 0$. This constraint ensures that growth can be expected to be positive if there were no external debt.

On the basis of the solution of the intertemporal optimization we derive: (a) the optimal ratio of external debt/net worth, (b) the optimal ratio of consumption/net worth, and (c) the optimal expected endogenous growth rate. These quantities are measurable, and are used in the empirical chapters below. Moreover (d) we explain that as the actual debt

---

[6] The requirement is that $\gamma < 1$. If $\gamma = 0$, the utility function is logarithmic. If $\gamma < 0$, then a discount rate is not necessary in the optimization.

Box 3.1. PROTOTYPE STOCHASTIC GROWTH MODEL

$$Y_t = b_t K_t = [b\,dt + \sigma_y dw_y]K_t, \quad dw_y = \varepsilon_y \sqrt{dt}, \varepsilon_y \sim N(0,1) \text{ iid} \qquad (3.6)$$

$$E[Y_t/K_t] = b\,dt \qquad (3.6a)$$

$$\text{var}\,[Y_t/K_t] = \sigma_y^2\,dt \qquad (3.6b)$$

$$dK_t = I_t\,dt \qquad (3.7)$$

$$dL_t = r_t L_t dt + [C_t + I_t - Y_t]dt = (I_t - S_t)dt. \qquad (3.8)$$

$$r_t dt = r\,dt + \sigma_r dw_r \qquad dw_r = \varepsilon_r \sqrt{dt}; \ \varepsilon_r \sim N(0,1) \text{ iid} \qquad (3.9)$$

$$r_t L_t dt = rL_t dt + \sigma_r L_t dw_r \qquad (3.9a)$$

$$E[w_r w_y] = \rho\,dt, \ 1 \geq \rho \geq -1 \qquad (3.10)$$

$$X_t = K_t - L_t. \qquad (3.11)$$

$C =$ consumption, $Y =$ GDP, $L =$ debt denominated in domestic currency, $I =$ investment, $K =$ capital, $r =$ real rate of interest, $X =$ net worth $=$ capital $-$ debt $= K - L$; Brownian motion, w_r, w_y. Constraints: $[C > 0, X > 0]$. Net foreign assets are $(-L)$, negative debt.

---

ratio rises above the optimal, the expected growth rate of consumption declines and its variance increases. This means that the economy is more vulnerable to random shocks to the productivity of capital and interest rate. The equations in the prototype stochastic growth model summarized in Box 3.1 are now discussed.

3.2.1. *Production function: Uncertainty concerning the return on capital*

Production function (3.6) states that the GDP or value added $Y(t)$ is proportional to capital $K(t)$. The ratio of real output/capital, $Y(t)/K(t) = b(t)$, is the return on capital. The deterministic part is the mean return b, with no time index, and the stochastic part involves the Brownian motion term $\sigma_y dw_y$, whose the mean is zero and variance is $\sigma_y^2 dt$, equations (3.6a) and (3.6b). The stochastic term arises from unpredictable movements in demand and costs of production, the prices of output and of inputs. Equation (3.6) is a stochastic AK production function, and the stochastic term may exhibit great variations over short periods of time.

The change in capital $dK(t)$ in equation (3.7) is the investment over the period $I(t)dt$. The concept of capital, the integral of investment in equation (3.7), has many ambiguities when there is technical change, depreciation, and obsolescence. In Appendix A we describe an alternative approach that does not explicitly use the concept of capital, avoids the problems involving technical change but leads to exactly the same mathematical results as are developed below.

3.2.2. *Debt payments uncertainty*

In Chapter 2, we considered a discrete-time finite horizon model where borrowing is in the form of short-term debt, which must be repaid with interest at maturity. In this chapter, we assume that the "debt" consists of portfolio investment, direct investment, or equity that have no maturity but be serviced continually at a *variable* real rate $r(t)$, which could be the interest rate for debt or dividend rate for equities. The term "debt", $L(t)$, refers to the total net liability position. In the balance of payments statistics, the product $r(t)L(t)$ is referred to as "the negative balance on investment income", which consists of interest, dividends and reinvested earnings.

The debt $L(t)$ consists of net liabilities to foreigners, which is often called the negative investment position of the country. Assume that the "debt" is denominated in the currency of the debtor – the domestic currency. In Chapter 9, we consider the case where the external debt is denominated in the currency of the creditor country, so that there is also an explicit exchange risk. Equation (3.8) is the equation for the current account deficit, which is identically equal to the change in net external liabilities. The change in net external liabilities, $dL(t)$, is the excess of domestic spending plus interest payments on existing liabilities relative to the GDP. Domestic spending is equal to consumption $C(t)$ plus investment $I(t)$ of the private plus public sectors. Since domestic spending plus income transfers less GDP is equal to investment $I(t)$ less saving $S(t) = Y(t) - r(t)L(t) - C(t)$, we may view equation (3.8) as stating that the change in the debt is equal to investment less saving.

The real interest payments $r(t)L(t)$ in equation (3.9) are stochastic, because the interest rate on portfolio investment, dividends, and reinvested earnings are stochastic. In interest rate equation (3.9), let r be the mean or expected real rate of interest, r, with no time subscript, and let the variance of the interest rate be equal to $\sigma_r^2 dt$. Equation (3.9a) describes $r(t)L(t)$, which is the net interest payments on the external debt.

3.2.3 *The correlation of the shocks to GDP and to the interest rate*

Equations (3.6) and (3.9a) describe the uncertainty. Consider the general case, equation (3.10), where the two shocks are correlated $E(dw_r dw_y) = \rho dt$, where $1 \geq \rho \geq -1$. The correlation coefficient ρ could be positive, zero, or negative, which varies among economies, regions, and sectors and over time for each one.

Often in the macroeconomy, a rise in the return on capital stimulates an economic expansion that raises investment, which then leads to a rise in interest rates. Then there is a positive correlation $\rho > 0$ between the return on capital and the interest rate. A very different situation exists when there has been a change in monetary policy, or a financial crisis that reduces GDP and hence the output per unit of capital. For example, a financial crisis leads to a rise in interest rates and a restriction of credit. Aggregate demand declines and the GDP is adversely affected. Then the correlation of the shocks is negative, because the rise in the interest rate is associated with a decline in Y/K, the productivity of capital.

3.3. The dynamic programming solution[7]

First, we show what is the dynamic programming (DP) solution for intertemporal optimization under uncertainty, over an infinite horizon. The derivations and underlying technical details are discussed in the mathematical Appendix B. Second, we explain how the DP solution for the optimal debt is related to the well-known Tobin–Markowitz mean variance model (M-V). On the basis of a simple graph, we are able to convey the economic meaning of almost all of our results.

Our underlying models are Markov diffusion processes where the future depends upon the present and not at all upon the past. The system is stochastic/unpredictable. Even if one specified the controls/decisions from the present to any future date, the future is unpredictable because there are many paths that the system can take due to the stochastic processes concerning the real GDP and the real interest rate. At each instant of time the "controller/decision maker" knows the state of the system, and *only has information up to the present*. Since, the controller cannot anticipate the future, the DP approach involves a multistage decision

---

[7] The dynamic programming method in stochastic systems is discussed and the basic equations are derived in Fleming and Rishel (1975). Chapters V and VI, and Øksendal (1995), Chapter V. These books are standard references for mathematicians.

process[8]. The *principle of optimality* of DP is that: *whatever the initial state and the initial decisions are, the remaining decisions must constitute an optimal policy with regard to the state resulting from the first decision. In a stochastic system, the optimal controls selected at any time depend upon the current information available and enter as feedback functions of the currently observable state.*

The state variable in the stochastic systems discussed in this model is net worth X_t defined as capital K_t less debt L_t, equation (3.11). Given net worth at any time, if we know the capital (debt) the value of the debt (capital) is also known.

Net worth $X(t) = K(t) - L(t) > 0$ is constrained to be positive. This constraint precludes Ponzi schemes where further borrowing refinances debt. In a Ponzi scheme net worth becomes negative, because debt grows without a growth in capital. In our model, net worth $X(t)$ cannot become negative, and a Ponzi scheme is not possible, because the optimal debt is proportional to net worth. If net worth were declining to zero, the optimal debt would also decline to zero. Alternatively, if net worth were declining to zero, the optimal current account deficit would also decline to zero.

A brief sketch of the dynamic programming approach is as follows. The reader who is not interested in the mathematical foundations may proceed directly to the Propositions below. They are explained later in terms of the well known mean-variance analyis.

The value function $V(X)$ in equations (3.3) and (3.4) is what we want to maximize. The initial net worth is $X = X(0)$. The DP equation for the maximum value of expected discounted utility over an infinite horizon $V(X)$ involves a multistage decision process. The first term in equation (3.12) is $U(C_t)dt$, the utility of consumption over a short period of length dt. This is "the first stage". The second term in (3.12) is the expectation of the discounted value of the utility of consumption starting from the wealth $(X + dX)$ that would exist at time $(t + dt)$, resulting from decisions made at time t. This is the "second stage". The discount rate is $\delta > 0$. The intertemporal aspect arises because the decisions taken in "one period" affect the net worth in the "next period"[9]. Our analysis is in continuous time so that the length of the period dt goes to zero.

The controls are consumption C_t and debt L_t or capital K_t, and the constraints are that consumption and net worth are positive. The set of

---

[8] This is very different from the intertemporal budget constraint approach.
[9] For example, see equations (3.1) and (3.2).

controls and constraints is referred to as Γ. The expectation E is taken over the stochastic variables dw_y and dw_r in Box 3.1.

$$V(X) = \max_\Gamma E[U(C_t)dt + (1 - \delta \, dt)V(X + dX)]. \qquad (3.12)$$

To derive $(X + dX)$ one must know what is the change in net worth dX. The dynamics of the state variable net worth $X(t)$ are expressed in equations (3.13) and (3.14). The change in net worth $dX(t)$ is equation (3.13). Substitute $dK(t)$ from equation (3.7), and the change in the debt $dL(t)$ from equations (3.8), using (3.6), (3.9a) and (3.11), to obtain equation (3.14).

$$dX_t = dK_t - dL_t. \qquad (3.13)$$

$$dX_t = [bX_t + (b - r)L_t - C_t]dt - L_t\sigma_r dw_r - (X_t + L_t)\sigma_y dw_y. \qquad (3.14)$$

The value function $V(X)$ depends upon the utility function, which reflects preferences. In equations (3.3) and (3.4) a HARA function was selected for two reasons. First, it is the only one that permits one to solve the system analytically. Merton (1990) used that function in his book. Otherwise, it must be solved numerically. Second, the HARA utility function allows us to use as controls the *ratios* of debt/net worth f equal to capital/net worth $K - 1$, since $(k - f) = 1$, and consumption/net worth $c = C/X$. The *control* variables are consumption ratio $c(t)$ and the debt ratio $f(t)$. A simplifying assumption is that the controls $c(t)$ and $f(t) = k(t) - 1$ can be varied instantaneously and are costless. The optimization (3.3) or (3.4) when the HARA utility function is used subject to the stochastic differential equation (3.14) and to the constraints implies equation (3.15).

$$dX_t = [(b - c_t) - (b - r)f_t]X_t dt - f_t X_t \sigma_r dw_r + (1 + f_t)X_t \sigma_y dw_y \qquad (3.15)$$

$$f = L/X, k = K/X = 1 + f, c = C/X, \quad C(t) > 0, X(t) > 0.$$

From (3.3) and (3.15), we derive the Hamilton–Jacobi–Bellman (HJB) equation (3.16) of dynamic programming. This is the basic equation for intertemporal optimization under uncertainty. Box 3.2 contains the solution of DP equation (3.16) for the optimal debt/net worth, capital/net worth[10], and consumption/net worth. The derivation of the HJB equation is quite technical and is contained in Appendix B. In the text, we show how the HJB equation can be understood in terms of the Tobin–Markowitz mean-variance (M-V) analysis. On the basis of simple M-V graphs, we are able to give a simple economic interpretation of the optimization equations. That is why it is not essential for the non-mathematician

---

[10] Net worth $X(t)$ equals capital less debt. Since capital/net worth less debt/net worth equals one, the propositions apply to the optimal ratio k^* of "capital"/net worth.

Box 3.2 SUMMARY OF OPTIMAL (*) CONTROLS

$$f^* = (b - r)/(1 - \gamma)\sigma^2 + \lambda(\rho\theta - 1)$$
$$= (b - r)/(1 - \gamma)\sigma^2 + f(0) \quad \text{debt/net worth} \tag{3.17}$$

$$[K_t/X_t]^* = k^* = 1 + f^* \geq 0 \quad \text{capital/net worth} \tag{3.18}$$

$$c^* = C_t/X_t = \delta, \quad \text{when } \gamma = 0. \quad \text{consumption/net worth} \tag{3.19}$$

Symbols: *Net worth* $X = K - L$; expected net return $= (b - r)$; total risk $= \sigma^2 = $ var $(b_t - r_t) = (\sigma_r^2 + \sigma_y^2 - 2\rho\sigma_r\sigma_y) > 0$; $\theta = \sigma_r/\sigma_y = $ standard deviation of interest rate/ standard deviation of growth; $\rho = $ correlation between interest rate and growth; $\lambda = (\sigma_y^2/\sigma^2) = 1/(1 + \theta^2 - 2\rho\theta) > 0$. Intercept term $f(0) = \lambda (\rho\theta - 1)$.

---

reader to know how to derive the HJB equation in order to understand the economic significance and interpretation of the propositions below and the content of this chapter. *The non-mathematical reader can jump directly to Propositions I–V below.*

Dynamic programming maximization

$$\delta/\gamma = \max_c[(1/\gamma)c_t^\gamma/A + (b - c_t)] + \max_f\{[(b - r)f_t] - (1 - \gamma)(\sigma_y^2/2)[(f_t^2\theta^2)$$
$$+ (1 + f_t)^2 - 2(1 + f_t)f_t\rho\theta]\}, \quad \theta = \sigma_r/\sigma_y. \tag{3.16}$$

Roughly speaking, the term $[(1/\gamma)c_t^\gamma/A]$ in (3.16) corresponds to the utility of present consumption $U(C_t)$ term in (3.12). Parameter A is determined from the optimal solution. In the logarithmic case, equation (3.4), the solution implies that A is the reciprocal of the discount rate. The remaining terms correspond to the $V(X + dX)$ term in (3.12), the utility of future consumption.

Propositions I–V are the implications for intertemporal optimization under uncertainty when there are risk and risk aversion. They are generalizations of the Merton approach in mathematical finance, which are very different from the implications of the intertemporal budget constraint models in the economics literature. The economic interpretation of the propositions is the subject of the subsequent sections.

Proposition I. The optimal debt/net worth f^* and capital/net worth k^* maximize a mean-variance function of expected return and risk.

Proposition II. The optimal f^* or $k^* = 1 + f^*$ are independent of the optimal ratio of consumption/net worth and discount rate[11].

---

[11] The converse is not true. See Appendix B.

Proposition III. When utility is logarithmic, the optimal debt/net worth f^* or capital/net worth k^* maximize the expected endogenous growth rate, for any constant consumption ratio c less than b, the expected productivity of capital.

Proposition IV. The optimal debt/net worth will only be positive if the expected return exceeds the expected real interest rate by an amount that depends upon the correlation of the growth and interest rate risks and their variances.

Proposition V. When the utility function is logarithmic, the optimal ratio of consumption/net worth is the discount rate.

Proposition VI. Permanent current account deficits/net worth are optimal if f^* and expected growth are positive.

Equation (3.17), graphed in Figure 3.1 as line U-S, relates the ratio f^* of the optimal debt/net worth to the risk adjusted expected net return on investment $z = (b - r)/\sigma^2$. The ratio of "capital"/net worth is $k^* = 1 + f^*$, so that the graph can be used to determine either debt or capital relative to net worth. Total risk σ^2 is the variance of the net return equal to var $(b_t - r_t) = (\sigma_r^2 + \sigma_y^2 - 2\rho\sigma_1\sigma_2) > 0$.

The slope of the curve is $1/(1 - \gamma)$, the reciprocal of positive risk aversion. The intercept $f(0) = \lambda \, (\rho\theta - 1)$ is the optimal ratio debt/net worth when the expected net return is zero. It can be positive, zero, or negative. As long as the correlation between the two disturbances is less than the ratio of the standard deviation of the return on capital/standard deviation of the interest rate, $\rho < \sigma_y/\sigma_r$, the value of $f(0)$ is negative. Figure 3.1 is drawn on

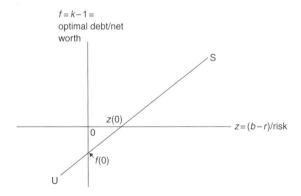

Figure 3.1 Optimal debt/net worth $f^* = k^* - 1$, and risk adjusted expected net return $z = (b - r)/\sigma^2$. If there are no transactions costs, curve U-S is the optimal relation. A debtor position is when $f > 0$, and a creditor when $f < 0$.

the basis of this realistic condition. The minimum value of the debt/net worth ratio is minus 1, when capital is zero.

We show in the M-V section below that $f(0)$ is the ratio of debt/net worth that minimizes total risk. As long as the risk adjusted expected net return z is less than $z(0)$, the ratio of debt/net worth should be negative – the economy should be a creditor. As the expected net return rises above $z(0)$, the economy should finance capital with debt. A debt/net worth is excessive/non-optimal, insofar as it lies above a line such as U-S in Figure 3.1.

Given the risk adjusted net return $z = (b - r)/\sigma^2$, the optimum debt ratio is given by equation (3.17) or line U-S in Figure 3.1. The prototype model in Box 3.1 is predicated upon the assumption that the economy can adjust to the optimum ratio instantly and without cost. If the debt ratio is above the curve U-S, then capital should be sold and debt repaid to bring the economy back to the curve. Similarly, if the debt ratio is below the curve, debt should be incurred and capital should be acquired via a capital inflow to bring the economy to the curve[12].

3.4. A mean-variance (M-V) interpretation of the DP solution

The Tobin–Markowitz mean-variance (M-V) analysis is the cornerstone of much of the work in the field of investment/portfolio allocation analysis. It is based upon a two-period model of portfolio choice between "safe" and "risky" assets, and implies clear and operational results. Our model in Box 3.1 seems to be quite different. There is an infinite horizon, and risk on both the debt and on capital. A negative debt is a positive holding of financial assets. Growth is endogenous. We show how the HJB equation (3.16) and the equations in Box 3.2 can be related to the M-V analysis.

---

[12] In fact capital cannot be sold or produced instantly and without costs. For example during the Asian or Argentine crises, if the economy tried to sell capital to foreigners in order to repay debt, it would do so at "fire sale" prices. The faster that the country tries to sell capital and repay debt, the less the country will realize from the sale. Similarly, if the economy were below the curve, a country cannot bring its capital/net worth up to $k^* = 1 + f^*$ instantly. The faster that the capital is built up, the more costly it will be.

Net worth $X(t)$ is very volatile due to the Brownian motion terms in equation (3.15). Say that the risk adjusted net return z is constant. If the debt/net worth $L(t)/X(t)$ ratio is kept at $f^* = z/(1 - \gamma) + f(0) = k^* - 1$, then there would be very frequent purchases and sales of capital as net worth $X(t)$ jumps around. The "transactions costs" would dissipate the net worth very quickly. Davis and Norman (1990), Fleming and Soner (1993), and Rogers (2004) showed that if there are linear "transactions costs", the optimal ratio of capital/net worth k should lie in a cone. Thereby, a balance is achieved between deviating from optimality and dissipating net worth with extremely frequent transactions costs.

The optimal values of debt/net worth f^* or "capital"/net worth $k^* = 1 + f^*$ maximize the value function equation $V(X)$ in (3.3) or (3.4) subject to the law of motion of the state variable $X(t)$ net worth, equation (3.15). In the M-V analysis, the object is to select a portfolio of risky and safe assets to maximize M-V expected utility V^*, which is a *mean M less risk R* times *risk aversion* $(1 - \gamma) > 0$:

$$V^* = M - (1 - \gamma)R = \text{M-V expected utility} \qquad (3.20)$$

To relate the HJB equation (3.16) for the optimal debt to the maximization of M-V expected utility equation (3.20), we must have expressions for "mean" M and "risk" R, which are based upon the prototype model. This correspondence is based upon the growth of net worth dX_t/X_t in equation (3.15). Think of net worth X_t as the value of a portfolio of two risky securities: capital, which has an uncertain return b_t, and debt, which has an uncertain return r_t. A negative debt is positive financial assets.

Define the *mean M(f,c)* as the expected growth of net worth $E(dX_t/X_t)$ in equation (3.21). It is the mean growth (not growth rate) of net worth – the value of the portfolio – if there were no risks of variations in the return on capital and the real interest rate.

$$M(f, c) = E(dX_t/X_t) = [(b - c) + (b - r)f]. \qquad (3.21)$$

Risk equation (3.22) describes the uncertainty concerning the growth rate. Define the *risk R(f)* as one half of the variance of the growth (dX_t/X_t) in

$$R(f) = \text{var } (dX_t/X_t)/2 = (\sigma_y^2/2)[f^2\theta^2 + (1 + f)^2 - 2f(1 + f)\rho\theta],$$
$$\theta = \sigma_r/\sigma_y. \qquad (3.22)$$

The correspondence between the DP solution based upon the HJB equation (3.16) and the M-V equation (3.20) exists because the DP equation can be written as equation (3.23) using the definitions for mean M and risk R and expected M-V utility V^* above. *Equation (3.23) shows that the intertemporal maximization with respect to the optimal debt/net worth f can be given an M-V interpretation:*

$$\delta/\gamma = \max\{(1/\gamma)c^\gamma/A + V^*(f, c)\}$$
$$= \max_{c, f}\{(1/\gamma)c^\gamma/A + M(f, c) - (1 - \gamma)R(f)\}. \qquad (3.23)$$

The choice of an optimal debt/net worth ratio in the HJB equation (16) can be viewed as selecting the debt/net worth ratio that maximizes the M-V expected utility $V^*(f,c) = M(f,c) - (1 - \gamma)R(f)$, given any ratio of consumption/net worth c, where $0 < c < b$. An M-V interpretation of HJB equation (3.23) for the optimal debt/net worth is described graphically in Figure 3.2, where we select a debt/net worth ratio that maximizes V^*, the "mean-variance expected utility".

3. Stochastic intertemporal optimization

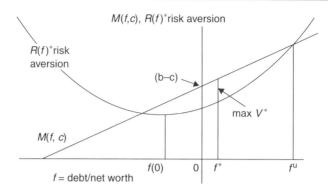

Figure 3.2 The optimum debt/net worth ratio f^* maximizes the M-V expected utility $V^* = M(f,c) - (1 - \gamma)R(f)$, for any arbitrary ratio c of consumption/net worth, $b > c > 0$. In the figure, risk aversion is unity, $\gamma = 0$, so that $V^* = M(f,c) - R(f) =$ expected growth.

The mean $M(f,c)$ in (3.21) is a linear function of f, the debt/net worth. The intercept $(b - c) > 0$ is the expected growth if there were no debt, $f = 0$. It is the mean productivity of capital b less the consumption ratio $c < b$. This constraint is necessary if expected growth is positive when there is no debt $f = 0$. The slope of the mean function is $(b - r)$, the expected return on capital less the expected interest rate. There are no diminishing returns to investment in the model. Variations in the consumption ratio only affect the intercept and not the slope of the mean function.

Risk $R(f)$ defined in (3.22) is a quadratic function of the debt/net worth, which is independent of consumption ratio c and the expected net return $(b - r)$. Total risk $R(f)$ is not the same as the variance of the return on investment σ_y^2. Borrowing to finance real investment involves a risky return and a risky interest rate liability. The two risks may be correlated positively or negatively, or may be independent of each other. The uncertainty concerns the variance of the net return.

The quadratic risk function $R(f)$ reaches a minimum at $f(0) < 0$ in Figure 3.2 and rises as the net debt/net worth deviates from $f(0)$. The minimum risk ratio of debt/net worth, at $f(0) = (\rho\theta - 1)/(1 + \theta^2 - 2\rho\theta)$, is the intercept term in equation (3.17) and Figure 3.1. To minimize risk, the country should be a creditor if the quantity $(\rho\theta - 1)$ is negative. If the correlation of the disturbances is less than the standard deviation of the return relative to that of the interest rate, $\rho < \sigma_y/\sigma_r$, then to minimize risk, the country should be a creditor. Figures 3.1 and 3.2 are drawn on the basis of this realistic assumption.

The mean-variance interpretation of the DP equation is that the optimal ratio f^* of debt/net worth in Figure 3.2 maximizes the expected M-V utility V^* equation (3.20), as explained above.

$$f^* \in \operatorname{argmax} \, [V^* = M(f,c) - (1 - \gamma)R(f)]. \qquad (3.24)$$

There are two important differences between the M-V static model and the intertemporal optimization using stochastic optimal control. One difference is that the intertemporal optimization solution states that the debt L_t^* should be varied constantly to keep it equal to $f^* X_t$. As net worth jumps around according to equation (3.15), the debt must be adjusted constantly to maintain the fixed proportion.[13] The optimal ratio of "capital"/net worth is $K_t^*/X_t = k^* = 1 + f^*$, so that the intertemporal optimization equation (3.17) implies the optimal ratio of capital/net worth k_t at any moment of time. As net worth varies according to equation (3.17) the optimum capital K_t^* must vary to maintain the optimal ratio. Our approach is a generalization of the Merton model to an open economy with two types of risk. Since we both use dynamic programming, we both obtain results very different from the open economy models, which use either the intertemporal budget constraint or the Maximum Principle.

3.5. Optimal consumption and the role of preference variables

The optimum consumption ratio $c^* = C_t/X_t$ is derived from the maximization of the HJB equation (16) with respect to the consumption ratio. The technical details of the derivation are in Appendix B. In the logarithmic case where $\gamma = 0$, the optimal consumption ratio c^* is equal to the discount rate, $c^* = \delta$ in equation (3.19). Box 3.2 contains the equations for optimal consumption/net worth, capital/net worth, and debt/net worth in the prototype model. They are our benchmarks of performance, which allow us to evaluate whether debt or consumption is excessive at any time.

Several features of the approach limit the *empirical* usefulness of the equations as benchmarks of performance, because the utility function is arbitrary and a wide range of discount rates is acceptable. A frequently asked question is whether countries with high government budget deficits have non-optimal social consumption ratios? Equation (3.19) cannot answer the important question of whether a country is consuming too much or too little. The reason is that the subjective discount rate is a crucial element in the optimal consumption ratio in the general case of risk aversion

---

[13] This is not the case when there are transaction costs, as explained in footnote 10 above.

$(1 - \gamma > 0)$ as shown in Appendix B. In effect, the discount rate in the value function (3.3) is an inverse measure of the length of the horizon. A high discount rate effectively makes consumption at later dates less valuable than consumption at earlier dates. The optimal consumption rate c^*, equal to the discount rate in (3.19), is high when the effective horizon is short; and it is low when the effective horizon is long. A government catering to populist pressures may incur any budget deficit/GDP, or any ratio of social consumption/GDP it wishes and justify it by saying that it corresponds to its high discount rate/short-horizon in its value function. Similarly, a dictator can justify depressing present consumption drastically for the sake of the future by saying that he is optimizing with a low discount rate/long horizon. There is no way that one can objectively criticize the selected discount rate or effective length of horizon. It is a preference variable, which can "justify" any shortsightedness or present sacrifice. Who is to say whose preferences/discount rate are the ones to use in equation (3.19)?

Another frequently asked question is whether the debt is excessive. Equation (3.17) contains both *objective* and *subjective* variables. The optimal debt ratio in (3.17) does not contain the arbitrary discount rate, and hence the optimal debt ratio is independent of the effective length of the horizon. The line U-S in Figure 3.1 describes the relation between the optimal debt ratio f^* and $z = (b - r)/\sigma^2$ the *risk-adjusted net mean return*. The slope of line U-S in Figure 3.1 is $1/(1 - \gamma)$, the reciprocal of risk aversion. Other than the constraint that the slope must be positive, no one can objectively say what is the "correct" risk aversion to use. By varying risk aversion, the positive slope of U-S, one can obtain any "optimal" debt ratio for a given $z = (b - r)/\sigma^2$. A borrower with low risk aversion would select a high debt ratio; and a borrower with high risk aversion would select a low debt ratio, corresponding to the same *risk-adjusted net mean return*. The model assumes, unrealistically, that lenders are willing to lend at rate r_t to both types of borrowers. This issue is discussed in Chapter 9 concerning United States current account deficits.

3.6. Optimal expected endogenous growth[14] and mean-variance expected utility

Since the utility function and discount rate are *subjective* variables the optimal values, which are benchmarks of performance, in Box 3.2 are

---

[14] Platen (2005) approaches portfolio optimization in this manner. He derives the growth optimal portfolio (GOP).

ambiguous. Optimality criterion equation (3.5) may be more useful for policy purposes and empirical analysis, because it does not involve a utility function. It only involves objectively measurable variables.

Continue to use the prototype model in Box 3.1. Select an arbitrary ratio of consumption/net worth $c = C_t/X_t > 0$ that is less than b, the productivity of capital. The control variable in the optimization is the debt ratio $f = L_t/X_t$, which maximizes the expected growth rate of net worth and consumption over some arbitrary horizon $(0,T)$, equation (3.25). The choice of a consumption/net worth ratio less than the productivity of capital $(c < b)$ is necessary if optimal expected growth is to be positive. The mean curve $M(f,c)$ in Figure 3.2 is constrained to have a positive intercept.

$$\max_f (1/T)E_{b,r}[\ln X_T/X|c < b] = \max_f (1/T)E_{b,r}[\ln C_T/C],$$
$$X = X(0), C = C(0). \tag{3.25}$$

First, we indicate the mathematical derivation. Second, we explain the mathematical results in terms of M-V expected utility, as described in Figure 3.2. The interesting result is that: when the consumption ratio is specified, the optimal expected growth rate is equal to the maximal M-V expected utility, when risk aversion is unity.

Dynamic programming is not necessary to find the optimal debt ratio. All that is required is to solve (3.15) for $\ln X_t$ using the Ito differential rule and then use calculus to determine the optimal debt ratio from (25). Technical details concerning the derivation of the optimal debt ratio and endogenous growth rate are in Appendix B.

Equation (3.26) is the solution for f^*, the debt/net worth that maximizes the expected growth rate. There is a linear relation between the optimal ratio f^* of debt/net worth and $z = (b - r)/\sigma^2$, the *mean* of the return less effective interest rate per unit of risk. *This is the same as the dynamic programming solution, equation (3.17), when risk aversion is unity, the logarithmic case, equation (3.4).* Equations (3.26) and (3.17) are graphed in Figure 3.1 where the slope is unity. Consider the case where the optimal debt ratio f^* is positive, as drawn in Figure 3.2.

$$f^* = L_t^*/X_t = (b - r)/\sigma^2 + f(0) = z + f(0), \quad \sigma^2 = \text{var}(b_t - r_t). \tag{3.26}$$

Derive the maximal expected endogenous growth rate by substituting equation (3.26) into the solution of equation (3.25) for $\ln X_t$. This is conditioned upon an arbitrary consumption ratio $c < b$. Of course, the consumption ratio selected could be the discount rate $c = \delta < b$.

In the case where the two risks are independent ($\rho = 0$), the *maximal expected growth rate* of consumption and net worth is Λ in equation (3.27).

Appendix B contains the mathematical derivation of equations (3.26) and (3.27).

Maximal endogenous expected growth of consumption and net worth

$$\Lambda = (b - c) + [(1/2)(b - r)^2/\sigma^2 - (b - r)/(1 + \theta^2) - \sigma_r^2/2] \qquad (3.27)$$
$$= \max_f (1/T)E_{b,r}[\ln X_T/X | c < b] = \max_f (1/T)E_{b,r}[\ln C_T/C]$$
$$- \max_f [V^* - M(f,c) - R(f)].$$

$\sigma^2 = \text{var}\ (b_t - r_t)$, $f(0) = \lambda(\rho\theta - 1)$, $\lambda = \text{var}\ (b_t)/\text{var}\ (b_t - r_t)$, $\rho = \text{correlation}$ (b,r), $\theta = \sigma_r/\sigma_b$, $C = C(0)$, $X = X(0)$, $V^* = M(f,c) - R(f)$.

The economic meaning of these equations can be explained in an *intuitive* way within the framework of the Tobin–Markowitz mean-variance (M-V) model. When risk aversion is equal to unity, we prove in Appendix B that the expected endogenous growth rate $\Lambda = E[(1/T)\ln X_T/X]$ is equal to the difference between mean curve $M(f_t;c)$ and risk curve $R(f_t)$, at each instant of time. This difference is precisely the M-V expected utility $V^*_t = M(f_t;c) - R(f_t)$ in Figure 3.2.

The expected growth rate is a continuous function of the debt ratio. If the debt ratio is $f = 0$, then the expected growth rate is the vertical intercept of the mean curve $M(0,c) = (b - c)$, less the vertical intercept of the risk curve $R(0)$. *The maximal expected growth rate $\Lambda^* = \max_f E[(1/T)\ln X_T/X]$ is the maximal difference between the two curves in Figure 3.2.* Therefore to maximize the expected growth rate for a given consumption ratio, select the debt ratio $f = f^*$ that maximizes mean-variance expected utility: $V^* = \text{Mean} - \text{Risk}$, when risk aversion is unity, that is $\gamma = 0$.

The minimum risk debt ratio is $f(0)$. As the debt ratio rises above $f(0)$, the expected growth rate Λ first rises and reaches a maximum at f^*. As the debt ratio rises above f^*, the expected growth rate declines. At a debt ratio $f = f^u$ the expected growth rate is zero. When $f > f^u$ the expected growth rate of consumption is negative, because the risk curve $R(f)$ lies above the mean curve $M(f;c)$ in Figure 3.2. In that region, expected growth is negative and the variance of the growth rate is higher than it is at f^*, the optimal ratio.

A hypothesis is that a country will default on its debt if the attempt to service it leads to a sustained decline in consumption. Insofar as the debt ratio rises above the optimum, the expected growth rate declines and its variance rises continuously. Therefore, the random shocks to the return on capital and to the interest rate increase the probability that total consumption $C_t = cX_t$ must decline if the debt is serviced.

The consumption ratio $c = C_t/X_t$ does not affect the optimum debt ratio. A rise in the consumption ratio $c < b$ lowers the intercept $(b - c)$ of the mean curve without changing its slope and does not affect the risk curve $R(f)$ involving the variances. The optimum debt ratio remains at $f = f^*$, but the optimum expected growth rate Λ^* of consumption and of net worth declines. This analysis just uses objectively measured variables.

3.7. Optimum current account

In the context of international finance, it is frequently argued that growing current account deficits are unsustainable, and increase the probability of a crisis. On the basis of our analysis based upon stochastic optimal control we answer the following questions. When optimal policies are followed, what is the expected current account? Must current account deficits be offset by future current account surpluses? Can it be optimal that the rich countries in the world be debtors? What is a sustainable current account deficit?

The results in Box 3.2 and Figures 3.1 and 3.2 show why the stochastic optimal control/dynamic programming approach arrives at propositions very different from the intertemporal budget constraint propositions that current account deficits must be offset by current account surpluses. In our DP analysis, the debt should grow at the same rate as net worth. Since the current account deficit is the change in the debt, in a growing economy it is optimal to have continuing current account deficits. The derivation of the optimal current account deficit is as follows. Since the ratio $f^* = L(t)/X(t)$ is the ratio of optimal debt/net worth, the optimal current account deficit/net worth is[15] (3.28) where $dL^*(t)$ is the change in the debt.

$$dL^*(t) = f^* dX(t). \tag{3.28}$$

The optimal ratio f^*, equation (3.17), in this model is constant. Hence the debt should grow at the same rate as net worth. The optimal growth of net worth is Λ in equation (3.27). Graphically in the M-V Figure 3.2, the optimum growth rate is V^*, equal to maximum mean-variance expected utility, when risk aversion is equal to unity. *Permanent current account deficits will be optimal if the optimal debt/net worth f^* and growth Λ are both positive.*

---

[15] The optimal debt is $L^*(t) = f^* X(t) = L(X(t))$, where $L_x = f^*$ and $L_{xx} = 0$. Therefore the change is $dL(t) = L_x dX(t) + (L_{xx}/2)(dX(t))^2 = f^* \, dX(t)$.

3.8. Conclusion

Good economic theory should explain with relative simplicity and clarity the phenomena that one observes in the complex real world. The theory should be operational, and lead to testable hypotheses where both the productivity of investment and the interest rate are stochastic and hence unpredictable. The recent major currency and debt crises came as surprises to the market, credit rating agencies, and academic economists. The sustainability of United States current account deficits is very controversial. The techniques based upon perfect knowledge and foresight cannot be implemented in a world of uncertainty. Since the controller cannot predict the future, we use the techniques of stochastic optimal control dynamic programming to derive conditions of optimality and answer the following questions.

What is an optimal long-term external debt? What is an optimal consumption ratio? What is an optimal expected endogenous growth rate? The answers to these questions are of particular importance in deriving early warning signals of debt crises, and an evaluation of the United States external debt and current account deficits. The following conclusion of this chapter are the answers to these questions, when risk aversion is unity.

- The optimal ratio of debt/net worth f^* is a linear function of the ratio of the *mean* net return $(b - r)$ divided by its variance σ^2.

- As the net worth changes due to the stochastic terms in the productivity of capital and effective interest rate, the optimal debt must change to preserve the constant ratio f^*.

- The debt *per se* is never repaid, but its ratio to net worth is constant and it is always serviced. There is never a problem of a "free lunch", since net worth cannot be zero or negative.

- When the optimal debt ratio is held, then the expected growth rate of net worth and of consumption is maximal for a given consumption/ net worth ratio c less than the mean productivity of capital.

- As the debt ratio rises above the optimal f^* then the expected growth rate of consumption declines, and its variance rises. This means that the probability is increased that bad shocks to the return and to the effective interest rate reduce consumption. Consequently, the economy is more vulnerable to shocks insofar as the debt ratio rises above the optimal level.

Appendix A. Alternate measure of capital and production function

The prototype model in Box 3.1 uses a concept of capital, which is the integral of investment over the period, equation (3.7). Operationally, this concept of capital is difficult to measure empirically, since it neglects technical progress, improvements in quality, and depreciation. An alternative concept of capital, which is not amenable to these deficiencies, will imply the same dynamic equation for the change in net worth dX_t in equation (3.15). In the empirical Chapters 5–9, we may use either concept of capital with identical theoretical results.

Instead of equations (3.6), (3.6a), (3.6b), (3.7) and (3.11) in Box 3.1, use the following. Equation (A1) is the growth of the GDP. The first term is bI_t/Y_t, the ratio of investment/GDP times a deterministic component b, which is the expected return on investment. The diffusion term $\sigma_y dw_y$ has an expectation of zero and a variance of $\sigma_y^2 dt$.

$$dY_t/Y_t = bI_t/Y_t + \sigma_y dw_y. \tag{A1}$$

Define "capital" K_t^*, as Frank Knight did in his writings. Capital in equation (A2) is the discounted value of Y_t, the current GDP, where the discount factor is b, the deterministic expected return on investment. This means that GDP is equation (A3). Net worth X_t is capital K_t^* less debt L_t, equation (A4).

$$K_t^* = Y_t/b. \tag{A2}$$

$$Y_t = b(X_t + L_t) \tag{A3}$$

$$X_t = Y_t/b - L_t. \tag{A4}$$

The change in net worth dX_t is (A5).

$$dX_t = dY_t/b - dL_t. \tag{A5}$$

Substitute (A1) and the change in the debt dL_t from equation (3.8) in Box 3.1 and derive (A6). Use the same definitions as before. The debt ratio $f = L/X$, and the consumption ratio $c = C/X$. Equation (A6) is precisely the stochastic differential equation (3.15) in the text.

$$dX_t = [(b - c_t) + (b - r)f_t]X_t dt - f_t X_t \sigma_r dw_r + (1 + f_t)X_t \sigma_y dw_y. \tag{A6}$$

We may therefore use either concept of "capital" in the prototype model. The great advantage of using the approach in this appendix is that we may measure the expected return on investment b in (A1) by regressing the dY_t/Y_t change in the GDP on the investment ratio I_t/Y_t. The regression coefficient is precisely the expected return on investment b. In the empirical work, we estimate b by either looking at the regression coefficient or by using $b = (dY_t/Y_t)/(I_t/Y_t)$, which is the ratio of the growth rate $(dY/dt)/Y$ to I/Y, the investment ratio.

Appendix B. Derivation of optimal consumption, capital, debt, and endogenous growth in continuous time over an infinite horizon

In this mathematical appendix, we briefly explain the derivation of equations (3.16), (3.17), (3.19), and (3.27) in the text. This is technically difficult material[16] that is generally used in the mathematical finance literature and by Robert Merton (1990) in his book, but is not common knowledge in economics.

The mathematical derivation proceeds in several steps. (a) Derive the Hamilton–Jacobi–Bellman (HJB) stochastic dynamic programming (DP) equation. (b) Prove that the HARA utility function implies that the value function $V(X)$ in equation (3.3) is homogeneous of degree $\gamma < 1$. The HARA function permits us to measure the variables consumption $C/X = c$, capital $k = K/X$, and debt $L/X = f$ as fractions of X net worth, where lower case letters refer to the ratios. Instead of C and L, we can equivalently take c and f as the control variables.

The stochastic control problem has a state $X(t) > 0$ and controls $f(t)$, $c(t) > 0$. The state dynamics are equation (3.15) in the text or (B1) here:

$$dX(t) = [(b - c(t) + (b - r)f(t)]X(t)dt - f(t)X(t)\sigma_r dw_r \\ + (1 + f(t))X(t)\sigma_y dw_y. \tag{B1}$$

The goal is to maximize the expected discounted HARA utility of consumption. The value function $V(X)$ is equation (3.3), where $X = X(0)$ is the initial net worth. The dynamic programming differential equation for $V(X)$ is (B2) and G^u is a second-order differential operator. See Fleming and Rishel (1975) or Øksendal (1995), Chapter V, for how to derive (B2), using the stochastic calculus Ito equation.

$$\delta V(X) = \max_u[G^u V(X) + (1/\gamma)(cX)^\gamma], \text{ where } u = (f, c) \text{ and} \tag{B2}$$

$$G^u V(X) = [b - c + (b - r)f]X V_x \\ + (1/2)[f^2\sigma_r^2 - 2f(1 + f)\rho\sigma_r\sigma_y + (1 + f)^2\sigma_y^2]X^2 V_{xx}. \tag{B3}$$

Candidates for the optimal control policy $u^*(X) = [f^*(X), \ c^*(X)]$ satisfy equation (B4).

$$u^*(X) \in \arg \max_u[G^u V(X) + (1/\gamma)(cX)^\gamma]. \tag{B4}$$

The HARA utility function in equation (3.3), $U(C) = (1/\gamma)C^\gamma$, $1 > \gamma$, $\gamma \neq 0$, implies that the value function $V(X)$ in equation (3.3), and hence $V(X)$ in (B2), is homogeneous of degree $\gamma < 1$, $\gamma \neq 0$. The proof is as follows[17]. If the state X, and controls C

---

[16] See Fleming and Rishel (1975) Chapter 5, Fleming (2001), Merton (1990) and Øksendal (1995) Chapter V for a fuller analysis of the underlying mathematics of stochastic optimal control, especially applied to mathematical finance.

[17] The logarithmic case, corresponding to $\gamma = 0$, implies $V(X) = A \ln X + B$, where A and B are to be determined.

and L are multiplied by a value $\lambda > 0$, then equation (B1) is unaffected but the new value function $V(\lambda X)$ is

$$V(\lambda X) = \max_\Gamma E\left\{\int_0^\infty (1/\gamma)[\lambda C(t)]^\gamma e^{-\delta t} dt\right\} = \lambda^\gamma V(X). \tag{B5}$$

Therefore, the value function of X is also homogeneous of degree γ. One may write the value function as (B6) where the constant $A > 0$ is to be determined. The first two derivatives are (B6.1) and (B6.2):

$$V(X) = (A/\gamma)X^\gamma \tag{B6}$$

$$V_x = AX^{(\gamma-1)} \tag{B6.1}$$

$$V_{xx} = A(\gamma - 1)X^{(\gamma-2)}. \tag{B6.2}$$

Substitute (B6) and its derivatives into (B2)–(B3) and derive the Hamilton–Jacobi–Bellman (HJB) equation of dynamic programming (DP). Equation (3.16) is repeated here as (B7). The ratios $c = C/X > 0$, $f = L/X > -1$ are the controls.

HJB equation, HARA case $\gamma < 1$, $\gamma \neq 0$.

$$\delta/\gamma = b + \max_c[(1/\gamma)c_t^\gamma/A - c_t] + \max_f\{[(b-r)f_t] - (1-\gamma)(\sigma_y^2/2)[(f_t^2\theta^2)$$
$$+ (1+f_t)^2 - 2(1+f_t)f_t\rho\theta]\}, \quad \theta = \sigma_r/\sigma_y. \tag{B7}$$

From this equation, we derive the optimal ratio of debt/net worth equation (3.17) and the optimal consumption ratio in the prototype model.

Optimal consumption

We now determine the optimal consumption ratio c^* in the prototype model of intertemporal optimization. Substitute the *optimal debt ratio* f^* from (3.17) into (3.16) and obtain equation (B8), where Ω_γ in (B9) is the *maximum* of the second term in (3.16), evaluated for a given risk aversion. The optimum consumption ratio $c^* = C_t/X_t$ is equation (B10), derived from the maximization of (B8) with respect to the consumption ratio.

$$\delta/\gamma = b + \max_c[(1/\gamma)c^\gamma/A - c] + \Omega_\gamma \tag{B8}$$

$$\Omega_\gamma = [(b-r)f^* - (1-\gamma)R(f^*)/2] \tag{B9}$$

$$c^* = A^{1/(\gamma-1)}. \tag{B10}$$

To determine the value of A, substitute the optimum consumption ratio (B10) into (B8) and derive (B11):

$$c^* = A^{1/(\gamma-1)} = [\delta - \gamma(b + \Omega_\gamma)]/(1 - \gamma). \tag{B11}$$

3. Stochastic intertemporal optimization

The condition for the existence of the required homogeneous solution $V(X)$ with $A > 0$ is precisely that the optimal consumption ratio c^* be positive. All we need for $A > 0$ is that $[\delta - \gamma(b + \Omega_y)] > 0$. If $\gamma < 0$, then no discount rate is needed for the existence of an optimum. In the logarithmic case where $\gamma = 0$, the optimal consumption ratio is $c^* = \delta$, the discount rate, equation (B12).

$$c^* = \delta. \tag{B12}$$

Equations (B12) in the logarithmic case, and (3.17) are the optimal consumption/ net worth and debt/net worth in the prototype Model. They are our benchmarks of performance, which allow us to evaluate whether debt or consumption is excessive at any time, based upon available information.

The optimal endogenous growth rate

The first step in determining the optimal expected endogenous growth rate is to solve the stochastic differential equation (3.15) for net worth X_t. We relate this derivation to the mean-variance analysis that shows that the optimal debt ratio maximizes the expected endogenous growth rate[18].

The way to do this is to use the Ito sense stochastic differential equation to derive $d(\ln X_t)$, which is equation (B13). Integrate this equation from $(0, T)$, take the expectation of X_t where the $E(dw)$ terms are zero, and derive equation (B14). The terms $M(f)$ and $R(f)$ are defined in (3.21) and (3.22) in the mean-variance section of the text.

$$d \ln X_t = [M(f_t; c) - (1/2)R(f_t)]dt + [\sigma_y(1 + f_t)dw_y - \sigma_r f_t dw_r]. \tag{B13}$$

For a constant debt ratio f and consumption ratio c, the expected growth rate is:

$$E[(1/T) \ln X_T / X] = [M(f_c) - (1/2)R(f)]. \tag{B14}$$

Find the optimal debt/net worth to maximize this expected growth rate. The solution $f_t = f^{**}$ is equation (B15). It is the same as f^* in (3.17) when $\gamma = 0$. When the disturbances are independent ($\rho = 0$) the optimal debt ratio is equation (B16).

$$f^{**} = \text{argmax } E[(1/T) \ln X_T / X] = (b - r)/\sigma^2 + f(0) \tag{B15}$$

$$f^{**}(\rho = 0) = [(b - r) - \sigma_y^2]/\sigma^2. \tag{B16}$$

The maximum expected growth rate, which is obtained when $f_t = f^{**}$, is denoted Λ^* in equation (B17). When the two stochastic terms (dw_y, dw_r) are independent $\rho = 0$, then the maximum expected growth rate is $\Lambda^*(\rho = 0)$ in equation (B18).

$$\Lambda^* = \max E[(1/T) \ln X_T / X] = M(f^{**}; c) - (1/2)R(f^{**}) \tag{B17}$$

$$\Lambda^*(\rho = 0) = [(b - c) + (1/2)(b - r)^2/\sigma^2] - [(b - r)/(1 + \theta^2) + \sigma_r^2/2]. \tag{B18}$$

---

[18] The derived optimal endogenous growth rate is very different from the growth rate in the Solow model. See Stein (2006).

The Term $\theta = \sigma_r/\sigma_y$ is the ratio of the standard deviation in the interest rate equation to the standard deviation in the growth of GDP equation.

The variance of the growth rate is (B19) where risk R is defined in (3.22):

$$(1/T)\text{var } \ln(X_T/X) = 2R(f). \tag{B19}$$

The debt ratio at which the variance of the growth rate is minimal is (B20). This minimal risk debt ratio is precisely $f(0)$, the intercept term in equation (3.17) for the optimal ratio of debt/net worth.

$$f(0) = \lambda(\rho\theta - 1) = \text{argmin}\{(1/T)\text{var } \ln(X_T/X)\}. \tag{B20}$$

The ratio $f(0)$ is negative, where the country is a creditor, if the correlation ρ between the two disturbances is less than σ_y/σ_r. This is a realistic case. Mean-variance Figure 3.2 is drawn where the minimum risk debt ratio $f(0)$ is negative.

References

Davis, M. H. A. and A. R. Norman, *Portfolio Selection with Transactions Costs*, Mathematics of Operations Research, 15 (1990), 676–713

Fleming, Wendell H. and Raymond W. Rishel (1975), Deterministic and Stochastic Optimal Control, Springer-Verlag, New York

Fleming, Wendell H. (2003) Some Optimal Investment, Production and Consumption Models, American Mathematical Society, Contemporary Mathematics, 351

—— (2001) Stochastic Control Models of Optimal Investment and Consumption, Aportaciones Matematicas, 16, Sociedad Matematica Mexicana

Fleming, Wendell H. and Jerome L. Stein (2004), *Stochastic Optimal Control, International Finance and Debt*, Journal of Banking and Finance, 28, May

Fleming, Wendell H. and Tao Pang (2004) An Application of Stochastic Control Theory to Financial Economics, SIAM Journal of Control and Optimization 43 (2) 502–31

Gandolfo, Giancarlo (2001) International Finance and Open-Economy Macroeconomics, Springer-Verlag, New York

Infante, E. F. and Jerome L. Stein (1973) Optimal Growth with Robust Feedback Control, Review of Economic Studies, 40(1), 47–60

Merton, Robert (1990) Continuous Time Finance, Blackwell, Oxford

Øksendal, Bernt (1995) Stochastic Differential Equations, Springer, New York

Pang, T. (2002) Stochastic Control Theory and its Applications in Financial Economics, Ph.D. thesis, Brown University

Platen, Eckhard (2005) Growth Optimal Portfolio in Economics and Finance, Australian Economic Papers 44, December

Rogers, L. C. G. (2004) Why is the Effect of Proportional Transactions Costs $O(\delta^{2/3})$? American Mathematical Society, Contemporary Mathematics, 351

Stein, Jerome L. (2003), *Stochastic Optimal Control Modeling of Debt Crises*, Mathematics of Finance, American Mathematical Society, Providence, RI

——(2005), Optimal Debt and Endogenous Growth Models in International Finance, Australian Economic Papers

——(2005) Optimal Debt and Endogenous Growth Models in International Fiance, Australian Economic Papers, 44, December

Stein, Jerome L. and Giovanna Paladino (1997), Recent Developments in International Finance, Journal of Banking and Finance, 21 (11–12), December

4

The NATREX model of the equilibrium real exchange rate

This chapter is concerned with "equilibrium" real exchange rates, external debt, and their interaction. Whereas the previous chapters concern *normative* economics, concepts of "optimality", the present chapter concerns *positive* economics involving explanation and prediction of *systematic* movements in real exchange rates.

Our interest here is the "equilibrium" real exchange rate and not with the actual real exchange rate at any one time. The real exchange rate R is the ratio of domestic/foreign prices measured in a common currency. It is defined as the product of the nominal exchange rate N (foreign currency per unit of domestic currency) and the ratio of domestic/ foreign price deflators (p/p^*). A rise in N or R is an appreciation of the currency.

The equilibrium real exchange rate is where the actual real exchange rate is heading and depends upon a vector Z_t of real fundamentals discussed below. The actual real exchange rate R_t is decomposed into three components:

$$R_t = \{R(Z_t) + [R(F_t; Z_t) - R(Z_t)]\} + [R_t - R(F_t; Z_t)]$$
$$= \text{NATREX} + \text{deviation.} \tag{4.1}$$

The NATREX is a model of the equilibrium real exchange rate, the terms in braces. The NATREX model has two components: the long-run equilibrium real exchange rate $R(Z_t)$ and the dynamics of adjustment of the medium-run equilibrium to the long-run equilibrium $[R(F_t; Z_t) - R(Z_t)]$. In the medium-run equilibrium, the ratio F_t of the external debt/GDP is predetermined, and the real exchange rate $R(F_t; Z_t)$ is associated with flow equilibrium, where there are both internal and external balances. The debt ratio is an endogenous variable. In full stock-flow equilibrium, where the endogenous debt ratio has stabilized, the long-run equilibrium real exchange rate $R(Z_t)$ just depends upon the vector of fundamentals Z_t.

The second term in square brackets is the deviation of the actual real rate from the medium-term equilibrium. A major part of the deviation is stochastic, based upon transitory non-systematic factors with a zero mean and a positive variance. Transitory factors include: speculative capital flows based upon anticipations of exchange rate variations, changes in reserves, governmental intervention in the foreign exchange market, changes in monetary policy, and cyclical factors. These factors do not affect the *equilibrium real* exchange rate. The stochastic component of $[R_t - R(F_t;Z_t)]$ has a zero expectation, but may be serially correlated. Another component of the deviation arises because of lagged adjustments between the real exchange rate and trade balance. These lags produce cyclical movements in the deviation.[1]

The real exchange rate is heading to an equilibrium rate $R(Z_t)$ based upon time-varying real fundamentals Z_t. However, as a result of the transitory factors and finite speed of response stock adjustment, the actual real exchange rate exhibits considerable variance around the mean.

The NATREX model explains what are the fundamental determinants of the equilibrium real exchange rate $R(Z)$ and the convergence process – the terms in braces in equation (4.1). The NATREX model does not explain the short-run variations in the actual real exchange rate R_t because they originate in the stochastic factors – the last term in equation (4.1) – that have zero expectations. Many of the models in the literature are based upon anticipations, speculative capital movements, and monetary policy – the Dornbusch type models. These models assume that the equilibrium real rate is constant. We subsume their effects in the stochastic part, which corresponds to the non-systematic deviation $[R_t - R(F_t;Z_t)]$ in equation (4.1). The consensus, based upon extensive empirical work, is that these models have been unsuccessful in explaining exchange rate movements.

Our concern is with $R(Z)$, where the real exchange rate is heading and its trajectory to the equilibrium. There are several reasons for this concern. An important question is whether the current nominal exchange rate is sustainable? The relation between the logarithm of the *equilibrium* nominal exchange rate N^e and the logarithm of relative prices is equation (4.2), graphed in Figure 4.1 for three values of the fundamentals Z_1, Z_2 and Z_3.

$$\log N_t^e = \log R(Z_t - \log(p/p*)_t. \tag{4.2}$$

---

[1] These issues are discussed in Appendix C.

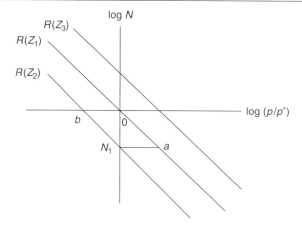

Figure 4.1. Relation between nominal exchange rate, relative prices, and equilibrium real exchange rate.

Say that the nominal exchange rate[2] has depreciated from $N=0$ to $N=N_1$. Several questions should be answered. What has produced the depreciation? Will this depreciation generate inflationary pressures? Should a restrictive monetary policy be used to counteract the depreciation? The answers depend upon the relation between the actual and equilibrium real exchange rate. Is nominal rate N_1 undervalued? That is the same as asking if the nominal exchange N_t rate is below the equilibrium rate N^e_t.

In this introductory section the discussion is intuitive and concepts are made precise in the subsequent sections of this chapter. Here we stress why it is important for policy that one understands what are the fundamental determinants of the equilibrium real exchange rate, and the logic of the NATREX model.

The *equilibrium nominal exchange rate is a line with an intercept that is the equilibrium real exchange rate.* If the equilibrium real rate were the line labeled $R(Z_1)$ and the logarithm of relative prices were $\log (p/p^*) = 0$, then the NATREX is $N=0$; and a nominal exchange rate N_1 is undervalued. There will be pressures to drive the nominal exchange rate and relative prices to a point along line $R(Z_1)$. Either the nominal exchange rate will appreciate to $\log N=0$ with no change in relative prices, the convergence will be to point a in Figure 4.1, with a higher rate of inflation, or there will be some combination of the two.

---

[2] When we discuss Figure 4.1, it should be understood that the variables are logarithms. When domestic and foreign prices are equal $p = p^*$ then $\log (p/p^*) = 0$.

If the equilibrium real exchange rate has depreciated to $R(Z_2)$ and domestic and foreign prices are equal, then the nominal exchange rate N_1 is not undervalued. A restrictive monetary policy that tends to appreciate the currency above N_1 will lead to deflationary pressures. For example, if the monetary policy raises the nominal rate to $\log N = 0$, there will be deflationary pressures to reduce relative prices to b in Figure 4.1. Given imperfect wage–price flexibility, the restrictive monetary policy will decrease the rate of capacity utilization, employment, and growth.

When nominal exchange rate changes have occurred, an effective monetary policy cannot be undertaken unless one knows whether the equilibrium real exchange rate has changed. Was the change in the real exchange rate due to the change in the equilibrium rate, or to the stochastic term involving transitory factors?

The equilibrium real exchange rate $R(Z)$, the intercept of a line in Figure 4.1, is the asymptotic mean of the distribution of the actual real exchange rate. The actual real rate will jump around due to the transitory factors, so there will be considerable variation around this mean. *The nominal rate is a stochastic variable whose mean is a line associated with a given value of $R(Z)$.* Although monetary policy affects the nominal exchange rate, it cannot affect the equilibrium real exchange rate.

The Asian crises[3] of 1997–8 can be viewed within the framework of Figure 4.1. When the nominal exchange rates collapsed, it was necessary to know whether the depreciation was due to speculative factors or was the depreciation due to an overvalued real exchange rate. Overvaluation means that the nominal exchange rate was above the line given by the appropriate $R(Z)$. At the onset of the crises, the International Monetary Fund advocated restrictive monetary and fiscal policies to counter the depreciation. Insofar as the depreciation was due to an overvalued real exchange rate, say $N = 0$ which was above line $R(Z_2)$ for the equilibrium real rate, these policies imposed unnecessary real costs upon the economies. In the absence of deflation and depressed conditions the nominal exchange rate would converge to the $R(Z_2)$ line through depreciation to N_1. After the economies collapsed, the restrictive policies were reversed. The policy failure was in not knowing what had been happening to the equilibrium real exchange rate. As shown in Chapter 8, the currencies of Thailand and Korea were overvalued.

Another example of why it is important to know the equilibrium real exchange rate concerns the enlargement of the euro area[4]. The countries of

---

[3] The Asian crises are discussed in Chapter 8.   [4] This is the subject of Chapter 6.

Central and Eastern Europe, CEEC, are preparing to enter the euro area. They must decide at what nominal exchange rates to enter. The challenge is to avoid the problems that beset eastern Germany as a result of currency unification. The CEEC are undergoing considerable structural changes, which involve the vector Z of real fundamentals discussed in the rest of this chapter. Therefore, the equilibrium real exchange rate $R(Z)$ is changing.

If the equilibrium real exchange rate is $R(Z_1)$ and a country selects nominal exchange rate N_1 and the logarithm of relative prices is zero, then the real exchange rate is undervalued. Inflationary pressure will raise relative prices to point a in Figure 4.1. This would mean that the CEEC could be violating the Maastricht treaty requirement concerning the rate of inflation.

Alternatively, if the equilibrium real exchange rate is $R(Z_2)$, the nominal exchange rate selected is $N = 0$ and the logarithm of relative prices is zero, then the exchange rate is overvalued. There will be deflationary pressures to lower relative prices to point b. At the origin $(0,0)$, there will be deficient aggregate demand, the economy will lose competitiveness, the export and import competing sectors will be depressed, and employment and growth will decline. The CEEC would have serious problems in remaining in the euro area. Consequently, it is important that the CEEC know the equilibrium real exchange rate before selecting an entering nominal exchange rate.

Summary

The extensive literature on exchange rates generally has focused upon the effects of the transitory factors that are excluded from the NATREX. These models involve either speculative capital movements arising from anticipations of changes in nominal exchange rates, or as a result of changes in nominal interest rates arising from monetary policy. In these models, the rate of capacity utilization varies due to monetary policies. The equilibrium real exchange rate in these models is assumed to be a constant, so that the equilibrium nominal exchange rate is derived from Purchasing Power Parity (PPP). In terms of Figure 4.1, the equilibrium nominal exchange rate is a given line; and nominal exchange rate variations are movements along a given line. Monetary models that focus upon the nominal exchange rate are very different from the NATREX, which focuses upon the moving equilibrium real rate $R(Z_t)$. The NATREX model does not specify to what extent the equilibrium real rate will vary due to changes in the nominal rate and to what extent it will change due to relative prices. The exchange rate regime determines the method of adjustment. The NATREX only determines the line $R(Z)$ in Figure 4.1, but not where the nominal exchange rate will be along the line. The NATREX model applies to either a free exchange rate or stabilized exchange rate regime. If one assumes that relative prices are determined by *relative exogenous* money stocks/GDP, then one would add this information to the NATREX to determine the long-run equilibrium nominal exchange rate. If the nominal exchange rate were fixed, then the NATREX model would imply what is the equilibrium endogenous ratio of money stocks/GDP.

4.1. The equilibrium real exchange rate in the medium and in the long run

An equilibrium[5] real exchange rate must satisfy several conditions. First, there should be *internal balance*, where the rate of capacity utilization is at its stationary mean.[6] There are neither deflationary pressures from excess capacity nor inflationary pressures from an overheated economy. Cyclical factors are excluded in deriving the equilibrium real exchange rate. Second, there should be *external balance*. This requirement excludes speculative capital flows based upon anticipations or bubbles and changes in reserves. *External balance* requires that the real rate of interest in the country equals the world real rate. From these two conditions, we derive the *medium-run equilibrium* real exchange rate $R(F_t; Z_t)$.

At medium-run equilibrium the current account need not equal zero, so that the external net asset position is changing. *Longer run equilibrium* requires that the ratio of the foreign debt[7]/GDP be constant. This additional condition for external balance requires that the debt grow at the same rate as the GDP. The equilibrium real exchange rate that satisfies these conditions is called the long-run natural real exchange rate (NATREX). There is a medium-run NATREX associated with medium-run equilibrium, and the long-run NATREX that satisfies all of the conditions above. The equilibrium real exchange rate $R(Z_t)$ in equation (4.1) is the long-run NATREX. It depends upon a vector Z of real fundamentals discussed shortly.

---

[5] See Driver and Westaway (2005) for a discussion of alternative concepts of equilibrium exchange rates. They also compare Williamson's fundamental equilibrium real exchange rate (FEER) with NATREX.

[6] This is a clearer concept than that the rate of unemployment should be at its "natural" rate. The constancy of the latter is a subject of dispute.

[7] Net foreign asset is the negative of the net foreign debt. Both external debt and equity are subsumed under debt.

The model can apply either to a small country *vis-à-vis* the rest of the world or to two large countries. Suppose that there were two large countries I and II. All variables are real. The internal and external balance conditions are equation (4.3a) for country I, equation (4.3b) for country II, and equation (4.4) for both. In each country, investment less saving plus the current account equal zero *when internal and external balance prevail, as defined above*. Investment less saving is the inflow of capital, equal to the net supply of securities offered to foreigners. Saving less investment is an outflow of capital, equal to a demand for foreign securities. The current account is the trade balance less net transfer payments to foreigners. The latter is the net liabilities to foreigners times the real interest rate. The current account balance for country II is the negative of that for country I, so that $(B - rF)^{II} = (rF - B)^{I}$.

Let I be investment/GDP, S be saving/GDP and the current account/GDP be $(B - rF)$, where B is the trade balance/GDP, r is the real rate of interest, and F is net foreign liabilities/GDP. Saving is social saving, private plus public. A government budget deficit is negative public saving.

$$(I - S + B - rF)^{I} = 0 \tag{4.3a}$$

$$(I - S + B - rF)^{II} = 0. \tag{4.3b}$$

Figure 4.2 describes equations (4.3a) and (4.3b). The vertical axis is the real exchange rate of country I, where a rise is an appreciation. The real exchange rate of country II is the reciprocal of the real exchange rate of

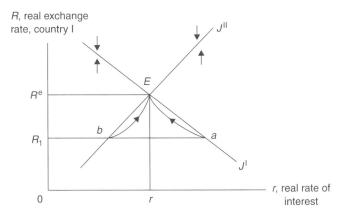

Figure 4.2. Simultaneous determination of the medium-run NATREX and world real rate of interest, point E. Convergence processes are trajectories b-E and a-E for the two countries.

country I. The abscissa measures the real rate of interest. Underlying the curves, (i) an appreciation of the real exchange rate decreases the trade balance, and (ii) a rise in the real rate of interest decreases investment.

Curve J^I describes equation (4.3a), where there is internal balance: investment less saving plus the current account is zero. The curve for country I is negatively sloped. An appreciation of the real exchange rate, R, reduces the trade balance and lowers aggregate demand relative to capacity output. In order to restore internal balance, the real rate of interest must decline and raise investment to offset the decline in the trade balance.[8] This accounts for the negative slope for country I. Since the real exchange rate for country II is the reciprocal of that for country I, the internal balance equation curve J^{II}, equation (4.3b), for country II is positively sloped. We discuss the conditions for medium-run equilibrium for country I. The conditions for country II are similar.

Internal equilibrium does not prevail at points above or below curve J^I. At points above the curve, aggregate demand is less than capacity output; and there is downward pressure on prices. The real exchange rate is overvalued. A depreciation of the exchange rate is required to raise aggregate demand to capacity output. Alternatively, the capital inflow $(I - S)$ plus the current account $(B - \mathrm{r}F)$ is negative. There is an excess supply of the currency, and the exchange rate tends to depreciate. The vertical vectors indicate the required movements in the real exchange rate to achieve internal balance. Therefore, internal equilibrium must occur when each economy is on its curve J^I or J^{II}, respectively in Figure 4.2.

External equilibrium requires[9] that real interest rates are equal in the two countries. This is equation (4.4).

$$r^I = r^{II}. \tag{4.4}$$

Suppose that the real exchange rate were R_1 for country I, or $1/R_1$ for country II. Internal balance requires that country I be at point a, and country II be at point b, in Figure 4.2. External balance does not prevail, because the real rate of interest at point b for country II is less than the real rate of interest at point a in country I. Arbitrage will lead to a convergence of real rates of interest. Investors will sell securities in country II and purchase securities in country I. The real rate of interest will rise in country II and decline in country I. The real exchange rate of country I will appreciate, and the real exchange rate in country II will depreciate. The

---

[8] If there is a foreign debt, the decline in the interest rate affects transfer payments as well.
[9] We also require that there be no speculative capital flows, which are based upon anticipations, or changes in reserves.

process of convergence is indicated by the trajectories[10] from b to E for country II and from a to E in country I. The *medium-run equilibrium* is at point E, where the medium-run NATREX is R^e and common real rate of interest is r. At this point there is both internal and external balance.

The underlying internal–external balance functions underlying curves J^I and J^{II} are the saving, investment, and current account functions, derived in the Section 4.2. At a medium-run equilibrium point such as E, the current account need not be zero. The current account deficit/debt may differ from the growth rate of the economy. Insofar as the debt/GDP ratio is changing, the curves J^I and J^{II} will also vary. Consequently, the medium-run equilibrium point E will be changing. The longer run equilibrium condition, discussed in Section 4.3, requires that the debt/GDP ratio F_t be constant. This means that the trade balance/GDP denoted by B_t is equal to the net transfers on the debt, adjusted for the growth rate of the economy. The interest payments on the debt are $r_t F_t$ and the growth rate of the economy is g_t. In long-run equilibrium, in addition to internal and external balance, the trade balance must be sufficiently large to service the debt when the growth rate is explicitly considered. Then the real exchange rate will be $R(Z_t)$ and the debt/GDP will be $F(Z_t)$, associated with the vector of fundamentals Z. In the NATREX model, both the real exchange rate and the debt ratio are endogenous variables.

The long-run equilibrium conditions in the NATREX model consists of equations (4.3a), (4.3b) and (4.4) for medium-run equilibrium plus equation (4.5). They determine the real exchange rate, real interest rates, and the debt/GDP ratio.

$$B(R, Z_t) = (r - g)F(Z_t). \tag{4.5}$$

The equilibrium real exchange rate $R(Z_t)$ will vary insofar as the fundamentals Z_t underlying the saving, investment, and trade balance functions vary. The PPP theory is a special case of the NATREX where $R(Z)$ is constant. The PPP theory arbitrarily assumes that there is only one line, a time-invariant line, $R(Z)$ in Figure 4.1.

4.2. Structural equations

In order to solve for the medium and the long run NATREX, we must explicitly state what are the structural saving, investment, and trade

---

[10] Appendix C discusses the trajectories to equilibrium when there are lagged adjustments in trade balance and real exchange rate.

balance equations. Focus upon one country and assume that the world real rate of interest is given. The NATREX is a model of *positive* economics. *We assume that the private sector optimizes in a rational manner discussed in Chapter 3, but the government decisions are the results of political pressures.*

SAVING FUNCTION AND TIME PREFERENCE

The saving function subsumes the private plus the public saving decisions. Optimal consumption is proportional to net worth,[11] and the factor of proportionality δ is the "discount rate". Net worth is capital less debt. So the ratio S of saving/GDP is equation (4.6). It is negatively related to the "discount rate" δ, positively related to F, debt/net worth and to the productivity of capital b. The term in parentheses $(1/b - F)$ is net worth/GDP, which is positive.[12]

$$S = 1 - \delta(1/b - F) = S(F, \delta), \quad S_F > 0, \quad S_\delta < 0. \tag{4.6}$$

The debt ratio F is an endogenous variable in the NATREX model. The discount rate parameter δ reflects the social time preference of both the government and the private sector. Populist policies raise the discount rate by emphasizing present consumption and living standards rather than the welfare of future generations[13]. The time preference δ which is an inverse measure of thrift, is a fundamental determinant of the equilibrium real exchange rate, as shown be below.

INVESTMENT FUNCTION

There are several ways to derive the investment function. Fortunately, they lead to similar *qualitative* conclusions that the investment/GDP ratio is positively related to "the return on investment" less the "real interest rate". They differ in the measures of the two variables in quotation marks. One approach is via the Keynes–Tobin q-ratio, which is based upon static considerations. The second and third are based upon intertemporal optimization in a dynamic context when there is not perfect knowledge and certainty.

The logic underlying the Keynes–Tobin[14] q-ratio is that firms are induced to undertake capital formation if it increases the expected value

---

[11] See Chapter 3, the case of the logarithmic utility function.

[12] Net worth is "capital" K less external debt L. Then net worth/GDP is $(K/Y - L/Y)$. The productivity of capital is b. Hence net worth/GDP is $(1/b - F)$, where $F = L/Y$.

[13] See Stein and Sauernheimer (1997) pp. 34–5 for a discussion of the changes in "time preference" resulting from the political processes in Germany.

[14] The idea that investment depends upon the q – ratio was developed by Keynes in his Treatise on Money, I (1930), pp. 200–9, and later by Tobin (1969). See Stein (1986), p. 187, for a discussion of this concept.

of the firm by more than the cost of the investment. The change in the expected value of the firm, the numerator, is equal to the expected (E) present value (PV) of the change in cash flows. The denominator pI is the value of the expenditure on new plant or equipment, where $I = \Delta K$ is the quantity and p is the supply price of the capital good, assumed to be proportional to the domestic price index.

$q = E$ (change PV of cash flows)/value of investment.

Cash flow is the value of real output Y less wages WL less the value of materials VM, where W is the wage rate, L is labor, M is the quantity of materials, and V is the price of materials. Assume that the output is sold in the world market at price P^* in foreign currency, so that P^*/N is the price in domestic currency at nominal exchange rate N. The materials are imported at world price V^* and V^*/N is the price in domestic currency. The change in average annual cash flow divided by the investment pI is $[(P^*/N)\Delta Y/pI - W \Delta L/pI - (V^*/N)\Delta M/pI]$.

The physical productivity of capital dY/I is denoted by m, the real wage $w = W/p$, the increment of labor required when there is a change in capital is $a_1 = \Delta L/I$, and the increment of materials required when there is a change in capital is $a_2 = \Delta M/I$. The real exchange rate $R = Np/p^*$ is the ratio of domestic/foreign prices in a common currency. The ratio of the price of imported materials V^*/N to the domestic price index p is the *inverse* of the terms of trade T and is $(1/T) = V^*/Np$. The change in the cash flow resulting from investment is $(m/R - wa_1 - a_2/T)$.

The q-ratio equation (4.7) is the expected present value of the change in the cash flow resulting from the investment undertaken at time t. The cash flows are discounted at interest rate r over a horizon. The *net productivity of investment* is the term in parentheses and is denoted by b.

$$q_t = E\textstyle\int_t (m/R - wa_1 - a_2/T)_s e^{-rs}ds = E\textstyle\int_t b_s e^{-rs}ds. \quad t < s < \infty \qquad (4.7)$$

An appreciation of the exchange rate lowers the ratio of the sales price of the goods (P^*/N) to the price p of the investment goods, and decreases the q-ratio. A rise in relative materials price ($1/T$) lowers net profits and hence the q-ratio. Similarly, a rise in the real wage (w) lowers the value of the firm and the q-ratio. Greater labor productivity ($1/a_1$) and greater productivity in using materials ($1/a_2$) raise the q-ratio.

The investment/GDP ratio I is positively related to the q-ratio, as described by equation (4.8), where $Z_q = (w, a_1, a_2, 1/T, r)^{-1}$ is the vector of variables that are considered exogenous for the q-ratio. A rise in vector Z_q raises the q-ratio. Since $q = Q(R; Z_q)$, the investment ratio is:

$$I = I(q) = I(R; Z_q), I_R < 0, Z_q > 0. \qquad (4.8)$$

This approach does not take into account the uncertainty concerning the future cash flows nor risk aversion. There are two alternatives to this procedure, which are based upon intertemporal optimization. Both are based upon dynamic programming.

The first is a suboptimal feedback control (SOFC) derived by Infante and Stein (1973). The Infante–Stein model starts from the standard intertemporal maximization of the discounted value of utility of consumption over an infinite horizon. Whereas the Maximum Principle requires perfect foresight and derives the saddle-point trajectory, the SOFC rejects the assumption of perfect foresight. The optimal steady state capital intensity is unknowable at the time that investment decisions are made. In view of that fact, the economy cannot converge to the steady state capital intensity along a known saddle-point trajectory, because it is unknown. The slightest forecast error will lead to instability. They derived a SOFC *based upon current measurements* that guarantees that the economy will converge to the unknown and possibly changing optimal trajectory[15]. Following that rule, the convergence process is stable.

The SOFC is that the optimal change in the capital intensity dk/dt is equation (4.8a), where $f'(k_t)$ is the current and measurable marginal product of capital, n is the growth of effective labor plus depreciation and the discount rate is associated with the real rate of interest.

$$\frac{dk}{dt} = A(k_t)[f'(k_t) - n - r] \qquad A(k_t) > 0. \qquad (4.8a)$$

One does not have to know the production function f. It is only necessary to know the current measurable value of the marginal product of capital. The latter corresponds to b_t in the integrand of the q-ratio in equation (4.7). Therefore the investment ratio should be directly related to the current $(b_t - r_t)$, namely that $I = I(b_t - r_t)$.

The second intertemporal optimization approach is the one developed in Chapter 3, using stochastic optimal control/dynamic programming. Only the briefest recapitulation is given here. The optimal ratio of capital/net worth is $k^* = 1 + f^*$, where f^* is the optimal ratio of debt/net worth, described by equation (3.17) and curve U-S in Figure 3.1. The optimal ratio of capital/net worth is equal to the mean rate of return on investment less the mean real rate of interest $(b - r)$ divided by the variance of the net return var $(b_t - r_t)$. The mean return on investment corresponds to the

---

[15] If there were perfect foresight, the optimal capital intensity at any time is $k(t)$. The capital intensity derived from the SOFC is $k^*(t)$. Infante and Stein proved that lim $(k(t) - k^*(t)) = 0$ as time t goes to infinity. In fact the convergence is quite rapid.

mean b in equation (4.7) above. It follows that the optimal investment rate in a stochastic environment is proportional to the mean rate of return on investment less the real interest rate.

The conclusions are that the investment ratio is given by equation (4.8), regardless of which approach is taken, and that the investment less saving function (I-S) can be written as equation (4.9). A positive $(I-S)$ represents the desired inflow of capital, equal to the investment that cannot fully be financed by domestic saving. A negative $(I-S)$ represents an outflow of capital, which is the excess of saving over the desired domestic investment.

$$I - S = I(R; Z_q) - S(F; \delta),\ I_R < 0,\ I_q > 0;\ S_F > 0,\ S_\delta < 0. \tag{4.9}$$

A rise in Z_q increases the q-ratio, which means that some of the elements $(w, a_1, a_2, 1/T, r)$ have declined.

TRADE BALANCE FUNCTION

The logic of the trade balance equation is that the real supply of net exports X is determined by the production possibility curve which relates X to the output of the rest of the economy $Y - X$, where Y is the GDP. The production possibility curve is negatively sloped and concave. The optimum composition of output is where the slope of the production possibility curve is equal to the relative price of net exports, $(P^*/N)/P = 1/R$, which is the reciprocal of the real exchange rate. The numerator (P^*/N) is the price in domestic currency of the net exports and P is the GDP deflator for the output not exported. This is the same as stating that the optimal output of net exports/GDP is such that marginal cost is equal to price. We show that the ratio $B = X/Y$ of net exports/GDP is positively related to the productivity in the net export sector and negatively related to the real exchange rate R, where a rise is an appreciation of the currency.

Equation (4.10a) states that marginal cost is equal to price. The price in the world market is P^* and the nominal exchange rate is N. The domestic price is P^*/N. The marginal cost MC is the change in labor cost $W\Delta L/\Delta X$ plus the change in material cost $(V^*/N)\Delta M/\Delta X$. The world price of materials is V^* and the domestic price is V^*/N. Divide both sides by the GDP deflator P and derive (4.10b). The real wage is $w = W/P$ and the terms of trade are $T = V^*/NP$.

$$P^*/N = MC = W\Delta L/\Delta X + (V*/N)\Delta M/\Delta X \tag{4.10a}$$

$$1/R = w\Delta L/\Delta X + (1/T)\Delta M/\Delta X. \tag{4.10b}$$

Insofar as there are diminishing returns to labor and materials, the transformation curve is negatively sloped and concave. This means that marginal cost is positively related to the relative output of net exports $B = X/Y$ and negatively related to the productivity in this sector Z_B. As the output X rises, more of other goods must be sacrificed at an increasing rate. This is equation (4.10c).

$$wΔL/ΔX + (1/T)ΔM/ΔX = B/Z_B. \tag{4.10c}$$

Using (4.10c) in (4.10b), the ratio B of net exports/GDP is equation (4.11).

$$B = Z_B/R = B(R, Z_B), B_R < 0, B_Z > 0. \tag{4.11}$$

This equation states that *optimum relative output is at the point where the production possibility curve is tangent to the relative price, or that marginal cost equals price.* Productivity Z_B combines physical productivity and the terms of trade. A rise in productivity increases the trade balance at any real exchange rate. For now, the parameter Z_B is exogenous. In Chapter 6, concerned with the transition economies, the dynamics of productivity are explicitly introduced.

GROWTH EQUATION

Insofar as the GDP is directly related to capital $Y_t = b_t K_t$, the growth of the GDP, denoted $g_t = (1/Y)dY/dt$ is equal to the productivity of capital b times I_t the ratio of investment/GDP plus another term Z_g equal to the growth in the productivity of capital, db/b. An appreciation of the real exchange rate that lowers the investment ratio reduces the growth rate, whereas a rise in vector Z_q that raises the investment rate increases the growth rate.

$$g_t = (1/Y)dY/dt = bI_t + Z_g = bI(R; Z_q) + Z_g = G(R; Z_q, Z_g). \tag{4.12}$$

The first part of the growth rate in equation (4.12) is described statistically by a regression of the growth rate g_t on the investment/GDP ratio I_t. For the US as well as for the other countries the slope is positive, but only a very small fraction of the growth rate–certainly less than 10% – can be explained by the investment ratio. The main part of the growth is in the residual Z_g, which is taken as another fundamental determinant of the exchange rate. Growth arises from several sources. An improved allocation of resources drives the economy to its production possibility surface. Liberalization of the economy, the deregulation of prices, wage price flexibility, and a rule of law are essential to this process. A continual use of more efficient production processes is another source of the expansion of the production possibility surface. For example, foreign direct investment FDI from the US, Japan, or Western Europe transfers technology to other countries such as the CEEC, and the Asian countries. These effects are subsumed under Z_g, which we take as an exogenous parameter.

The growth process presented here seems to be different from the presentation in the previous versions of the NATREX model. In the earlier versions, there was a concept of capital whose rate of change is investment. The version developed in this chapter has no *explicit* capital. However, equation (4.12) is the growth rate of GDP. In Appendix B, we explain that *the two approaches are mathematically consistent with each other*. The advantage of the approach taken here is that there is no need to measure capital K_t. Such a measure is problematic, because the quality of investment and capital changes, due to technical change, obsolescence, and depreciation. These factors mean that the effective capital to produce real GDP depends upon the quality and vintage. In equation (4.12) all we need to measure are flows, investment.

MEDIUM-RUN AND LONG-RUN DYNAMIC PROCESS

The NATREX model is summarized by four equations, (4.13)–(4.15) in Box 4.1. Equation (4.13) is the internal–external equilibrium equation where the external debt/GDP ratio F_t is predetermined. This is *medium-run equilibrium* and is described by point E in Figure 4.2. It is very useful for the subsequent analysis to graph equation (4.13) as the CA curve in Figure 4.3. The negatively sloped $CA = [B(R_t; Z_B) - rF_t]$ curve relates the current

---

Box 4.1. THE NATREX MODEL

$$[B(R_t; Z_B) - rF_t] + I(R_t; Z_q) - S(F_t, \delta) = 0 \qquad (4.13)$$

$$\begin{aligned} dF_t/dt &= r_t F_t - B(R_t; Z_B) - G(R; Z_q, Z_g)F_t \\ &= I(R_t; Z_q) - S(F_t, \delta) - G(R; Z_q, Z_g)F_t \end{aligned} \qquad (4.14)$$

$$[r - G(R; Z_q, Z_g)]F = B(R; Z_B). \qquad (4.15)$$

$R = Np/p^*$ is the real exchange rate, N is the nominal exchange rate and p/p^* is the ratio of domestic/foreign price levels. A rise in N or R is an appreciation. F is the ratio of external debt/GDP. The growth rate is g. These are endogenous variables. Exogenous parameters are the Z's. A rise in Z_q raises the investment/GDP, Z_B raises the trade balance/GDP, Z_g raises the growth rate. The parameter δ lowers saving/GDP. Medium-run equilibrium is equation (4.13). The dynamics are in (4.12) and (4.14). The long-run equilibrium is described by equations (4.13), (4.15) and (4.12).

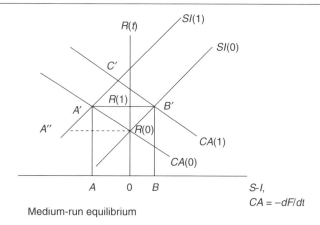

Figure 4.3. Medium-run equilibrium. Rise in investment less saving shifts the *SI* curve to the left, appreciates the real exchange rate from $R(0)$ to A', and increases the current account deficit from 0 to A. Rise in productivity or terms of trade shifts the *CA* curve to the right, appreciates the real exchange rate from $R(0)$ to B', and increases the current account surplus from 0 to B.

account to the real exchange rate. An appreciation of the real exchange rate reduces the trade balance and decreases the current account. A rise in the external debt ratio F_t decreases the current account because income transfers rF are raised, and shifts the *CA* curve to the left. The *CA* curve is affected by fundamentals Z_B described in Section 3.3 above.

Curve *SI* in Figure 4.3 is the saving less investment function $[S(F_t,\delta) - I(R_t;Z_q)]$. An appreciation of the exchange rate reduces the q-ratio and lowers investment. The slope is positive because saving less investment rises when the real exchange rate appreciates. The *SI* curve shifts when the fundamentals, time preference δ, and the determinants of the q-ratio Z_q change. A rise in time preference reduces saving and shifts the *SI* curve to the left. A rise in the productivity of capital raises the q-ratio, raises investment, and the *SI* shifts to the left. Any factor that decreases saving less investment, given a real exchange rate, shifts the *SI* curve to the left. Each *SI* curve is evaluated at a predetermined F_t debt ratio, which is time varying.

The ratio F_t and the real exchange rate R_t are endogenous variables. The external debt ratio changes insofar as there is a current account surplus or deficit adjusted for growth. *Dynamic equation* (4.14) describes the change in the debt/GDP ratio. It is the current account deficit, equal to investment less saving, adjusted for the growth rate g_t.

The *long-run NATREX* is the medium-run real exchange rate at which the debt/GDP ratio has stabilized. Long-run NATREX satisfies both equation (4.13) for internal–external balance and equation (4.15) for a debt/GDP ratio that is not changing. At this point the trade balance is sufficiently large to make the income transfers adjusted for growth.

The long-run equilibrium real exchange rate and debt/GDP ratio that satisfy equations (4.13), (4.15) and (4.12) are equations (4.16) and (4.17). Both are functions of the fundamentals $Z = (\delta, Z_q, Z_B, Z_g)$. Insofar as these fundamentals are time varying, the equilibrium real exchange rate is also time varying.

$$R = R(Z) \tag{4.16}$$

$$F = F(Z). \tag{4.17}$$

SUMMARY

The NATREX model is a model of the *equilibrium* real exchange rate. It starts with the *medium-run equilibrium* real exchange rate, which satisfies equation (4.13), when there is internal and external equilibrium. Then there are dynamic processes on the debt and growth rate that drive the medium run equilibrium exchange rate to the *long-run equilibrium* $R(Z)$, and the debt ratio $F(Z)$ to its equilibrium value. The real exchange rate $R(Z)$ is the intercept in Figure 4.1 which relates the long-run *equilibrium* nominal exchange rate to the long-run equilibrium real rate. The *actual* real exchange rate converges to a distribution whose mean is $R(Z)$, but there is a considerable variance. The NATREX model is very different from the monetary models with anticipations and from the PPP. The fundamentals (Z, δ) are treated as exogenous or control/policy variables. The basic equations are derived from *intertemporal optimization when there is uncertainty*, using stochastic optimal control and dynamic programming as described in Chapter 3.

4.3. Scenarios of medium and long-run equilibrium[16]

The economic meaning of the equations of the NATREX model can be understood by describing two scenarios: a populist scenario and a productivity-oriented scenario. The effects of the other exogenous and

[16] The NATREX model of equilibrium consists of the equations in Box 4.1. When there are lagged adjustments, then Appendix C shows that there will be cyclical movements around the equilibrium.

policy variables can be understood, using these two scenarios as examples. These scenarios are used in explaining the real value of the euro in chapter 5 and the real exchange rates of transition economies in Chapter 6. The discussion starts with medium-run equilibrium and then proceeds to longer run equilibrium. Appendix A contains the underlying mathematical analysis.

The real exchange rate satisfies equation (4.13) when the debt ratio F is predetermined. Graphically, the saving less investment function is $SI(0)$, and the current account function is $CA(0)$, in Figure 4.3. The medium-run equilibrium real exchange rate is $R(0)$ and the current account deficit is zero. Solve equation (4.13) for the medium-run equilibrium real exchange rate and derive equation (4.18). The differential of the real exchange rate is equation (4.19). A very important point is that a rise in the debt ratio depreciates the real exchange rate $R_F < 0$. Graphically, a rise in the debt decreases the current account curve, shifts it to the left, which tends to depreciate the exchange rate along a given SI curve. Moreover, a rise in the debt lowers net worth, which decreases consumption and raises saving (equation 4.6). The SI curve shifts to the right. When the debt ratio rises, a combination of the two effects depreciates the real exchange rate. This is $R_F < 0$. Medium-run equilibrium is derived from equation (4.19) when F is predetermined, so that $dF = 0$. The medium run equilibrium is affected by changes in the fundamentals $Z = (\delta, Z_q, Z_B)$. Two scenarios, a rise in time preference δ and a rise in the productivity Z_B, are discussed in the context of equation (4.19).

$$R_t = R(F_t; \delta, Z_q, Z_B) \tag{4.18}$$

$$(I_R + BR)dR - (r + S_F)dF = S_\delta d\delta - I_q dZ_q - B_z dZ_B \tag{4.19}$$

where $(I_R, B_R) < 0, S_F > 0, S_\delta <, I_q, B_z) > 0, R_F = (r + S_F)/(I_R + B_R) < 0$.

In *scenario I*, time preference δ rises/social saving declines, as a result of populist policies that favor consumption of goods and services for the present generation. Initially, saving less investment is described by curve $SI(0)$, and the current account by curve $CA(0)$. They are equal at the real exchange rate $R(0)$.

As a result of the populist policies, the SI curve shifts from $SI(0)$ to $SI(1)$ in Figure 4.3. If all of the increased demand were directed to home goods, then the CA curve remains at $CA(0)$. At exchange rate $R(0)$, the *ex ante* current account is zero but *ex ante* saving is less than investment. Domestic firms/government borrow abroad what they cannot borrow at home. The desired capital inflow appreciates the exchange rate to $R(1) > R(0)$, to restore internal and external balance. This is a movement to the medium-run equilibrium point A', evaluated at the initial level of net foreign assets $F(0)$ and productivity. From equation (4.19) the change in the medium-run equilibrium exchange rate is equation (4.20). It is evaluated at a given debt ratio $F(0)$.

$$\frac{dR}{d\delta} = \frac{S_\delta}{I_R + B_R} > 0, \text{ when } F = F(0). \tag{4.20}$$

Any perturbation that decreases saving less investment can be described by the movement in the *medium run* from $R(0)$ to $R(1)$ at point A' in Figure 4.3.

Scenario II concerns a change in the trade balance function. A crucial variable determining the shift in the trade balance function $B(R; Z_B)$ is the change in marginal cost relative to price of exports/import substitutes–call them "tradables". The marginal cost depends upon the real wage relative to productivity. A rise in the productivity results from a more efficient allocation of resources, deregulation of prices, labor, and capital mobility. If there is a rise in productivity relative to the real wage, the marginal cost of producing tradables is lowered, and the trade balance and current account functions shift to the right. Alternatively, production may be geared to higher quality and priced goods, without a corresponding rise in nominal unit costs. The scenario concerns a rise in Z_B.

Initially, the *SI* curve remains at $SI(0)$, when the trade balance parameter Z_B rises. The current account curve in Figure 4.3 increases from $CA(0)$ to $CA(1)$. At the initial exchange rate $R(0)$, the current account $CA(1)$ exceeds the capital outflow $SI(0)$, and the real exchange rate appreciates to point B' with real exchange rate $R(1)$. The appreciation of the exchange rate to $R(1)$ restores medium-run equilibrium by restoring $SI(0) = CA(1)$. The medium-run change in the equilibrium real exchange rate from $R(0)$ to point B' is equation (4.21).

$$\frac{dR}{dZ_B} = -B_Z / (I_R + B_R) > 0. \tag{4.21}$$

In the *medium run* there is a difference between scenario I and scenario II. In scenario I, there is a capital *inflow* equal to the current account deficit of Adt, which implies a rising foreign debt. In scenario II, there is a capital *outflow* equal to a current account surplus of Bdt, which implies a declining foreign debt. This leads us into the dynamics of the movement to long-run equilibrium.

DYNAMICS TO LONG-RUN EQUILIBRIUM

Whereas the macroeconomic balance models stop at the movement $R(0)$-$R(1)$, the NATREX model continues by taking into account the

Table 4.1 Medium-run and long-run effects: alternative scenarios. Assume: dynamic stability, $(r - g) > 0$ and $F(0) > 0$. See Appendix A for the mathematical derivation.

Scenarios	Medium-run real exchange rate R, debt ratio given	Long-run real exchange rate R^*	Long-run debt ratio F
Scenario I $\Delta(I\text{-}S)$ rise in investment less saving/rise in time preference	appreciate	depreciate	rises
Scenario II ΔZ_B rise in trade balance function	appreciate	appreciate	declines
Δg, when $F(0) > 0$ rise in growth rate	not affected	appreciate	declines

endogenous changes in foreign net claims and growth, which feed back upon the macroeconomic balance equation.

Consider *scenario I* where the initial disturbance is a rise in time preference. The decline in saving shifts the *SI* curve to *SI*(1). At initial real exchange rate $R(0)$ saving less investment is at point A''. The real exchange rate appreciates to point A'. The appreciation lowers the *q*-ratio and decreases investment. Hence the medium-run equilibrium real exchange rate is R (1). At point A', since some investment has been crowded out, the capital inflow is less than the initial decline in saving, and equals the current account deficit Adt. The foreign debt is rising at rate Adt, equation (4.14), evaluated when the growth rate is $g = 0$.

The *trajectories of the real exchange rate and the debt ratio to the long-run equilibrium, $R(Z)$ and $F(Z)$, are derived from the medium-run equilibrium equation (4.18) and dynamic equation (4.14)*. The results are summarized[17] in Table 4.1.

Dynamic equation (4.14) concerns the shifts of the *CA* and *SI* curves in Figure 4.3 as a result of the change in the debt, which is the current account deficit (Adt) or surplus (Bdt) adjusted for growth. There are both destabilizing and stabilizing effects of the debt.

The *destabilizing* effect stems from the rise in the debt, which raises the interest payments $rF(t)$. These shift the *CA* curve to the left of $CA(0)$. The leftward shift of the *CA* function along the *SI*(1) function depreciates the exchange rate below $R(1)$ and widens the deficit on the current account. The steady decline in the *CA* function–due to a steady rise in the debt – *along a given SI function produces instability*. The current account deficit rises steadily, debt will explode, and the real exchange rate will depreciate steadily.

---

[17] Appendix A is a mathematical analysis of the movement from medium-run to long-run equilibrium. In the text, the discussion is literary and graphic.

The *stabilizing* effect arises from several components. First, the rise in the debt lowers net worth, which reduces consumption and raises saving. The stabilizing effect is $S_F > 0$, that there is an *endogenous* shift of the *SI* curve to the right. There must be a decline in absorption as a result of the decline in net worth[18]. It may occur either because the government reduces its high employment deficit or the private sector increases saving.

Second, the depreciation of the exchange rate increases the trade balance $B_R < 0$, which increases the current account. *These two effects reduce absorption and increase the trade balance.* The third component is that the depreciation of the exchange rate raises the q-ratio, which raises investment and raises the growth rate $G_R < 0$.

On the basis of equation (4.15) there is a direct explanation why the long-run real exchange rate NATREX depreciates as a result of a rise in time preference. The long-run debt/GDP rises as a result of the accumulation of current account deficits, such as *Adt* in Figure 4.3. The long-run debt F^* rises above its initial level, and the interest rate must exceed the growth rate, $(r- g) > 0$ if the present value of GDP is finite. Since the net income transfer $(r-g)F^*$ rises, the trade balance $B(R^*; Z)$ must increase to generate the foreign exchange for the transfer. Consequently, the real exchange rate R^* must be below its initial level to generate the greater trade balance. In this manner, the NATREX model shows that scenario I – a rise in investment less social saving – leads to longer run depreciation, not appreciation as claimed by the traditional models.

The dynamics of scenario II, where there is a rise in Z_B, are quite different from those in scenario I, where there is a rise in time preference δ. The long-run results are summarized in the second row in Table 4.1.

A crucial variable determining the shift in the trade balance function $B(R;Z_B)$ is the marginal cost relative to price of tradables. The marginal cost depends upon the real wage relative to productivity – real unit labor cost. If there is a rise in productivity relative to the real wage, the marginal cost of producing tradables is lowered, and the trade balance and current account functions shift to the right.

The *SI* curve remains at *SI* (0). When the trade balance parameter Z_B rises, the current account curve in Figure 4.3 increases from $CA(0)$ to $CA(1)$. At the initial exchange rate $R(0)$, the current account $CA(1)$ exceeds the capital outflow $SI(0)$, and the real exchange rate appreciates to point B' with real exchange rate $R(1)$. The appreciation of the exchange rate to $R(1)$ restores medium-run equilibrium by restoring $SI(0) = CA(1)$.

---

[18] This issue is discussed in the chapter on the US balance of payments.

The dynamic story involves further movements in both the CA and the SI functions. As a result of the current account surplus Bdt, the debt declines. The decline in the net interest/dividend payments on the debt/equity shifts the CA curve to the right of $CA(1)$, and further appreciates the real exchange rate.

The long-run effect of an increase in productivity is to appreciate the real exchange rate to $R^* > R(0)$. The reason is understood by looking at equation (4.15), when the debt/GDP has stabilized at F^*. The debt ratio F^* is lower due to the accumulation of current account surpluses such as Bdt. If we started from a zero debt $F(0) = 0$, then the new long-run equilibrium debt/GDP ratio is negative, $F^* < 0$, and the country becomes a creditor. There are inflows of interest and dividends $rF^* < 0$. To finance the inflows, the trade balance must decline. The rise in parameter Z_B has increased the trade balance. Therefore, the real exchange rate R^* must appreciate above its initial level to reduce $B(R^*; Z_B)$ to equal the lower value of $(r-g)F^* < 0$. At the new long-run equilibrium, there are *sustainable* current account surpluses and net asset position grows at the growth rate g of real GDP[19].

Another scenario occurs when there is a rise in the growth rate, which may occur in several ways. Foreign direct investment (FDI) is accompanied by an improved technology. Liberalization of the economy and price flexibility improve the allocation of resources. When the growth rate rises relative to the interest rate, the debt/GDP ratio declines according to differential equation (4.14). Insofar as the equilibrium debt ratio is lower, there are smaller transfer payments. Graphically, the decline in the debt shifts the CA function in Figure 4.3 to the right. The resulting long-run equilibrium real exchange rate appreciates.

4.4. Conclusions

The NATREX model is concerned with the "equilibrium" real exchange rate and not with the actual nominal exchange rate at any one time. *The contribution of the NATREX model is an analytical framework whereby one can analyze the medium and longer run effects of policies and exogenous variables upon the real exchange rate and external debt/GDP ratio.* This is *positive* economics. The underlying equations are derived from intertemporal optimization by the private sector, whereas government policies are based upon political considerations.

---

[19] The equilibrium condition is $B^* = (r - g)F^*$. The current account is $CA = B - rF$. The constancy of the ratio F is that $CA/(-F) = g$. Since $F^* < 0$, $CA = g(-F) > 0$.

The equilibrium real exchange rate is where the actual rate is heading – a central tendency – and depends upon the value of real fundamentals, which change as a result of policies and exogenous variables. The equilibrium real exchange rate is the asymptotic mean of a distribution, which has considerable variance due to speculative factors, anticipations, and pronouncements by Central Bankers, cyclical elements, and lags in adjustment.

A distinction is made between medium-run and long-run equilibrium. The former is a flow equilibrium and the latter is a stock-flow equilibrium. There are several lessons to be learned from the NATREX model. First, the standard models imply that an expansionary fiscal policy appreciates the real exchange rate. In the NATREX model, such a policy – scenario I – appreciates the medium-run equilibrium real exchange rate, but leads to a higher debt ratio that depreciates the longer-run equilibrium. Policies that lead to an appreciated real exchange rate in the longer run are those that either raise the trade balance function at any real exchange rate, increase the growth rate, or raise the social saving rate.

Second, an expansionary fiscal policy that leads to a rise in social consumption produces dynamic instability, unless the resulting rise in the debt – a decline in net worth – induces a decline in social absorption. *If social absorption does not decline, the current account deficit/GDP will rise steadily and the real exchange rate will decline steadily.* This lesson is discussed in the chapter on the United States dollar.

Third, the PPP hypothesis and monetary models – that the equilibrium real rate $R(Z)$ is constant, and that the nominal exchange rate is simply the ratio of price levels – are unduly simplistic to provide a guide to policy. In our analysis the equilibrium *nominal* exchange rate is described in Figure 4.1, which depends upon both the equilibrium real rate and relative prices or nominal unit costs.

The NATREX model is applied in Chapter 5 to explain the euro exchange rate and in Chapter 6 to evaluate the real exchange rate in the transition economies. Moreover, it is used in Chapter 8 to explain the Asian crises.

Appendix A. Mathematical analysis of effects of fundamentals upon the medium-run and long-run equilibrium real exchange rate and debt/GDP ratio

Equation (A1) is the *medium-run equilibrium* when there is internal and external balance. This is point E in Figure 4.2 or the intersection of the SI and CA curves in

Figure 4.3. The differential of equation (A1) is (A2). A rise in the debt ratio depreciates the real exchange rate. This is $R_F = dR/dF$ in equation (A3). It is negative because the numerator $(S_F + r) > 0$ and the denominator $(I_R + B_R)$ is negative. It is convenient to write $S_\delta d\delta - I_q dZ_q$ as the change in saving less investment $d(S-I)$.

$$R_t = R(F_t; \delta, Z_q, Z_B) \tag{A1}$$

$$(I_R + B_R)dR - (r - S_F)dF = S\delta d\delta - I_q dZ_q - B_z dZ_B = -d(I - S) - B_z dZ_B$$
$$\text{where } (I_R, B_R)<0, S_F>0, S\delta<0, (I_q, B_z)>0 \tag{A2}$$

$$R_F = \frac{dR}{dF} = \frac{r + S_F}{I_R + B_R} < 0. \tag{A3}$$

The *medium-run* equilibrium real exchange rate changes as the fundamentals change, when the *debt ratio F and growth rate g are predetermined*. These effects are:

$$\frac{dR}{d\delta} = \frac{S_\delta}{I_R + B_R} > 0. \quad \text{rise in time preference} \tag{A4}$$

$$\frac{dR}{dZ_B} = \frac{-B_z}{I_R + B_R} > 0 \quad \text{increase in trade balance function} \tag{A5}$$

$$\frac{dR}{dZ_q} = \frac{-I_q}{I_R + B_R} > 0 \quad \text{rise in } q\text{-ratio.} \tag{A6}$$

The *long-run equilibrium* exchange rate and debt ratio are derived from (A2) and from the condition that $dF/dt = 0$. The latter is equation (4.5) whose differential is (A7). Here we treat the growth rate $(1/Y)dY/dt = g$ as a parameter. Therefore the differentials of the long-run system are (A2) and (A7).

$$B_R dR - (r - g)dF = -Fdg - B_z dZ_B. \tag{A7}$$

There are three fundamentals: the exogenous shift of saving less investment $d(S-I)$, the shift in the trade balance function $B_z dZ$, and the shift in the growth rate parameter. Whereas the debt/GDP ratio is predetermined in the medium-run equilibrium, in the long run the debt is endogenous.

Figure 4.4 is a graphic description of dynamics, when the growth rate g is treated as an exogenous fundamental. In the chapter on the transition economies, structure is given to the growth rate, which complicates and enriches the dynamics. The dynamics of the debt is equation (A8).

$$dF/dt = (r - g)F - B(R; Z_B). \tag{A8}$$

Substitute (A1) for the medium-run real exchange rate and derive (A9), which is graphed in Figure 4.4. The stability condition is (A10) when the growth rate is a parameter.

$$dF/dt = (r - g)F - B(R(F; Z); Z_B) \tag{A9}$$

$$\Delta = (r - g) - B_R R_F = (r - g) - [B_R/(B_R + I_R)](r + S_F)]$$
$$= B_R(S_F + g) - I_R(r - g) < 0. \tag{A10}$$

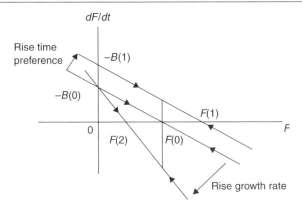

Figure 4.4. Dynamics of scenarios, row 1 and row 3 in Table 4.2. Scenario 1 is a rise in time preference, which raises the negatively sloped curve, which relates dF/dt to F, from the one with vertical intercept $-B(0)$ to the one with vertical intercept $-B(1) > -B(0)$. The economy converges along the higher curve to debt ratio $F(1) > F(0)$. Scenario 3 is a rise in the growth rate. There is no change in the vertical intercept, but the curve rotates counterclockwise. The dynamics reduce the debt to $F(2) < F(0)$, and appreciate the real exchange rate.

Equation (A9) is graphed in Figure 4.4 for three values of the fundamentals. The slope is term Δ in (A10), which must be negative in the stable case, for reasons discussed in the text. The decline in net worth must induce a decline in absorption, a rise in saving.

Let the initial equilibrium debt be $F(0) > 0$. One scenario is a rise in time preference, which is a decline in social saving. The medium-run equilibrium in Figure 4.3 involves an appreciation of the real exchange rate to $R(1)$ and a decline in the current account to A. This movement corresponds to the negative current account, rate of change of the debt, point $-B(1) > 0$ in Figure 4.4. The debt rises along the direction of the arrows. The debt ratio converges to a steady state value $F(1) > F(0)$. Since the real exchange rate is $R = R\,(F;Z)$, the rise in the debt ratio to F (1) depreciates the long-run equilibrium real exchange rate below its initial value. This scenario is summarized in the first row of Table 4.2.

Another scenario is that there is a rise in the growth rate. There may be structural reforms that deregulate prices, privatize the firms, and increase wage flexibility and labor mobility. Parameter g rises. There is no change in the medium-run equilibrium. At the initial debt/GDP ratio, the growth rate rises. If the initial situation had an equilibrium debt ratio of $F(0) > 0$ when $dF/dt = 0$, the new curve describing (A9) has the same vertical intercept and a steeper slope. The new curve rotates counterclockwise with a horizontal intercept of F (2). This means that, when the growth rate rises, then at point $F(0)$ the debt ratio is no longer constant but declines, $dF/dt < 0$. The economy moves along the trajectory in the direction of the arrows to intercept $F(2)$, where $dF/dt = 0$. It is seen that the new steady state debt ratio

Table 4.2 Medium-run and long-run effects: stability, $(r\text{-}g) > 0$ and $F(0) > 0$.

Disturbance	Medium-run real exchange rate R, debt ratio given	Long-run real exchange rate R^*	Long-run debt ratio F
$\Delta(I - S)$ rise in investment less saving	$(-1)/(I_R + B_R) > 0$ appreciate	$(r\text{-}g)(\Delta) < 0$ depreciate	$B_R/\Delta > 0$
ΔZ_B rise in trade balance function	$(-B_Z)/(I_R + B_R) > 0$ appreciate	$(B_Z/ - \Delta)(S_F + g) > 0$ appreciate	$(B_Z I_R/ - \Delta) < 0$
Δg, when $F(0) > 0$ rise in growth rate	0	$(r + S_F) F/(-\Delta) > 0$ appreciate	$[(I_R + B_R)/ (-\Delta)]F < 0$
$\Delta = B_R(g + S_F) - I_R(r\text{-}g) < 0$, stability condition			

$F(2) < F(0)$. Since the real exchange rate is negatively related to the debt ratio, the decline in the debt ratio appreciates the real exchange rate $R(2) > R(0)$. This scenario is summarized in row 3 of Table 4.2.

Table 4.2 describes the medium-run and long-run effects of the changes in the three fundamentals upon the real exchange rate and the debt ratio.

Appendix B. Growth equation replaces capital, global stability condition

The long-run dynamics presented here seem to be different from the presentation in the previous versions of the NATREX model. In the earlier versions, there was a concept of capital whose rate of change is investment. Therefore, there were two dynamic equations: one for the rate of change of the debt ratio $dF/dt = (r - g)F - B$ and the second was $dK/dt = I$. Capital $K_t = \int^t I_s \, ds$ is the integral of investment. The growth rate was not explicit.

The version developed in this chapter has no *explicit* capital. The first dynamic equation concerns the debt ratio $dF/dt = (r - g)F - B$, as before. However, the second dynamic equation is (B1) concerning the growth rate of GDP. *The two approaches are mathematically equivalent.* The advantage of the approach taken here is that there is no need to measure capital $K_t = \int^t I_s \, ds$ in any structural equation. A measure of capital is problematic, because the quality of investment and capital changes, due to technical change, obsolescence, and depreciation. These factors mean that the effective capital required to produce real GDP depends upon the quality and vintage. In the version used in this chapter *all we need to measure are flows – investment.*

The growth of GDP is equation (B1). The investment ratio $I_t = J_t/Y_t$, where J_t is the rate of investment, is equation (4.8), which is negatively related to the real exchange rate. Solving equation (B1) for the logarithm of GDP, obtain (B2), where $Y = Y(0)$ in the initial period. The changes in quality are captured by the changes in the productivity of investment b_s. In (B1), as in the chapter, the investment/GDP *ratio* is $I(R,Z)$.

$$g_t = (dY_t/dt)/Y_t = bI_t + Z_t = bI(R_t, Z) + Zg \tag{B1}$$

$$\ln Y_t/Y = \int^t [b_s I(R_s; Z) + Z_g] ds. \tag{B2}$$

The two approaches can be compared in the following way. If $b_s = b$ were constant, then we obtain (B3). Define capital K_t as the integral $\int^t J(R_s; Z) ds$. Then we have, as in the original NATREX model, that GDP depends upon capital plus a trend term zt, where z is the mean of the Z terms.

$$Y_t = Y(0) + b\int^t J(R_s; Z) ds + \int^t Y_s Z_g ds = (Y(0) + bK_t) + z.t, \tag{B3}$$
$$z = (1/t)\int^t Z_s Y_s ds.$$

The big differences between the two approaches are that (B2): (a) does not assume that "capital" can be obtained by cumulating investment, and (b) does not require diminishing returns to capital. It is quite possible that the productivity of investment b_s does change with "capital", but that is not necessary. With quality improvements, the productivity of investment need not decline as "capital" increases. Equation (B2) states, what is empirically the case, that the growth rate g_t is proportional to I_t the investment ratio with a considerable variance. In terms of applying the NATREX model to the data in the chapters in Parts III and IV, either approach can be taken.

When the growth rate is partially endogenous in Equation (4.12), the stability condition that the debt ratio and the real exchange rate converge to their long-run equilibrium values from the medium-run equilibrium is equation (B4), based upon equation (4.14).

$$\Delta - FR_F G_R < 0. \tag{B4}$$

Condition (B4) is a global stability condition, when there are both endogenous debt and growth. If the initial debt is $F(0) = 0$, then the stability condition is (A9).

PROOF OF GLOBAL STABILITY CONDITION

Use the method of Lyapounov for *global* stability. Let $X(F) = (dF/dt) = [(r-g)F - B(R(F))]$, and $g = (G(R))$. Define $V[X(F)]$ in (B5). It is positive definite and continuous, and is zero only when the debt ratio is not changing, that is the term in brackets is zero. Therefore $V[X(F)]$ is zero only at the long-run equilibrium[20].

$$V[X(F)] = (dF/dt)^2/2 = (1/2)[(r-g)F - B(R(F))]^2 > 0. \tag{B5}$$

Convergence to equilibrium will occur if $dV[X(F)]/dt < 0$, which is equation (B6). The term

$$X_F \text{ is } d(dF/dt)/dF = \Delta - FR_F G_R.$$

$$dV[X(F_t)]/dt = V_X X_F dF/dt = X_t^2 X_F = X_t^2 (\Delta - FR_F G_R). \tag{B6}$$

---

[20] The fundamentals Z are constant, so they are ignored here.

The global stability condition is (B4). If the initial debt is $F(0) = 0$, the stability condition is just (A10), $\Delta = [(r-g)F - B\,(R(F)]^2\,[(r-g) - B_R R_F] < 0$. QED.

Global stability conditions involve: $R_F < 0$, saving is positively related to net worth $(B_R + I_R)$, appreciation reduces the trade balance plus investment, $G_R < 0$, appreciation reduces investment, which reduces growth. The comparative long-run equilibrium analysis in Table 4.2 just uses the stability condition $\Delta < 0$, when the growth rate is a parameter.

APPENDIX C. Lagged adjustments generate cyclical movements around the equilibrium

The NATREX model concerns the medium-run and the long-run *equilibrium* real exchange rate and current account. When there are lagged adjustments, the real exchange rate can oscillate around the equilibrium value $R^* = R(Z)$. Two modifications can be made to the model when there are lagged adjustments[21]. Assume that the real exchange rate R_t appreciates relative to its equilibrium value $R^* = R(Z)$ in equation (4.16) when there is a surplus in the balance of payments (BOP) $M_t = (B - rF + I - S)_t > 0$, and depreciates when there is a deficit $M_t < 0$. Internal and external stability require that the equilibrium balance of payments, $M^* = M(R^*, Z) = 0$ in equation (4.13).

Define $x_t = R_t - R^*$ as the deviation of the real exchange rate from the equilibrium value. "Overvaluation" means that the real exchange rate is above its equilibrium value $x_t = R_t - R^* > 0$, and "undervaluation" means that the real exchange rate is below its equilibrium $x_t = R_t - R^* < 0$. Define the BOP "surplus" or "deficit" as $y_t = M_t - M^*$.

Equations (C1) and (C2) describe the lagged adjustments in continuous time. A BOP surplus $y_t > 0$ appreciates the real exchange rate, and a BOP deficit $y < 0$ depreciates the real exchange rate[22]. Equation (C1) states that the rate of appreciation of the real exchange rate from its equilibrium value dx/dt is proportional to the surplus or deficit y_t, where the speed of response a_1 is finite and positive

Equation (C2) states that when the exchange rate is overvalued $x > 0$, the balance declines $dy/dt < 0$; and when the exchange rate is undervalued $x < 0$, the balance rises. The speed of response a_2 is finite and positive.

Equations (C1) and (C2) describe the lagged adjustments of the real exchange rate to the NATREX equilibrium real exchange rate and of the balance of payments

[21] The inspiration for these additions is Gylfason (2002) and its use by the GS (Goldman Sachs) FX Monthly Analyst report by Stolper (2004).

[22] In discrete time, equation (C1) states that the real exchange rate R_t will be what it was in the "previous period" R_{t-1} plus a term that is proportional to the surplus or deficit y_{t-1}.

to its equilibrium value. The fundamentals Z are subsumed under the equilibrium values $R^* = R(Z)$ and $M(R^*(Z)) = 0$.

$$\frac{dx}{dt} = a_1 y \tag{C1}$$

$$\frac{dy}{dt} = -a_2 x. \tag{C2}$$

Speeds of response $(a_1, a_2) > 0$, finite; $b = \sqrt{a_1 a_2}$.

The solution of this system depends upon the speed of response coefficients and initial conditions $x(0)$ and $y(0)$. The general solution for the real exchange rate deviation $x_t = R_t - R(Z)$ is equation (C3), and the balance is (C4).

$$x_t = x(0) \cos bt + (a1/b) y(0) \sin bt = R_t - R^* \tag{C3}$$

$$y_t = y(0) \cos bt - (b/a_1) x(0) \sin bt = M_t - M(R^*(Z)). \tag{C4}$$

In the general case, the orbit of the exchange rate and balance is an ellipse such as the one drawn in Figure 4.5.

In the special case when the speed of adjustment coefficients are equal to unity, $a_1 = a_2 = b = 1$, the orbit of the real exchange rate deviation and the balance of payments deviation is a circle. The real exchange rate deviation is equation (C5); the orbit is (C6) in the special case. The radius r of the circle is the square root of the sum of the squares of the initial deviations, $r = \sqrt{((x(0)^2 + Y(0))^2}$.

$$x(t) = x(0) \cos t + y(0) \sin t \tag{C5}$$

$$x(t)^2 + y(t)^2 = (x(0) + y(0))^2 \tag{C6}$$

The orbit of (x,y) has important implications that can be used in the later chapters on the real exchange rate of the US dollar. The first lesson is that the orbit traverses four regions (quadrants): overvalue/surplus, overvalue/deficit

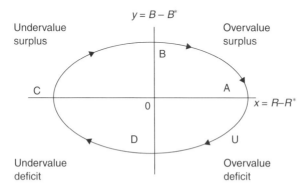

Figure 4.5. Effects of lagged adjustment. Oscillations of the real exchange rate and balance from their equilibrium values result.

undervalue/deficit, and undervalue/surplus. *This means that there is no relation between an overvalued exchange rate x_t and the balance y_t.*

The vectors in Figure 4.5 show the clockwise direction of movement. Start at any point on the orbit, say point U where the exchange rate is overvalued and there is a deficit. Many economists believe that this is the position of the US economy. The dynamics state that when the exchange rate is overvalued, the balance will decline. This means that the point moves from U towards D. At point D, the exchange rate is at its equilibrium value $x = 0$, but there is a negative balance $y < 0$. A negative balance depreciates the exchange rate, and moves the point to the left of D.

The exchange rate is now undervalued, and the balance increases though it is still negative. The economy moves towards point C, where the balance $y = 0$. The exchange rate does not tend to change, but the undervalued exchange rate continues to raise the balance. Moving from point C, the balance is positive, and the exchange rate appreciates towards point B. At point B, the exchange rate is in equilibrium, but the balance is still positive. Therefore the exchange rate continues to appreciate towards point A. Now the balance is zero, but the exchange rate is overvalued. The overvalued exchange rate reduces the balance, and the economy moves towards point U. The process described here is a *repeating cycle* of exchange rate misalignment and surpluses or deficits in the balance of payments around their equilibrium values.

The second lesson is that a regression of the *level* of the exchange rate x_t on the *level* of the balance y_t would yield a coefficient that is not significantly different from zero. The reason is that the sample space is an ellipse. For example, the level of the real exchange rate deviation remains positive even though the balance is negative from point U to point D; and the level of the exchange rate deviation is negative even though the balance is positive from point C to point B in Figure 4.5. This oscillation has some explanatory power, as shown in the chapter on the US dollar.

To summarize, when lagged adjustments are added to the NATREX model of the *equilibrium* real exchange rate, there *can be* limit cycles around the equilibrium point. It is also possible to have lagged adjustments where the oscillations converge to zero. The point is that the NATREX equilibrium, equations (4.16) and (4.17) are *means*, but that the actual convergence of the real exchange rate to the NATREX can result in considerable variances around these means.

References

Driver, Rebecca and Peter Westaway (2005), Concepts of equilibrium exchange rates, in R. Driver, P. Sinclair and C. Thoemissen (ed.) Exchange Rates, Capital Flows and Policy, Routledge

Gylfason, Thorvaldur (2002), The Real Exchange Rate always Floats, Australian Economic Papers, 41 (4), 369–381

Infante, E.F. and Jerome L. Stein (1973), Optimal Growth with Robust Feedback Control, Review Economic Studies 40, 47–60

Keynes, J.M. (1930), A Treatise on Money I , London: Macmillan

Stein, Jerome L. (1986) The Economics of Futures Markets, Blackwell, Oxford

Stein, Jerome L., Polly R. Allen et al. (1995, 1998), Fundamental Determinants of Exchange Rates, Oxford University Press

Stein, Jerome L. and Karlhans Sauernheimer (1997), The Equilibrium Real Exchange Rate of Germnany, in J.L.Stein (ed.) The Globalization of Markets, Physica-Verlag/Springer-Verlag

Stolper, Thomas (2004), Dollar Depreciation: More to Go, Goldman Sachs FX Monthly Alanlyst, June

Tobin, James (1969), A general equilibrium approach to monetary theory, Journal of Money, Credit and Banking, 1, 15–29

Williamson, John (1994), Introduction in J.Williamson (ed.) Estimating Equilibrium Exchange Rates, Institute for International Economics, Washington DC

Part III

Evaluating exchange rates

5

The equilibrium real value of the euro: An evaluation of research[1]

In this chapter, we evaluate the studies concerning the "equilibrium" value of the real euro. In the next chapter we evaluate the studies concerning the "equilibrium" real exchange rate in the *transition economies*, which consists of the Central and Eastern European countries (CEEC) that have joined the EU but not as yet the euro area.

The movement in the nominal exchange rate between the euro and the US dollar, from its inception in January 1999 to December 2004 is plotted in Figure 5.1. Variable EXEUUS is the number of $US per euro, the nominal exchange rate of the euro. A rise is an appreciation of the euro. As the euro fell from $1.16 in January 1999 to $0.85 in June 2001, authors adduced a variety of factors to account for the decline. Many predicted further depreciation. As the euro rose from that low point of $0.85 to $1.34 in December 2004, the same or other authors adduced a new variety of factors to account for the appreciation. Many predicted further appreciation, which would lead to serious economic problems for the euro area and financial difficulties for the United States.

There was a need for a scientific objective analysis of the determinants of the euro. Economists at the European Central Bank and at European universities responded to this challenge. The basic questions are:

- How can one explain the medium to longer run movements in the synthetic euro, which is a basket of currencies of the member countries, from 1973 to 2000?

- Based upon the answer to the previous question we analyze what is the expected value of the euro/$US exchange rate in the future, conditional upon policies followed in the two area.

[1] This chapter draws upon Stein (2002).

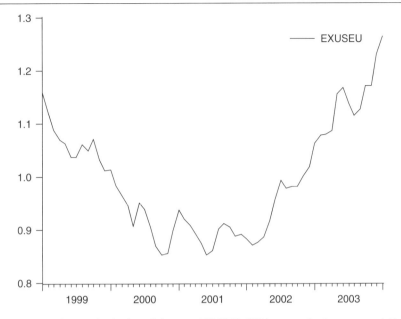

Figure 5.1. The nominal value of the euro EXUSEU, $US/euro; a rise is an appreciation of the euro relative to the US dollar.

In section 5.1 we evaluate the studies concerning the "synthetic euro" based upon an eclectic-econometric approach, often called BEER – the behavioral equilibrium exchange rate approach. In section 5.2, we derive estimating econometric equations for the equilibrium real exchange rate based upon the natural real exchange rate (NATREX) model developed in Chapter 4. Whereas the BEER type of equations is not based upon an explicit model or transmission mechanism, the NATREX is a theoretical stock/flow/growth model with an explicit transmission mechanism. In section 5.3, we explain how the NATREX model answers the questions marked by the bullets above. There is model uncertainty and different methods of estimation are used. The *quantitative* estimates vary depending upon the econometric method of estimation, but the *qualitative* estimates are relatively robust to the econometric method used. The *nominal* exchange rate of the euro is explained by synthesizing the NATREX model for the equilibrium real exchange rate with relative price variables, as shown in Figure 1.1 in Chapter 1.

5.1. The empirical literature

5.1.1. *The eclectic-econometric (BEER) studies of the equilibrium value of the real euro*

Researchers who aimed to answer the questions in bullets above faced a daunting task. They realized that the standard exchange rate models, which featured prominently in the graduate textbooks in international finance–monetary models with Purchasing Power Parity (PPP), over-shooting monetary models, models founded upon expectations, chaotic models, portfolio balance models – were inconsistent with the accumulated evidence. Other models, such as "intertemporal optimization models" were not even operational in an objective sense. For this reason, the majority of researchers decided to be eclectic and see what the state of the art econometric techniques could yield in an attempt to estimate "equilibrium exchange rates". The new macroeconometric time series analyses using vector autoregression (VAR) and vector error correction (VEC) frameworks held great promise. Moreover, there exists an excellent econometric tookit, EVIEWS, that allowed these techniques, in all of their forms, to be used by anyone with an appropriate data set. This was the rationale for using the BEER approach. But it comes with a price.

Stock and Watson (2001, page 102) evaluated the strengths and weaknesses of the VAR technique for macroeconomic analysis. "In data description and forecasting, VARs have proven to be powerful and reliable tools that are now, rightly, in everyday use. Structural inference and policy analysis are, however, inherently more difficult because they require differentiating between correlation and causation ... This problem cannot be solved by a purely statistical tool, even a powerful one like VAR. Rather, economic theory ... is required to solve the ... 'identification' (causation versus correlation) problem." This is our theme in contrasting the BEER type of studies with those based upon NATREX.

In all of the studies evaluated here, the researchers constructed a historical synthetic euro exchange rate, which is the exchange rate of a basket of currencies of countries now constituting the euro area. The hypothesis is that a valid theory concerning the actual real value euro, whose birth was only a few years ago, should be able to explain trends in the *real* value of the synthetic euro based upon many years of data. The advent of the European Central Bank can be expected to change monetary policy and relative prices in the euro area. However, the change in monetary policy should not affect the longer run equilibrium real value of the euro.

The nominal exchange rate is $N(t) = $ dollars/euro, where a rise is an appreciation of the euro. The real exchange rate $R(t)$ of the euro can be defined in several ways. Generally, the researchers use equation (5.1), where the ratio $p(t)/p^*(t)$ is the euro/foreign GDP or CPI price deflators[2]. The period covered is usually 1973:1–2000:1.

$$R(t) = N(t)p(t)/p^*(t). \tag{5.1}$$

Researchers divided the world into two blocs. The euro bloc consists of a weighted average of the countries that currently comprise the euro area, and the second bloc[3] is a weighted average of the US, UK, Japan, and Switzerland. Liliane Crouhy-Veyrac considered the $US vis-à-vis a weighted average of the euro-11. Others used a weighted average of France, Germany, and Italy as the euro area vis-à-vis the US. Since we have Crouhy-Veyrac's data, we shall use them as a basis for our empirical estimates[4]. Figure 5.2 graphs the two exchange rates: the nominal $N(t) = $US/euro, denoted EUUSNERMA, and the real $R(t)$, denoted EUUSREDPMA, value of the euro, measured as four quarter moving average (MA).

Several points should be noted immediately. (a) The real and nominal exchange rates have similar trends. (b) Neither variable reverts to

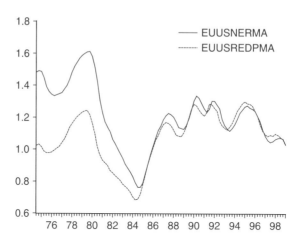

Figure 5.2. The real value of the euro relative to the $US: $R(t) = N(t)p(t)/p^*(t)$, denoted EUUSREDPMA, and nominal value of the euro relative to the $US: $N(t) = $US/euro, denoted EUUSNERMA. A rise is an appreciation of the euro. MA = 4Q moving average

[2] Some researchers use labor costs instead of broad price indexes. There are advantages and disadvantages to each measure. See, for example, Clostermann and Friedmann (1998) and Deutsche Bundesbank (1995).

[3] See Table 5.1 for the different reference currencies used in the empirical studies.

[4] They are similar to those used by the ECB researchers.

a constant mean. Both are integrated of order $I(1)$, where we use a four-quarter lag. (c) Both nominal and real exchange rates display significant variation over the sample period. These points induced the researchers to think beyond the PPP hypothesis.

The researchers carefully examined the theoretical literature concerning the determination of exchange rates, in order to find models that are potentially useful to explain the observed movements in the euro. They discarded those models that were non-operational, in the sense that the crucial variables were not objectively measurable, or whose structural equations have been shown to be inconsistent with the evidence. They ended up by going in two directions. In one direction, they took an *empirical, atheoretical econometric driven approach*. In the other direction they used the NATREX model that implies explicit econometric equations. The former set of studies may be grouped under the heading BEER, an acronym for the behavioral equilibrium real exchange rate,[5] evaluated in this chapter. The second set of studies takes as a point of departure the natural real exchange rate (NATREX) model discussed later in this chapter. Each one has a very different concept of "equilibrium".

Most of the empirical studies take the BEER approach, where one does not specify the underlying model. A partial list of these studies is presented in Table 5.1. These studies take an eclectic approach that simply searches for cointegrating equations in "sensible" variables,[6] which pass the usual econometric tests. The VECM vector error correction method used by the authors restricts the long-run behavior of the endogenous variables to converge to their cointegrating equations, while allowing a wide range of short-run dynamics.[7] As MacDonald (2002) noted, the authors obtain a *statistical/atheortetic* concept of the "equilibrium". The statistical/atheoretical approach does not correspond to any particular analytical framework. The concept of equilibrium in the BEER studies is just a cointegrating equation. Both the BEER and NATREX approaches are positive, and not normative, economics[8]. There is no welfare significance,

---

[5] The BEER approach is based upon Clark and MacDonald (1999).

[6] Outstanding papers using this approach are by Clostermann and Schnatz (2000) for the DMark, and by Maseo-Fernandez, Osbat and Schnatz (2002) for the synthetic euro. See MacDonald and Stein (1999), Chapter 1, and Stein and Lim (2002) for a discussion of these approaches.

[7] The toolkit used in most of the studies is EVIEWS, where a majority of test statistics are covered. Explanations of the tests are found in the User's Guide.

[8] Williamson's fundamental equilibrium exchange rate (FEER) approach requires a subjective assumption of what are sustainable capital flows. That is why the empirical researchers did not use his approach.

5. The equilibrium real value of the euro

Table 5.1. Survey of BEER studies of equilibrium real value of euro.

Study	Methodology	Fundamentals $Z(t)$	Reference currency
Gern et al. (2000)	BEER, UIP	Interest rate differential	$US
Clostermann and Schnatz (2000)	BEER	Internal price ratio, interest rate differential, government spending, oil prices	$US
Makrydakis et al. (2000)	BEER	Interest rate differential, relative labor productivity, net foreign assets	Effective partners
Lorenzen and Thygesen (2000)	BEER	Net foreign assets, dependency ratio, Internal price ratio, R&D expenditures; interest rate differential; output gap, interest rate differential	$US
Koen et al. (2001)	BEER	GDP per capita, dependency ratio, interest rate differential, oil prices	Effective partners
Maseo-Fernandez, Osbat and Schnatz (2002)	BEER/PEER	Productivity, internal price ratio, interest rate differential, government spending, oil prices	Effective partners
OECD (2001)	BEER	Internal price ratio, net foreign assets, government consumption/GDP, real oil price, demographic balance	Effective partners; $US
Alberola et al. (1999)	PEER	Internal price ratio, net foreign assets	$US
Teiletche (2000)	BEER	Productivity, government spending, interest rate differential	$US
Hansen and Roeger (2000)	PEER	Internal price ratio, net foreign assets	Effective partners
Wren-Lewis and Driver (1998)	FEER	Internal/external balance	$US
Borowski and Couharde (2000)	FEER	Internal/external balance	$US
IMF (2000)	Saving-investment		$US

Sources: See European Central Bank (2002: Box 2) for the references and a critique of many of these studies.

or value judgments, that the derived equilibrium real exchange rate is "optimal" in some sense[9].

5.1.2. *The BEER statistical/atheoretical approach*

Table 5.1 indicates the differences in the equations used in the various papers using the BEER methodology, but I shall try to present them in terms of their common characteristics.

The first thing to observe from Table 5.1 is that there are many variables that the authors consider as "fundamentals". The BEER methodology is clearly specified by the authors of the OECD (2001) study.

Different sub-sets of determinants were tested in turn...until a significant and economically meaningful cointegrating vector was identified...The long-run relationship was then tested for cointegration directly with the Johansen test...the residuals of the cointegrating vector were also tested for stationarity using the augmented Dickey–Fuller and Phillips–Perron tests. [OECD, p.29]

Second, there are therefore $n > 2$ candidate variables for a cointegrating equation $R = R[Z]$, where Z is a vector of candidate variables listed in Table 5.1. Since the number of sensible elements in Z is n, the number of possible regressions is 2^n. When $n = 8$, there are 256 possible regressions, using a given technique and lag structure. If there are $m > 2$ techniques, lag structures, and choice of smoothing variables into "permanent" and "transitory" components, then there are $2^{(m+n)}$ possible regressions. If $m = 4$, then there are $2^{12} = 4096$ possible regressions. That is why the number of BEER studies grows as a power function. We restrict our evaluation to a small number of representative BEER studies, which are listed in Table 5.2.

A strength of the statistical/atheoretic approach is that the underlying model is not specified, so the results do not depend upon any one model that may be misspecified. This methodology has many useful advantages, since one can never be sure that he has the correct model. But it comes at a high price. In the next section, shall show two things. (1) The qualitative/sign results concerning the significance and sign of variable Z_i depend significantly upon which other variables are or are not included in the specific regression. (2) It is often very difficult to provide an economic interpretation of the results.[10] That is why it is difficult to use the

---

[9] The optimality issues are discussed in Chapters 2 and 3 above, using stochastic optimal control/dynamic programming.

[10] See the quotation from Stock and Watson (2001) above.

Table 5.2. BEER: Longer run determinants of real value of euro and DM.

Fundamental	Makrydakis et al. (2000)	Maseo-Fernandez et al. (2002) model I	Maseo-Fernandez et al. (2002) model IV	Lorenzen and Thygesen (2000)	Clostermann and Friedmann DM (1998)	OECD (2001) pp. 29–31
Relative labor productivity	Appreciate	Appreciate	–	Appreciate		
Real price of oil		Depreciate	Depreciate			Depreciate
Relative government expenditures		Not significant	Depreciate			Depreciate
Net foreign assets NFA	Not significant	Depreciate (wrong sign); weakly exogenous	–	Appreciate	Not significant	Not significant, depreciate (wrong sign)
Real long-term interest differential	Appreciate	Appreciate	–		Appreciate	
Internal price ratio CPI/WPI	Not significant		Appreciate	Appreciate	Feeble effect	Not significant
Dependency ratio				Appreciate		

statistical/atheoretical method to answer the questions in bullets at the beginning of this chapter.

5.1.3. *An evaluation of the econometric-eclectic studies*

Table 5.2 compares six carefully executed studies that use the BEER approach in terms of their common characteristics. All the studies agree that there are real variables that can produce a cointegration equation with the real exchange rate. Each cointegrating equation passes the usual econometric tests and does track the real value of the synthetic euro and the real value of the DMark. The authors often show that their equation for $R[Z(t)]$ outperforms a random walk and the superiority improves as the horizon increases. The real value of the euro/\$US is not a stationary, *constant mean reverting*, variable. The PPP hypothesis cannot explain the trends graphed in Figure 5.2.

Six main variables, the vector $Z(t)$ in the rows in Table 5.2, are considered as possible fundamentals. Maseo-Fernandez, et al. (2002) considered five models, using the same data set. We have selected their models I and IV to show the sensitivity of the results, the effect of variable Z_i upon the real exchange rate, depending upon what are the other regressors. Although each study succeeds in finding a cointegrating equation, the studies arrive at contradictory and often puzzling results. Consider several variables across the four studies.

Two measures of productivity are used. One is measured directly as GDP per worker. The other concerns the Balassa/Samuelson effect discussed below. The direct measure of productivity – GDP per worker – appreciates, and the real price of oil depreciates the real exchange rate. These are "sensible" results within almost any model.

Net foreign assets (NFA) is the sum of the current accounts. NFA is included as a variable in five of the six studies in Table 5.2. In three studies it is not significant, in one study it depreciates the real exchange rate, and in only one study does it appreciate the real exchange rate. Moreover, Maseo-Fernandez et al. (2002) found that the net foreign assets variable was weakly exogenous. These results are not consistent with basic economic theory. In almost any transmission process, the current account is an endogenous variable that reacts to, and subsequently affects, the real exchange rate. Net foreign assets generate interest and dividend income and should appreciate the exchange rate. How can net foreign assets be exogenous in an equation/economic model that determines the long-run equilibrium real exchange rate?

Another variable is relative government expenditures, or fiscal policy. The role of fiscal policy in exchange rate determination is important for theory and policy. For example, will high-employment budget deficits appreciate or depreciate the real exchange rate? In the Maseo-Fernandez et al. article, the significance of government expenditures depends upon what measure of productivity is included in the regression. When relative labor productivity is used (row 1), then the fiscal variable is not significant. If the ratio of the CPI/WPI (row 6) replaces labor productivity, then the fiscal variable is significant. What shall one conclude from these regressions about the effects of an expansionary fiscal policy, budget deficits, upon the real exchange rate? The authors of the statistical/atheoretic studies focus upon econometric technique rather than upon the economic meaning of the results.

5.1.4. *The Balassa/Samuelson effect*

The Balassa Samuelson (B/S) effect claims that the law of one price (PPP) applies to the traded goods sector, but not to the non-traded goods sector. Therefore the real exchange rate, measured in terms of broad based indices such as the CPI deflators, will vary in proportion to the relative prices of non-traded/traded goods in the two countries. Explanations of trends in the real exchange rate would then have to be based upon the determinants of relative prices in the two sectors. The latter varies insofar as productivity of inputs differs between the two sectors in the two countries. Then a hypothesis is added that labor productivity grows more rapidly in the traded goods sector. Hence the more productive countries tend to have appreciating real exchange rates. The questions are: how to measure the B/S effect? Is this effect economically significant? In this part, we show that recent work casts serious doubt concerning the importance of the B/S effect for the Western European economies. The evaluation and interpretation of the B/S effect for the transition economies (CEEC) is discussed in more detail in the next chapter.

We formalize the B/S effect in equations (5.2), (5.2a), (5.2b),(5.2c) and (5.2d). Then we explain how different authors measure the variables. Finally, we describe the empirical results.

The real exchange rate $R(t) = R(\text{CPI})$ based upon broad based price indexes such as the CPI is the product of the constant "external" price ratio $R(T)$ of traded goods in the two countries and an "internal" price ratio $R(\text{NT})$, the price ratio of non-traded/traded goods in the two countries. The "law of one price" for traded goods is that $R(T) = C$, a constant. The weight of non-traded goods in the CPI is the fraction w. The B/S hypothesis states that variations in the real exchange rate $R(\text{CPI})$ derive from variations in $R(\text{NT})$. The real exchange rate $R(\text{CPI})$ changes in proportion to R(NT), equation (5.2c). Most authors *arbitrarily* use the ratio of CPI/WPI as their measure of the internal price ratio $R(\text{NT})$. This implies the B/S hypothesis, equation (5.2d).

B/S HYPOTHESIS

$$R(\text{CPI}) = N(t)p(t)/p^*(t)$$
$$= R(T)R(NT), \text{definition of real CPI deflated exchange rate.}$$

$$(5.2)$$

$$R(T) = [N(t)p_T(t)/p_T^*(t)] = \text{real exchange rate of traded goods.} \quad (5.2a)$$

$$R(NT) = [p_N(t)/P_T(t)]^w/[p_N^*(t)/p_T^*(t)]^w,$$
$$p_N(t) = \text{price of non-traded } (N) \text{ goods.} \quad (5.2b)$$

N = nominal exchange rate, $p_T(t)$ = price of traded T goods at time t.

"Law of one price for traded goods"$R(T) = C$ constant. $\quad$ (5.2c)

$$\log R(\text{CPI}(t)) = C + w \log R(\text{NT})$$
$$= C + a \log[\text{CPI}(t)/\text{WPI}(t)]/[\text{CPI}^*(t)/\text{WPI}^*(t)]. \quad (5.2d)$$

The empirical results are not supportive of the B/S hypothesis. In two studies, row 6 in Table 5.2, the ratio of the CPI/WPI is not significant. In two the variable appreciates the real exchange rate, and in one the effect is feeble.

A recent study by Duval (2002) measures the relative price $R(\text{NT})$ directly, using sectoral value added data from the OECD database over 1970–96 for 19 sectors and 14 countries. He derives sectoral price deflators and then he classifies the sectors as tradable/non-tradable based upon the degree of openness. Based upon direct measures of $p_N(t)/p_T(t)$ he arrives at the following conclusions.

- The long-run fluctuations of the real exchange rates do not seem to be explained by those of relative prices of non-tradables.
- Long-run PPP does not seem to be verified for tradable goods, particularly for the main currencies (dollar, yen, mark).

Duval's results are seen in Figure 5.3 for the euro/$US real exchange rate, where a rise is an appreciation of the $US or a depreciation of the synthetic euro. The dark curve ($Q = R(t)$) is the real exchange rate calculated using

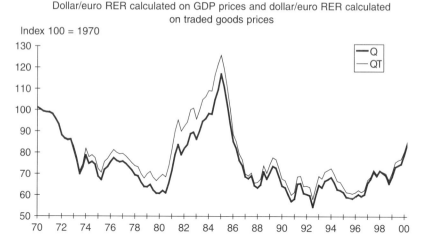

Figure 5.3. The real value of the $US relative to the synthetic euro, Q. A rise is a depreciation of the euro or appreciation of $US. Real value in terms of tradables QT.

GDP prices, and the light curve $(QT = R(T))$ is the real exchange rate calculated on traded goods prices. The B/S effect is the distance between the two curves. It is seen that the real exchange rate $R(t) = Q$ is primarily explained by the relative price of traded goods $QT = R(T)$. On the basis of Figure 5.3, the PPP and B/S effects are seen to be incapable of explaining variations in the real synthetic euro.[11] Duval's results are consistent with those of Clostermann and Friedmann (1998) for the DMark. They treated the prices of services and rents as prices of non-tradables, and prices of consumer durables and other consumer goods as tradables. They wrote that:

[Figure 5.3 page 215 in Closterman and Friedman (1998)] shows Germany's relative internal price ratio compared with a trade-weighted average of this group of 10 countries ... [R(NT)] ... is remarkably constant, and – accordingly – the real effective exchange rate on the basis of the overall CPI ... [R(CPI)] ... seems to be nearly identical with the real exchange rate based upon prices for tradables ... [R(T)]. On balance so far, not much evidence in favour of a "Balassa–Samuelson effect" in broadly defined real effective D-Mark exchange rates seems to exist in the data under consideration.

What can we conclude from these econometric-eclectic studies concerning the questions in bullets at the beginning of this chapter? The studies in Table 5.2 yielded different and often contradictory results, even

[11] Figure 5.3 is copied from his paper. A rise in his measure of the exchange rate is an appreciation of the dollar or a depreciation of the synthetic euro. Duval found the same results for Germany and France.

though each obtained a cointegrating equation with significant values for different vectors of "fundamentals" $Z(t)$ and each one tracked the euro. The variables in the cointegrating equations are mixtures of endogenous, control, and exogenous variables. Without an explicit theoretical structure telling us what variables should be included in the regressions, it is difficult to know how to interpret the econometric results.

5.2. Equilibrium real exchange rate based upon the NATREX model

In view of the problems interpreting the eclectic-econometric results, several authors listed in Table 5.3 proceeded to examine structural equations of the NATREX model to explain the fundamental determinants of the real euro, and the underlying currencies. Detken, et al. (2002) wrote the following.

A further step towards increasing the structure underlying the estimated model is to estimate a number of behavioural relations as commonly found in standard structural macroeconometric models. To begin with, we consider a small-scale model based upon the NATREX approach (NATural Real Exchange rate)...This approach tries to link the real exchange rate to a set of fundamental variables explaining savings, investment and the current account. Natrex is based upon a rigorous stock-flow interaction in a macroeconomic growth [model]. A distinction is made between a medium run equilibrium where external and internal equilibrium prevails (equivalent to the macroeconomic balance approach) and the long-run equilibrium where the budget constraint on net foreign debt is met and the capital stock has reached its steady state level.

Table 5.3 NATREX studies of the synthetic euro and component currencies.

Author	Currency	Estimation
Detken et al. (2002)	synthetic euro	structural equations
Detken and Marin Martinez (2001)	synthetic euro	structural equations
Duval (2002)	synthetic euro	reduced form dynamics
Maurin (2000/01)	synthetic euro	reduced form dynamics
Fischer and Sauernheimer (2002)	DMark	reduced form dynamics
Stein and Sauernheimer (1997)	DMark	reduced form dynamics
Federici and Gandolfo (2002)	Italian lira	structural equations
Crouhy-Veyrac and Saint Marc (1997)	French franc/DM	reduced form dynamics
Stein (1999)	$US/G7	reduced form dynamics
Verrue and Colpaert (1998)	Belgian franc	structural equations
Stein and Paladino (2001)	French franc/DM, Italian lira/DM	reduced form dynamics

Detken (2002) and Detken and Marin Martinez (2001) estimated several key structural equations in the NATREX model. From these equations, they inferred the equilibrium real exchange rate and compared the inferred equilibrium rate with the actual synthetic real euro. Other authors, such as Duval (2002) and Maurin (2000), estimated the implied reduced form equations of the NATREX model, to explain the evolution of the synthetic real euro. Stein (1999) estimated the implied reduced form equation for the $US/G7. Several authors used the model to explain the trends in the underlying currencies of the euro area. Federici and Gandolfo (2002) estimated structural equations for the Italian lira, and Verrue and Colpaert (1998) did something similar for the Belgian franc. Fischer and Sauernheimer (2002) estimated reduced form equations for the DMark. Stein and Paladino (2001) did the same for the franc/DM and Italian lira/DM and explained the currency crises of 1992–3. Crouhy-Veyrac and Saint Marc (1997) used the model to explain the real French franc/DM exchange rate. The studies in Table 5.3 obtain consistent results[12].

Sections 5.2 and 5.3 apply the NATREX model, developed in Chapter 4, to the euro. Section 5.2.1 describes the econometric results using the structural equations. Section 5.3 explains the econometric results from the reduced form approach. We conclude by explaining how the NATREX approach answers the first set of questions marked by bullets at the beginning of this chapter. Chapter 6 is concerned with the transition economies.

5.2.1. *Structural equations*[13]

The studies in Table 5.3 by Detken et al. (2002) and by Detken and Marin Martinez (2001) estimate vector error correction (VEC) models for the variables entering the investment, consumption, and trade balance equations. The object was to examine the structural equations summarized in Chapter 4, Box 4.1, and from them estimate the equilibrium real exchange

[12] The papers concerning the euro dated in the references (2002) are published together in a special issue of the *Australian Economic Papers*, December 2002: Exchange rates in Europe and Australasia. The Introduction by Stein and Lim puts the papers into perspective. The authors: Detken, Dieppe, Henry, Marin and Smets, as well as Maseo-Fernandez, Osbat and Schnatz, are researchers at the European Central Bank. Their articles, in the journal issue cited, do not represent official points of view. Their papers reflect what the staff thinks about the usefulness of existing theoretical literature for an explanation of the value of the euro. The issue also contains an article by Otmar Issing and Vitor Gaspar, of the ECB, which is policy oriented.

[13] I am using the authors' notation, except for the growth in total factor productivity, but do not specify when they use the long-term or the short-term interest rates.

rate. The medium-run NATREX is the real exchange rate that equilibrates saving less investment to the current account, when cyclical effects are eliminated, speculative capital flows based upon anticipations and changes in reserves are zero. The reader is referred to Chapter 4 for the details of the model.

The consumption equation is (5.3a), and the implied saving function is (5.3b), $S(t)/Q(t) = 1 - C(t)/Q(t)$. The ratio of consumption to output $C(t)/Q(t)$ depends positively upon net worth $(K - F)/Q$; capital less debt. Hence $C(t)/Q(t)$ depends negatively upon the foreign debt/output $F(t)/Q(t)$ where $F(t)$ is measured as cumulative current account deficits. The stability of the system depends crucially upon the sign of the debt variable: social saving (consumption) must rise (fall) with the debt. The authors also assume that $C(t)/Q(t)$ depends negatively upon the real rate of interest $r(t)$, and positively upon the nominal interest rate $i(t)$, which represents the business cycle.

Investment function equation (5.4) depends upon the Keynes–Tobin q-ratio. As explained in chapter 4, section 4.2, investment/output $I(t)/Q(t)$ is negatively related to the capital stock/output $K(t)/Q(t)$, which is an inverse measure of the productivity of capital $Q(t)/K(t)$, negatively to the real rate of interest $r(t)$, and is positively related to a^*, the growth of total factor productivity. Investment is negatively related to the real exchange rate. This is the investment crowding out effect, which produces a positively sloped SI curve in Figure 4.3.

The trade balance equation (5.5) states that the trade balance $TB(t)/Q(t)$ is negatively related to the real exchange rate $R(t)$, the domestic social consumption ratio $C(t)/Q(t)$ given in (5.3a), and positively related to foreign social consumption ratio $C^*(t)/Q^*(t)$ and to the terms of trade TOT.

Three equations are used but not estimated directly. One is the uncovered real interest parity. In addition, there are two dynamic equations. One is the growth of the debt/GDP ratio $F(t)/Q(t)$, which is equation (4.14), and the second is the growth of capital/GDP ratio $K(t)/Q(t)$, which corresponds to growth equation[14] 4.12.

The authors estimate separate VEC models for the variables in Box 5.1 over the period 1972:1–1997:4. The empirical results are as follows. The variables are integrated of order $I(1)$ – they are not stationary – except for the productivity growth rate. There is one cointegrating equation for each behavioral equation. *All of the crucial coefficients have the hypothesized sign and are significant.* There are certain crucial requirements for the validity of

---

[14] See also the discussion in Chapter 4, Appendix B.

Box 5.1. ESTIMATED STRUCTURAL EQUATIONS

$$C/Q = 1 - S/Q = a_6 + a_7 K/Q - a_8 F/Q - a_9 r + a_{10} i \qquad (5.3a)$$

$$S(t)/Q(t) = 1 - C(t)/Q(t) \qquad (5.3b)$$

$$I/Q = a_1 + a_2 a^* - a_3 K/Q(-1) - a_4 r(-3) - a_3 R(-4) \qquad (5.4)$$

$$TB/Q = -a_{11} - a_{12} R - a_{13} C/Q(-4) + a_{14} C^*/Q^*(-4) + a_{15} TOT \qquad (5.5)$$

$$S/Q - I/Q = TB/Q - rF/Q. \qquad (5.6)$$

Hypothesized values of regression coefficients are positive. $C/Q =$ social consumption/GDP, $I/Q =$ gross social investment/GDP, $TB/Q =$ trade balance/GDP, $F/Q =$ external net debt/GDP. Quarterly lag is in parentheses; interest rates, $r =$ real and $i =$ nominal.

---

the structural aspects of the NATREX model, and others are not crucial. Their empirical results (a)–(d) below are consistent with the hypothesized structural equations of the NATREX model.

(a) The rate of investment is negatively related to the real exchange rate. Exchange rate appreciation crowds out domestic capital formation in the estimate of equation (5.4). This is consistent with the positively sloped SI curve in Figure 4.3.

(b) The trade balance is negatively related to the real exchange rate in the estimate of the trade balance equation. Exchange rate appreciation crowds out the trade balance and tends to raise the debt. This is consistent with the negatively sloped CA function in Figure 4.3.

(c) The stability of the system requires that the foreign debt reduce wealth, which reduces social consumption by the sum of households, firms, and government. The debt significantly reduces social consumption in the estimate of social consumption equation (5.3a). This is consistent with the dynamics in Figure 4.3.

(d) A rise in the capital/output ratio K/Q – a decline in the productivity of capital Q/K – reduces the rate of capital formation, in the estimate of investment equation (5.4).

The structural equation approach derives the medium-run equilibrium real exchange rate from a solution of equation (5.6), based upon the econometric estimates from the equations (5.3)–(5.5) in Box 5.1. The medium-run equilibrium is evaluated given the current debt $F(t)/Q(t)$ and capital $K(t)/Q(t)$. The authors derive the longer run equilibrium real exchange rate by adding the conditions that the current account deficit/debt is a constant, and that the ratio of investment to capital is a constant. The model is then simulated to compare the actual with the simulated estimates outside the sample period. The simulation results and conclusions are as follows.

Overall, the variability of the estimated... equilibrium is very high due to the volatility in the productivity growth rate, the terms of trade and domestic interest rates... On the positive side, this could be used to refute the claim that exchange rate models based on fundamentals are not volatile enough. Furthermore, the basic pattern of the synthetic euro has been traced by our version of the Natrex model. On the other hand one caveat is appropriate. The exact level of the resulting equilibrium rate is quite fragile to small changes in the behavioural equations... The basic pattern would remain similar, but the degree of over- or undervaluation can vary significantly.

A very encouraging result is that the actual real exchange rate converges to the estimated medium run real exchange rate until about 1998. Then the actual value of the synthetic euro depreciates drastically, but the medium-run NATREX appreciates. The estimation states that the euro is *drastically undervalued* from the advent of the euro to the end of the sample period. See Detken et al. (2002), Figure 8. At the time of the writing of their paper, one did not know if the estimated undervaluation was due to a misspecification of the model or if the misalignment would be corrected. Looking at Figure 5.1 at the beginning of this chapter, we see that the euro was indeed undervalued, and its subsequent appreciation provides further confirmation of the validity of the NATREX model.

Studies of the structural equations of the NATREX model for the Italian lira by Federici and Gandolfo (2002) and the Belgian franc by Verrue and Colpaert (1998), cited in Table 5.3, yield results that are consistent with (a)–(d) above. My conclusion is that the authors have shown that: (i) the crucial transmission mechanisms of the NATREX model are consistent with the evidence, and (ii) the NATREX model explains trends quite well, but one should be hesitant in accepting the quantitative results from the simulation as precise estimates.

5.3. Reduced form dynamic equations for NATREX

Table 5.3 cites the studies that use the NATREX model to obtain estimates of the reduced form dynamic equation for the equilibrium real exchange

---

Box 5.2. NATREX MODEL: MEDIUM-RUN, LONG-RUN EQUILIBRIUM AND DYNAMICS; ECONOMETRIC COINTEGRATING AND ERROR CORRECTION EQUATIONS

$R_t = R(F_t; Z_t) \Leftrightarrow (7a)F_t = F(R_t; Z_t)$ medium-run equilibrium, $R_F = 1/F_R < 0$.

$$(5.7)$$

$B(R^*; Z) = (r - g)F(R^*; Z)$ long-run equilibrium (5.8)

$g_t = \left(\dfrac{1}{Y}\right)\dfrac{dY}{dt} = G(R_t; Z_t)$ growth rate of GDP (5.9)

$R^* = H(Z)$ long-run solution $(5.10a)$

$\Delta R^* = -w_1\Delta\delta + w_2\Delta Z_B + w_3\Delta g$ $(5.10b)$

$\dfrac{dR}{dt} = R_F[(r - g)F(R^*; Z) - B(R; Z)]$ dynamics of real exchange rate (5.11)

$\Delta R_t = \alpha(R - H.Z)_{t-1} + \Gamma.\Delta Z$ error correction dynamics (5.12)

$Z = (\delta, Z_B, Z_g)$ vector of real fundamentals

---

rate of the euro and for the underlying currencies. The NATREX model is a stock-flow dynamic model, where a distinction is made between the medium-term and the longer term trajectory of the exchange rate. In the medium term, the stock of debt and level of GDP are given, but they are endogenous in the longer run. The model in Chapter 4 is summarized in Box 5.2.

Equation (5.7) is the medium-run equilibrium exchange rate, which depends upon the debt ratio F and the vector of exogenous variables $Z = (\delta, Z_B, Z_g)$. This is based upon equation (4.13), and graphed in figure (4.3). One can solve this equation for the debt, equation (5.7a). Equation (5.8) is the long-run equilibrium condition of a constant debt/GDP ratio, which is equation (4.5). The growth rate g_t of GDP is equation (5.9), based upon equation (4.12). Equation (5.10a) is the solution for the long-run equilibrium real exchange rate $R^* = H.Z$, and equation (5.10b) is the differential ΔR^* which expresses the effects of changes in the fundamentals Z upon the change in the long-run equilibrium real exchange rate.

A rise in time preference δ means a decline in saving, which appreciates the medium-run real exchange rate, but depreciates the long-run real exchange rate. See Chapter 4, Appendix A. The reason for the long-run depreciation is that a decline in saving produces a capital inflow, which raises the external debt steadily. In equilibrium, the debt ratio F^* is higher. A constant debt ratio F^* requires that the trade balance $B(R^*; Z)$ equal the net transfer payments on the debt adjusted for the growth rate $(r - g)F^*$.

This is equation (5.8). Since the debt is higher, the real exchange rate must depreciate to raise the trade balance sufficiently. This is the term $\Delta R / \Delta \delta = -w_1 < 0$ in equation (5.10b).

There are two basic forces that appreciate the long-run real exchange rate. One is a rise in the trade balance function $B(R;Z_B)$, given the real exchange rate. The disturbance Z_B is associated with a rise in the productivity of the economy; see Chapter 4. This is expressed as the term $\Delta R / \Delta Z_B = w_2 > 0$. We stress and discuss this effect in more detail in the next chapter concerning the transition economies. The second force is a rise in the growth rate due to an increase in total factor productivity $\Delta g = \Delta Z_g$. For this reason $\Delta R / \Delta g = w_3 > 0$.

The dynamics of the exchange rate to the long-term equilibrium is equation (5.11). It is derived from equation (5.7) and the dynamics of the change in the debt. See equations (4.22 and A10) for the debt dynamics and equation (4.14 and A9) for the growth rate.

Dynamic equation (5.11) corresponds to the econometric error correction equation (5.12). In this way, equation (5.11) of the NATREX model corresponds directly to the VEC method of finding a cointegrating equation. The term $R^* = HZ(t)$ is the longer run equilibrium associated with the "fundamentals" $Z(t)$. The NATREX theory and econometrics are now linked up directly[15].

The error correction (EC) term $\alpha[R(t-1) - HZ(t-1)]$ represents the movement along the trajectories, resulting from endogenous variations in stocks. The term $\Sigma b(i) \Delta Z(t-i) = \Gamma . \Delta Z$ represents short-term shocks from variables that are stationary/transitory $I(0)$ and have zero expectations.

Long-run equilibrium equation (5.10a) has been estimated[16] in several ways. (a) The most commonly used procedure is the Johansen/VEC method. The tests involve the following questions. (i) Are $R(t)$ and vector $Z(t)$ integrated $I(1)$? (ii) Is there just one cointegrating equation? (iii) Are the Z's weakly exogenous? (b) Some authors use a NLS method due to Phillips and Loretan. (c) A third method is the Engle–Granger two-stage least squares. After establishing that $[R(t),Z(t)]$ are $I(1)$ and cointegrated, an OLS estimate of B is done directly. Then the residual $[R(t-1) - BZ(t-1)]$ is used as the EC term. (d) Some authors use dynamic OLS estimators, the Stock–Watson approach, which involves leads–lags of the variables. This approach allows a standard interpretation of the t-statistics.

---

[15] Contrast this with the OECD quotation above concerning the econometric-eclectic methods.
[16] See MacDonald (1999), (2002) for an analysis and use of various estimation methods. Also see the EVIEWS User's Guide for a discussion and how to implement the techniques.

5.3.1. *Measurement of the variables*

A difficult problem, handled differently by the various authors, is how to measure the variables: the real exchange rate $R(t)$, relative prices $p(t)/p^*(t)$ and the vector Z of disturbances to productivity and thrift that produce the change in the longer run equilibrium real exchange rate. Variables R and Z are $I(1)$ – they do not revert to constant means. We generally measure the basic $I(1)$ variables as four-quarter moving averages (MA) to reduce the shorter run noise components. We shall indicate below the effects of alternative measures of smoothing upon the results. Figures 5.4–5.6 graph the three key variables: the real exchange rate, relative social consumption, and relative productivity. The variables smoothed by the Hodrick–Prescott filter have a suffix HP. These three variables are not stationary. They do not revert to a constant mean over the sample period. A rise in the real exchange rate R signifies an appreciation of the euro relative to the US dollar.

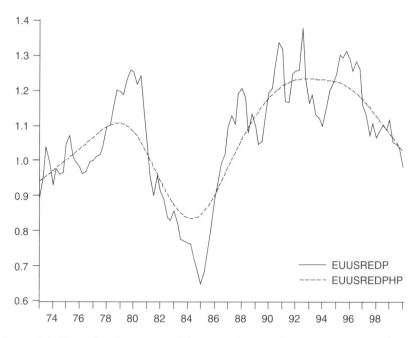

Figure 5.4. The real exchange rate of the euro relative to $US, EUUSREDP, based upon GDP deflators. A rise is an appreciation of the euro. The variable smoothed by the HP filter has suffix HP.

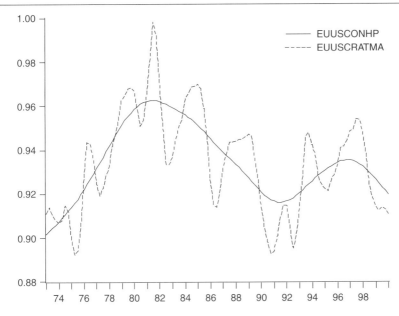

Figure 5.5. The ratio of EU/US social consumption 4Q MA is EUUSCRATMA. The variable smoothed by the HP filter has suffix HP.

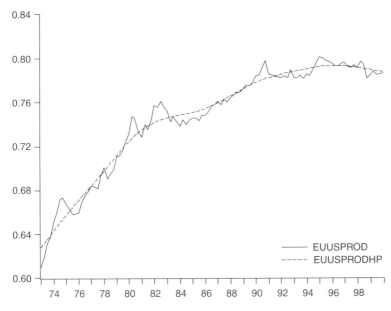

Figure 5.6. Ratio of EU/US productivity y is EUUSPROD. The variable smoothed by the HP filter has suffix HP.

(1) The real exchange rate $R(t) = N(t)p(t)/p^*(t)$ is the relative price in the trade balance function $B(R;Z_B)$. The most appropriate measures of relative prices are either the GDP deflators or unit nominal labor cost[17].

(2) There are alternative measures of social "time preference". Theoretically, the optimum ratio of consumption/net worth is equal to the discount rate, when the utility function is logarithmic. The measure should reflect shifts of the social consumption/saving function. We prefer to use the ratio $c(t)/c^*(t)$ of private plus public consumption to GDP in the two blocs. A question is raised whether this variable is truly exogenous. One can write $c(t)$ as private consumption/GDP plus $c_g(t)$ government consumption/GDP. Some authors use $c_g(t)$ as their measure of time preference, since it is more exogenous than $c(t)$. However, the ratio $c_g(t)/c_g^*(t)$ misses the effects of changes in tax policy and social policy upon total consumption, whereas $c(t)/c^*(t)$ corresponds directly to the variable in the theory.

(3) Productivity can be measured in various ways. Theoretically, we want to find a measure for factors Z_B in the trade balance function that ultimately shift the CA function to the right by more than it shifts the SI curve in Figure 4.3. Some authors use the productivity of labor $y(t) = $ GDP/employment. Others use total factor productivity $y_s(t)$, the Solow residual, or its rate of change. The Solow residual is appealing, but there are some problems. The magnitude of the residual depends upon assumptions concerning the aggregate production function and the ambiguous measurement of "capital". The measurement of "capital" is dubious in a world of technical progress, because of obsolescence and depreciation. Insofar as most of growth cannot be explained by capital formation, the two measures $y(t)$ and $y_s(t)$ can be expected to yield similar results.

It is theoretically appealing to use the differential rate of return on investment $[b(t) - b^*(t)]$ in growth equation (4.12). The problem arises from the econometrics. Variable $b(t)$ is stationary/$I(0)$ both in Europe and in the US. Therefore, we were constrained not to use it in the cointegrating equation based upon the VECM.

In summary, the long-run $R^* = H.Z$ is a "rational expectations equilibrium", insofar as this rate is solely based upon real fundamentals, vector Z. The NATREX model explains the dynamics of adjustment from the medium

---

[17] The Deutsche Bundesbank (1995) compared the differences in the trends of the real value of the DMark resulting from the use of the alternative deflators: for example, GDP, CPI, or unit labor costs in manufacturing, price indices of total expenditures.

run equilibrium, when the stock of debt is predetermined, to the long-run equilibrium when both the debt/GDP ratio and growth rate of GDP have stabilized. Both concepts of equilibrium abstract from volatile anticipations, speculative capital flows, and from cyclical elements. There is no room for "self-fulfilling prophesies" in the NATREX model. It is a model just based upon real fundamentals.

5.3.2. *Estimates of the real exchange rate NATREX of the synthetic euro*

The NATREX model concerns the equilibrium exchange rate satisfying the conditions of internal and external equilibrium described in Section 5.1 above. In all of the econometric studies listed in Table 5.3, the relations among variables $R(t)$ and $Z(t)$ pass the econometric tests mentioned above. A unique cointegration equation is obtained. These are the longer run effects. The *qualitative* significant sign results for component European currencies are similar to those obtained for the synthetic euro[18]. Each estimation finds that: (1) the ratio $c(t)/c^*(t)$ of EU/US social consumption/GDP depreciates the longer run value of the euro; (2) relative EU/US productivity $y(t)/y^*(t)$ or relative Solow residuals $y_s^*(t)/y_s^*(t)$ appreciate the longer run real value of the euro; (3) when the terms of trade are included, they appreciate the real euro; (4) in the shorter run, relative EU–US real long-run rates of interest appreciate the currency.

The detailed studies of the reduced form dynamics for the real synthetic euro are listed in Table 3.3. A good example of the test of the NATREX model is the study by Duval (2002). We refer the reader to his study for measurement of variables and the econometric details. Duval examined the real exchange rate of the euro area, represented by a weighted average of French, German, and Italian relevant variables over the period 1970:1 through 1999:4. He started out with the identity equation (5.13), where the logarithm of real exchange rate Q is the sum of the logarithm of the real exchange rate of traded good Q_T plus Q_{NT}, where the latter is the product of the logarithm of the ratio of non-traded/traded goods in the euro area relative to the US times 0.68, the share of non-traded goods in the CPI deflator. The following conclusions based upon his econometrics are apparent from Figure 5.3 above[19]. A rise is Q is an appreciation of

---

[18] The studies of the Italian lira, Dmark, and Belgian france as well as to the franc/DM and Italian lira/DM in Table 5.3 obtain similar results.

[19] The same was true for various countries examined.

the \$US or a depreciation of the real synthetic euro.

$$Q = Q_T + Q_{NT}. \tag{5.13}$$

- The long-run fluctuations of the real exchange rate of the euro Q do not seem to be explained by the relative price of non-tradables Q_{NT}. That is Q is almost entirely explained by the real exchange rate of traded goods Q_T.

- Therefore, the explanation of trends in the real exchange rate must be based upon the determinants of the real exchange rate R_T for traded goods.

- Long-run PPP does not seem to be verified for the R_T real exchange rate of tradable goods.

Using the NATREX model and the standard econometric tests, he found a cointegrating equation determining the long-run equilibrium real exchange rate of tradables $R_T = H.Z$, where the vector Z consists of the relative time preference variables c/c^* and relative total factor productivity $(y/y^*)_s$. The signs of the coefficients in the cointegrating equation conformed to the NATREX hypothesis. A rise in the ratio of US/EU time preference depreciated the \$US/appreciated the euro; A rise in US/EU total factor productivity appreciated the \$US/depreciated the euro. The deviation of the shorter run real exchange rate from the NATREX is related to the real long-term interest rate differential $(r - r^*)$ between the US dollar and the synthetic euro.

The *qualitative* results from tests of the NATREX model are generally robust to sensible methods of estimation and sample period, but the *quantitative* results do differ. An example of this is shown in Table 5.4. We use the VECM to find a cointegrating equation[20] $R = HZ$ between the NATREX variables, where $Z = (c/c^*, y/y^*)$. Each variable is $I(1)$, that is no variable reverts to a constant mean, which is clear from Figures 5.4–5.6. The sample period is 1973:1–2000:1. The VEC equation is (5.12), repeated at the head of table 5.4.

The relative productivity variable is designed to capture the parameter Z_B in the trade balance function $B(R;Z_B)$. Another candidate variable to be included in Z_B is the terms of trade or its inverse, which is the relative price of inputs of materials. In view of the oil shocks during the sample period, the relative price of oil – measured as \$US price of oil/US PPI index – is an additional sensible component.

Columns A and B are 4Q MA of the variables, which are in logarithms. Both columns uses a lag of four quarters in the $\Gamma.\Delta Z$ inner product term of

---

[20] The testing protocol follows the suggested approach in EVIEWS.

Table 5.4. Estimates of the cointegration part of equation (5.12) $\Delta R_t = \alpha(R - H.Z)_{t-1} + \Gamma.\Delta Z$ for synthetic real euro using alternative methods. Rise $(+)$ is an appreciation of the euro/depreciation of the US dollar. The sample period is 1973:1–2000:1. Regression coefficient and [t-statistic] in cointegrating equation $R = HZ$, using VECM.

Regressor	A (lag 4) log R	B (lag 4) log R	C (lag 2); smoothed variables using HP filter. Variables are not logs
Relative log EU/US time preference c/c^*	−4.5 [−4.8]	−4.13 [−4.3]	−11.5 [−26.6]
Relative log EU/US productivity y/y^*	4.4 [12.4]	2.8 [7.3]	8.6 [22.5]
Log relative price oil	–	−0.00144 [−2.44]	–
Speed of adjustment α coefficient; half-life $T = \log 0.5/\log(1+\alpha)$	$\alpha = -0.024$ [−2.7] $T = 28Q$	$\alpha = -0.045$ [−3.47] $T = 15Q$	

equation (5.12). In each case there was a unique cointegrating equation. In column C, we did not use logarithms and the variables were smoothed by the HP filter graphed in figures 5.4–5.6. In this filtered case using two lags, there are two cointegrating equations, clearly due to the HP filter. It is seen that the *qualitative* results and unchanged, but there are significant differences in the *quantitative* estimates, particularly the significance of coefficients, when the HP filter is used.

Figure 5.7 graphs the results of Table 5.4, column B. The real exchange rate, EUUSREDPMAL $= R$, is compared to the estimate of the long-run NATREX, denoted $H.Z = $ EUUSF), where the variables are normalized. In this way one can see to what extent the trends in the real exchange rate can be explained by the long-run NATREX.

The actual real exchange rate R_t is decomposed into three factors, equation (5.14).

$$R_t = \{R(Z_t + [R(F_t; Z_t - R(Z_t)]\} + [R_t - R(F_t; Z_t)]$$
$$= \{\text{long-run NATREX} + \text{convergence}\} + (\text{non-systematic factors}).$$

$$(3.14)$$

The terms in braces represent the NATREX, both the long-run $R(Z_t)$ and the convergence of the medium-term NATREX to the long-term value $[R(F_t; Z_t) - R(Z_t)]$. The last term $[R_t - R(F_t; Z_t)]$ is the deviation of the actual real exchange rate from the medium-term NATREX. This deviation is very important in the short-run, but washes out in the medium and long run.

Figure 5.7. Real value of euro (R = EUUSREDPMAL) and long-run NATREX (*H.Z* = EUUSFL) based upon Table 5.4, column B. The variables are normalized: (variable − mean)/standard deviation.

The estimates in Table 5.4 of the cointegrating equation just concern the relation between R_t and $R(Z_t)$. Therefore the residual, the deviation $\{[R(F_t;Z_t) - R(Z_t)] + [R_t - R(F_t;Z_t)]\}$ between the two curves in Figure 5.7, represents the sum of two deviations. On the basis of the model, this sum is not pure noise, but will have the serial correlation from both terms.

5.4. Conclusions

To what extent have we answered the questions marked by bullets at the beginning of this chapter? First: the researchers agree that there are real fundamental determinants, which vary over time, of the longer run value of the synthetic euro. The trends in the nominal and the real euro are similar. The implication is that purchasing power parity and the monetary approaches are inadequate to explain the medium to longer term trends in the synthetic euro.

Second: the researchers studied the theoretical literature carefully to find useful frameworks for empirical analysis. They end up taking two approaches. One is a statistical/atheoretical or eclectic-econometric approach, where the equilibrium real exchange rate simply means the value of the real exchange rate implied by a cointegrating equation. One difficulty with a statistical/atheoretic approach is that researchers find different sets of fundamentals to be significant, and the sign and significance change as other regressors are added or dropped. A second serious deficiency is that it is often difficult to provide an economic explanation for the econometric results. Third: the atheoretical approach is not a tool for the economic analysis of the effects of changes in exogenous and policy variables upon the exchange rate.

A theoretical framework that another set of researchers use is the NATREX model. This is a generalization of the more traditional macroeconomic balance models to take into account endogenous variations in the stock of debt and in the growth rate. The NATREX theoretical approach clearly specifies what are the exogenous and control variables, and which variables are endogenous. The model contains an explicit transmission mechanism linking the endogenous variables to the control variables. A very important result for theory and policy concerns the effects of fiscal policy. In the traditional Mundell–Fleming model, an expansionary fiscal policy appreciates the real exchange rate. In the NATREX model, this is just a medium-run effect. As the stock of debt and growth rate vary endogenously, the real exchange rate depreciates below its initial level.

Another advantage of the NATREX model is that it provides an analytical framework to explain the effects of policy variables upon the long-run real exchange rate and debt ratio. We explain the transmission mechanism from the policies to the trajectories of the real exchange rate. No one can predict which social policies will be followed, so our predictions concerning the trajectory of the exchange rate are conditional upon which policies are followed.

Some studies of the NATREX model estimate the structural equations, and others estimate the reduced form dynamics for the synthetic euro as well as for the key underlying currencies. Our message can be tersely summarized.

- There are real fundamental factors – productivity, thrift, and the terms of trade – that explain the longer term movements in the equilibrium real exchange rate of the synthetic euro. The qualitative/sign/significance results are similar across studies.
- Trends in real and nominal rates of the euro are highly correlated.

- There is considerable model uncertainty. The quantitative estimates vary depending upon the method of estimation, and its details such as the lag structure. A direct implication of model uncertainty is that exchange rate management, the use of target zones, and other policies that require confidence in quantitative estimates, do not rest upon firm foundations.

The NATREX model concerns the *equilibrium* real exchange rate in the terms in braces in equation (5.14) – when there is internal equilibrium and external equilibrium. External equilibrium requires that real long-term interest rates are equal in the two areas. Figure 5.7 shows how the euro converges to its longer run value. In the two years prior to the adoption of the euro, the real value of the synthetic euro was undervalued relative to the NATREX. The estimated half-life of convergence is 15 quarters (Table 5.4, column B). The euro is expected to appreciate, which it does from 2001. Although we focus upon the equilibrium real exchange rate, which is associated with internal and external equilibrium, and abstracts from anticipation and speculative elements, the effects of real long-term interest differentials – uncovered interest rate parity – can easily be added to the NATREX[21].

References

Allen, Polly R. (1997), The Economic and Policy Implications of the NATREX Approach, in Stein, Jerome L., Polly Allen et al (1997) *Fundamental Determinants of Exchange Rates*, Oxford University Press, chapter 1

Clark, Peter and Ronald MacDonald (1999), Exchange Rates and Economic Fundamentals: A Methodological Comparison of BEERs and FEERs in Ronald MacDonald and Jerome L. Stein (1999), Equilibrium Exchange Rates, Kluwer Academic

---

[21] When real long-term interest rates are not equal, the deviation $[R_t - R(Z_t)]$ between the real exchange rate and the long-run NATREX will reflect *among other factors* the uncovered interest rate parity (UIRP) condition. To see this, we regress the real exchange rate R_t on the long-run NATREX based upon Table 5.4 – where the variables are logarithms – and the real long-term interest rate differential. The estimated equation (5.15) shows that both the long-run NATREX and the real long-term interest rate differential are explanatory variables. The term $(r - r^*)$ is not in the NATREX, and hence was not used in the cointegrating equation. $R = \log$ real exchange rate = EUUSREDPMAL, log long-run NATREX = $Z_t = R(Z_t) = $ EUUSFL, based upon Table 5.4, $(r - r^*) = $ (EU–US) real long-term interest rate.

$$R_t = 0.28.BZ_t + 0.06(r_t - r_t^*) + 0.031 + \varepsilon_t \qquad (5.15)$$

$$(s) \quad (0.04) \quad (0.006) \quad (0.01)$$

The error term will contain both the omitted dynamic adjustment $[R(Z_t) - R(F_t;Z_t)]$ from medium-run equilibrium to long-run equilibrium, and the speculative and cyclical factors.

Clostermann, J. and Bernd Schnatz (2000), The Determinants of the Euro-Dollar Exchange Rate, Discussion Paper 2/00, Economic Research Group of the Deutsche Bundesbank, May

Clostermann J. and Willy Friedmann (1998) What Drives the Real Effective D-Mark Exchange Rate? *Konjunnkturpolitik*, 44, Heft 3

Crouhy-Veyrac, Liliane and Michèle Saint Marc (1997) The Natural Real Exchange Rate between the French Franc and the Deutschmark, in Stein, Jerome L., Polly Allen et al (1997) *Fundamental Determinants of Exchange Rates*, Oxford University Press, ch. 4

Crouhy-Veyrac, Liliane, Efficiency, Information and Welfare: Euro(ECU)/US Dollar Futures and Forward markets, presented at Banque de France Conference (2000)

Detken, Carsten, Alistair Dieppe, Jérôme Henry, Carmen Marin and Frank Smets (2002) Determinants of the Effective Real Exchange Rate of the Synthetic Euro: Alternative Methodological Approaches, *Australian Economic Papers*, Special Issue on: Exchange Rates in Europe and in Australasia, December

Detken, Carsten and Carmen Marin Martinez (2001) The Effective Euro Equilibrium Exchange Rate Since the 1970's: A Structural Natrex Estimation, European Central Bank, Working paper, available at < webdeptos.uma.es >

Deutsche Bundesbank (1995) Overall Determinants of the trends in the real external value of the Deutsche Mark, Monthly Report, August

Duval, Romain (2002) What do we know about the long-run equilibrium real exchange rates? PPP vs. macroeconomic balance approach, *Australian Economic Papers* (2002) Special Issue on: Exchange Rates in Europe and in Australasia, December

European Central Bank (2002), Monthly Bulletin, Economic Fundamentals and the Exchange Rate of the Euro, January, 41–53

Federici, Daniela and Giancarlo Gandolfo (2002), Endogenous Growth in an Open Economy and the NATREX Approach to the Real Exchange rate: The case of Italy, *Australian Economic Papers*, Special Issue on: Exchange Rates in Europe and in Australasia, December

Fischer, Christoph and Karlhans Sauernheimer (2002) The History of the DMark's Real External Value, *Australian Economic Papers*, Special Issue on: Exchange Rates in Europe and in Australasia, December

Gandolfo, Giancarlo (2001) International Finance and Open Economy Macroeconomics, Springer-Verlag, New York

Lorenzen, H. P. and Thygesen, N. (2000) The Relation between the Euro and the Dollar, paper presented at the EPRU Conference, Copenhagen

MacDonald, Ronald (1999) What do we really know about exchange rates in MacDonald, Ronald and Jerome L. Stein (1999) *Equilibrium Exchange Rates*, Kluwer Academic, Dordrecht

—— (2002) "Modeling the Real Exchange Rate of New Zealand" A BEER Perspective", *Australian Economic Papers* December

MacDonald, Ronald and Jerome L. Stein (1999), Introduction: Equilibrium Exchange Rates, in MacDonald, Ronald and Jerome L. Stein, *Equilibrium Exchange Rates*, Kluwer Academic

Makrydakis, S., P. de Lima, J. Claessens and M. Kramer [ECB:M](2000), The Real Effective Exchange Rate of the Euro and Economic Fundamentals, Deutsche Bundesbank Conference

Maseo-Fernandez, Francisco, Chiara Osbat and Bernd Schnatz, Determinants of the euro real effective exchange rate, *Australian Economic Papers* (2002) Special Issue on: Exchange Rates in Europe and in Australasia, December

Maurin, Laurent (2000/1) La Modélisation des taux de change d'équilibre et leur estimation pour l'euro, le dollar et le yen, Economie & Prévision, #142

OECD, Tracking the Euro (2001), Economics Department Working Papers No. 298, June

Schnatz, Bernd and Frank Smets (2001), A Survey of Recent Studies on the Equilibrium Exchange Rate of the Euro, European Central Bank, June

Stock, James and Mark Watson (2001), Vector Autoregression, Journal of Economic Perspectives, 15 (4), 101–115

Stein, Jerome L., Polly Allen et al (1997) *Fundamental Determinants of Exchange Rates*, Oxford University Press

Stein, Jerome L. and Karlhans Sauernheimer (1997) The Equilibrium Real Exchange Rate of Germany, in Jerome L. Stein (ed) *The Globalization of Markets*, Physica-Verlag, Heidelberg

Stein, Jerome L. and Giovanna Paladino (1997) Recent Developments in International Finance: A Guide to Research, *Jour. Banking and Finance* 21, 1685–1720

——(2001) Exchange Rate Misalignments and Crises, *Jahrbuch fur Wirtschaftswissenschaften*, Band 52 Heft 2, 111–151; also available as CESifo Working paper (1999) #205, Munich; http://www.cesifo.de

Stein, Jerome L. (1999) The Evolution of the Real Value of the US Dollar relative to the G7 Currencies, in MacDonald, Ronald and Jerome L. Stein (1999), *Equilibrium Exchange Rates*, Kluwer Academic Press

Stein, Jerome L. (2002) The Equilibrium Real Exchange Rate of the Euro: An Evaluation of Research, ifo Studien, 3, 349–381

Stein, Jerome L. and Guay C. Lim (2002), Introduction, Australian Economic Papers Special Issue on: Exchange Rates in Europe and in Australasia, December

Verrue, Johan Verrue, and J. Colpaert (1998), A Dynamic Model of the real Belgian franc, CIDEI Working Paper series 47, La Sapienza, Rome; http://cidei.eco.uniroma1/wp/cidei47.pdf

6

The transition economies: A NATREX evaluation of research[1]

6.1. Introduction

The new member states of the European Union do not have an opt-out clause from the obligation to adopt the euro at some point in the future. The policy decision of the acceding countries is whether to join the European Monetary Union at an early or at a later stage after accession. At that time they must decide what irrevocable exchange rate is best suited for entry into the ERM II. Countries participating in the Exchange Rate Mechanism peg their exchange rates to the euro, allowing for fluctuations within a symmetric band of no more than 15% around the central parity. A prerequisite for moving from the ERM II to adopting the euro is that there be no "major tensions" for two years in the foreign exchange markets. The main issues are: When should the country enter ERM II? What rate should be selected? What policies should be adopted to reduce their *vulnerability to crises*? The criteria should be that: the selected conversion rate is *sustainable*; and the irrevocable conversion rate should neither trigger inflation due to undervaluation, nor a loss of competitiveness caused by an overvaluation. A sustainable rate is defined as the *equilibrium* rate in the NATREX model[2]. Economies are *vulnerable* to crises[3] if they have overvalued exchange rates or *excess debt*. This chapter applies the NATREX model of equilibrium exchange rates to evaluate several key

---

[1] I am indebted to the following for criticisms of an earlier draft: Kirsten Lommatzsch, Jan Frait, and Peter Karadi.
[2] The NATREX theory is developed in Chapter 4, and it is applied to the euro area in Chapter 5.   [3] The Asian crises were explained in this manner in Chapter 8.

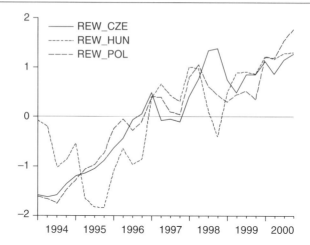

Figure 6.1. Real effective exchange rates of Czech Republic (CZE), Hungary (HUN), and Poland (POL), using CPI prices, relative to OECD trading partners, normalized: (real exchange rate − mean)/standard deviation.

Source: Deutsche Bundesbank.

studies of the Central and Eastern European Countries (CEEC) in general[4] with particular emphasis upon the Czech Republic and Hungary and with references to Poland and Bulgaria. In this manner we explain how one should address the main issues cited above.

Real trend currency appreciation has been observed in all of the CEEC transition economies, although the extent of real currency appreciation has varied considerably from one candidate country to another. Figure 6.1 graphs in normalized form the real effective exchange rates of Poland, Hungary, and the Czech Republic. The real exchange rate is $R = Np/p^*$ where N is the nominal exchange rate (foreign currency per unit of domestic currency) and p/p^* is the ratio of domestic to foreign prices. Real appreciation, which is a rise in R, can occur either from an appreciation of the nominal rate N, a rise in the ratio of domestic/foreign prices or a linear combination of the two.

At the beginning of transformation in 1991, all three currencies appreciated sharply in real terms due to the price effects (p/p^*); and the countries increased the flexibility of their nominal exchange rate regimes over the period from 1991 to 2002. The real currency appreciation in the transition countries occurred regardless of their exchange rate

---

[4] The reader is urged to read the outstanding survey article by Égert et al. (2004). The authors critically review the various methods for calculating equilibrium exchange rates, and provide a comprehensive evaluation of the extensive literature.

regimes – floats, managed floats, pegs, and currency boards. Not only did the regimes differ among countries, but also some changed their regimes over time.[5] Hence the division of the appreciation (rise) in R between the rise in N and the rise in p/p^* varied over time. In some cases, there was nominal depreciation but real appreciation.

Why did the real exchange rates of Hungary, Czech Republic, and Poland significantly appreciate from 1994–5 to 2002, as seen in Figure 6.1? Was the real appreciation *sustainable* and consistent with competitiveness? The PPP hypothesis states that the real exchange rate reverts to a constant mean, and deviations from PPP imply misalignment. The PPP hypothesis should not be used to derive a measure of the equilibrium exchange rate in the case of these transition economies, where the structure is changing as a market economy replaces the Socialist economy. Instead we use the NATREX model to answer the questions: What are the "fundamental determinants" of the equilibrium real exchange rate, and what is the transmission mechanism between these real determinants and the equilibrium real exchange rate? Unless these questions are answered satisfactorily, a country cannot rationally decide what is a *sustainable/equilbrium* exchange rate for entry into the euro area, and desirable policies to follow subsequently.

The sharp widening of current account deficits in a number of countries in 2003, and which are expected to remain high, raised questions about their sustainability and the competitiveness of these economies. For example, one effect of foreign direct investment (FDI) is to decrease the net investment position which will lead to subsequent outflows of dividends. Should FDI and current account deficits be causes for concern, as feared by the International Monetary Fund (WEO, April 2004)?

On the basis of the NATREX model, we evaluate several key studies to answer the questions:

- How can the trends in the real exchange rates of the transition economies be explained?

- What are sustainable trends in their real exchange rates? To what extent were the real exchange rates misaligned?

[5] Frait and Komarek 2001, (Figure 3) graph the nominal and real exchange rates and inflation differentials of six transition economies. See also their Figure 4. The country/time period diversity of exchange rate regimes is apparent. For example, beginning in 1991 Hungary had a relatively flexible exchange rate regime. In the major part of the 1990s Hungary had quasifixed/ adjustable peg regimes: an adjustable peg until 1996, then a crawling peg with a band of ±2.25%, but low volatility. In 2001 Hungary changed to a relatively flexible band ±15%, a shadow ERM II regime. I argue that the NATREX – which is an equilibrium rate – contains all regimes, but the speed of convergence to the NATREX is affected by the regime, since price flexibility is limited. In each case, the real exchange rate has a trend of appreciation.

Table 6.1. Percentage change (Δ) in R(CPI) and R(PPI) $= Np/p^*$, Czech Republic, Hungary, Poland, relative to Germany until 1999, then to euro. Real R or nominal appreciation is ($+$). Foreign producer prices P^* are those Germany.

	Appreciation +	(1) ΔR(CPI)	(2) ΔR(PPI)	$\varepsilon = \Delta R$(PPI)/ΔR(CPI)
Czech Republic	1991–2004	51.6%	42.6%	83%
CZ	1995–2004	34.5	27.6	80
Hungary	1991–2004	37.9	14.7	39
HU	1995–2004	35.8	23.7	66
Poland	1991–2004	31.7	14.9	47
PL	1995–2004	23.3	14.8	64

Source: Lommatzsch and Tober (2005) spreadsheets, based upon International Monetary Fund data.

- What are sustainable/equilibrium current account deficits and net investment positions in the medium and in the long-run?

- What are the policy implications for the transition economies of the NATREX analysis?

6.1.1. *Neither Purchasing Power Parity nor the Balassa/Samuelson hypothesis has explanatory value*

An inspection of Figure 6.1 and Table 6.1 leads to the following conclusions. First: the PPP hypothesis is rejected. The real exchange rate does not revert to a constant mean. Instead, there is a significant trend appreciation of the real exchange rate in the transition economies. Second: it is not possible to rescue the PPP hypothesis by stating that the equilibrium real exchange rate for "tradable" goods, R_T, is constant but that the R_{NT}, the relative price of non-traded/traded goods, has been responsible for the appreciation of the real exchange rate.

The B/S effect hypothesis can be stated as follows[6]. The logarithm of the real exchange rate based upon the CPI index R(CPI) is defined to be equal to the logarithm of the real exchange rate of traded goods R_T plus the R_{NT}, a weighted logarithm of the relative price of non-traded to traded goods at home and abroad.

$$R(\text{CPI}) = R_T + R_{NT}$$

The GDP is supposed to be divided into tradable goods, where the law of one price prevails, and non-tradable goods where there is no law of one price. The law of one price for tradables means that R_T is a constant.

---

[6] See Chapter 5 section 5.1 for a discussion of the role of the B/S effect in the euro area.

By definition, there is no law of one price for non-tradables. Therefore variations in the real exchange rate R(CPI) are determined by variations in R_{NT} relative prices non-tradable/tradable in the two countries.

Empirical studies testing this hypothesis are arbitrary because it is not clear what are tradable and non-tradable goods. Arbitrary proxies are used to estimate R_{NT}, whose meaning is ambiguous. Authors differ in what they include in traded or non-traded goods[7], which leads to significant differences in the empirical results. Some assume that R_{NT} can be proxied by the ratio of the CPI/WPI. Several authors state that the producer price index PPI does not include prices in the services sectors, whereas the CPI index includes services. They[8] then argue that the real exchange rate based upon the producer price index R(PPI) reflects the R_T, the relative price of traded goods, and that the difference between the real exchange rate based upon the CPI index and R(PPI), the real exchange rate based upon the PPI index, reflects the relative price of non-traded/traded goods, $R_{NT} = [R(\text{CPI}) - R(\text{PPI})]$. The econometric results vary drastically depending upon the measures used for "tradable/non-tradable" goods[9].

One estimate of the significance of the B/S hypothesis – as stated in the paragraph above – is that the percentage change ΔR(PPI) is negligible – the "law of one price" prevails for "traded" goods – and that the variation in the real exchange rate arises from variations in the relative price of non-traded/traded goods $\Delta[R(\text{CPI}) - R(\text{PPI})]$. Operationally the B/S states that the *ratio* of ΔR(PPI) to $\Delta[R(\text{CPI}) - R(\text{PPI})]$ is small. Let ε be the ratio of ΔR(PPI) to $\Delta[R(\text{CPI})]$. The B/S hypothesis can be expressed as equation (6.1) in percent change (ΔR), where the hypothesized ratio ε is "small".

$$\Delta R(\text{PPI})/\Delta R(\text{CPI}) = \varepsilon \tilde{0}. \tag{6.1}$$

Table 6.1 shows that neither PPP nor the B/S hypothesis has explanatory value. Columns 1 and 2 show the appreciation of both R(CPI) and R(PPI) over the transition period 1991 to 2004 and from 1995 to 2004 in each country. Table 6.1, column 3 shows that the value of ε is large. For the period 1995–2004, the main part of the variation in the CPI real exchange rate comes from the real exchange rate based upon the PPI index. Epsilon ε is 80% for the Czech Republic, 66% for Hungary, and 64% for Poland, whereas the B/S hypothesis claims that ε is close to zero.

More direct tests of the B/S and PPP hypotheses are discussed in connection with the studies based upon panel data, summarized in Table 6.2

[7] See Egert, et al. (2004), Table 8, for a list of how various authors arbitrarily classify open/closed, tradable/non-tradable sectors in transition economies.

[8] See the discussions in Egert et al. (2004) and in Lommatzsch and Tober (2005).

[9] See, for example, Chapter 5, Table 7.2.

Table 6.2. Panel data. Determinants of the real effective exchange rate in central and eastern European accession countries[*]. Period: 1994–9. Rise is an appreciation.

Explanatory variable	Estimation A coefficient (t-stat)	Estimation B Coefficient (t-stat)	Estimation C coefficient (t-stat)	Estimation D coefficient (t-stat)	Estimation E coefficient (t-stat)
Labor productivity in agriculture	0.46 (2.87)	0.44 (3.64)	0.55 (3.24)		
Labor productivity in industry	0.76 (3.34)	0.60 (2.65)	1.65 (6.07)		
Labor productivity in services			0.9 (2.06)		
Total labor productivity				1.68 (17.49)	1.58 (15.81)
Consumption/GDP	0.89 (4.13)	–	1.82 (3.75)	0.55 (3.98)	–
Government consumption/GDP	–	0.45 (3.51)			0.24 (3.39)
Real rate of interest (average of USA and Germany)	−0.21 (−4.18)	−0.23 (−4.2)	0.08 (2.5)	−0.03 (−2.77)	−0.04 (−3.52)

[*] Czech Republic, Estonia, Hungary, Latvia, Lithuania, Poland, Slovak Republic, and Slovenia.

Sources: Deutsche Bundesbank, Monthly Report, July 2002, and Fischer, Deutsche Bundesbank Discussion Paper 19/02, Table 2. Estimations (A) (B) (C) are based upon annual data 1994–9; and estimations (D) (E) are based upon quarterly data 1994:1–2000:4, p. 58. Data, except for interest rates, are in logarithms of variables relative to a weighted average of OECD trading partners.

below. In all cases, not only are the PPP and B/S hypotheses lacking in explanatory value, they are also theoretically deficient.

Suppose that the "law of one price" were valid. Let there be a significant rise in unit labor costs in the country relative to the rest of the world in all sectors of the economy. Then marginal costs are rising relative to both the internal and the external prices. The country would be losing competitiveness and the volume of exports would fall drastically, even though the law of one price prevails. The B/S and PPP hypotheses would not provide any early warning signals of an impending currency crisis. These hypotheses says nothing about the sustainability of the nominal exchange rate.

The theoretical deficiencies stem from the simplistic characterization of an economy: an arbitrary dichotomy between "traded" and "non-traded" goods, a law of one price for traded goods, no theory of a transmission process between total factor productivity and the trade balance, and no equation for balance of payments equilibrium. The B/S equation is not a substitute for an explicit testable and operational model of exchange rate determination.

Another important characteristic of the transition economies, stressed especially by Lommatzsch and Tober (2005), concerns the trends in the current account and trade deficits in the Czech Republic, Hungary, and Poland. The appreciations of the PPI real exchange rates of the accession countries have not been accompanied by a loss of competitiveness. Current account deficits have not continually increased with the appreciation of the R(PPI). In some countries, current account deficits have declined. Moreover, both exports and imports have grown in real as well as in nominal terms along with the appreciation of the R(PPI) exchange rate.

A third characteristic over the period 1993:1–2004:4 is that labor productivity in industry or in the overall economy has been found to be the most stable determinant of the real exchange rate[10]. It makes very little difference whether the real exchange rate is R(CPI) or R(PPI).

The characteristics of the transition economies described above are inconsistent with the PPP and B/S methods of analysis. At best these two hypotheses cannot be used to answer the questions marked in bullets above.

6.1.2. Organization of chapter

The very large number of studies of the determinants of the equilibrium real exchange use the same, or a very similar, econometric methodology.

---

[10] Égert and Lommatzsch (2004).

They consider a vector (R, Z) of variables, in the real exchange rate R and a vector of candidate variables Z. Insofar as the real exchange rate is not stationary, they ask if the Z's are also non-stationary. *A stationary variable is one that reverts to a constant mean.* When they find a set of non-stationary variables, they use the standard econometric tests to see if they are cointegrated. Is there a linear combination that is stationary? The stationary linear combination is called the cointegrating equation, which is interpreted as a long-run equilibrium relation among the variables[11]. They are just eclectic-econometric studies, and that is why the results differ among studies. Moreover, they cannot be used for policy analysis since they are not based upon an explicit and consistent theory. They cannot answer the questions marked with bullets at the beginning of this chapter.

Our approach is not to survey the extensive work that has been done.[12] Instead we use the NATREX model to explain the results of several key studies of the transition economies. There are several problems involved in trying to estimate the equilibrium real exchange rate of the CEEC/ transition economies compared to what has been done for the synthetic euro. First, the time span of data for the post Socialism period is short. Generally it is from 1991 or 1995 to 2001. The use of the vector error correction model (VECM) to find a long-run relation is questionable for a short period where the structure is changing. Second, several authors try to overcome the problem of the short period by using panel data of a set of countries over the post Socialism period. The problem of interpretation of panel data is that the estimation of coefficients such as dR/dZ assumes that they are the same for each country, even though it is agreed that the countries are very different in their structure. Econometric results from panel data vary according to which countries are or are not included. The conclusion must be that one cannot place too much confidence in quantitative estimates of "the equilibrium" exchange rate, using just one method of estimation. Our approach here is to examine the studies, which use both approaches. To what extent can the NATREX model explain the econometric results? Section 6.4 of this chapter concludes by explaining what are the implications for policy.

The first set of studies that we consider are by Christoph Fischer/ Bundesbank, and are based upon panel analysis. The methodology and results are discussed in Section 6.2. In Section 6.3, we interpret the panel results on the basis of the NATREX model. Then we draw upon several

---

[11] See the discussion in Chapter 5, Section 7.3.
[12] See the detailed survey article by Égert, et al. (2004) for a discussion of the extensive literature.

studies that are more country specific, written by economists at the Central Banks.[13] The study of Hungary by Peter Karadi/Central Bank of Hungary is based upon the structural estimation of the NATREX model, similar to what Detken and Marin did for the synthetic euro discussed in Chapter 5. The study of the Czech Republic by Jan Frait and Lubos Komarek (2001) uses the reduced form dynamics VECM approach. The study by Lommatzsch and Tober (2005) concerning several transition economies focuses upon the crucial trade balance structural equation. The conclusions, the answers to the questions in bullets, are in section 6.4, the policy implications.

6.2. Econometric analysis based upon panel data[14]

Christoph Fischer addressed the question concerning what factors might have caused trend appreciations of the real effective exchange rates of the transition economies. He used panel methods for the estimation, because the observation period may be too short to obtain reliable estimates of the long-run effects of economic variables upon market determined equilibrium real exchange rates in the transition economies. The panel initially consisted of ten CEEC, which have been in the process of entry into the EU. The question concerning the equilibrium real exchange rate is important because these countries would enter the euro area in the foreseeable future. In one set of estimations, he used 10 countries. Due to their heterogeneity, the econometric panel results were significantly changed when Romania and Bulgaria were excluded. Panel data tests are sensitive to the set of countries included or excluded. The data reported in Table 6.2 consists of the eight countries cited at the foot of the table.

The variables selected for panel analysis of equilibrium real exchange rates were not arbitrary. First, he tested carefully the Balassa/Samuelson hypothesis that sectoral relative prices R_{NT} can account for the trends in the real effective exchange rate. Sectoral measures of productivity were included in his regressions. Second, total labor productivity or total factor productivity and measures of social consumption were also used. These variables play important roles in the NATREX model.[15]

[13] The disclaimer is that the authors who are at the Central Banks are not expressing official views of their respective banks.

[14] This section is based upon two articles: Christoph Fischer (2002) and Deutsche Bundesbank (2002).

[15] Fischer is quite familiar with the NATREX model, which was used by Fischer and Sauernheimer (2002) in their study of exchange rates in Germany. That explains his choice of variables. His studies are not data mining.

The real effective exchange rate, social consumption/GDP, labor productivity are measured against a weighted average of the OECD trading partners of each country, and are expressed as logarithms. The external real interest rate is a simple average of Germany and the US.

Table 6.2 summarizes the econometric results from panel data. Estimations (A), (B), and (C) are based upon annual data. The annual frequency of sectoral productivity data has been the main reason for using annual instead of quarterly data.

One sees that the *signs* of the estimated coefficients of sectoral productivity variables did not depend on the sector. Productivity increases in each sector caused a real appreciation although, in the case of the services sector, the coefficient was often insignificant. An increase in labor productivity in agriculture appreciates the real exchange rate just as does an increase in productivity in the industrial sector.

The three sectoral productivity variables were then replaced by one aggregated labor productivity series, which is GDP/number of employees in the whole economy. The proposed relationship was then estimated with a panel of quarterly data in the estimations in columns (D) and (E). The results are that the real exchange rate is positively related to total labor productivity in the entire economy, and to the ratio of social consumption/GDP and is negatively related to the relative real rate of interest.

6.3. NATREX explanation of the econometric studies of the transition economies

Fischer's analysis of panel data in Table 6.2, and the country studies, especially of Hungary by Karadi (2003) and of the Czech Republic by Frait and Komarek (2001) discussed below, can be understood on the basis of the NATREX model. We also show how other studies such as by Lommatzsch and Tober (2005) and those surveyed by Égert (2004) can be interpreted in this framework.

The NATREX model, developed in Chapter 4 and applied to the euro area in Chapter 5, concerns the *equilibrium rate*. This is where the rate is heading. It is a sustainable rate and is not the actual rate at any one time. In the medium run, it is associated with *internal equilibrium*, where the rate of capacity utilization is at its stationary mean and there are no inflationary or deflationary pressures, and also *external equilibrium* where real long-term interest rates are equal to the foreign rates. The debt/GDP ratio and the growth rate are predetermined in the medium run. The economy travels

Table 6.3. Summary NATREX model: Medium-run and long-run effects. See Chapter 4, Table 4.2. Figures 6.3 and 6.4 summarize this table.

Disturbance: changes in fundamentals	Medium-run real Exchange rate R, debt ratio given	Long-run exchange rate R*	Long-run debt-ratio F
Δ(I-S) rise in investment less saving rise in time preference δ	Appreciate	depreciate	Increases
ΔZ_B Rise in trade balance Function, rise in productivity y	Appreciate	appreciate	decreases
Δg, when F(0) 0 Rise in growth rate	0	appreciate	decreases

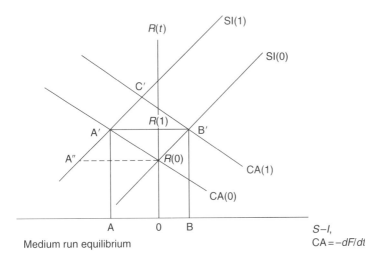

Figure 6.2. Medium-run NATREX resulting from a rise in time preference/decline in social saving rate $R(0) \to A'$, a rise in the trade balance function $R(0) \to B'$.

along a *trajectory* where these two variables stabilize at their long-term values. The *long-run equilibrium* is the limit of medium-run equilibria, and is a function of a time-varying vector of fundamentals denoted Z_t. Insofar as this vector changes, so do the medium-run and long-run equilibria. This implies that misalignment will occur if the nominal exchange rate and relative prices cannot adjust to the changing equilibrium.

We summarize[16] in Table 6.3 and graph in Figures 6.2–6.4 the implications of the NATREX model that are relevant for the transition economies. There are three real *fundamentals*: (i) relative[17] time preference δ/δ^*, which is the ratio of social consumption/GDP; (ii) relative

---

[16] See Chapter 4 for technical details.　　[17] Foreign variables are denoted by asterisks.

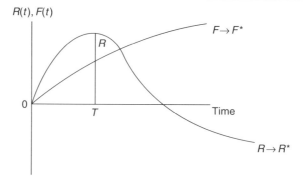

Initial increase $(I-S)$, rise in time preference, or investment demand

Figure 6.3. Dynamic effects of a decline in social saving/rise in social consumption, or a rise in investment, upon the trajectories of the real exchange rate R_t and F_t, the debt/GDP ratio. Other parameters are assumed to be fixed. Long-run values are R^*, F^*.

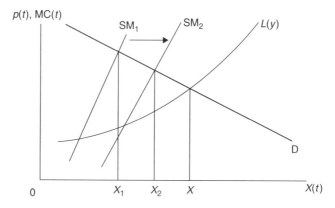

Figure 6.4. Optimal output is affected by FDI that lowers short-run marginal cost. Output has both a qualitative as well as a quantitative dimension.

productivity[18] in the *whole economy*, which is either total factor productivity or total labor productivity y/y^*; (iii) growth rate g. *Endogenous* variables are the real exchange rate R and the debt ratio F, defined as the negative of the net investment position/GDP. The net investment position includes equity as well as debt.

Figure 6.2 describes the medium-run effects[19]. The medium-run equilibrium real exchange rate equilibrates saving less investment – the SI

---

[18] The effects of variations in the terms of trade are understood in terms of the productivity variable.
[19] See Chapter 4 section 4.4 for details.

curve – to the current account – the CA curve. The current account is the trade balance plus income transfers of interest plus dividends.

A rise in time preference δ means a decline in social saving (public plus private). The SI curve shifts from SI(0) to SI(1). The decline in saving relative to investment induces a capital inflow Adt, which appreciates the real exchange rate from $R(0)$ to $R(1)$. Investment and growth are adversely affected by the appreciated real exchange rate. The resulting current account deficits Adt produce the transfer of resources. The current account deficit is the rate of change of the debt. This means that, given the new saving and investment functions, a current account deficit raises the debt steadily. The CA curve keeps shifting steadily to the left, along the SI(1) curve, as the debt rises and exchange rate depreciates.

The growing current account deficit depresses the real exchange rate along the SI(1) curve, and the debt ratio rises steadily. This is a movement from A′ to A″. In the stable case, the growth of the debt reduces net worth. In turn, consumption declines, saving rises, the SI curve then shifts to the right, and the debt ratio stabilizes at a higher value.

Figure 6.3 describes the dynamics of the convergence process in the case of Table 6.2, row 1. Start with the exchange rate and the debt ratio at the origin. The real exchange rate R_t first appreciates from $R(0)$ to $R(1)$ in Figure 6.2, and the debt ratio F_t rises. After a certain point, at time $t = T$, the rise in the interest payments on the debt[20] and the lower growth rate lead to a decline (depreciation) in the real exchange rate to R^*, which is below its initial level. The trajectory of the real exchange rate is not monotonic, but the debt rises monotonically to F^*, a new long-run equilibrium.

The second effect concerns the parameter Z_B in the trade balance $B = B(R; Z_B)$, which reflects the factors that change the trade balance function at any given real exchange rate. This is graphed as shifts in the current account function CA in Figure 6.2. Specifically, let there be foreign direct investment (FDI) in the economy. The first effect is that investment rises relative to saving. The SI curve shifts to the left from SI(0) to SI(1). The medium-run effect is just like the decline in social saving graphed in Figure 6.2. The capital inflow appreciates the real exchange rate and produces a current account deficit. The debt rises for a while.

Unlike the case of a decline in saving/rise in time preference, the FDI is induced by a privatization and liberalization of the economy. There are unexploited opportunities for productive investment. Investment is

---

[20] Debt includes portfolio plus direct investment, so interest includes the payment of dividiends.

productive if the q-ratio exceeds unity, the expected marginal return exceeds the opportunity cost. Under Socialism, such an economic calculus did not influence investment decisions; and the quality of products was low. With privatization and liberalization there is a marked shift from low-quality, low value-added products towards products of higher quality and value added[21]. That is, investment occurs in sectors where the q-ratio exceeds unity.

A graphic *microeconomic* description of the process, underlying the macroeconomic analysis of FDI, is as follows. The productivity in the entire economy, GDP per worker or total factor productivity, affects the marginal cost of producing goods that can be exported relative to demand. Marginal cost is the ratio of nominal input prices divided by the marginal productivity. In Figure 6.4, the demand function is D and the short-run marginal cost functions are labeled SM. The short-run marginal cost function depends upon the input prices and the current level of productivity of the inputs that are variable in the short-run, but the quantity of "capital" is given. The long-run marginal cost function $L(y)$ is derived when "capital" is variable and the marginal cost of production is the same for all inputs. When the short-run marginal cost is SM_1, optimal output is X_1. But short-run marginal cost at that point exceeds long-run marginal cost. This means that there is a less than optimal quantity of "capital" – the factor that is relatively fixed in the short run. Alternatively it means that the marginal return to investment is greater than the opportunity cost, the q-ratio exceeds unity.

Foreign direct investment, FDI, may be induced because short-run marginal cost exceeds long-run marginal cost. That is, FDI is induced because more capital will be productive. The decline in short-run marginal costs occurs when productivity rises relative to nominal factor prices. For example, there may be a decline in the prices of services, an improved domestic transportation system, improved telecommunications, or better IT. Productivity rises with FDI as shown in equation (6.3). This means that short-run marginal cost declines from SM_1 to SM_2. The cost of producing quantity X_1 of output declines. It is optimal to expand the value of output. But "output" has a quality as well as a quantity dimension. The expansion of output to X_2 could mean that the quality of output X_2 is superior to that of X_1. With the lower level of productivity SM_1, only the low-quality output was profitable. With the higher level of productivity induced by FDI, the short-run marginal cost declines to SM_2 and a higher-quality X_2 is

---

[21] This theme is stressed by Lommatzsch and Tober (2005).

profitable. The shifting of the short-run marginal cost function, resulting from the rise in productivity, corresponds to an increase in Z_B in the trade balance function. These developments are subsumed under parameter Z_B in the trade balance function.

The productive investment leads to capital inflows, a current account deficit, and a change in the composition of the GDP. The improved allocation of resources has two effects. First, the growth rate of the economy rises. Second, productivity of the economy increases and parameter Z_B in the trade trade balance function rises.

The macroeconomic interpretation of the effect of FDI is summarized in the last two rows of Table 6.3. Formally, the growth rate of the economy $(1/Y)dY/dt$ is equation (6.2), based upon Chapter 4, Section (4.2). The GDP is Y. The first term is the productivity of investment b_t times the ratio I_t of investment/GDP. The second term Z_g is the growth of employment plus the effects of an improved allocation of resources. The latter involves shifting resources from uses where the value of the marginal product is low to where it is high, based upon market-determined prices. These are structural changes from lower to higher quality and value added uses.

$$g_t = \left(\frac{1}{Y}\right)\frac{dY}{dt} = b_t I_t + Z_g. \tag{6.2}$$

Solve (6.2) for the GDP and derive equation (6.3) for the productivity of the economy $y(t) = Y(t)/\text{worker}$. The initial labor productivity is $y(0)$.

$$\frac{y(t)}{y(0)} = \exp[\int^t -b_s I_s ds + z.t]. \tag{6.3}$$

The productivity of the economy is an *integral* of the productivity of investment times the investment ratio over a period of years. The second term z reflects the average annual value of Z_g. Foreign direct investment affects $b_s I_s$, the productivity of the investment undertaken times the investment ratio. Thereby the FDI and improved resource allocation lead to the build-up of productivity over a period of years. It is this productivity of the economy that increases the trade balance function $B(R;Z_B)$ and the growth rate of the economy.

Graphically the CA function in Figure 6.2 gradually shifts to the right from CA(0) to CA(1) as productivity rises. At any given real exchange rate, the trade balance increases, and the debt ratio declines. The trajectories of the real exchange rate and the debt ratio are described in Figure 6.5.

The net effect of FDI is a combination of Figures 6.3, 6.4, and 6.5. Initially, the real exchange rate appreciates, there are current account deficits, and the debt rises. Later on, as the productivity effect in equation (6.3) grows, the growth rate

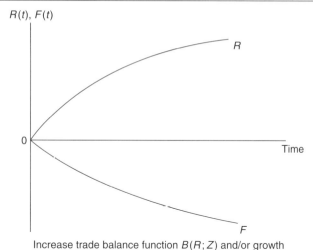

Increase trade balance function $B(R; Z)$ and/or growth

Figure 6.5. Foreign direct investment induced by the productivity of investment raises productivity according to equation (6.3). The current account function CA in Figure 6.2 shifts to the right. There is long-run exchange rate appreciation and a decline in the debt ratio.

rises, the economy is more competitive, the current account function shifts to the right, the debt ratio declines and the real exchange rate appreciates.

Figures 6.2–6.5 are graphic representations of the conclusions of the NATREX model in Table 6.3, based upon Chapter 4. These figures are extremely important, because they explain why many results from the eclectic-econometric approaches can be ambiguous and misleading.[22] On the basis of the analysis above we analyze and evaluate some key empirical studies of the transition economies.

6.3.1. *Interpretation of results from panel data*

There are two main results from Table 6.2 based upon panel data. First, the real exchange rate appreciates with a growth in productivity. It is the growth in *total labor productivity* that is relevant, regardless of the sector where it occurs. Second, the real exchange rate is positively related to the relative consumption ratio.

The *first effect* is explained by relating total labor productivity to the liberalization of the economy, a rise in productive investment, and an improved allocation of resources. Initially, FDI finances productive

---

[22] See Égert (2004), Table 5 for the ambiguous results of the various studies.

investment, and shifts the SI function in Figure 6.2 to the left from SI(0) to SI(1). The exchange rate appreciates and induces a current account deficit, which finances the excess of investment less saving. In the medium run the economy is at point A' in Figure 6.2.

The growth of the "debt", the decline in the net investment position, does imply that there will be a future transfer of interest and dividends. People who look at the current account deficit *Adt* in Figure 6.2 at point A' may feel that this augurs a depreciation of the exchange rate in the future. This is myopic thinking because it fails to see the difference between the effects of a decline in social saving and a rise in productive investment. The difference is as follows.

The integral of investment times the productivity of investment is productivity at time t, $y(t) = y(0) \exp [\int^t b_s I_s \, ds + z.t]$. As a result of the FDI, the CA function shifts gradually to the right from CA(0) to CA(1). The trajectories of the real exchange rate and the debt ratio are that at first the rise in investment produces the graphs in Figure 6.3. In the longer run as productivity rises, the real exchange rate appreciates and debt ratio declines (the net investment position increases) as described by Figure 6.5. This is an important implication of NATREX analysis.

The study by Lommatzsch and Tober (2005) (L-T) can be related to that of Fischer summarized in Table 6.2. They found that:

(L-T:1) Both the CPI and PPI real exchange rates of the accession countries have been appreciating since macroeconomic stabilization was achieved. This result, along with the results of the panel study of Fischer, cannot be explained by the PPP and the B/S hypotheses.

(L-T:2) The appreciation has not been accompanied by a loss of competitiveness. There has not been a corresponding steady decline in the trade balance/GDP and current account/GDP functions. What has happened is consistent with the analysis summarized in the last two rows in Table 6.3 where the rise in productivity has shifted the CA function to the right.

(L-T:3) The dominant factor has been an increase in Z_B in the trade balance function $B(R;Z_B)$. There has been an increase in the capacity to produce goods of higher quality and technological content, a catch-up factor. Most likely the improved allocation to higher value-added goods can show up as an improvement in the terms of trade. However in this case, the improved terms of trade are not exogenous[23]. The increase in total factor productivity corresponds to the scenario in the last two rows of Table 6.3.

---

[23] I owe this insight to Jan Frait.

Lommatzsch and Tober (2005) focus upon the improved allocation of resources as an important factor explaining both the exchange rate and trade balance. They use two methods of estimation for the Czech Republic, Hungary, and Poland. In the first, they estimate export and import equations using the real exchange rate R(PPI) using the PPI price deflators,[24] labor productivity in industry or in the entire economy, and foreign demand. This is a structural equation approach. The result is:

(L-T:4) The productivity in industry can be regarded as the driving force behind exports, especially in Hungary and Poland. That means that productivity in the economy is the driving force in the $B(R;Z_B)$ function. See Table 6.3, row 2 and the analysis of shifts in the CA function above.

They then move on to a reduced form analysis. The equilibrium real exchange rates R(PPI) were calculated using variables that were earlier determined as affecting the current account: productivity differentials and external debt or net foreign assets. The medium-run equilibrium R equates the sum of the current account plus the capital inflows to zero. They found that:

(L-T:5) In all countries, the productivity differential relative to Germany contributes to the real PPI based exchange rate. This result is consistent with the results from the estimated export equations.

The main conclusions are consistent with the NATREX model summarized in Table 6.3. *A long-run appreciation of the real exchange rate requires that there be a rise in relative productivity in the entire economy that shifts the trade balance function $B(R;Z_B)$ to the right. Then the appreciation of the real exchange rate is not accompanied by rising current account deficits.* In Figure 6.2, when the CA function shifts from CA(0) to CA(1) the real exchange rate appreciates from $R(0)$ to $R(1)$ and the current account/GDP rises from 0 to *Bdt*. Parameter Z_B is associated with total productivity as described by the integral of the growth equation (6.3).

Figure 6.6 shows that the appreciation of the real exchange rate 1994–2004 (see Figure 6.1) was not associated with deteriorating ratios of trade balance of goods and services/GDP. The trade or current account balance could result from the scenario in Figure 6.3 either as a movement from $R(0)$ to A' or from $R(0)$ to B'.

The *second result* in Table 6.4 is that a rise in consumption/GDP appreciates the real exchange rate. In the short-time span covered, one tends to see only the medium-run equilibrium. The rise in the consumption

---

[24] The foreign country is Germany.

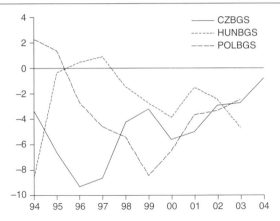

Figure 6.6. Balance goods and services/GDP, Czech Republic, Hungary, and Poland.
Source: IMF data underlying article by Lommatzsch.

Table 6.4. Hungary: the effects of the fundamental determinants of the real exchange rate in the medium run and in the long run.

Exogenous disturbance	Medium-run NATREX	Long-run NATREX
Δ(Exogenous disturbance) 1 percentage point rise in fiscal consumption/GDP ratio, i.e., reduction in saving ratio	(1) $\Delta(R)$ 3.95% appreciation	(2) $\Delta(R^*)$ 1.8% depreciation
1 percentage point permanent rise in fiscal productive investment/GDP ratio	3.95% appreciation	1.1% depreciation
Permanent rise in TFP growth causing a 1 percentage point higher investment/GDP ratio	4.04% appreciation	1.55% appreciation
1 percentage point reduction in real rate of interest	0.01 % appreciation	–
Permanent increase in external demand causing a 1 percentage point higher trade balance/GDP	6.65% appreciation	8.25 % appreciation

Source: Karadi (2003), Table 4.

ratio corresponds to a rise in investment less saving, row 1 in Table 6.3. This corresponds to the leftward shift of the SI function in Figure 6.3. The real exchange rate appreciates and there is a current account deficit. Graphically, this is described by the early part in Figure 6.3 over the period (0,*T*) where both the real exchange rate and the debt rise.

The observed relation between the real exchange rate and the debt ratio depends upon (i) the period considered such as (0,T) or the longer period (0, T + s), and

(ii) the type of fundamental that has changed, the rows in Table 6.3/Figures 6.3–6.5. Simple eclectic-econometric analysis is not sensitive to these distinctions and hence often leads to ambiguous, bizarre, or contradictory results.

Tests based upon panel data implicitly assume that the exogenous/control variables have the same effects upon the endogenous variables in each country. This is a questionable assumption, given the significant differences in their structures and development. Tests of long-run effects based upon data from each transition economy suffer from short sample period. Therefore, we evaluate both types of studies from the NATREX point of view.

We have explained the panel data results in terms of the NATREX model. Next, we turn to two country studies. The first country is Hungary. Peter Karadi (2003) estimated the structural equations of the NATREX model. The second is the Czech Republic, where Frait and Komarek (2001) used a reduced form estimation of the NATREX model.

6.3.2 *Hungary: Structural equation estimation.*

Peter Karadi of the Central Bank of Hungary[25] estimated the equilibrium trajectory, and hence any misalignment, of the Hungarian real exchange rate using the NATREX approach. He stated that the "advantage of the NATREX approach *vis-à-vis* other methods is its well-founded – dynamic general equilibrium – theoretical basis. It can produce forecasts of the medium-term NATREX equilibrium and of the long-term equilibrium". He followed the method used by Detken and Marin and used quarterly data 1994:1–2002:4. The object was first to estimate the components of the SI and CA curves in Figure 6.2: the investment function, the consumption (saving) function, and the current account function. The arguments of these functions are discussed in Chapter 4. From these equations the medium-run equilibrium NATREX is obtained, which is the point of the intersection of the SI and CA curves in Figure 6.2.

Investment/potential GDP equation (6.4) is based upon intertemporal optimization in a stochastic environment or upon the q-ratio.[26] The investment ratio I is *positively* related to: (i) the growth rate of total factor productivity α; (ii) the productivity of capital Q/K; and is *negatively* related to (iii) the real rate of interest r, and (iv) the real exchange rate $R = Np/p^*$, where a rise is an appreciation. The signs of the hypothesized partial derivatives are noted in the functions.

$$I = I(\alpha^+, Q/K^+, r^-, R^-) \quad I = \text{Investment}/Q \text{ potential GDP.} \quad (6.4)$$

[25] The usual disclaimer applies. His paper does not represent the official view of the Bank.
[26] See Chapter 4 Section 4.2.

Social consumption/potential GDP, C in equation (6.5), is derived from the intertemporal optimization in a stochastic environment,[27] where consumption depends upon net worth: capital less debt. Negative net foreign assets are net foreign debt. Saving is GDP less consumption.

$$C = C(K/Q^+, \text{NFA}/Q^+, \text{PDI}/Q^+, r^-). \tag{6.5}$$

The consumption ratio is *positively* related to: (i) capital/potential output K/Q; (ii) net foreign assets/potential output NFA/Q; (iii) personal disposable income/potential output PDI/Q. (iv) An increase in real interest rate r decreases consumption.

The trade balance equation (6.6) is based upon the optimization of firms.[28]

$$B = B(R^-, \text{ABS}^-, C^{*+}) \qquad \text{Trade balance/potential GDP.} \tag{6.6}$$

An appreciation of real exchange rate R reduces trade balance. A rise in ABS = absorption/potential GDP reduces trade balance. A rise in foreign (German) consumption ratio C^* increases the trade balance. The current account/potential GDP, denoted CA, is equal to trade balance B plus investment income $r(\text{NFA})$ = interest rate (net foreign assets/Q).

$$\text{CA} = B + r(\text{NFA}). \tag{6.7}$$

To obtain the medium and long term NATREX, Karadi filtered all flow variables to eliminate the temporary effects. *Estimated parameters in each structural equation have the hypothesized signs and residual tests support the hypothesis that the variables of each equation are cointegrated.* Similar *qualitative* results are obtained from both the Engle–Granger and Phillips–Hansen methods.

Medium-run NATREX is the intersection of the SI and CA curves in Figure 6.2. The medium-run NATREX is derived from solving equation (6.8), the intersection of the SI and CA curves.[29] The structural equation estimation of the medium-run NATREX is equation (6.9) derived from the estimates of equations (6.4)–(6.7).

$$C(K/Q, \text{NFA}/Q, \text{PDI}, r) + I(\alpha, Q/K, r, R)$$
$$+ B(R, \text{ABS}, C^*) + r(\text{NFA}) = 1. \tag{6.8}$$

$$R_t = R(K_t/Q_t, \text{NFA}_t/Q_t; Z_t). \qquad \text{Medium-run NATREX.} \tag{6.9}$$

Table 6.3, column "Medium-run" explains the NATREX analysis of the effects of vector Z = (time preference, parameters of the trade balance function) upon the medium-run equilibrium exchange rate.

---

[27] See Chapter 4, Section 4.2.   [28] Ibid.
[29] The SI curve is derived from the estimation of equations (6.4) and (6.5). The CA curve in (6.7) is derived from the estimation of equation (6.6).

Variables K_t/Q_t, NFA_t/Q_t in equation (6.9) for the medium-run NATREX are endogenous in the long-run, and Z is a vector of the other variables in equations (6.4)–(6.6). In order to estimate the long-term NATREX, the long-run relative values of the endogenous ratios K_t/Q_t, NFA_t/Q_t have to be determined. In the long-run equilibrium, three conditions must be satisfied[30]. There must be medium-run equilibrium as described by equation (6.8). The ratio of capital/potential output is constant. Capital grows at the same rate as potential GDP, equation (6.10). Net foreign assets/potential output is constant. Net foreign assets should grow at the rate of potential output. Consequently, the ratio of current account/net foreign assets should be equal to g, the growth rate.

$$I/K = g = \text{growth rate} \tag{6.10}$$

$$CA/NFA = g = \text{growth rate.} \tag{6.11}$$

The growth rate was determined from the appropriate filtered GDP series. Using (6.9)–(6.11), the long-term NATREX is derived, $R^* = R(Z)$.

The structural NATREX model can provide estimates of the effects of the exogenous factors – such as productivity growth or fiscal variables – upon both the medium- and long-term NATREX exchange rate, and can give forecasts of the adjustment path of the medium-run NATREX R to the long-run level R^*. *Table 6.4 summarizes Karadi's results, which are precisely what are implied by the NATREX model summarized in Table 6.3 and Figures 6.3–6.5 above.*[31]

One of the most interesting implications of the NATREX model is that a rise in investment less saving $\Delta(I - S)$ *per se* appreciates the real exchange rate in the medium-run but depreciates it in the longer run. This can occur either because time preference, consumption/GDP, rises or that investment/GDP rises – with no change in the trade balance function $B(R;Z_B)$. The trajectory of this effect is graphed in Figure 6.3.

Table 6.4 rows 1 and 2, concern this effect. For example, the *medium-run* effect of a rise in fiscal consumption/GDP – a decline in saving – shifts the SI curve to SI(1) and appreciates the real exchange rate from $R(0)$ to $R(1)$ in Figure 6.2. The structural equation estimate of the medium-run effect is seen in the first row, column (1) in Table 6.4. When the fiscal consumption ratio rises by 1%, the estimated appreciation is 3.95% in the medium run.

As seen in Figure 6.3, in the *long-run* the NATREX real exchange rate depreciates below its initial level. Table 6.4, row 1, column 2 estimates

---

[30] See Chapter 4, Appendices A and B.
[31] The theoretical details and derivations are in Chapter 4.

that when the fiscal consumption ratio rises by 1%, the *longer run real exchange rate depreciates* by 1.8%.

Row 2 in Table 6.4 concerns the rise in investment ΔI. The same analysis applies. There is medium-run appreciation and long-run depreciation.

Row 3 in Table 6.4 concerns a rise in the growth rate. This corresponds to the NATREX model summarized in Table 6.3, last row. Insofar as the rise in total factor productivity raises investment, there will be medium-run appreciation. There is a current account deficit and the debt rises, which is a depressive force in the long run. However, as the growth rate rises, the debt/GDP ratio declines and the exchange rate appreciates. The result summarized in Table 6.3, last column can be understood by the long-run equilibrium condition for a constant debt ratio discussed in Chapter 4, where $B(R^*;Z_B) = (r-g)F^*$. The trade balance B^* must be sufficiently great to pay the interest on the debt adjusted for the growth rate $(r-g)F^*$. The rise in the growth rate lowers the right-hand side for $F > 0$. Therefore, the real exchange rate must appreciate to reduce the trade balance to equal the smaller right-hand side.

A rise in foreign demand is included in parameter Z_B in the trade balance equation. Figure 6.4, Table 6.3, row 2 shows that a rise in Z_B, that may result from either a rise in productivity – the decline in marginal cost SMC – or a rise in external demand – a rise in D – which raises the trade balance function, appreciates the real exchange rate and reduces the debt/ raises net foreign assets. It is the decline in the debt ratio that leads to more appreciation in the long run than in the medium run. See NATREX Figure 6.5. Table 6.4, row 5 shows that this appreciation effect does indeed occur.

No single test *per se* is conclusive, because the sample period is relatively short. It is best that alternative tests be performed to determine if the results are robust. One can also estimate the reduced forms.[32] The fundamental determinants of the *long-run* NATREX are relative time preference and relative labor productivity for the *entire economy*. Using the data underlying Christoph Fischer's panel data analysis in Table 6.2, we seek to find a cointegrating equation (6.12) linking the three variables.

The real exchange rate R is the real effective exchange rate against a weighted average of Hungary's OECD trading partners. The relative time preference δ/δ^* is the social consumption/GDP ratio in Hungary relative to the same weighted average of trading partners. Relative total labor

---

[32] See the discussion of this procedure and its application to the euro in Chapter 5.

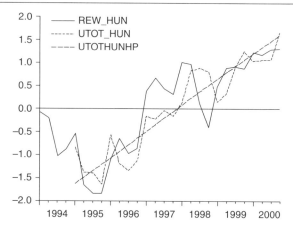

Figure 6.7. Real effective exchange rate, Hungary REX_HUN, relative labor productivity UTOT_HUN, smoothed relative labor productivity using HP filter UTOTHUNHP. Variables are normalized. Data supplied by C. Fischer.

productivity y/y^* is also measured relative to the same weighted average of trading partners. The sample period is 1996:4–2000:4.

$$R^* = R(\delta/\delta^*, y/y^*) \quad R_\delta < 0, R_y > 0. \tag{6.12}$$

A unique cointegrating equation was obtained. The signs were precisely those hypothesized and graphed in Figures 6.3 and 6.5 above or Table 6.3 long-run real exchange rate. A rise in social consumption depreciates the long-run real exchange rate and a rise in relative productivity appreciates the long-run real exchange rate. The coefficients are statistically significant. The *quantitative* estimates differ according to the lag structure. Thus the reduced form estimates are *qualitatively* the same as those obtained from the structural equations estimation.

SUMMARY

- There are clear trends in the real effective exchange rate $R = \text{REW\_HUN}$.

- The crucial determinant of the long-run real exchange rate is relative total labor productivity $y/y^* = \text{UTOT\_HUN}$. The trend in the long-run equilibrium real exchange rate follows the trend in relative productivity.

Figure 6.7 graphs[33] in normalized form the real effective exchange rate, relative productivity and the *smoothed* relative labor productivity

---

[33] Since the results are based upon Fischer's data, I use his acronyms in Figure 6.7.

UTOTHUNHP, using the HP filter. These results are consistent with those that were found both in Table 6.4 based upon estimates of the structural equations and from cointegrating equation (6.12).

The trend of the real exchange rate will deviate away from that in relative productivity insofar as relative time preference is changing. Neither PPP nor the B/S hypothesis equation (6.1) is useful in explaining trends in the real exchange rate and the balance of payments.

6.3.3. *Czech Republic*

The Czech koruna appreciated in real terms, since the beginning of transformation in 1993, as seen in Figure 6.1 above. Real appreciation occurred primarily through the rise in relative prices, since there was no trend in the nominal exchange rate.

The questions examined by Jan Frait and Lubos Komarek (F-K) were: why did the Czech koruna *real* exchange rate appreciate? Is the real appreciation sustainable and consistent with "equilibrium"? How should one model the equilibrium trajectory of the real exchange rate? Will the appreciation lead to a lower external competitiveness and higher external deficit and debt? Is the real appreciation compatible with low inflation? They stated that the objective of economic theory is to explain what factors and processes influence the development of the real exchange rate in transition economies such as the CEEC.

Clearly, the PPP hypothesis is not consistent with the trend appreciation. Frait and Komarek also show that the B/S hypothesis is overly simplistic. For the Czech Republic approximately 80% of the percentage appreciation of the CPI weighted real exchange rate came from the appreciation of the PPI weighted real exchange rate. See Table 6.1 above.

In the period examined 1993:1–2000:4, there were structural changes and capital mobility. The variable to be explained is the real exchange rate R(CPI) relative to Germany. They used the NATREX model of a "sustainable" or "equilibrium" real exchange rate as their benchmark. They examined to what extent the trend of actual real exchange rate can be explained in terms of the trajectory of the real exchange rate implied by the NATREX dynamic stock-flow growth model. Thereby, a measure of misalignment is obtained and the prediction is that the real exchange rate will converge to the NATREX. The emphasis was upon explanation/ theory, which would be useful for policy, and not upon data mining to account for variations in the real exchange rate. First, their econometric tests and results are summarized. Second, their economic significance and implications are discussed.

As summarized in Table 6.3 and in the previous section, the vector Z of the fundamental determinants of the real exchange rate are the variables that shift the SI and CA curves in figure 2. F-K used as vector Z: saving rate/ time preference/consumption ratio, productivity y, terms of trade T, foreign direct investment FDI, and world real interest rate r. A decline in the saving rate/rise in social consumption ratio produces the trajectories in Figure 6.3. A rise in productivity generates the trajectories in Figure 6.5. A rise in foreign direct investment FDI first leads to the trajectory in Figure 6.3. As productivity and growth rise as a result of cumulative investment[34], the trajectory in Figure 6.5 is generated. An improvement in *exogenous* terms of trade also leads to trajectories in Figure 6.5.

The saving ratio variable was problematic, since it displayed large jumps that are difficult to interpret from an economic point of view. Since it lacked explanatory power F-K did not include it in the vector Z of fundamental determinants.

The goal of econometric analysis is to estimate the trajectories, involving changes in the stocks of assets and the growth rate[35], to the long-run equilibrium. These adjustments take time. Estimates of long-run equilibrium based upon quarterly data are problematic, due to the short period. The cointegration/vector error, VEC, correction approach conforms to the dynamic model described in Chapter 4 and for the euro in Chapter 5. The VEC equation estimated is:

$$\Delta R_t = a(R - R(Z))_{t-1} + B.\Delta Z, \quad a<0, \tag{6.13}$$

$Z = [y = \text{productivity}, \text{FDI}, \text{TOT} = \text{terms of trade}, r = \text{world real interest rate}]$. *The cointegration equation* (6.14) is the long-run equilibrium, which is summarized in column 1 in Table 6.5:

$$R^* = R(Z) = R(y^+, T^+, \text{FDI}^+, r^-). \tag{6.14}$$

The *error correction component is* in column 2 of Table 6.5, which represents the shifts in the SI and CA curves in Figure 6.2.

The results in Table 6.5 are consistent with those implied by the NATREX model in Table 6.3. The aim is not to establish exactly by how much the Czech koruna may have been misaligned, but to determine if the current

---

[34] One could equivalently state that capital is gradually raised as a result of the path of investment. In turn the higher capital raises productivity, which shifts the CA function.

[35] In the earlier NATREX work capital is a variable. The usual measure of capital is the sum of investment. Since capital is not objectively measurable, we have been using (see Chapter 4, Appendix B) an alternative but mathematically equivalent concept. This substitutes an equation for the rate of growth of GDP for the growth of capital.

Table 6.5. Czech Republic: Empirical results, equation (6.13), 1993:1–2004:4. Coefficients are significant and have the hypothesized sign.

Real exchange rate	(1) Cointegrating equation	(2) Error correction (ΔR)	
Productivity	appreciate	Δ(Productivity)	appreciate
FDI	appreciate	Δ(FDI)	appreciate
Terms of trade	appreciate	Δ(Terms of trade)	appreciate
World real interest rate	depreciate	Δ(real interest rate)	depreciate

Source: Frait and Komarek (2001), Appendix.

exchange rate trend is consistent with the trend in the *equilibrium* real exchange rate. Moreover, it is important to understand and to predict how policy changes will affect the trend of the real exchange rate.

The logic of the NATREX is that distinctions are made between: (a) endogenous and exogenous variables[36], and (b) the medium and longer run equilibrium. Insofar as (a) is concerned, there may very well be interrelations among the regressors in the econometric equations. Jan Frait posed[37] some pertinent questions about point (a) above. Are the terms of trade exogenous? What is the relation between the terms of trade, TOT, and FDI? His argument is that the Czech economy experienced sustained improvements in the TOT since the transition from Socialism. The sustained decline in the TOT was probably the best evidence of devastation of the economy during the Socialist times. The improvements in the TOT reflect structural changes in the economy, where there is greater efficiency and productivity due to FDI inflows. Thus it is a question to what extent the TOT and FDI are both independent variables in the regressions.

Frait's argument is consistent with the NATREX interpretation of the theme of Lommatzsch and Tober (2005) discussed in Section 6.3.1 above. Productivity y_t:

$$y_t = y(0) \exp[\int b_s I_s ds + zt] \qquad (6.3)$$

is the exponential of the integral of the investment ratio times the productivity of investment, plus the improved resource allocations over the period $(0, t)$. FDI is induced by the potential return on optimal investment and leads to rises in $b_s I_s$ as well as in z. This is manifested as shifts from low-value added to high-value added goods, which was made possible by the higher productivity. These goods can now compete in the world

---

[36] The eclectic-econometric equations are not concerned with point (a) and just search for cointegrating equations. [37] This was done in correspondence with the author.

market. *In Figure 6.4, output has both a quality and a quantity dimension.* Theoretically, the CA curve in Figure 6.2 shifts to the right. The story is described in Table 6.3 in the row labeled ΔZ_B. This shift is detected empirically as an improvement in TOT = prices exports/prices of imports. Therefore FDI, productivity, changes in structure of the economy and the TOT are interrelated in the manner summarized in equation (6.3).

Due to the short sample period, cointegration analysis, which attempts to estimate both medium-run and longer run equilibria, does not have much power. It is more convincing if a series of methods and studies arrive at similar qualitative results[38]. My aim is to interpret them in the NATREX framework.

A relatively robust NATREX explanation of the evolution of the Czech real exchange rate, which is not amenable to the limitations discussed above, can be presented in the following way. I use Fischer's data[39] and acronyms for the Czech Republic (CZE) the way we used it for Hungary. The real effective exchange rate $R = $ REW_CZE is measured relative to a weighted average of the OECD trading partners. Total labor productivity $y/y^* = $ UTOT-CZE is measured relative to the same weighted average. Relative social consumption/GDP is also measured the same way $\delta/\delta^* = c/c^* = $ KQ-CZE. Figure 6.8 graphs the actual real exchange rate R and *smoothed* values, using the HP filter, of relative productivity UTOTCZ*HP* and of relative time preference KQCZ*HP*. Any sensible smoothing method for c/c^* and y/y^*, such as moving averages, will serve just as well.

Figure 6.8 shows that there is a non-monotonic trend in the real exchange rate. Two fundamental factors explain the longer-run movements. First, there is a trend in relative time preference *KQ*. In the NATREX model, this trend leads to long-run depreciation. See Table 6.3, row 1. Figure 6.3 describes this populist scenario: a rise in social consumption/ decline in social saving. Second: there are two trends in relative productivity

---

[38] One study by Egert and Lommatzsch (2004) did cointegration analyses using either the CPI or the PPI weighted real exchange rate and employed several different methods of estimation. They obtained a cointegrating equation in the case of each real exchange rate, and method of estimation, for the Czech currency. Their results (their Table 1a), summarized in (a)–(c), are consistent with those of Frait and Komarek (2001) and the NATREX model. (a) Labor productivity in either industry or in the overall economy is found to be the most stable determinant of either R(CPI) or R(PPI). Again the B/S hypothesis is rejected. (b) The similar results for R(CPI) and R(PPI) are consistent with the theoretical framework where appreciation comes from the shifts in the CA curve in Figure 6.2, and the dynamics are as described in Figures 6.4 and 6.5. (c) Foreign debt depreciates the real exchange rate. This is consistent with the dynamics that the growth in the foreign debt shifts the CA curve to the left along the SI curve and depreciates the real exchange rate. In a stable system, the growth in the debt must lead to a rightward shift in the SI curve, which increases the depreciation.

[39] These are the data in Fischer's panel analysis, summarized in Table 6.2 above.

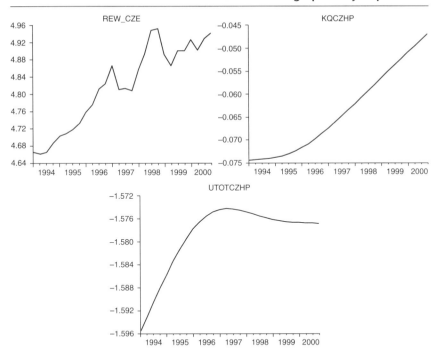

Figure 6.8. Czech Republic. Real effective exchange rate REW_CZE, smoothed relative time preference KQCZHP, smoothed relative productivity UTOTCZHP.

UTOT. For the first three or so years, relative productivity is rising. This is the force for long-run appreciation. By 1997, the trend is reversed. Productivity is growing at a slower rate than the OECD trading partners. This is no longer a force for longer run appreciation. Third is the net effect of the two different trends. The earlier growth in productivity offsets the effects of populist policies, and the real exchange rate appreciated rapidly. In the second part of the period, the decline in the trend rate of appreciation was due to the fact that the lower growth in relative productivity was not able to offset to the same extent the effects of populist policies discussed in Chapter 1.

6.4. A summing up: Policy implications

Vaclav Klaus, President of the Czech Republic, delivered a significant address (June, 2004) concerning policy issues in the transition economies. He opened his remarks in the following way.

181

In recent weeks we could hear and read hundreds of comments on the historical significance of the enlargement of the European Union by ten new, mostly former communist countries of Central and Eastern Europe. We could hear many words, but I fear hardly any serious, well founded analyses. It was the *a priori* position of almost all speakers that it was a clearly positive and productive change for all concerned. Any indication to think about this statement, any indication of criticism, question mark or comments regarding the costs involved in enlargement were considered short-sighted or ill-intentioned...I can neither present an in-depth scientific analysis of the effects of this year's EU enlargement nor an empirical analysis. This remains a long-term task for other people, even though it will not be an easy task for them either for lack of a simple scientific methodology and tested instruments.

The NATREX analysis in this chapter responds to Klaus's cogent remarks. At what pace should the countries enter the euro area and at what exchange rate? *First, the NATREX explains what are the fundamental determinants of equilibrium/sustainable real exchange rates, and the transmission mechanism between policies and sustainable real exchange rates.* A real exchange rate significantly higher – more appreciated relative to the NATREX – is unsustainable and will lead to serious problems. The dangers of selecting unsustainable exchange rates and policies may be what Vaclav Klaus had in mind when he wrote the following.

The new member states...accepted the European (and originally German) model...of a social market economy that is unambiguously connected with the low competitiveness of the firms, with the rigidity of the entire economy, with high unemployment and low economic growth. This will not lead these countries, whose level of development is lower than the European average, to real economic convergence. There is even the risk that, quite to the contrary, nominal convergence...will be the brake on real convergence. It should not be necessary to stress this in a country [Germany] that experienced unification, in which the effects of unification (or rapid nominal convergence) are well known.

Second, the NATREX analysis is relevant regardless of whether the nominal rate is fixed, there is a currency board or there is a more flexible exchange rate regime. If the nominal exchange rate is relatively fixed, then the variation in the real exchange rate will occur through differential rates of inflation.

We already have shown in detail how NATREX analysis explains the trends of the real exchange rate for Hungary and for the Czech Republic. A desirable characteristic of the analysis is that it can be applied to countries in various stages of structural change. The case of Bulgaria is relevant for our argument. We draw upon the work on Chobanov and Sorsa (2004) (C-S) to further demonstrate these points.

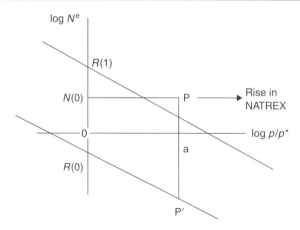

Figure 6.9. Nominal exchange rate N, the NATREX is R and relative prices (p/p^*).

Bulgaria had high rates of inflation, 321% in 1996 and 548% in 1997, followed by a deep financial crisis. A Currency Board Authority (CBA) was introduced in July 1997 to ensure financial stability, and Bulgaria also liberalized most capital movements. At first, the currency was fixed to the German mark and then to the euro. Since the introduction of the CBA, the real value of the currency appreciated by 30% and the current account deficit widened to 8.5% of GDP. The important questions studied by C-S are whether the real appreciation indicates a misalignment, and whether the current account deficit is a cause for concern.

Chobanov and Sorsa used the NATREX methodology to evaluate if the currency was significantly misaligned. Their econometric results are that the real appreciation of the exchange rate reflects changes in fundamentals, such as productivity, terms of trade, gross saving, world interest rates, and foreign direct investment. The appreciation of the real exchange rate since stabilization reflects the appreciating NATREX and they did not find misalignment in the post-July 1997 period.

The Bulgarian situation can be demonstrated by using Figure 6.9 which relates[40] the logarithm of the equilibrium nominal exchange rate $\log N^e$ to the logarithm of relative prices $\log (p/p^*)$. It is the graph of the equation

$$\log N_t^e = \log R(Z_t) - \log(p/p^*)_t. \tag{6.15}$$

The NATREX is $\log R(Z_t)$, which is the vertical intercept, and the slope of the line is -1. The PPP hypothesis is that the equilibrium nominal rate lies along a given line: the equilibrium real exchange rate is constant. We have

[40] This is the same as Figure 1.1 in Chapter 1.

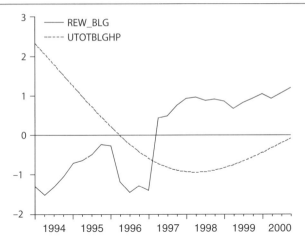

Figure 6.10. Bulgaria. Real effective exchange rate REW_BLG, relative productivity, smoothed UTOTBLGHP, normalized variables.

shown that this is not a correct description of the transition economies, and that the equilibrium real exchange rate $R(Z_t)$ varies with relative productivity and time preference. Two values for the NATREX are drawn in figure 6.9, where $R(1) > R(0)$.

Prior to 1997, the NATREX was $R(0)$, and the nominal exchange rate was $N(0)$. Inflation raised relative prices to a. The economy is at point P. The nominal exchange rate was overvalued by distance P-P'. The misalignment produced the financial disasters that C-S described.

If the nominal exchange rate were fixed at log $N = 0$, relative prices remained at a and the NATREX remained at $R(0)$, the CBA would not have been sustainable.[41] After stabilization, the consequent growth of relative productivity raised the NATREX from $R(0)$ in the direction of $R(1)$. The lines were shifting up to the right. This means that the higher relative price ratio a is more likely to be sustainable at the nominal exchange rate of log $N = 0$.

Figure 6.10, based upon Fischer's data, shows in a direct manner what happened. The real effective exchange rate is REW_BLG and the relative productivity[42] smoothed using the HP filter[43] is denoted UTOTBLGHP.

---

[41] As we know from the case of Argentina, a currency board is not necessarily viable if there is a serious misalignment where the real exchange rate rises significantly above the NATREX. This is the argument made in Chapter 8 to explain the currency crises in South-East Asia.

[42] Fischer measures the variables relative to a weighted average of the trading partners.

[43] Smoothing by moving averages is equally good.

The variables are normalized, so that orders of magnitude are seen graphically.

From 1993 to 1997, the real exchange rate was rising/appreciating, while smoothed relative productivity was falling – Figure 6.10. Thus the real exchange rate was appreciating/rising while the NATREX was falling. The misalignment was P-P′ in Figure 6.9. Stabilization occurred in July 1997. From then on, the trend in productivity was positive and rising. This means that the NATREX was rising in the direction of $R(1)$ in Figure 6.9. The trend in the real exchange rate was following the smooth trend in the NATREX. That is why C-S argue that the stabilization was effective and that the CBA is viable.

Poland provides a contrast to Bulgaria. Figure 6.11, again based upon Fischer's data, plots the real effective exchange rate of Poland REW_POL, the relative productivity UTOT_POL and the smoothed value of the latter, using the HP filter UTOTPOLHP. Unlike Bulgaria, the trend in productivity generated the trend in the real effective exchange rate. The Polish curves in Figure 6.9 were shifting to the right. The real exchange rate appreciated primarily via relative inflation. However, serious misalignment is not apparent.

At what pace should the country enter ERM II and the euro area? The answer depends upon the trend of the NATREX. If the dominant trend is a continued rise in relative productivity, the NATREX will rise above line $R(1)$ in Figure 6.9. With the ERM II, which establishes a central parity for

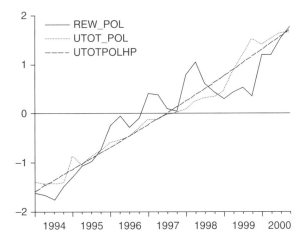

Figure 6.11. Poland. Real effective exchange rate REW_POL, relative productivity UTOTPOL, smoothed relative productivity UTOTPOLHP.

the nominal exchange rate, the relative prices must rise in the direction of the vector in Figure 6.9. The nominal exchange rate log $N = 0$ would be *undervalued* at relative prices a. This means that there will be a steady rise in central bank reserves and there will be inflationary pressures. The rate of inflation will be greater than in the rest of the EMU, leading the economy to points greater than a.

A lesson from NATREX is that insofar as relative productivity is rising and the nominal exchange rate is fixed, relative inflation must rise. It would be a mistake, and futile, to implement measures that will inhibit investment and growth.

To mitigate the inflation, the country should postpone entering the euro area until its productivity is growing at the same rate as in the euro area, when the ratio y/y^* has stabilized. If productivity is growing at the same rate y/y^* is constant, then marginal costs can be equated with a discrete, once and for all, change in relative input prices. If, however, there is a trend in relative productivity, then there must be a trend in relative nominal input prices.This means differential rates of inflation.

Another scenario is that a country enters the euro area at nominal exchange rate log $N = 0$ and then engages in populist policies that raise time preference – increases in the high-employment budget deficit – and lower the growth of productivity. If the rise in time preference effect is stronger than the productivity effect, the NATREX declines – the line in Figure 6.9 shifts down. At the origin where log $N = 0$, log $p/p^* = 0$, the nominal exchange rate is *overvalued*. The economy will be less competitive, exports will be adversely affected, there will be a loss of reserves, and employment and growth will decline. Since the nominal exchange rate is fixed at log $N = 0$, there is no alternative but to lower wages and prices. Given a low level of wage-price flexibility, the economy will stagnate.

Initially upon entry into the ERM II, the central parity will seem to be sustainable. Insofar as the country announces its parity log $N = 0$, there will be speculative capital flows that will be based upon the anticipation that this nominal rate will be the rate that is ultimately fixed. Consequently the actual nominal rate will lie in a band around this rate, even though the NATREX is very likely to vary due to relative productivity and thrift. Say that there is a downward trend in the NATREX due to trends in productivity and thrift. Then the combination of the established nominal exchange rate log $N = 0$ and no relative inflation log $p/p^* = 0$ will not be sustainable. Although "tensions" may not be discernable in the first few years due to speculation, a crisis is inevitable. *If the NATREX is depreciating, then there is no alternative but a reduction of wages and prices.* Social policies that prevent that from occurring will lead to the East German situation cited by Vaclav Klaus.

The policy conclusion is that insofar as the countries are committed to entry into the euro area, they should not ignore the likely dangers of misalignment. The Central Banks should calculate the trend of the NATREX, as was done in the Czech Republic and Hungary.

References

Chobanov, Dimitar and Piritta Sorsa (2004), Competitiveness in Bulgaria: An Assessment of the Real Effective Exchange Rate, International Monetary Fund, Working Paper WP/04/37

Detken, Carsten, A. Dieppe, J. Henry, Carmen Marin and Frank Smets, "Determinants of the Effective Real Exchange Rate of the Synthetic Euro: Alternative Methodological Approaches", (2002) Australian Economic Papers, 41 (4), December

Deutsche Bundesbank, (2002) Fundamental determinants of real exchange rate movements in the central and eastern European accession countries, Deutsche Bundesbank, Monthly Report, October

Égert, Balazs, László Halpern and Ronald MacDonald (2004) Equilibrium Exchange Rates in Transition Economies: Taking Stock of the Issues, CEPR DP #4809

Égert, Balazs and Kirsten Lommatzsch (2004), Equilibrium Exchange Rates in the Transition countries, William Davidson Institute Univ. Michigan Business School, WP #676

Fischer, Christoph (2002) Real currency appreciation in accession countries: Balassa-Samuelson and investment demand, Discussion paper 19/02, Economic Research Centre of Deutsche Bundesbank, July

——and Karlhans Sauernheimer (2002) A History of the D-Mark's Real External Value, Australian Economic Papers, 41 (4)

Frait, Jan and Lubos Komarek (2001), Real Exchange Rate Trends in Transition Countries, Warwick Economic Research Papers, No. 596, University of Warwick

International Monetary Fund (2004), World Economic Outlook, Washington DC, April

Karadi, Peter (2003), Structural and Single Equation Estimation of the NATREX Equilibrium Real Exchange Rate, Central Bank of Hungary, Working Paper

Klaus, Vaclav (2004) Implications of this year's EU enlargement: A preliminary analysis, CESifo Forum, Autumn

Lommatzsch, Kirsten and Silke Tober (2005) What is behind the real appreciation of the accession countries? An investigation of the PPI-based real exchange rate, Economic Systems, **28**, 383–403

Part IV

External debt and exchange rate crises

7

Country default risk in emerging markets[1]

7.1. Interaction between short-term capital flows and crises

In the aftermath of the 1997–8 turbulence in international financial markets, the International Monetary Fund published a retrospective assessment[2] of the weaknesses in private risk management, bank supervision, and financial market surveillance that had been intended to avoid crises. The major credit rating agencies have been assuming increasingly important roles in providing standardized evaluations of credit risks associated with emerging market investments. The rating agencies are important, because it is expected that they would rectify the problems of asymmetric information between the borrower and the many investors all over the world.

In this section, we review and evaluate the Fund study. This provides a motivation for an application of the "optimal short-term capital model" presented in Chapter 2 to explain how one can evaluate country default and derive early warning signals of crises.

The Fund wrote that during the 1990s, global securities markets became an increasingly important source of funding for many emerging market countries. As a result, the portfolio preferences and practices of major institutional players in these markets became key determinants of the scale and composition of capital flows. Credit rating agencies had strong impacts upon both the cost of funding and the willingness of major institutional investors to hold the various types of instruments. In many cases, obtaining a sovereign credit rating has been a prerequisite for

---

[1] This chapter is based upon Stein and Paladino (2001).
[2] International Monetary Fund, (1999a), especially Chapter III and Annex V.

issuing a Eurobond. Some institutional investors are constrained by official regulations or by internal risk management practices to hold securities that have been classified by the rating agencies as "investment grade". Moreover, under recent proposals by the Basel Committee on Bank Supervision, credit ratings would become key determinants of the weight attached to bank exposure to sovereign and other borrowers.

The large capital inflows into emerging markets in the 1990s were predicated on the assumption that emerging markets represented a near-mainstream asset class that was suitable for many investors. By early 1997, this prescription resulted in stable credit ratings and in "low" yield spreads.

Table 7.1 describes the net private capital flows 1990–8 into the emerging markets and into the five Asian countries (Asian5) that suffered severe crises in mid-1997 through 1998. Focus upon the "Asian5" countries. Approximately one half of the net inflows were "Bank loans and other", which are short-term capital flows. Except for a decline in 1993, private capital inflows grew steadily up to the 1997–8 crises. When the crises came in 1997 and 1998, they became huge outflows. The high and rising capital inflows from 1990 to 1996 indicate that the financial market did not anticipate the crises.

The usefulness of rating agencies to market participants in overcoming the problems of asymmetric information is ultimately tied to how accurately the rating agencies measure the default probabilities. Historically, sovereign ratings have been relatively stable. A question is whether

Table 7.1. Net private capital flows to emerging markets and five affected Asian countries* 1990–8, $US billion.

	1990	1991	1992	1993	1994	1995	1996	1997	1998
Emerging *markets*: Total net private capital inflow	47.7	123.8	119.3	181.9	152.8	193.3	212.1	149.2	64.3
a. Net foreign direct investment	18.4	31.3	35.5	56.8	82.6	96.7	115.0	140.0	131.0
b. Net portfolio investment	17.4	36.9	51.1	113.6	105.6	41.2	80.8	66.8	36.7
c. Bank loans and others	11.9	55.6	32.7	11.5	−35.5	55.4	16.3	−57.6	−103.5
Asia: Five affected countries Total net private capital inflow	24.2	26.8	26.6	31.9	33.2	62.5	62.4	−19.7	−46.2
a. Net foreign direct investment	6.0	6.1	6.3	6.7	6.5	8.7	9.5	12.1	4.9
b. Net portfolio investment	0.3	3.4	5.3	16.5	8.3	17.0	20.0	12.6	−6.5
c. Bank loans and others	17.9	17.3	15.0	8.7	18.4	36.9	32.9	−44.5	−44.5

*Indonesia, Korea, Malaysia, Philippines, and Thailand
Source: International Monetary Fund (1999a), Table 3.1.

the ratings or the market spreads displayed foresight. The credit rating agencies down-graded these countries only after the crises.

Table 7.2 presents the average spreads for "non-crises countries", "crises countries" and total at four dates: June 1997 just before the Asian crises, June 1998 just before the Russian crisis, December 1998 and May 1999 after the crises. The column labeled June 1997 shows that the dollar denominated interest rate spreads over US treasury securities were very low for both sets of countries. This shows that investors did not consider the securities of these countries as carrying much risk. Only when the Asian crises came, did the spread rise significantly in the crisis countries. It rose to a lesser extent in the non-crises countries. The crisis countries in the December 1998 and May 1999 columns reflect the Russian default.

Tables 7.1 and 7.2 show that the financial markets did not anticipate the risks, and that they continued to invest heavily in the crisis countries up to the debacle. Surveys of the market analysts at major international, commercial, and investment banks, published by the Institutional Investor and Euro-money just prior to the crises, indicated that these analysts gave high creditworthiness ratings to all the Asian countries receiving investment grade ratings by Moodys and S&P. When the crises came, the surprised investors then drastically reversed the capital flows.

The conclusions of the Fund study are that there is a need for a "paradigm shift" in evaluating country risk. Based upon econometric tests the significant variables in leading to high ratings were: high per capital income, rapid growth, low foreign debt/exports, absence of history of defaults, and high level of economic development. Insignificant variables were: budget surplus/GDP and current account surplus/GDP.

After the crises, financial system weaknesses, particularly in the banking system, are now viewed as a key source of vulnerability. The Fund study

Table 7.2. Average spreads, basis points.

	June 1997	June 1998	December 1998	May 1999
Non-crisis countries*	162	307	478	267
Crisis countries**	142	615	1470	1049
Total	156	403	788	511

* Non-crisis countries include Argentina, China, Colombia, Hong Kong, Mexico, Philippines, Poland, South Africa, Turkey, and Venezuela;
** Crisis countries include Brazil, Indonesia, Korea, Russia, and Thailand.
The average spreads are distorted by the extremely high level of Russian spreads.

Source: International Monetary Fund (1999a), Table A5.2.

made three recommendations. First: greater emphasis should be placed on the risks associated with the reliance on short-term debt for otherwise creditworthy borrowers. Second: there should be greater emphasis on the creditworthiness of the country's short-term borrowers. Third: there should be a greater appreciation of the risks posed by a weak banking system. The level and rate of growth of leverage in the economy as a whole are seen as key determinants of the likelihood of stress in the financial system.

There are two basic types of risk: microeconomic risk[3] concerned with the second point above, and macroeconomic risk concerned with the first and third points. Our concern is the *macroeconomic* risk for the entire economy and banking system. Loans that seem sound in one macroeconomic context may be unsound in a different macroeconomic context.

We derive early warning signals of a "default" or debt crisis by drawing upon the stochastic optimal control model of an "optimal" and excessive short-term debt developed in Chapter 2. The analysis is applied to emerging market countries that "defaulted" and to those that did not "default". *Default* is viewed as taking place when there is either a failure to meet a principal or interest payment on the due date or a distressed coercive rescheduling of principal and interest on terms less favorable than those originally contracted.

We derive: (a) benchmarks for *optimal* foreign debt, which will not be defaulted in the event of adverse shocks, and (b) a quantitative measure of the *maximum* debt that satisfies the no-default constraint. Insofar as the actual debt exceeds the benchmark, the risk of default is increased. An excessive debt occurs for several reasons. (a) The agents use certainty equivalence, as is done in much of the theoretical literature. (b) There is the moral hazard issue, which has been stressed in the literature on crises. The government provides implicit insurance, such as a pegged exchange rate, that induces firms to ignore/underemphasize risk. When the shocks occur, however, the government cannot fulfill its promise. (c) The borrower is overly optimistic about the distribution function of the return to investment. (d) Both borrowers and lenders neglect to constrain the optimization that there be no default/rescheduling.

---

[3] The book by Crouhy, et al. (2000) concerns the *microeconomic* risk. They draw upon the finance literature to objectively evaluate individual bank risk, and derive risk management techniques for *individual banks*. Their work is relevant for the regulation of individual banks.

7.2. Recapitulation of short-term optimal capital movements model

The short-term optimal capital movements model developed in Chapter 2 is applied in this chapter to explain the default risk in emerging market countries. There are three main characteristics to this benchmark model. First, there is a fixed maturity date at which the debt plus interest must be repaid. Second, the controls are investment and consumption. Third, a "no bankruptcy" constraint is built into the optimization. Macroeconomic financial fragility occurs when this constraint is violated.

The model assumes that there are two repeating discrete time periods. In period one, the country has a stock of capital K_1 and a gross domestic product Y_1. The *controls* are consumption C_1 and investment I_1. If consumption plus investment is greater than the GDP, the country incurs an external debt L_1 to finance the difference. If consumption plus investment is less than the GDP the country is an international creditor, and the debt L_1 is negative. The debt, or net foreign assets, bears a known real rate of interest. At the second period, the debt plus interest must be repaid. We consider a repeating two-period model, so that the capital at the end of period two must be the same as it was at the beginning of period one. This constraint means that the sum of investment over the two periods must be zero.

The GDP is a fraction b of capital K. The productivity of capital $Y/K = b$ is a stochastic variable. When the investment decision I_1 is made in period one, the productivity of capital in period two, $b_2 = Y_2/K_2$, is unknown. Capital in period two is the capital at the beginning of period one plus the investment made in period one. Two possibilities are considered. Either the productivity of capital b_2 exceeds the interest rate r, with probability $1 > p > 0$, or the productivity of capital is less than the rate of interest with probability $(1 - p)$. The stochastic variables b_2 and C_2 are written in bold letters in equations (7.1)–(7.3).

The debt in period one L_1 is equation (7.1). Consumption in period two C_2 is equal to the GDP in period two $Y_2 = b_2 K_2 = b_2 (K_1 + I_1)$ less the repayment of the debt plus interest $(1 + r)L_1$ plus the disinvestment to make capital at the end of period two equal to the initial capital K_1. Equations (7.2) or (7.3) describe consumption C_2 in period two. The return on capital can assume two values: $b_+ > r$ in the good case, and $b^- < r$ in the bad case. Therefore consumption in period two can assume either C_2^+

in the good case or C_2^{-} in the bad case.

$$L_1 = (C_1 + I_1 - b_1 K_1) \tag{7.1}$$

$$C_2 = b_2 K_2 - (1+r)L_1 + I_1 \tag{7.2}$$

$$C_2 = b_2 K_1 + [(1+r)(b_1 K_1 - C_1)] + (b_2 - r)I_1. \tag{7.3}$$

There are three components to consumption in period two, equation (7.3). If there were neither saving[4] ($S_1 = Y_1 - C_1$) nor investment in period one, then consumption in period two would just be the GDP in period two, $b_2 K_1$.

If there were saving but no investment, in period one, then consumption in period two would be the sum of the first two terms. The saving is invested abroad at the known rate of interest, and permits the economy to consume $[(1+r)(b_1 K_1 - C_1)]$. This term is not stochastic.

If there were investment in period one, then the additional consumption available in period two is the stochastic net return times the investment – the third term $(b_2 - r)I_1$.

In this short-term capital model, the country is stuck with the debt incurred in period $t = 1$, no matter what happens in period $t = 2$. If the bad state of nature occurs $b_2 = b_2^{-} < r$ then the burden of the debt resulting from $(b^{-} - r)I_1$ could depress consumption C_2 to an intolerable level. In that case, the country would default rather than accept the required reduced standard of living.

The optimization decision is to select the *controls*: consumption $C_1 > 0$ and investment $I_1 > 0$ during period one to maximize J, the expectation over the *stochastic* variable b_2 of the discounted value of HARA utility over the two periods, equation (7.4). The discount factor is $\beta = 1$, since it makes sense to give each period equal weight.

$$J = \max\{(1/\gamma)C_1 + (\beta/\gamma)[p(C_2^{+})^{\gamma} + (1-p)(C_2^{-})^{\gamma}]\}. \tag{7.4}$$

An important constraint is that there should be no default. This means that the set of consumption and investment in period $t = 1$ should ensure that consumption in period $t = 2$ exceeds some minimum tolerable level even when the bad state of nature $b^{-}_2 - r = -(a/2) < 0$ occurs. Call the minimum tolerable level of C_2 zero. Then the maximum debt/GDP, denoted $f-_{\max}$, in period $t = 1$ is equation (7.5). If the debt ratio

---

[4] This means that consumption is equal to GDP $= Y_1 = b_1 K_1$ in the first period.

exceeds f_{max} then firms will not be able to repay their debts to the external lenders.

$$f_{-max} = (\max L_1)/\mathrm{GDP}_1$$
$$= [(b^-(2)/b(1)) + (1 + b^-(2))j(1)]/(1 + r), \qquad (7.5)$$

where $j =$ investment/GDP in the first period, $b^-(2) =$ productivity of capital in the "bad case" $< r =$ real rate of interest, and $b(1) =$ initial productivity of capital.

The conclusions in Chapter 2 are described and summarized in Figure 7.1 for $h = L_1/Y_1$, the optimal debt/GDP, in the logarithmic case where the results are clear.

Optimal saving/capital is a constant independent of the expected net return $E(b - r)$. Optimal investment/capital is zero for expected net return $x < \rho$ in Figure 7.1. Risk premium ρ is related to the ratio of the possible loss from investment in capital relative to a safe return. This means that, for $x < \rho$, the country should be a creditor and invest all of its saving abroad, earning the safe rate of return $r > 0$. The debt/capital will be $f_{-min} < 0$, where the country is a creditor.

When the expected net return rises above ρ, optimal investment is positive, thereby reducing the capital outflow. When the expected net return is $x = D$, optimal investment is equal to optimal saving and the country will neither be a creditor or a debtor. When $x > D$, investment exceeds saving and there is a short-term capital inflow. There is a positive optimal ratio of $h =$ debt /GDP > 0. *Curve ABDEF is the optimal ratio*

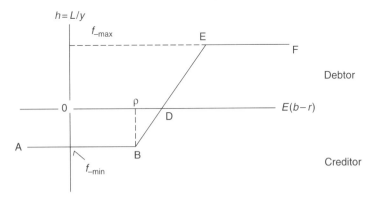

Figure 7.1. Optimal debt/GDP $h = L_1/Y_1$ is curve ABDEF. Expected net return $E(b - r) = [pb^+ + (1 - p)b^-] - r$. Along ABD the country is a creditor. Along DEF the country is a debtor. If debt/GDP exceeds f_{-max}, the probability of default is $(1 - p) > 0$.

debt/GDP. Expected utility is maximized along this curve. Insofar as the debt deviates from the curve, expected utility is reduced.

The constraint $h < f_{-max}$ makes precise the concept of macroeconomic vulnerability. The resources available for consumption plus investment, $C + I$ in period $t = 2$ when the debt must be repaid, is equation (7.6a). In a repeating two-period model, where terminal capital is equal to initial capital, $I_1 + I_2 = 0$, the maximum amount of resources that would be available for consumption in $t = 2$ is equal to the left-hand side of (7.6b). The "no bankruptcy" constraint in equation (7.5) is precisely equation (7.6b) that there be sufficient resources to repay the external short-term debt and where $C_2 > 0$.

$$Y_2 - (1 + r)L_1 = C_2 + I_2 \qquad (7.6a)$$

$$Y_2 - (1 + r)L_1 + I_1 = C_2 > C_{min} = 0. \qquad (7.6b)$$

The constraint that there be no default means that there is a maximal debt, f_{-max}, such that in the event of a ***bad state of nature*** $b_2 = b^-$, the level of consumption would exceed $C_{min} = 0$. If the debt exceeds f_{-max}, then with probability $(1 - p) > 0$ consumption will be less than C_{min} and there will be a *default* in the sense defined above.

Vulnerability is formalized as a situation where the debt exceeds f_{-max}. When default occurs, then there is a domino effect. The firms that borrowed from the banks cannot repay their loans. The domestic banks that borrowed "dollars" abroad cannot repay their external debts. There is a flight from the currency and the banking system is in crisis. Macroeconomic vulnerability occurs because the economy cannot service the external debt when the "bad" state of nature occurs. Loans that seemed to be sound in the good state of nature are non-performing in the bad state of nature.

7.3. Research design

We consider a set of 21 countries during the period 1978–9 which "defaulted" on the debt, and a "control" group of 13 countries that did not default. *Default* is defined as a situation where private firms or the government of a country *reschedule* the interest/principal payments on the external debt owed to either commercial banks or to official institutions. On the basis of the theoretical presentation in chapter 2, we compare the external liabilities of private or public debtors in countries that defaulted/did not default on their bonds with our concepts of the optimal or maximal debt/GDP. In section 7.3.1 we compare two pair of countries, Mexico/Tunisia and in section 7.3.2 Argentina/Brazil, to give *specific examples* of how our analysis is used to provide early warning signals of default crises. In section 4 there is a comparison of the two groups based upon panel data, where we show that an "excess debt", defined as the debt/GDP ratio h_t in excess of debt-max is a condition for a default/ renegotiation. The derivation of debt-max involves the probability of the "bad" state of nature. The conclusion is that it is not the level of the debt ratio *per se* h_t that indicates "financial fragility" or is an EWS of a debt crisis, but it is $(h_t - f - _{max})(2001)$.

Appendix A and Table A2, derived from the World Bank, list the entire set of 21 countries that rescheduled and the dates of agreement on their external private[5] plus public debt with commercial banks and with official creditors during the period January 1980 to December 1999. These countries are contrasted with a *control group* in Table A3 consisting of 13 emerging market countries that did not default.

The basic variables are[6]: the actual external public debt/GDP ratio $h(t)$, the productivity of capital $b(t)$, the interest rate $r(t)$ on foreign currency denominated debt, the growth rate $g(t)$ of real GDP, and the ratio $j(t)$ of investment/GDP. An estimate of the gross productivity of capital $b(t)$ is the inverse ICOR,[7] where $b(t) = d\,Y(t)d\,K(t) = [d\,Y(t)/d\,t\,/Y(t)]\,/\,[J(t)/Y(t)] = g(t)/j(t)$, equal to the growth rate of GDP divided by the ratio of gross investment/GDP. The net return is $x(t) = b(t) - r(t)$. The productivity of investment $b(t)$ is gross of depreciation and obsolescence.

The debt/GDP ratio combines short and long term external debt, but the theoretical analysis is based upon a two-period model where the debt plus interest must be repaid. A similar relation between the optimal debt/GDP and the net return is found in both the infinite-horizon model and in the two-period model. The difference is that in the two-period model, the debt plus interest must be repaid by the end of period two; and in the infinite-horizon model, the only requirement is that the debt must always be serviced. Operationally, the only significant difference is in the concept of the maximal debt f_{-max}. Given the mix of maturities, we use the inclusive measure of the external debt.

---

[5] In some cases, private borrowing was supported by implicit government guarantees.
[6] Our data are from: World Bank (2001), the IMF (International Financial Statistics) and IIF (countries data sets).   [7] ICOR is the incremental capital output ratio.

The application of the theoretical analysis is carried out in two parts. First, we compare two pairs of countries Mexico, a country that defaulted/rescheduled the debt, with Tunisia, which did not default, and Argentina/Brazil. Second, we examine the panel data of the countries that defaulted relative to those that did not.

7.3.1. *Comparison between Mexico and Tunisia*

Mexico experienced currency crises in September 1976, February and December 1982, and December 1994, and concluded 10 debt-rescheduling agreements with commercial banks, and three with official creditors, during the two decades January 1980 to December 1999 (see Appendix A). These agreements were concentrated in the periods 1983–90 and 1996. Tunisia is not among the countries that rescheduled. A comparison of the two countries provides a clear understanding of the subsequent panel data analysis. Table 7.3 summarizes the basic relations used in our analysis.

The median debt/GDP, row 1, was higher in Tunisia (0.61), which did not default than in Mexico (0.45), which rescheduled many times in our sample period 1980–99. It is not the debt ratio *per se*, $h(t)$, that determines the probability of default, but rather an excess of the actual ratio, $h(t)$, compared to the debt-max.

Table 7.3. Comparison of Mexico and Tunisia.

Variable: median, [range], (σ)	Mexico	ADF	Tunisia	ADF
1.Debt/GDP = $h(t)$	0.45 [0.81, 0.29](0.14)	−2.5	0.61 [0.74,0.44](0.09)	−1.8
2.Gross return = $b(t)$	0.15 [0.30, −0.31](0.16)	−3.3*	0.167[0.27, −0.08] (0.09)	−3.5*
3.bad case b⁻(2)	(median b(2)−1σ = −0.012		(median b(2)−1σ = 0.077	
4.Interest rate = $r(t)$	0.08 [0.15, 0.07] (0.02)	−1.89	0.05[0.06,0.04] (0.004)	−3.67*
5.Investment/GDP = $j(t)$	0.22 (0.02)	−1.55	0.28 (0.04)	−3.67*
6.Net return = $x(t)$	0.057[0.17, −0.39](0.16)	−2.1	0.107 [0.21, −0.13](0.09)	−3.47*
7.Growth = $g(t)$	0.035[0.08, −0.06] (0.036)	−3.07*	0.049[0.086, −0.02] (0.028)	−3.5*
8.f_{-max}	0.13	0.73		
9.DEF = h(t)−f−max	0.322	−0.116		
10.Cor(h, x)	−0.67		−0.24	
11.Cor(b, r)	0.02		−0.11	

Actual debt/GDP = $h(t)$; maximal debt/GDP = f_{-max}. We use median b(1), j(1), r(1) to eliminate the outlier which may have been the consequence of the currency crisis. ADF is significant if there is an asterisk. $f_{-max} = [b^-(2)/b(1) + (1+b^-(2)) j(1)]/(1+r)$ is evaluated at the median investment ratio j(t). The net return is $x(t) = b(t) - r(t)$.

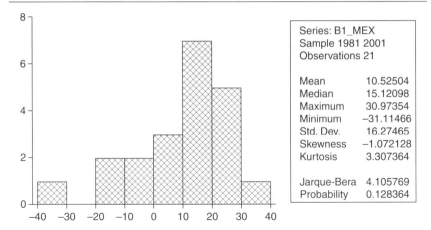

Figure 7.2. Mexico. Histogram of gross return $b(t)$ = growth/investment ratio, % pa.

Equation (7.5), repeated below, is the "no default" constraint. It is the relation between the debt and rate of investment $j(1)$ which will lead to a zero consumption in the bad case, when $b(2) = b^-(2)$. The value of f_{-max} in (5) is conditional upon the rate of investment $j(1)$ undertaken in the first period, which is then available for debt repayment and consumption in the second period. We see in Table 7.3, row 5, that there was a small variance to the rate of investment/GDP in the countries. We use the median rate of investment as $j(1)$. The interest rate is in row 4.

Figures 7.2 and 7.3 are histograms of the gross return $b(t)$, denoted B1, in Mexico which defaulted/rescheduled and Tunisia which did not, respectively. It is essential to study these histograms to estimate $b(2)$ in the good and bad cases[8].

In the *Mexican* case, the left tail of the gross return $b(t)$, figure 7.2, reflects the debt crises periods 1994–5, where the return fell drastically as a *consequence* of the crisis. We minimize the weight of these outliers in the distribution of $b(t)$, the gross return, by taking as our measure of the expected return $E[b(2)] = 0.15$ in Table 7.3, row 2 to be the median gross return in Figure 7.2. We assume that $b(1)$ was equal to the expected return. The distribution of $b(t)$ is stationary/mean-reverting. The standard deviation of the gross return 0.16 is taken to be an estimate of $(a/2)$. Therefore the bad case $b^-(2) = 0.15 - 0.16 = -0.01$, in Table 7.3/row 3.

---

[8] Box 2.1 in Chapter 2 presents our theoretical concept of the distribution of the gross return $b(2)$ in the good and bad cases.

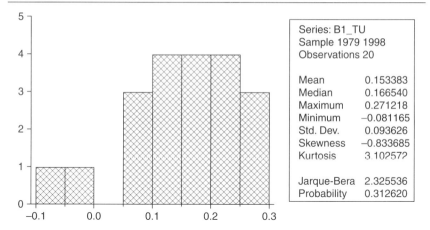

Figure 7.3. Tunisia. Histogram of gross return $b(t)$ = growth/investment ratio, % pa.

The investment ratio $j(1)$ is the median investment/GDP ratio 0.22, in row 5; and the interest rate r is taken as the median 0.08 in Table 7.3, row 4.

The f_{-max} for *Mexico* based upon (7.5) is (7.5 – MEX), equal to the maximal debt/GDP that Mexico can have and yet repay if the bad event occurs. It is based upon the histogram in Figure 7.2 and data in Table 7.3. Row 8, column 1 in Table 7.3, states that f_{-max} for Mexico is 0.13. A similar calculation for *Tunisia* implies that f_{-max} is 0.73. See row 8, in Table 7.3, column 2.

$$f_{-max} = [(b^-(2)/b(1)) + (1 + b^-(2))j(1)]/(1 + r) \tag{7.5}$$

$$f_{-max} = [(-0.012)/(0.15) + (1 - 0.012)(0.22)]/(1.08)$$
$$= 0.13. \tag{7.5-MEX}$$

It is not the debt ratio h(t) that is relevant for default (DEF), but the excess of the actual debt over f_{-max}. We calculate the difference (DEF) between the actual median debt and f_{-max}. If DEF > 0, then the debt is "excessive" and the country is likely to default in the event that the bad case occurs. The resulting values of DEF = [actual median debt/GDP – (f_{-max})] is in the row 9 of Table 7.3. In Mexico, DEF = 0.45–0.13 = 0.32 and in Tunisia, DEF = – 0.116. Since the Mexican debt exceeded f_{-max}, then default would occur if the bad event arose. In Tunisia, the debt ratio was less than f_{-max}, so that the "no bankruptcy constraint" was satisfied.

Figure 7.4 is even more revealing. We plot the annual DEF$(t) = h(t) - (f_{-max})$ = actual debt/GDP in each year less the f_{-max} (row 9 in Table 7.1),

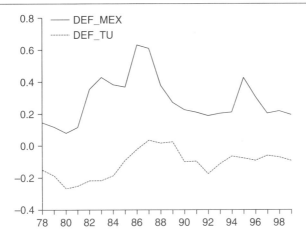

Figure 7.4. Excess debt = DEF = debt/GDP $-$ (debt/GDP)$_{max}$, in Mexico and Tunisia.

for Mexico and Tunisia. In Mexico, there was an excess debt DEF > 0 in every year 1978–99. In Tunisia, the excess debt DEF < 0, except for a short period when it was slightly positive. The conclusions are that, in the "bad state of nature" Mexico would default/reschedule, whereas Tunisia could repay the debt.

7.3.2 Argentina and Brazil

Another example of the explanatory power of our model concerns the recent Latin American debt crises. In the second half of the 1990s Argentina was the darling of the financial markets, and held up by economists as a model of stability and growth[9]. Argentina and Brazil restructured their debts to both commercial banks and official institutions during the period 1983–2001. Argentina, in particular, was transformed from the darling of the emerging markets 1997–2000 to "the world's largest deadbeat" in 2001. For example, in June 2002 Argentina carried out one of the largest debt swap operations ever conducted by a developing country, including a quarter of its outstanding peso and dollar denominated bonds. The dates of the debt relief agreements with both private and official creditors and debt swaps are listed in Appendix A, based upon the World Bank, *Global Development Finance* (2001).

---

[9] See Dornbusch's laudatory evaluation of Argentina, CESifo (2003, page 38). Mussa (2002) provides an excellent critical evaluation of the case.

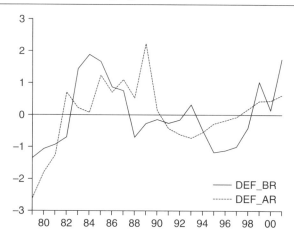

Figure 7.5. Argentina and Brazil: Excess debt $= h_t - (f_{-max}) =$ DEF, normalized variables.

Figure 7.5 graphs the "excess debt" DEF for both countries during the period 1978–2001. This is done in normalized form (variable – mean)/ standard deviation, for each country to give the reader an order of magnitude. Both countries have long successions of restructuring/defaults during the two decades.

The warning signals of a debt crisis are high and/or rising values of DEF. These signals mean that if the "bad" state of nature occurs then the country would not be able to service its debts. The "bad" state of nature does not necessarily arrive in the year or so when there is a positive and/or rising DEF. It is a stochastic variable based upon the distribution of the return. This means that a debt crisis is expected within a few years.

On the basis of Figure 7.5, warning signals are emitted for these two countries, which turned out to be accurate[10]. First, the Argentine *excess debt DEF* was rising from 1993 to 2001 by about two standard deviations from the Argentine mean. This was the period when Argentina was the darling of the financial markets. Our analysis indicates that there was a warning signal of the crisis of 2001. Second, the period 1979–89 exhibited rapidly rising and relatively high excess debt. We would then expect debt problems and renegotiations in the period of the 1990s, which indeed occurred.

Brazil had two periods where the warning signals were flashing "red". The first was 1979–84 and the second was 1995–2001. From the graph, we would expect that Brazil would have a series of debt renegotiations

---

[10] See Appendix A, Table below and World Bank (2001), Appendix 2 and 3.

certainly in the second half of the 1980s and then 1995–2001. As predicted, in 1999–2001 there was a series of "voluntary debt swaps" with commercial banks.

Early warning signals of a debt crisis based upon the stochastic optimal control model of an excess debt are much more reliable the predictions from the monetary models used by the Fund, the financial markets, and by many economists.

7.3.3. Panel data analysis

The theory Figure 7.1 describes the relation between $h(t)$, the constrained optimal debt/GDP, and the expected net return $E[x(t)]$. The net return $x(t)$ is equal to the gross return $b(t)$ less the interest rate $r(t)$. The gross return $b(t)$ is the growth rate/investment ratio. Thus $x(t) = b(t) - r(t) = g(t)/j(t) - r(t)$, where $g(t)$ is the growth rate and $j(t)$ is the investment ratio.

If one simply compared the actual net return $x(t) = g(t)/j(t) - r(t)$, with the actual debt/GDP, there is a negative bias. An example is Mexico during the default crisis 1980–2. When a crisis occurs, the growth rate $g(t)$ declines and the actual GDP may fall. The financial crisis induces a rise in interest rates, which aggravates the crisis. The net effect is that the crisis tends to raise the debt ratio $h(t) = L(t)/Y(t)$ and lower the net return $x(t)$. The drastic decline in the return and the rise in the debt/GDP may have been *consequences* of the crisis rather than its cause.

We use a panel data analysis for several reasons. First, an analysis of panel data country by subperiod may diminish the effect of the bias between debt/GDP and net return. Second, hypothesis testing is more easily done on panel data.

Appendix B, Tables A2 and A3 contain the panel data for the two sets of countries: default/reschedule and a control group that did not default. The *default countries* are: Algeria, Argentina, Bolivia, Brazil, Chile, Ecuador, Egypt, Honduras, Indonesia, Iran, Korea, Mexico, Morocco, Peru, Philippines, Poland, Romania, Russia, South Africa, Turkey, Uruguay, and Venezuela. The *control countries* are: China, Czech Republic, Estonia, Hungary, Slovenia; India, Kuwait, Lebanon, Malaysia, Saudi Arabia, Tunisia, United Arab Emirates, and Zimbabwe. The growth and stability in the control set of countries are tenuous, investment there is very risky, but they have not as yet defaulted.

For every country, each five-year period (1980–4, 1985–9, 1990–4, 1995–9) is considered as one observation. Appendix B, Tables A2 and A3 contain the values of the basic variables during four five-year periods: There are

Table 7.4. Panel data: Default countries vs control/no default countries. Periods: 1980–4, 1985–9, 1990–4, 1995–9.

Variable: mean (σ)	Default	Control[*]
Debt/gdp, $h(t)$	0.53 (0.26)	0.37 (0.18)
f_{-max}	0.37	0.34
DEF = debt/gdp − f_{-max}	0.16	0.03
Return $b(t)$	0.12 (0.15)	0.14 (0.13)
Net return $x(t)$	0.05 (0.16)	0.07 (0.14)
Investment/GDP $j(t)$	0.23 (0.06)	0.26 (0.06)
Correlation [$h(t),x(t)$]	0.09	−0.13

[*]Exclude Kuwait, 1990–4

127 observations, 51 default countries, and 76 control/no-rescheduling countries. Each observation contains the basic variables. The *debt-max* for each country in each of the four periods is based upon the frequency distribution of the return over the entire sample period.

Table 7.4 summarizes the key relations that are pertinent to our analysis for the default countries and for the control countries – those that did not default.

Table 7.4 shows that: (1) the mean gross return b and net return x are higher, and their variability is lower, in the control group. (2) The investment ratio j is slightly higher in the control group. (3) Therefore, the optimal debt ratio should be higher in the control group. (4) The maximal debt/GDP ratios are somewhat similar in the two groups. The crucial difference was that: (5) the actual debt/GDP is significantly higher in the default group. *Since the excess debt/GDP was significantly positive, DEF = 0.16, among the default countries, but DEF = 0.03 was not significantly positive among the control countries, the basic panel results are consistent with the predictions from the theoretical model.*

Figures 7.6 and 7.7 plot $h(t) =$ debt/GDP against the net return $x(t) = b(t) - r(t)$ for the panel data in Appendix B, Tables A2 and A3, where each observation is a country during one of the four five-year periods. Figure 7.6 concerns the default/renegotiation countries and Figure 7.7 refers to the control group that did not default. If the debt ratio were optimal, then the relation should look like curve ABDEF in Figure 7.1. The *conclusions* are the following, based upon scatter diagrams in Figure 7.6 and 7.7 relative to Figure 7.1.

(i) In neither set of countries is the debt–net-return relation even qualitatively optimal. Both sets of countries are poor credit risks.

(ii) In neither set of countries is the debt/GDP ratio positively and significantly correlated with the net return

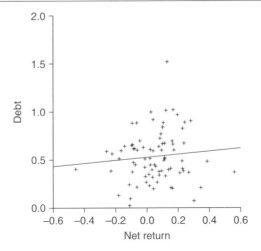

Figure 7.6. Default/reschedule countries panel: 1980–4, 1985–9, 1990–4 1995–9. $h(t) = $ debt/GDP on $X(t) = $ net return.

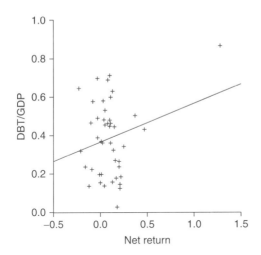

Figure 7.7 Control group panel: 1980–4, 1985–9, 1990–4, 1995–9. $h(t) = $ debt/GDP on $x(t) = $ net return.

(iii) Positive debt is associated with a zero net return, despite the great risk measured by the standard deviation of the return. Compare Figures 7.6 and 7.7 with the constrained optimal case, Figure 7.1, where a positive debt is only optimal if the expected net return exceeds a quantity $D > 0$, which is positively related to the downside risk/safe return.

(iv) The main difference between the two groups is seen in Table 7.4. There is a significant excess debt DEF > 0 in the default group, but the excess debt is not significant in the control group.

7.3.4 Early warning signals of bubbles, vulnerability to shocks, and default

On the basis of the theoretical analysis, we derive early warning signals (EWS) that an economy is vulnerable to shocks that will lead to a default/rescheduling. The EWS of the rescheduling should be a DEF (default) variable that is significantly positive and persistent. To avoid false signals we require that an on-signal, DEF $= [h(t) - (f_{max})] = [debt/GDP - (debt \ max /GDP)]$ be positive and either exceed one standard deviation or that it has been rising.

Contingency Tables 7.5 and 7.6 are used to test the explanatory power of the model. Each country in each subperiod is considered one observation. The default and control country data are in Appendix Tables A2 and A3, respectively. The rows of Table 7.5 are the signal *on/off*. The first row refers to the *on-signal*. It is conditioned on the sign of DEF and whether either it has been rising during the period or exceeds one standard deviation. The second row is the off signal, the complement of the first row. The columns in Table 7.5 refer to the occurrence/non-occurrence of rescheduling during the subperiod. Rescheduling is a legal act and comes after a period of difficulties. A caveat is that political factors are operating so that there is often a political bailout. However, if the country falls in row 1, this may be an EWS of a political bailout.

The χ^2 test concerns the independence of the rows and columns. Since the value of $\chi^2(1) = 17.6$ falls in the rejection region, we have to reject the null hypothesis of independence of the two classification. In 84% of the periods of rescheduling the DEF variable has been positive and was either greater than one standard deviation or rising.[11] One can summarize Table 7.5 by stating that the *conditional probability* that the debt was excessive during renegotiation periods is

$$Pr(\Psi|R) = Pr(R\Psi)/ Pr(R) = (43/127)/(51/127) = 84\%.$$

$$\Psi = DEF > 0 \qquad R = \text{renegotiation/default}.$$

---

[11] To further investigate the explicative power of the DEF $= [h(t) - (f_{max})]$ variable, we carried out a probit analysis. The results are encouraging. The DEF is significant and positive, with a marginal effect of 11%.

Table 7.5. Contingency table by country/subperiod. Number of observation in category (expected cell frequency); total Number of observations 127.

	Recheduling	No rescheduling	Total
Ψ = DEF > 0; and (i) DEF > 1 σ or (ii) DEF rising	43(30.8)	36(46.2)	79
DEF < 0 and (i)DEF < 1 σ or (ii) DEFdeclining	8(19.2)	40(28.8)	48
Totals χ^2 (1) = 17.6 **	51	76	127

Note: Each country has been analyzed by subperiod, based upon Tables A.2 and A.3.
** means significant at the 1% level.

Table 7.6. Contingency table by country/subperiod. Number of observation in that category (expected cell frequency); total Number of observations is 127.

	Ψ = DEF > 0, and increasing	DEF < 0	DEF > 0, and declining	total
Reschedule	39 (28)	4 (10.8)	8 (11.2)	51
No reschedule	33 (42)	19 (16.2)	24 (16.8)	76
Total	72	23	32	127

χ^2 (2) = 13.89, significant at the 1% level.

There is some arbitrariness in the classification concerning what is a significant excess debt. Table 7.6 is a threefold classification by country and period. In any subperiod the debt could be excessive and increasing in column 1, there is no excessive debt in the subperiod column 2, and the debt could be excessive but declining in the subperiod column 3.

The χ^2 statistic with two degrees of freedom is significant. The default/ renegotiation and the excess debt are not independent.

The *conditional probability* that there was an excess debt prior to the renegotiation is

$$\Pr(\Psi|R) = \Pr(R\Psi)/\Pr(R) = (39/127)/(51/127) = 0.76.$$

The conclusion from Tables 7.5 and 7.6 is that an excess debt is a necessary condition for a default/renegotiation. This is based upon the condition that a significant $\Pr(\Psi \mid R)$ means that R implies Ψ.

7.4. Conclusion

How should one evaluate country default risk in terms of *objective* criteria? When crises and defaults occur, then with hindsight it is often stated that the banking system was "fragile" and that the economy was "vulnerable". The concepts in quotes are not given precise definitions, so that they do not provide measurable and reliable early warning signals. The literature discussed in section 7.1 one, especially Table 7.2, shows that the market lacked objective reliable early warning signals. Our contribution is to apply the stochastic optimal control short-term capital model in Chapter 2 to explain and provide early warning signals of country default risk.

The optimal debt/net worth ratio serves as a benchmark of performance. This is a non-linear function of the return on capital less the interest rate. It has an upper bound, which we called debt-max. This is a no-bankruptcy constraint. When the debt ratio is equal to or exceeds debt-max – there is an excess debt – then the country will default when the "bad" state of nature occurs. The stochastic "bad" state of nature occurs when the return on capital is less than the interest rate on the debt. The optimal and excess debt are based upon the distribution function of the return on capital, using historical information. Our macroeconomic approach is consistent with the microeconomic approaches to bank regulation.[12]

The reason is that when there is an excess debt, and the "bad" state of nature occurs, then the GDP plus the sale of capital is less than or equal to the repayment of the debt plus interest. If there were no default, then social consumption would be zero. Such a situation is intolerable and the country will default.

We considered two sets of emerging market countries: one set renegotiated defaulted and the other set did not. In neither set did the debt ratio resemble the optimal ratio. The difference was that the countries that defaulted/renegotiated had significant excess debt, whereas the countries that did not default/renegotiate did not have significant excess debt. Therefore, our *early warning signal of a debt crisis is the excess debt, and not the level of the debt/GDP ratio per se.*

---

[12] See the book Crouhy (2000).

Appendix A

Table A1 List of multilateral relief agreements with official and private creditors, January 1980 to December 1999

Country	Official creditors	Private creditors
Algeria	1994; 1995	1992;1995
Argentina	1985;1987;1989;1991;1992	1983;1985;1987;1993,1997,1998,1999, 2000,2001, 2002
Bolivia	1986;1988; 1990;1992; 1995:1998	1980;1981;1988;1992;1993
Brazil	1983;1987;1988;1992	1983;1984;1986;1988;1992;1994,1997, 1999,2000,2001
Chile	1985;1987	1983;1984;1985 1987;1988;1990
Ecuador	1983;1985;1988;1989;1992;1994	1983;1985;1987;1995
Egypt	1987;1991	
Indonesia	1998	1998
Iran	1993;1994	
Korea	1998	
Mexico	1983;1986;1989	1983;1984;1985;1987;1988;1990;1996
Morocco	1983;1985;1987;1988;1990;1992	1986;1987;1990
Peru	1983;1984;1991;1993;1996	1980;1983;1996
Philippines	1984;1987;1989;1991;1994	1986;1987;1990;1992;1996
Poland	1981,1985;1987;1990;1991	1982;1983;1984;1986;1988;1989;1994
Romania	1982;1983	1982;1983;1986;1987
Russian Federation	1993;1994;1995;1996;1999	1991;1993;1995;1998
South Africa		1985;1986;1987;1989;1993
Turkey	1980	1982
Uruguay		1983;1986;1988;1991
Venezuela		1986;1987;1988;1990

Source: World Bank (2001) Table A2.3 and Table A3.2; Op. cit. (2001), Tables A2.2, A3.2.

Appendix B

Table A2 Summary table default group

Country		1980–4				1985–9				1990–4				1995–9			
		$b(t)$	$r(t)$	$j(t)$	$h(t)$	$b(t)$	$r(t)$	$j(t)$	$h(t)$	$b(t)$	$r(t)$	$j(t)$	$h(t)$	$b(t)$	$r(t)$	$j(t)$	$h(t)$
Algeria	(ALG)	0.117	0.085	0.370	0.394	0.056	0.072	0.309	0.421	–0.012	0.070	0.278	0.611	0.148	0.065	0.241	0.722
Argentina	(AR)	0.013	0.106	0.201	0.373	–0.073	0.082	0.125	0.640	0.333	0.064	0.176	0.369	0.117	0.069	0.188	0.446
Bolivia	(BOL)	–0.053	0.114	0.142	0.594	0.089	0.063	0.146	0.996	0.277	0.049	0.151	0.826	0.212	0.050	0.190	0.694
Brazil	(BR)	0.683	0.122	0.169	0.369	0.225	0.087	0.223	0.396	0.079	0.058	0.215	0.348	0.098	0.062	0.217	0.317
Chile	(CHL)	0.082	0.127	0.156	0.696	0.289	0.093	0.212	0.968	0.303	0.077	0.244	0.486	0.206	0.054	0.255	0.410
Ecuador	(ECU)	0.097	0.110	0.218	0.508	0.125	0.085	0.207	0.917	0.178	0.056	0.201	1.015	–0.034	0.059	0.185	0.879
Egypt	(EGY)	0.334	0.052	0.302	0.904	0.184	0.054	0.298	1.521	0.154	0.049	0.226	0.885	0.262	0.034	0.208	0.408
Indonesia	(INDO)	0.249	0.084	0.258	0.200	0.160	0.066	0.325	0.599	0.229	0.056	0.335	0.601	–0.008	0.057	0.248	0.883
Iran	(IR)	0.331	0.030	0.201	0.070	–0.097	0.013	0.145	0.022	0.334	0.008	0.199	0.207	0.093	0.052	0.229	0.195
Korea	(KOR)	0.213	0.099	0.304	0.510	0.307	0.072	0.311	0.383	0.203	0.049	0.371	0.208	0.125	0.046	0.320	0.341
Mexico	(MEX)	0.061	0.135	0.226	0.448	0.062	0.086	0.205	0.628	0.174	0.079	0.220	0.384	0.101	0.079	0.237	0.446
Morocco	(MOR)	0.152	0.050	0.253	0.840	0.214	0.045	0.231	1.02	0.146	0.056	0.228	0.768	0.097	0.058	0.212	0.592
Peru	(PER)	0.012	0.098	0.282	0.472	0.010	0.072	0.281	0.601	0.157	0.057	0.180	0.665	0.171	0.058	0.234	0.521
Philippines	(PHIL)	–0.018	0.074	0.268	0.656	0.176	0.063	0.170	0.839	0.077	0.056	0.286	0.606	0.161	0.047	0.220	0.671
Poland	(POL)	–0.112	0.117	0.247	0.383	0.105	0.086	0.314	0.514	–0.025	0.057	0.187	0.619	0.259	0.048	0.222	0.362
Romania	(ROM)	0.111	0.095	0.356	0.228	–0.023	0.078	0.308	0.093	–0.143	0.039	0.286	0.127	–0.061	0.051	0.219	0.240
Russian Fed	(RUS)	na	na	na	na	na	na	na	na	–0.390	0.065	0.236	0.401	–0.104	0.072	0.189	0.515
South Africa	(SAF)	0.100	0.105	0.267	0.266	0.077	0.087	0.191	0.325	0.012	0.077	0.153	0.213	0.141	0.075	0.161	0.267
Turkey	(TUR)	0.207	0.085	0.264	0.331	0.257	0.070	0.231	0.482	0.140	0.063	0.241	0.376	0.164	0.056	0.239	0.494
Uruguay	(URU)	–0.141	0.081	0.146	0.562	0.317	0.075	0.122	0.889	0.299	0.062	0.137	0.672	0.134	0.058	0.155	0.637
Venezuela	(VEN)	–0.124	0.133	0.206	0.586	0.020	0.100	0.211	0.651	0.249	0.081	0.169	0.661	0.132	0.075	0.184	0.431

Symbols: Debt/GDP = $h(t)$, gross return = $b(t)$, the interest rate = $r(t)$, the net return $x(t) = b(t)–r(t)$, and the investment/GDP ratio = $j(t)$.

Appendix C

Table A3 Summary table control group

Country +	1980-4				1985-9				1990-4				1995-9			
	x(t)	r(t)	j(t)	h(t)	x(t)	r(t)	j(t)	h(t)	x(t)	r(t)	j(t)	h(t)	x(t)	r(t)	j(t)	h(t)
China (CI)	na	0.11	na	0.03	0.21	0.03	0.36	0.12	0.22	0.05	0.38	0.18	0.17	0.04	0.39	0.18
Czech Republic (CK)	na	na	na	na	0.04	0.10	0.27	0.14	-0.16	0.08	0.25	0.24	-0.03	0.08	0.32	0.39
Estonia (ESTO)	na	na	na	na	na	na	na	na	-0.12	0.03	0.26	0.15	0.10	0.05	0.27	0.45
Hungary (HUNG)	-0.03	0.10	0.28	0.49	-0.03	0.08	0.27	0.70	-0.23	0.07	0.21	0.64	0.03	0.08	0.28	0.58
India (IN)	0.21	0.02	0.24	0.15	0.20	0.03	0.25	0.24	0.14	0.05	0.24	0.32	0.20	0.06	0.25	0.26
Kuwait (KW)	-0.10	0.10	0.16	0.47	0.47	0.07	0.13	0.43	1.28	0.06	0.17	0.87	-0.08	0.08	0.12	0.58
Lebanon (LB)	na	na	na	na	na	na	na	na	0.25	0.06	0.27	0.34	0.01	0.10	0.36	0.37
Malaysia (MAL)	0.11	0.07	0.36	0.46	0.10	0.07	0.28	0.71	0.37	0.06	0.38	0.50	0.05	0.06	0.37	0.45
Saudi Arabia (SARA)	-0.12	0.12	0.25	0.14	0.01	0.07	0.19	0.20	0.13	0.07	0.21	0.16	-0.01	0.08	0.19	0.20
Slovenia (SLO)	na	na	na	na	na	na	na	na	-0.21	0.09	0.18	0.32	0.11	0.05	0.24	0.36
Tunisia (TU)	0.10	0.06	0.33	0.48	0.04	0.05	0.24	0.48	0.11	0.05	0.28	0.60	0.13	0.05	0.27	0.63
United Arab Emirates (UAE)	-0.09	0.14	0.28	0.22	0.02	0.08	0.24	0.36	0.15	0.06	0.25	0.45	0.08	0.05	0.27	0.46
Zimbabwe (ZW)	0.16	0.08	0.2	0.27	0.18	0.07	0.17	0.03	0.05	0.06	0.21	0.53	0.08	0.04	0.22	0.69

Symbols: Debt/GDP $= h(t)$, gross return $= b(t)$, the interest rate $r(t)$, the net return $x(t) = b(t)-r(t)$, and the investment/GDP ratio $= j(t)$.

References

Crouhy, Michel, Don Galai and Robert Mark (2000) Risk Management, Irwin

Dornbusch, Rudiger (2003) International Financial Crises, Munich Lectures, CESifo Working Paper #926.

International Monetary Fund, (1999a), International Capital Markets, Washington DC

International Monetary Fund, (1999b). Anticipating Balance of Payments Crises, Occasional Paper #186.

Mussa, Michael (2002) Argentina and the Fund: From Triumph to Tragedy, Institute for International Economics, Washington, DC.

Stein, Jerome L. and Giovanna Paladino (2001) Country Default Risk, An Empirical Assessment, Australian Economic Papers (40), 4, December.

World Bank, Global Development Finance (2001) Washington DC.

8

Asian crises: Theory, evidence, warning Signals[1]

8.1. Application of NATREX and stochastic optimal control/dynamic programming

In July 1997, the economies of East Asia became embroiled in one of the worst financial crises of the postwar period. Yet, prior to the crisis, these economies were seen as models of economic growth experiencing sustained growth rates that exceeded those earlier thought unattainable. Table 8.1 describes the situation for ASEAN4 and Korea before and after 1997. The high growth from 1986 to 1996 was suddenly followed by a collapse of the real economy, with negative growth in 1998. In 1997, the exchange rates depreciated by double digits and, for some countries, the depreciation continued into 1998.

What went wrong? What caused the financial crisis? With hindsight, there is now a consensus as to what went wrong with the Asian countries. Dean (2001)[2] briefly describes the consensus as follows. The Asian growth was generated by high investment and saving. The difference between investment and saving was financed by capital inflows, made possible when the economies were liberalized in the early 1990s. Since these economies generally had fixed exchange rates, the capital inflows led to increases in the money supply. There was inflation of asset prices, speculative bubbles, but not inflation of prices of goods and services. The investment was poorly intermediated and misallocated.

---

[1] This chapter is based upon Stein and Lim (2004).

[2] An important article on the subject is by Williamson (2004), who cogently evaluates the literature. Dean (2001) contains the basic references on this subject, and the reader is referred to his article for the extensive bibliography. Flouzat (1999) and recent International Monetary Fund WEO reports describe the consensus view country by country.

8. Asian crises

Table 8.1. The Asian crisis 1997–8

Country	GDP: annual growth rate %		Exchange-rate depreciations %	
	1986–96	1998:1–1998:6	1997	1998:1–1998:6
Indonesia	7.4	−12.0	−52.0	−50.0
Korea	8.6	−5.0	−43.0	6.0
Malaysia	7.8	−5.0	−33.0	−1.0
Philippines	3.7	−12.5[a]	−29.0	−5.0
Thailand	9.1	−8.0	−44.0	16.0

Source: (1998 International Monetary Fund, Tables 3.11, 3.12. (a) 1997:4–1998:2

The capital inflows produced a high ratio of external debt and debt service obligations relative to export earnings. With the bursting of the speculative bubble in asset prices, the former capital inflows turned to outflows. The countries faced a dilemma. If interest rates were raised to stem the outflow, the debt service burden to domestic borrowers would be raised. If the interest rates were not raised, devaluation would have to occur; and the debt service burden on the foreign currency denominated debt would rise. The net result was a financial collapse and exchange rate depreciation.

But why did the market not anticipate the crises?[3] Could it be that the market and credit rating agencies failed to anticipate the crisis because there were no useful warning signals? More importantly could it be that the range of qualitative and quantitative indicators normally monitored (for example, per capita income, growth rates, inflation rates, ratios of foreign debt to exports, history of defaults, level of economic development, government budget deficits, ratio of current account deficits to GDP) were not helpful because these measures were assessed in an *ad hoc* manner?

We contend that it would be more useful to derive warning signals based on concepts derived from a coherent theoretical framework that can predict the crisis. We draw upon the theoretical Chapters 2–4 to derive operational warning signals. To this end, we review the Asian financial crisis from two related perspectives – whether the crisis was precipitated by a failure of the real exchange rate to be aligned with its fundamental determinants and/or whether the crisis was precipitated by a divergence of the foreign debt from its optimal path. The first perspective is based the NATREX model of the equilibrium real exchange rate (Chapter 4) which

---

[3] Available measures of expectations by market participants display a poor record in anticipating crises. The secondary market yield spreads on US dollar denominated Eurobonds did not vary much before the Asian crisis, see IMF (1997), Figure 14 and IMF (1999) pp. 107–12. See also Berg and Pattillo (1999).

shows how "misalignments" lead to currency crises. The second perspective is based on a model of optimal foreign debt ratio which showed why "divergences" lead to debt crises (Chapters 2 and 3). The important point here is that these models suggest important variables which may serve as warning signals of impending crises.

The chapter is organized as follows. In Section 8.2 we discuss some traditional warning signals. Section 8.3 is a brief review of the natural real exchange rate (NATREX) approach to the determination of the equilibrium real exchange rate and the measure of misalignment that may serve as a warning signal for currency crises. This section also describes the stochastic optimal control/dynamic programming (SOC/DP) approach to derive the optimal foreign debt ratio and shows how the deviation of the actual debt from this benchmark measure of performance may serve as a sufficient condition for a debt crisis.

A large literature concerns warning signals for both balance of payments/currency crises and debt crises. The method of analysis generally estimates a family of probit models to assess the predictability of some vector in anticipating each type of crisis. The method of analysis is *eclectic-econometric*. In Chapter 1, we briefly discussed this literature. The difference between our approach and the literature is that our analysis is theoretically based and not eclectic-econometric. In Section 8.4 we explore the explanatory value of our theoretically based warning signals all *utilizing only available information* to explain and predict the Asian crises. Concluding remarks are contained in the final Section 8.5.

8.2. Traditional warning signals

This chapter is concerned with two types of crises. The first is a *currency crisis*, which results from an "overvalued" exchange rate, and the second is a *debt crisis*, which occurs when the country cannot service its foreign debt. In both cases, the likely outcome is a dramatic currency devaluation or depreciation.

A common view associated with currency crises is that they result from "unstable macroeconomic policies". Consequently the early warning measures are the state of key macroeconomic variables and the response to a currency crisis is to implement restrictive monetary and fiscal policies.[4] Section 8.2.1 below explains why the crises in Asia could

---

[4] Some economists have argued that the way to avoid currency crises is to adopt a currency board or to replace the domestic currency with a foreign currency.

not be explained by "unstable macroeconomic policies". Debt crises are associated with "unsustainable" external debt, and Section 8.2.2 reviews a few traditional measures of "unsustainability".

Warning signals have two components. (a) What variables are considered? (b) What periods are compared? In this section, we focus primarily upon International Monetary Fund WEO reports that organized the data in forms (a) and (b) above: variables and comparison periods. For example, Table 8.2 is based upon the IMF's presentation. We show the limitations of the standard approaches.

8.2.1. Was there macroeconomic instability?

It is now well-documented that the Asian crises were not preceded by increases in "macroeconomic instability". Table 8.2 compares some macroeconomic indicators for the pre-crisis period 1986–96 with the earlier tranquil period 1975–85. Inflation declined, and there were no significant increases in fiscal deficits or current account deficits. By the usual standards of macroeconomic performance the Asian economies were doing very well. In fact, prior to the crises, according to the International Monetary Fund (1998b, Chapter III, pp. 82ff), the successful economic performance of these East Asian countries can be attributable to their emphasis on stability oriented macroeconomic policies such as maintaining low rates of inflation, avoiding overvalued exchange rates, and sustaining high rates of physical and human capital accumulation and export oriented production. This evidence leads one to reject an assertion that the crises were produced by monetary and fiscal mismanagement.

However, the currency did collapse and that leads one to question the usefulness of the above macroeconomic variables as warning signals of

Table 8.2. Macroeconomic variables 1975–85 and 1986–96.

Country	Inflation % p.a.		Fiscal balance/GDP %		Current account/GDP %	
	1975–85	1986–96	1975–85	1986–96	1975–85	1986–96
Hong Kong	8.2	8.0	1.1	2.1	3.0	5.6
Indonesia	13.4	8.2	0.3	−0.5	−2.0	−2.8
Korea	13.5	5.7	−2.2	−0.1	−3.7	0.9
Malaysia	4.8	2.6	−5.3	−2.4	−3.2	−2.6
Philippines	15.6	8.9	−2.0	−2.3	−5.1	−2.6
Singapore	3.4	1.9	1.9	9.1	−7.2	9.5
Taiwan	6.3	3	0.3	−0.5	4.3	7.8
Thailand	7.2	4.5	−3.7	2.1	−5.5	−4.9

Source: International Monetary Fund (1998b), Table 3.11.

vulnerability. In Section 8.3, we suggest that it may be more useful to look at the behavior of the fundamental determinants of the real exchange rate to predict the probability of a currency crisis. Our warning signals are based on a theoretically justifiable concept and measure of exchange rate misalignment.

8.2.2. *Was the foreign debt sustainable?*

Since the crises could not be attributed to "macroeconomic instability", the focus turned to the role of the external debt[5] and to the weaknesses in the financial structure as explanations of the crises. For the Asian economies, the banking system was the means by which foreign lending was inter-mediated through the corporate sector. Equity markets played a limited role, and fixed income money and bond markets were less developed and liquid. Table 8.3 describes the net private capital flows to Asia.

Table 8.3 shows the volatility in total capital flows. Net foreign direct investment was the main component of the capital flows, 55% in 1996, and was relatively steady. The highly volatile element was the category of bank loans, which was about 33% in 1996. It switched from an inflow of $32.8 billion in 1996 to an outflow of $89.7 billion in 1998. What caused the turnaround? Clearly the outflow reflected a reaction to a perceived weakness in the nature of the foreign debt. Can we identify some features which may be used as indicators of financial stress?

Consider, first, an assessment of financial vulnerability from a perspective on the composition of debt. The Fund considers countries with high levels of short-term debt, variable interest rate debt, and foreign currency denominated debt as being particularly vulnerable to internal and external shocks and thus as susceptible to financial crises.[6] Was the

Table 8.3. Net private capital flows to Asia.

$billion	1990	1991	1992	1993	1994	1995	1996	1997	1998
Total investment	19.6	34.1	17.9	57.3	66.4	95.1	100.5	3.2	−55.1
Net foreign direct	9.3	14.4	14.8	33.0	45.3	49.8	55.1	62.6	50.0
Net portfolio; Bond and equity	−2.7	1.4	7.8	21.0	9.4	10.9	12.6	0.9	−15.4
Bank loans, Investments	13.0	18.4	−4.7	3.3	11.7	34.4	32.8	−60.3	−89.7

Source: International Monetary Fund, International Capital Markets (1999), Table 3.1

[5] Both domestic and foreign investors held domestic debt. Since part of the domestic debt was sometimes denominated in foreign currency or linked to the exchange rate, the distinction between domestic and foreign debt becomes blurred (see Berg and Pattillo 1999).
[6] See IMF, WEO (1998a: p. 85).

Fund's view correct? Arteta (2005) investigated two questions. First, does high dollarization of deposits and credits increase the likelihood of banking crises and currency crashes and second does the dollarization make these crises and crashes more costly? He used a comprehensive data set on deposit and credit dollarization for a large number of developing and transition economies and based on extensive econometric estimation finds little evidence of any particular link between high bank dollarization and the likelihood of banking crises or currency crashes.

Next consider a macroeconomic aggregate approach based on a widely used measure of "solvency" or "sustainability" to assess the excessiveness of foreign debt.[7] The measure of *solvency* is the net resource transfer (that is the trade surplus) that an indebted country must have to keep the ratio of external liabilities to GDP a constant. The argument is that the greater is the long-term resource transfer, the greater is the probability of a debt crisis. More specifically, the "sustainability" argument asks what will be the value of the steady state debt/GDP (in this chapter denoted as h^*) if current policy as measured by the current account deficit/GDP were to continue at the current growth rate? *The standard argument is that the greater is the equilibrium value of the debt h^* based upon current policy, the greater is the probability of a crisis.*

To empirically apply this concept, the standard approach is to calculate h^* as the ratio of current account deficit/GDP divided by the growth rate of GDP. This is because in the steady state, when the ratio of debt/GDP has stabilized, the ratio of the current account deficit to the debt is equal to the growth rate. Hence h^* is as defined below. Table 8.4 presents the average value of h^* over two sample periods, the pre-crisis period 1986–96

Table 8.4. Measure of "sustainability".

Country	$h^* = $(Current account deficit/GDP)/growth rate	
	1975–85	1986–96
Hong Kong	−0.37	−0.89
Indonesia	0.35	0.38
Korea	0.49	−0.10
Malaysia	0.51	0.33
Philippines	1.76	0.68
Singapore	1.0	−1.13
Taiwan	−0.52	−1.01
Thailand	0.83	0.54

Source: Positive values of h^* are debtor positions.

[7] See IMF, WEO, (1998a: 86–7; 2003, Chapter III).

and the corresponding 1975–85 tranquil period, for the Asian countries that experienced crises.

As shown in Table 8.4, for Indonesia, there was no significant change in the "sustainable debt" measure; for Korea, the pre-crisis policies would have led to a creditor rather than to a debtor situation. Similarly, Malaysia, Philippines, and Thailand would have become less of a debtor. In other words, the current account deficit/GDP ratios in the pre-crisis period were the same or less than what they were a decade earlier for the ASEAN4 and Korea. In other words, these measures of sustainability would have failed to signal problems ahead for the Asian countries affected by the crisis.

The failure of the above "sustainability" approach arises because, as explained in Stein and Paladino (2001), the growth rate is simply related to the current account without taking into account the purpose of the foreign borrowings. If the current account deficit finances productive investment, then present current account deficits will generate future growth. The latter can make the economy more competitive and increase future trade balances. Moreover, another point to note here is that the actual debt to GDP ratio by itself is also *not* a relevant variable in predicting a debt crisis. For example, the ratio of debt service payments/exports for the Asian countries did not rise in the years before the crisis, as seen in Table 8.5.

8.2.3 *Summary of market anticipations.*

The International Monetary Fund, *International Capital Markets* (1999, Chapter V and Annex V) contains a comprehensive analysis of market anticipations prior to the Asian crises. We draw upon and paraphrase the analysis contained there to evaluate the "early warning signals" used.

Global securities markets became important sources of funding for many emerging market countries in the period of the 1990s. The portfolio preferences of the major institutional investors became key determinants and conditions of capital flows. Credit rating agencies had great influence upon the effective cost of capital charged by international lenders to the borrowers in the emerging market countries. In many cases, intuitional

Table 8.5. Debt service/export ratios (%).

	1989	1990	1991	1992	1993	1994	1995	1996
Asian countries	20.9	17.7	17.3	18.1	17.8	16.0	15.7	16.1
Developing countries	24.5	21.3	22.7	23.8	23.8	23.1	22.0	23.1

Source: International Monetary Fund (1997), Table B7.

investors are constrained to hold securities that have been classified by rating agencies as investment grade. Therefore, the cost of capital is effectively reflected in the ratings of the agencies and/or the bond spread. These two variables should reflect the market anticipation of crises, whereby the debtor may experience difficulties in servicing the debt.

Although the rating agencies stress that they do not use a specific formula to derive their ratings, empirical researchers explained the ratings as a weighted average of key indicators. Warning signals used by the international market are reflected by low credit ratings. The statistically significant variables to explain a high rating were: high per capita income, more rapid growth, low inflation, low ratio of foreign currency debt/exports, absence of a history of defaults, and high level of development. The recent history of budget surplus/GDP and current account surplus/GDP were not statistically significant.

The conclusion drawn by the International Monetary Fund study is that:

Spreads as well as market analysts – as represented in Institutional Investor and Euromoney ratings – provided signals similar to those of the credit rating agencies. They failed to signal the Asian crises in advance[8]; they down-graded these countries after their crises. (p. 195).

In summary, with hindsight it is clear that neither the market nor the credit rating agencies anticipated the Asian crises. It is also clear that there is an inadequacy in the standard theories to provide warning signals that identify weaknesses early enough to guide policy makers in either the prevention of crises or in making a rational response to them.

The object of our chapter is to provide a coherent theory, which implies quantitatively measurable warning signals of a crisis based upon available information. We draw upon the theoretical analyses in Chapters 2–4 to provide an operational theory to answer the questions:

(a) *Was a currency crisis produced by an overvalued real exchange rate?*
(b) *Was a debt crisis produced by an "excessive/unsustainable" external debt?*
(c) *What was the interaction between the two?*

---

[8] For example, "In Korea, despite the growing awareness of financial sector vulnerabilities following the collapse of Hanbo Steel in January 1997, there were no actions by the rating agencies until Moody's placed it on negative outlook in June 1997. The downgrade on October 24 by S&P's (from AA − to A +) was accompanied by a sharp rise in yield spreads." In Thailand, "S&P made no rating changes in the period between 1994 and July 1997. No further rating changes occurred during the severe speculative attacks on the baht in May and the subsequent floating of the baht in July 1997. Interest rate spreads began to rise in the third week of August prior to the downgrade of Thailand's rating by S&P's (to A − on September 3)" (p. 187).

The phrases in italic must be given theoretical and operational content. We use the NATREX model of equilibrium real exchange rates to evaluate whether the exchange rate is misaligned-that is whether the actual exchange rate deviates significantly from its "equilibrium" value thereby precipitating a currency crisis. We use a stochastic optimal control/ dynamic programming (SOC/DP) approach to derive the optimal foreign debt ratio and we then evaluate the divergence of actual debt from optimal to see whether the economy is vulnerable to a debt crisis. Both NATREX and SOC/DP have proved to have explanatory power. The aim of this chapter is to apply these techniques and concepts to explain the Asian crises, and thereby provide early *warning signals* of a crisis.

8.3. Currency and debt crises: An overview

8.3.1. *Currency crisis*

A currency crisis is generated by an overvalued exchange rate. In order to determine whether a rate is overvalued, we need a definition of an "equilibrium" real exchange rate. We use the concept of the natural real exchange rate (NATREX)[9], which is the rate that satisfies the four conditions (C1)–(C4) below.

(C1) Internal balance prevails where the rate of capacity utilization is equal to its long-run stationary mean.

(C2) External balance exists where there are no speculative capital movements or changes in reserves, and domestic and foreign long-term real rates of interest are equal[10].

(C3) The ratio of net foreign liabilities/GDP is constant.

(C4) As a result of market forces, the actual exchange rate converges to a distribution whose conditional mean is the "equilibrium" rate.

The NATREX theory can be presented graphically. In Figure 8.1, the current account CA is negatively related to the real exchange rate R. An appreciation of the currency – rise in R – raises domestic production costs and prices relative to foreign production costs and prices. Competitiveness is reduced and the trade balance declines. The saving less investment curve SI is positively related to the real exchange rate, because an

---

[9] This is a brief review and summary of Chapter 4.
[10] Speculative capital flows are based upon anticipations of exchange rate changes. Uncovered interest rate parity implies that when interest rates are equal, the anticipation of exchange rate changes is zero.

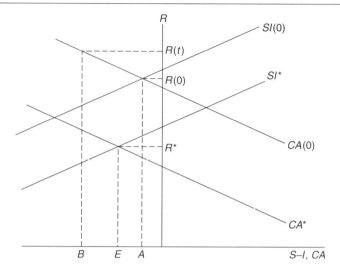

Figure 8.1. The medium-run and long-run real exchange rate NATREX.

appreciation of the real exchange rate adversely affects investment. Insofar as goods are sold in the world market, an appreciation of the real exchange rate lowers the Tobin q-ratio, which lowers investment. Hence an appreciation of the real exchange rate increases saving less investment. The intersection of the CA and SI lines gives the determination of the real exchange rate R_0 when conditions (C1) and (C2) are satisfied. We call this the medium-run NATREX and it is described algebraically in equation (8.1.)

$$R_0 = [R|I - S + CA = 0] \qquad (8.1)$$

In this case, net saving is negative (the current account deficit is A in Figure 8.1) and hence the foreign debt is rising. The latter increases interest payments and shifts the current account curve CA *steadily* to the left along the SI curve SI(0). If the saving less investment function SI does not increase – shift to the right – then the situation is unstable. The real exchange rate would depreciate steadily, the current account deficit would rise steadily, and the debt would explode. Stability can only be achieved if the rise in the foreign debt stimulates saving, and shifts the *SI* curve to the right. For example, the government may react to a rising public debt by increasing the primary surplus.[11] As saving rises in response

---

[11] This occurs more strongly in the industrial countries than in the emerging market countries; see IMF (2003, p. 128) for observed relations between these two variables.

to the accumulation of the debt, the *SI* curve shifts to the right towards SI^*. However, the rise in interest payments on the debt shifts the current account curve to the left towards CA^*. In the long-run equilibrium, the real exchange rate converges to R^* in Figure 8.1, where the ratio of debt/GDP is constant. Condition (C3) implies that the *equilibrium* trade balance to GDP ratio (denoted B) divided by the *equilibrium* debt/GDP ratio (h^*) is equal to $(r - g^*)$ the real interest rate (return on financial assets) less the *equilibrium* growth rate g^*. This term must be positive if present values of assets are finite. The *long-run* NATREX satisfies conditions (C1)–(C4) and is described by equations (8.1) and (8.2):

$$B(R^*; Z) = (r - g^*)h^* \tag{8.2}$$

where R^* is the long-run NATREX, and h^* is the equilibrium debt to GDP ratio. The elements of the vector Z are the fundamental determinants underlying the $S - I$ and CA functions. They are productivity (v) and time preference (ρ) measured as the ratio of social consumption/GDP. In Figure 8.1, the current account/GDP is $E < 0$ and the debt to GDP has stabilized at h^*.

In the *short run*[12], the uncovered "interest rate" parity theory states that the real exchange rate R_t will exceed (be less than) its longer-run equilibrium value R^* if the domestic real rate of return on assets i_t exceeds (is less than) the corresponding foreign rate i^*_t.[13] This is denoted as R_t in Figure 8.1 and mathematically in equation (8.3). The coefficient α is a speed of response.

$$log(R_t) = log(R^*) + \alpha(i_t - i^*_t). \tag{8.3}$$

If there is a speculative bubble in asset prices, then the domestic anticipated return i_t rises relative to the foreign rate i^*_t. There is a speculative capital inflow, which appreciates the real exchange rate to R_t above R_0, the medium-run equilibrium value. We can think of this inflow as the bank loans and investments in Table 8.3 during the period 1993–6. The net effect is that the current account deficit rises to $B > A$, and the external debt rises at a faster rate.

The real exchange rate R_t is not sustainable for several reasons. First, it can only persist as long as there is a speculative capital inflow. The latter is generated by the differential in rate of return on assets. Insofar as the higher rate of return is generated solely by anticipated capital gains – where asset prices are rising without a corresponding rise in earnings

---

[12] This is not medium-run equilibrium, since it violates condition (C2) above.
[13] This rate of return could be on fixed income instruments, equity, or real property.

generated – debt service payments are increasing relative to earnings. The bubble must burst, sooner or later. Second, as long as there is a current account deficit (for example point B in Figure 8.1) due to speculative capital inflow, the debt/GDP and interest payments/GDP will rise. The rise in the debt service reduces the current account, and shifts the CA curve to the left along the initial saving less investment curve SI(0). The decline in the current account relative to saving less investment depreciates the real exchange rate.

A measure of misalignment ($\Phi_t = R_t \quad R_t^*$) is the deviation of actual real exchange (R_t) from the equilibrium value (R_t^*). A large value of Φ_t is clearly a warning signal of an impending currency crisis. Furthermore, since the equilibrium value (R_t^*) is related to the set of fundamental variables Z_t, we can also explain the cause of the misalignment. In Section 8.4, we examine how well this measure identifies periods of overvaluation, and hence how well this measure served as a warning signal of a currency crisis for the Asian countries.

8.3.2. Debt crisis

A currency crisis is likely to result when the actual real exchange rate exceeds the benchmark exchange rate – the NATREX – for a considerable period of time. Similarly, a debt crisis is likely to occur when actual external debt is excessive or "unsustainable". In order to assess whether the debt is "unsustainable" we need a concept of an optimal debt as our benchmark. Excess debt can then be measured as the deviation of the actual debt from the optimal debt. Our discussion of an optimal debt, and the effects of deviations from the optimal, draws upon the analysis of optimal debt in Chapter 3.

The country will have a debt crisis if the attempt to service the debt requires a drastic decline in consumption. To see this first consider equation (8.4) which describes the change in the debt dL_t, where L is the real external debt.

$$dL_t = (I_t - S_t)dt = (C_t + I_t + r_tL_t - Y_t)dt. \tag{8.4}$$

The debt increases because consumption C_t plus investment I_t plus the debt service r_tL_t exceeds Y_t the GDP. Alternatively, the change in the debt is $(I_t - S_t)dt$ investment less saving over the period. In the Latin American countries the external debt has risen due to high consumption and/or low social saving by the public plus the private sectors. In the Asian countries, the high investment has produced the external debt. For example, there were speculative bubbles in asset prices for land and/or equity that raise the anticipated returns. The differential investment less saving leads to a capital inflow and an increase in the external debt.

The external debt has to be serviced and that would clearly affect consumption. We can see this by writing consumption at some time after t, say at time $s = t + \Delta t$, equation (8.5):

$$C_s ds = (Y_s - r_s L_s - I_s) ds + dL_s. \tag{8.5}$$

Consumption is equal to the GNP, which is equal to the GDP less the debt service $(Y_s - r_s L_s)$, less investment I_t plus new borrowing dL_t.

Focus now on the behavior of the two stochastic variables – real GDP and real interest rate. If bad shocks reduce the GDP and raise real interest rates, and investment falls to a minimum level $I_s = I_{min}$ then consumption may have to be reduced, unless there is new borrowing to offset the decline.[14] *In the event that bad shocks occur, we may expect a debt crisis because it is more likely that the country would renegotiate its debt than reduce consumption.*

To formalize the discussion we model the two sources of uncertainty that affect consumption. The first source of uncertainty is the growth of GDP described in equation (8.6):

$$dY_t/Y_t = bI_t/Y_t dt + \sigma_y dw_y \tag{8.6}$$

Real growth dY_t/Y_t has two components: a deterministic component bI_t/Y_t, where b is the mean return on investment times I_t/Y_t the ratio of investment/GDP, and a stochastic component involving the variance of growth $\sigma_y^2 dt$. This stochastic part may be viewed as arising from variations in the terms of trade, the conditions of aggregate demand, and the composition and quality of the investments.

The second source of uncertainty concerns the real interest rate required to service the external debt L_t. The real interest rate in terms of consumer goods r_t has three components. The first is the real interest rate on US Treasury long-term debt. The second is the premium on dollar denominated debt charged to sovereign borrowers. The third is the anticipated exchange rate depreciation of the currency. Equation (8.7) is the equation for the real debt service, where the first term is deterministic and the

---

[14] In Korea, the investment/GDP ratio fell from 35% in 1997 to 21% in 1998. In Thailand the investment ratio fell from 41% in 1996 to 22% in 1998.

second term is stochastic. Each component varies and produces a variance of $(\sigma_r L_t)^2 dt$ on the real debt service.

$$r_t L_t = r L_t + \sigma_t L_t dw_r. \tag{8.7}$$

Each source of uncertainty is modeled as a Brownian motion. Each expectation, of dw_y and dw_r, is equal to zero, but the two disturbances are correlated. During the Asian crisis period, the growth of GDP and real interest rate were negatively correlated and that can be explained briefly as follows.

A decline in GDP may occur because of external shocks or internal shocks. External shocks may arise from declines in foreign demand. The latter may occur because of a decline in the terms of trade or there is a depreciation of the currencies of competitors selling in the world market. Internal shocks may occur because the anticipated return on investment turns out to be an illusion and the asset bubble collapses, $dw_y < 0$. Since firms borrow primarily from the banks to finance real investment and the banks in turn primarily finance their loans by borrowing US dollars in the international capital market, a domino effect is created in the event of a financial panic. When debtors are unable to repay their loans to the banks, the banks in turn are unable to repay their loans to international creditors. Financial panic leads to a short-term capital flight. The government may try to help out by using the dollar reserves, but that is only a stopgap measure. Sooner or later the monetary authorities will raise interest rates and, when that fails to stem the outflow, the currency will suffer a devaluation/depreciation. The depreciation of the currency implies that the real rate of interest, measured in terms of the prices of goods produced, rises ($dw_r > 0$). The situation is exacerbated when banks denominate their loans to the domestic firms in US dollars. Firms would find it very difficult to service debts denominated in foreign currency because they are faced with both a rising rate of interest and a depreciating currency.

Faced with these sources of uncertainty, how then should a country select its optimal debt and level of consumption to maximize the expectation of the discounted value of the utility of consumption over an infinite or finite horizon? The intertemporal nature of the process is seen in equations (8.4) and (8.5). A rise in the debt at one time will affect consumption at a later date. The standard approach in the economics literature is to maximize the expectation of the discounted value of the utility of consumption subject to an "intertemporal budget constraint" (IBC). The (IBC) requires that the expectation of the discounted value of consumption be equal to the expectation of the discounted value of GDP.

Given the uncertainty concerning the growth rate (equation 8.6) and real interest rate (equation 8.7), the future is unpredictable. *The IBC is unknowable and unenforceable.* How can anyone know if any country is, or is not, violating the constraint? *The IBC is a non-operational concept.* This profound deficiency of the IBC approach led us to use the dynamic programming (DP) approach developed in detail in Chapter 3. The controls are the debt and consumption. The optimal controls are functions of the state of the system, which are observable/measurable variables.

The solution for the optimal ratio of debt/net worth is equation (8.8). Only summary is presented here. Using stochastic optimal control/ dynamic programming we derive the optimal ratio f^* of debt/net worth.[15] The derived optimal debt in equation (8.8) is a benchmark measure of performance.

$$f^* = (b - r)/(1 - \gamma)\sigma^2 + f(0), \quad \sigma^2 = var \ (dY_t/Y_t - r_t) \qquad (8.8)$$

where b is the *mean* return to investment (in equation 8.6), r is the *mean* real interest rate (in equation 8.7), quantity $(1 - \gamma)$ is a measure of risk aversion, and σ^2 is the variance of the quantity $(dY_t/Y_t - r_t)$, the current growth rate less the current interest rate, so that it also contains a covariance term. Equation (8.8) is graphed in Figure 8.2 as line US.

The optimum ratio of debt/net worth, f^*, is positively related to the *mean* rate of return on investment less the *mean* real rate of interest $(b - r)$. The slope is the reciprocal of the product of risk aversion and risk. The intercept $f(0)$ is the optimal ratio of debt/net worth, when the expected net return $(b - r) = 0$. When the correlation coefficient between the growth rate and interest rate is less than σ_y/σ_r, the intercept is $f(0) < 0$. Any non-positive correlation implies $f(0) < 0$ as drawn in Figure 8.2. The country should be a debtor only when the net return $(b - r) > m > 0$, where m is the risk premium implied by equation (8.8).

The optimum debt ratio, our benchmark of performance, has several important characteristics. The proofs are in Chapter 3. It is the value where: (i) the expected present value of the utility of consumption is maximized; and (ii) the expected growth rate – of consumption, net

---

[15] Net worth is "capital" less debt. Capital is the Frank Knight concept, the discounted value of current income, Y_t/b, where Y_t is current GDP and b is the mean return on investment in equation (8.6). This is a measurable and logical concept. The ratio of $h_t = $ debt/GDP is positively related to the ratio of $f_t = $ debt/net worth. Therefore, we can speak about either ratio f or h interchangeably. The optimum ratio of consumption/net worth is constant, $c^* = C_t/X_t$. Therefore consumption, net worth, and GDP grow at the same rate.

worth, and GDP – is maximized for any arbitrary ratio of consumption/net worth.[16] The major implications of the analysis are as follows.

- As the debt ratio rises above the optimum f^*, the expected growth rate declines, and the risk, the variance of the growth rate, increases.
- For any ratio of consumption/net worth, as the debt ratio rises above the optimum, the expected growth of consumption declines and its variance rises.
- When the net return $(b - r)$ is falling and the debt/GDP ratio is rising, it is more probable that the debt ratio is in the region above the curve US. Hence divergent movements of the net return $(b - r)$ and the debt/GDP ratio can serve as an operational warning signal that foreign debt is becoming "excessive" and that the economy is becoming susceptible to default.

Figure 8.3 describes these conclusions, and provides a theoretically based concept and an empirical measure of vulnerability to shocks. Given an arbitrary ratio of consumption/net worth, the probability distribution of the growth rate of consumption depends upon the selected ratio of debt/net worth. When the ratio is optimal $f=f^*$, as described by curve US in Figure 8.2 or equation (8.8), the expected growth rate is g^* with a given variance. If the debt ratio f is above the curve US in Figure 8.2, then the expected growth rate declines to $g_1 < g$, and the variance rises. *This means that the probability that bad shocks produce a negative growth rate rises. Since*

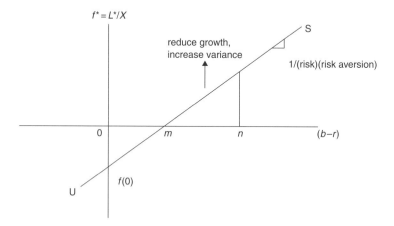

Figure 8.2. Optimal ratio debt/net worth f/curve, US.

[16] This is true in the case of the logarithmic utility function.

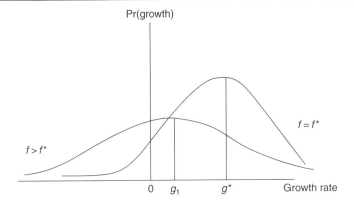

Figure 8.3. Probability distribution of the growth rate of consumption, for a given consumption/net worth ratio. A rise in the debt ratio above the optimal ratio f^* shifts the distribution to the left with a lower expectation and larger variance. Thereby the probability of a decline in consumption resulting from shocks increases.

consumption is proportional to net worth, a debt ratio in excess of the optimal ratio f^* makes the economy more vulnerable to shocks.

In Section 8.4, we examine the time-paths of actual debt/GDP ratios relative to the time-paths of their $(b - r)$ values to explain the pattern of debt defaults during the period of the Asian financial crisis.

8.4. Empirical analysis

Section 8.4.1 discusses whether the Asian currencies were overvalued, and Section 8.4.2 discusses whether they had excessive debt. Table 8.6 below summarizes the results. In the conclusion, Section 8.5, we explain the interaction of these two sources of crisis. The reader may want to look at this table while reading these two parts.

8.4.1 *Were the Asian currencies overvalued?*

In this section, we examine the proposition that the nominal exchange rate depreciated in 1997, because the real exchange rate (R_t) was overvalued relative to the equilibrium rate suggested by NATREX. The real exchange rate R_t is defined as $R_t = N_t(P_t/P_t^*)$ where the nominal rate N is defined as the number of $US per domestic currency (a rise is an appreciation), and P (P^*) is the domestic (foreign) price index. The currencies of Thailand, Malaysia, Philippines, and Indonesia were linked to the US dollar, which appreciated from 1995 to 1998 relative to both the Japanese yen and to a trade weighted index. Misalignment would occur if the actual real exchange rate deviated significantly from the NATREX suggested rate.

Following the discussion above, we estimate the deviation of the actual rate from the NATREX equilibrium rate as our measure of the degree of over- and undervaluation, i.e., "misalignment". To compute our empirical measure of misalignment, first recognize that the misalignment $\Phi_t = R_t - R_t^*$ can be rewritten as $\Phi_t = (R_t - R_{t-1}) - (R_t^* - R_{t-1})$. The first term is the actual change in the exchange rate. The second term can be written as: $(R_t^* - R_{t-1}) = (R_t^* - R_{t-1}^*) + (R_{t-1}^* - R_{t-1})$. Term $(R_t^* - R_{t-1}^*) = \alpha\Delta Z_t$ is the change in the NATREX based upon changes in the fundamentals in vector Z, and the term $(R_{t-1}^* - R_{t-1}) = \varepsilon_1$. Thus $(R_t^* - R_{t-1}) = \alpha\Delta Z_t + \varepsilon_t$. Then use *recursive least squares* to estimate the coefficient α in the regression equation $\Delta R_t = \alpha_t\Delta Z_t + \varepsilon_t$. Finally compute misalignment $\Phi_t = R_t - R_t^*$ as:

$$\Phi_t = \Delta R_t - \hat{\alpha}_{t-1}\Delta Z_t. \tag{8.9}$$

Vector Z contains three fundamental variables that were explained in Chapter 4:[17] productivity (υ), time-preference (ρ) measured as the ratio consumption/GDP, which is negative thrift, and the differential of long-term real net return ($b - r$). *The b is the domestic real return and r reflects the cost of capital.* Our method of estimation avoids the problems associated with non-stationary time-series data and, more importantly, the coefficients contained in the vector $\hat{\alpha}_{t-1}$ are estimated by recursive least squares and hence are based only on information up to time t. *Post-crisis information is not used before the event to predict the event.* As presented above, Φ_t may be interpreted as the deviation of the actual change in the real exchange rates from the change that should prevail at time t, given changes in the explanatory variables, ΔZ_t, suggested by NATREX.[18] Note, however, that Φ_t is an estimate of the difference between the level of actual R_t and the NATREX estimated R_t^*.

Productivity (υ) is measured as real GDP per capita and time preference (ρ) is the ratio of household and government consumption expenditure per GDP. The real return to investment expenditure (b) is computed as (growth rate of GDP)/(investment/GDP). The long-term real return r is the 10-year US bond rate less US inflation[19]. These variables are all readily

---

[17] We also tested a terms of trade variable, but this was not always significant.

[18] Note that this approach avoids a problem associated with estimation over the whole sample period and then defining the residuals of a regression model as a measure of misalignment. Here post-crisis information is not used before the event to predict the event.

[19] The real interest rate should take into account the anticipated depreciation of the currency. Since the exchange rates were linked to the $US, the market did not take the likelihood of depreciation into account.

available from the IMF, International Financial Statistics. Charts 1–5 present our analysis for the ASEAN4 countries (Indonesia, Malaysia, Philippines, Thailand) plus Korea. The *pre-crisis period 1994–6 is shaded*.

Each chart shows a plot of the deviations of the level of the actual rate from the NATREX rate expressed in standardized units, that is in the form

Chart 1: INDONESIA

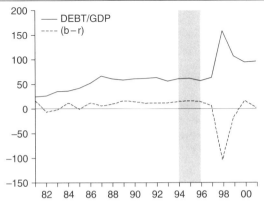

Warning signal variables: Pre, during and post crisis (Indonesia)

	$\Delta\nu$ (%)	$\Delta\rho$ (%)	$(b-r)$ %
1994	5.72	0.39	13.68
1995	6.39	2.35	14.96
1996	6.06	0.74	14.21
1997	3.16	−2.04	5.67
1998	−15.47	6.99	−104.57
1999	−0.58	9.19	−18.06
2000	3.44	−7.42	15.69
2001	1.95	−0.44	2.07

Chart 2: KOREA

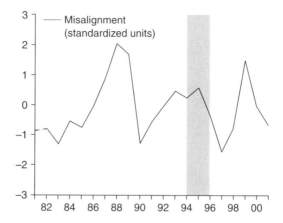

Warning signal variables: Pre, during and post crisis (Korea)

	$\Delta\nu$ (%)	$\Delta\rho$ (%)	$(b-r)$ %
1994	6.94	0.93	11.50
1995	7.61	−0.34	15.13
1996	5.65	2.50	9.34
1997	4.06	0.52	5.58
1998	−7.70	−1.06	−34.24
1999	9.60	1.39	32.91
2000	8.22	1.22	26.47
2001	2.40	3.14	5.12

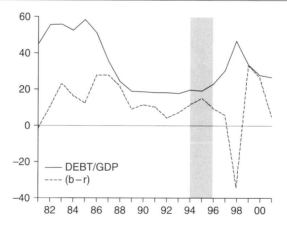

Chart 3: MALAYSIA

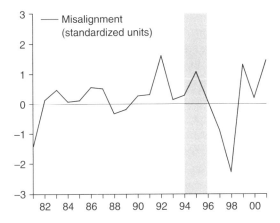

Warning signal variables: Pre, during and post crisis (Malaysia)

	$\Delta\nu$ (%)	$\Delta\rho$ (%)	$(b-r)$ %
1994	6.17	−0.84	13.73
1995	6.77	−0.18	14.30
1996	6.96	−5.38	15.45
1997	4.53	−1.81	9.72
1998	−10.11	−8.91	−37.35
1999	3.59	2.38	21.03
2000	5.76	0.52	27.02
2001	−1.66	8.72	−1.84

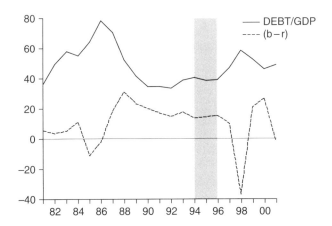

Chart 4: PHILIPPINES

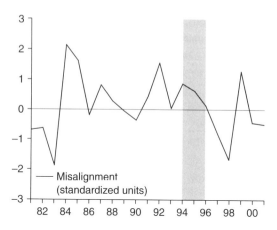

Warning signal variables: Pre, during and post crisis (Philippines)

	$\Delta\nu$ (%)	$\Delta\rho$ (%)	$(b-r)$ %
1994	2.07	−1.27	5.63
1995	2.39	0.37	9.08
1996	3.55	−0.07	12.06
1997	2.97	0.45	10.97
1998	−2.61	2.08	−15.73
1999	1.36	−2.20	7.53
2000	1.99	−3.55	11.58
2001	1.46	−0.94	8.89

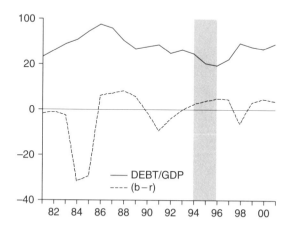

Chart 5: THAILAND

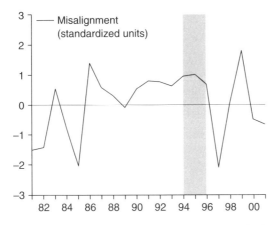

Warning signal variables: Pre, during and post crisis (Thailand)

	$\Delta\nu$ (%)	$\Delta\rho$ (%)	$(b-r)$ %
1994	7.42	−1.44	12.11
1995	7.69	−1.05	12.06
1996	4.64	1.41	4.77
1997	−0.02	1.20	−13.59
1998	−0.12	0.73	−61.10
1999	0.03	3.39	17.03
2000	0.03	−0.19	16.39
2001	0.01	1.63	3.87

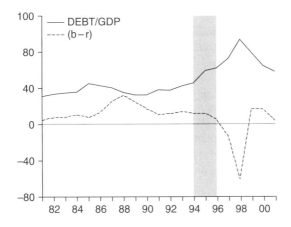

$[\Phi_t - mean(\Phi_t)]/std(\Phi_t)$, as well as information about the explanatory variables , Δv, $\Delta \rho$, and $(b - r)$ pre-, during, and post crisis. Recall that the NATREX is a positive concept – the real exchange rate satisfying conditions (C1)–(C4) in Section 8.3.1 above – and not a normative concept such as Williamson's FEER.

The crisis started in *Thailand*, whose currency was linked to the $US which was appreciating relative to the yen and other major currencies. As shown in the charts, Thailand is the country with the prolonged pre-crisis period of misalignment from about 1990 to 1995/96. The decline in productivity, increase in the propensity to consume, plus decline in relative return, all signaled that a depreciation of the nominal exchange rate (given sticky prices) was necessary to realign the real exchange rate. The deviation Φ_t is a warning signal of exchange rate misalignment.[20]

The signals for Korea were the same as for Thailand, but in this case the exchange rate was not seriously misaligned. A crucial variable that is common to both the misalignment and excess debt is the net rate of return on investment. In both Thailand and Korea, the risk adjusted net return $(b - r)/\sigma$ declined drastically from 1995 to 1997. This means that the medium-run equilibrium exchange rate should be falling from R_t towards R^* in Figure 8.1. Thereby we have warning signals of exchange rate misalignment for Thailand and Korea.

In contrast, over the period 1981–96 the Indonesia rupiah was aligned with the NATREX rate and there were no signals, based upon trends of productivity, time-preference, or returns, that the currency was misaligned. Malaysia and the Philippines show no prolonged periods of misalignment. In fact the pre-crisis signals, such as a decrease in the propensity to consume, supported the appreciation then underway.

8.4.2 Were the Asian foreign debts unsustainable?

Following the discussion in Section 8.3.2, our strategy is to compare the evolution of the actual debt/GDP ratios h with the evolution of the relative returns $(b - r)$ on investment in the Asian countries. If the relative return is declining significantly but the debt ratio is rising significantly or not declining, then the debt ratio is moving into the region above the line

---

[20] Rajan et al. (2002) conducted an *ex-post study* of the baht's misalignment with respect to the Japanese yen since Thailand's main trading partner was Japan, which was also the major creditor. They concluded that it was relatively larger than that for the $US and that the misalignment with respect to the yen is consistent with a widening of the Thai trade deficits before the crisis.

US and the probability of default increases for the reason described in Figure 8.3. Growth is expected to decline and the variance/risk to rise. The economy is more vulnerable to shocks to the growth rate and real interest rate. *A sufficient condition for a crisis is a strong decline in the relative net return and a rise or at least not a decline in the debt ratio.*

We know, with hindsight, that the Asian countries that defaulted were Indonesia (1998), Korea (1998), and the Philippines (1984–96) and the countries that did not default were Malaysia and Thailand. We now explore whether our suggested warning signal variables h and $(b - r)$ for *Korea* would have indicated the likelihood of default whereas the signals for *Malaysia* would have indicated no financial vulnerability.

For each country, h_t is the actual debt/GDP ratio based on data published by the Economic Intelligence Unit. The debt is total external debt stock "comprising public and publicly guaranteed long term debt, private non-guaranteed debt, use of IMF credit and short term debt, end of period". The net return $(b - r)$ is as defined above. Again, these are publicly available data and subjected to no manipulations. The plots of and are shown in Charts 1–5. The *pre-crisis period 1994–6 is shaded.*

The return b_t varied significantly, but the interest rate spread and credit ratings were practically constant until the crises, as noted above. Therefore, any anticipated exchange rate depreciation was not reflected in the cost of capital. Variations in $(b_t - r_t)$ are almost exclusively due to variations in the return on investment b_t. We do not arbitrarily select a comparison period to estimate the mean returns, rather we use the information contained in the two time series. When they diverge in the manner described above, we anticipate a crisis. The data are annual, which irons out random fluctuations.

Korea and *Thailand* both gave warning signals that they were incurring excess debt. In both cases prior to the crisis, there was a clear upswing in the debt/GDP ratio and a clear downswing in relative returns. Industrial policy in *Korea* involving the government, the banks, and the "chaebols" aimed for rapid growth with little concern for the rate of return b on investment. The banks were used as the means to finance the growth. The banks were not concerned about the risk, because there was an implicit government guarantee. That is why the total external debt ratio rose, even though the net returns were declining. In *Thailand*, the net return declined from 12% pa in 1994 to 4.77% pa in 1996 (see Chart 5), but the external debt rose by 40% during that period. Rajan et al. (2002) show that half of the debt was short-term, 45%, was denominated in yen, and Japanese banks were the major creditors.

Warning signals for Korea and Thailand mean that the expected growth of consumption was low and its variance was high. The probability that a random event could lead to a debt crisis increases, where the economy could not service its debt without reducing consumption. Such random events were the bankruptcies of major Korean concerns in 1997 before the crisis, and the collapse of the bubble in the construction sector in Thailand that led to bank failures[21].

Whereas Korea and Thailand both showed warning signals of an excess debt, in Malaysia, Indonesia, and the Philippines there was no evidence that the debt ratio was "excessive" in the pre-crisis period 1994–6. However for the Philippines, there were clear warning signals of the debt crises period 1984–94.

8.5. Conclusions: Interactions of types of crisis

Much has been written, with hindsight, about the causes of the Asian financial crisis. The crises were unexpected by the market and many countries in the region experienced it at about the same time. The traditional warning signals in use then[22] were inadequate. To this end, we analyzed the Asian financial crisis from two related perspectives – whether the crisis was precipitated by a failure of the real exchange rate to be aligned with its fundamental determinants, and/or whether the crisis was precipitated by a divergence of the foreign debt from its optimal path. Our models produced a set of objective, theoretically based warning signals and our empirical analysis allowed us to assess whether there were signs of financial distress before the crisis.

Table 8.6 presents a summary of the warning signals, based upon Charts 1–5. In all of these countries during the crisis, the exchange rate depreciated and the GDP declined significantly, as shown in Table 8.1. *Our warning signals and measures of misalignment are based upon available information before the crisis.* In our analysis, neither *the level of the real exchange rate nor of the debt/GDP is relevant.* The relevant variables are: (a) the *misalignment* $\Phi(t)$ of the real exchange rate from the NATREX in Figure 8.1, and (b) the *deviation* $\Psi(t)$ of the debt ratio from its optimal level if the debt ratio has risen above curve US in Figure 8.2.

[21] See Flouzat (1999), Chapter 2, and Rajan et al. (2002) for stimulating discussions of the developments in the Asian countries.
[22] These signals were the budget deficit, inflation, and current account deficit. Table 8.2 shows that they were inadequate.

Table 8.6. Summary of warning signals analysis for 1997–8 crises

Country	Actual changes	analysis of misalignments pre- crisis $\Phi_t > 0$	Warning signals of excessive debt during pre-crisis period $\Psi_t > 0$
Indonesia	Rupiah depreciated and debt **defaulted 1998**	No evidence of significant misalignment	No warning signals
Korea	Won depreciated, debt **defaulted 1998**	No evidence of significant Misalignment won depreciated dele. Defaulted 1998	**Warning Signals** Evidence of growing debt/GDP ratio despite falling excess returns
Malaysia	Ringgit depreciated but there was no debt default	Evidence of misalignment, but not prolonged	No Warning Signals
Philippines	Peso depreciated debt **defaulted 1984, 1986, 1987, 1990, 1991, 1992, 1994**	Evidence of misalignment, but not prolonged	No Warning Signals (Warning signals for 1984 default)
Thailand	Baht depreciated but there was no debt default	Evidence of **prolonged, persistent misalignment**	**Warning Signals** Growing debt/GDP ratio despite falling net returns

Equation (8.10) is a simple framework to understand how the two types of crises are interrelated. Consumption is equation (8.5) above. The real rate of interest r_t is equation (8.7a). Term r_{1t} is the foreign currency ($US) denominated interest rate and $(1/R_t)dR_t/dt$ is the real appreciation of the currency. A rise in the dollar denominated interest rate or a depreciation of the real exchange rate raises the real rate of interest r_t.

$$r_t = r_{1t} - (1/R_t)dR_t/dt. \tag{8.7a}$$

Substitute (8.7a) into (8.5) and derive (8.10) for consumption.

$$C_t dt = Y_t dt - (r_{1t} - (1/R_t)dR_t/dt)L_t dt - I_t dt + dL_t. \tag{8.10}$$

An overvalued exchange rate may lead to a debt crisis in the following way. In Figure 8.1, the exchange rate R_t is overvalued relative to the longer run NATREX R^*, because a speculative/unsustainable bubble led to a differential anticipated rate of return on assets. Capital inflows raise the debt. Initially the inflow is $0B$ per unit of time. When the anticipated return turns out to be an illusion, such as in Korea and Thailand, the capital inflows will not continue at the same level and the real exchange rate will fall drastically to a lower NATREX. If the nominal exchange rate is free, there will be exchange rate depreciation and the real interest rate – measured in terms of the GDP deflator – on the foreign debt will rise. If the nominal exchange rate is pegged, reserves will decline. The monetary authorities may raise interest rates. Eventually, the currency will be depreciated. In either case, real interest rates rise.

Once the exchange rate collapses, there are several reasons why defaults may occur. First the collapse of the exchange rate raises the cost of servicing the foreign debt, which leads to bankruptcies and financial market stringency. If the debt is sufficiently high, then term $(r_{1t} - (1/R_t)dR_t/dt)L_t dt$ in equation (8.10) will rise drastically and tend to reduce consumption C_t. Second, when the exchange rate depreciates, there may also be a capital outflow, the term dL_t falls, and aggravates the decline in consumption. Third the financial stringency may throw the country into a recession. The GDP falls. Even though the level of the debt has been relatively stable, the decline in the GDP raises the debt/GDP ratio. These three factors reduce $[Y_t dt + (1/R_t)dR_t/dt)L_t \, dt + dL_t]$. Hence, the attempt to service the debt would reduce consumption below a tolerable level and the country will default. In this way, an overvalued exchange rate may lead to a debt crisis. If the value of $r_s L_s$ is not too high, then misalignment $\Phi(t)$ will only generate a currency crisis.

A *debt crisis* occurs with positive probability when the debt ratio has risen above the *US* curve. A rise in the debt ratio occurs if there have been sustained capital inflows, current account deficits. If the debt ratio rises along curve US because of rises in $(b - r)$, the rise in the debt ratio is optimal. Therefore current account deficits or rises in the debt *per se* do not imply that there will be a crisis. Table 8.5 shows that the debt service/exports did not rise in the Asian countries before the crisis. However, there cannot be a debt crisis without a prior rise in the debt. It is not revealing to state that current account deficits lead to a debt crisis.

However, if the debt ratio tends to rise above curve *US* in Figure 8.2, then the situation is unstable. A random event which leads to a significant decline in $(Y_t - r_t L_t)dt$ can lead to a decline in C_t, as seen in Figure 8.3, which can generate a debt crisis. Once the country is unable to service the debt, then there will be a capital outflow, particularly short-term capital. See net private capital flows: bank loans and investments 1995–8 in Table 8.3. As a result of these outflows, the exchange rate collapses. In this way a debt crisis leads to a currency crisis.

Our analysis focuses upon two countries: Thailand and Korea. Table 8.6 suggests that *Thailand* was primed for a collapse of the currency. Its exchange rate was severely misaligned and its foreign debt was suboptimal. The warning signs for *Korea* were the same as for *Thailand* – consumption was increasing at a time of falling productivity and relative returns. The Korean exchange rate was not severely misaligned, but there were clear warning signals, $\Psi_t > 0$, and the financial crisis took the form of a debt crisis.

Our analysis did not find objective warning signals of the 1997–8 crises for *Indonesia*, *Malaysia*, and *Philippines*. There were no declines in productivity or in the differential returns prior to the crisis. The situation for Indonesia, Malaysia, and the Philippines may be symptomatic of a "contagious effect". When the crises occurred in Thailand and Korea, because the situations were not sustainable in terms of our objective criteria, the Japanese commercial banks – which were the common lender – raised risk premia for loans to the other countries in the region. The Japanese banks tried to reduce their risk exposure to the other borrowers. Short-term capital flowed out of the other Asian countries and their exchange rates depreciated.

The "contagion" argument is a description rather than a precise analytical concept[23]. Rajan and Siregar (2002) compared the experiences of Hong Kong with those of Singapore. They are similar economies, subject to similar shocks. The main difference between them is the flexibility of the exchange rate to real shocks – our fundamentals discussed in Section 8.4. The Hong Kong currency was linked to the $US via a currency board. The Singapore currency was much more flexible. Rajan and Siregar estimated the NATREX for each economy and then examined **ex-post**, the degree of misalignment. They found that, in the period leading up to the crisis, the Hong Kong currency was misaligned, whereas the Singapore dollar was not. When the Asian crises occurred, the Hong Kong growth rate fell severely from 5.15% pa in 1997 to – 5% p.a. in 1998. In Singapore the growth rate declined from 8.8% to 0.5%, a significantly better performance than in Hong Kong. A message here seems to be that "contagion" can be mitigated by avoiding exchange rate misalignment and by adopting a more flexible exchange rate system.

References

Arteta, Carlos (2005) Exchange Rate Regimes and financial Dollarzation in Topics in Macroeconomics, volume 5, no. 1, article 10.

Berg, Andrew and Catherine Pattillo (1999) Are Currency Crises Predictable? International Monetary Fund, Staff Chapters, June.

Dean, James (2001) East Asia Through a Glass Darkly, in Geoffrey Harcourt et al (ed), Essays in Honour of Mark Perlman, Routledge.

---

[23] There is a large literature on "contagion"; see Kaminsky et al. (2003).

Flouzat, Denise (1999) La nouvelle emergence de l'Asie, l'évolution économique des pays asiatiques depuis la crise de 1997, Presses Universitaires de France.

International Monetary Fund, World Economic Outlook (WEO), Crisis in Asia, December 1997.

International Monetary Fund (1998a), World Economic Outlook (WEO), Financial Crises, May 1998, Washington DC.

International Monetary Fund (1998b), World Economic Outlook (WEO), Financial Turbulence in the World Economy, October 1998, Washington DC.

International Monetary Fund (1999). International Capital Markets, September 1999, Washington DC.

International Monetary Fund, World Economic Outlook (WEO), Public Debt in Emerging Markets, September 2003, Washington DC.

Kaminsky, Graciela, Carmen M. Reinhart and Carlos A. Vegh (2003), The Unholy Trinity of Financial Contagion, Journal of Economic Perspectives, 17(4), 51–74.

Rajan, Ramkishen and Reza Siregar (2002) Choice of Exchange Rate Regime: Currency Board (Hong Kong) or Monitoring Band (Singapore), Australian Economic Chapters, 41(4), December.

Rajan, Ramkishen and Reza Siregar, (2002) Misalignment of the Baht, Trade Imbalances and the Crisis in Thailand, University of Adelaide, Australia, Working Paper.

Stein, Jerome L. and Giovanna Paladino (2001) Country Default Risk: An Empirical Assessment Australian Economic Papers 40(4) December 417–36.

Stein, Jerome L. and Guay C. Lim (2004) Asian Crises: Theory, Evidence and Warning Signals, Singapore Economic Review 49(2), 329–41.

Williamson, John (2004) The Years of Emerging Market Crises, Journal of Economic Literature, XLII(3), 822–37.

9

United States current account deficits: A stochastic optimal control analysis[1]

For nearly a quarter of a century, the US has persistently run significant current account deficits. The cumulative consequence of these deficits is that the US has been transformed from the world's largest net creditor to its largest debtor. Table 9.1 describes the ratio of external assets to external liabilities of the United States, Europe, the industrial countries of Asia and Pacific, and emerging markets and other developing countries from 1980 to 2003. A debtor (creditor) country will have a ratio of external assets/ external liabilities less (greater) than unity.

Over the period, the US went from a creditor to a debtor where the ratio fell from 1.11 to 0.73. Europe's net external position did not change very much. It remained slightly a debtor. The big counterparts to the US were the industrial countries of Asia and Pacific, which is primarily Japan. These countries went from debtors with a ratio of 0.73 to creditors with a ratio of 1.17.

External assets include portfolio debt securities, portfolio equity securities, foreign direct investment (FDI), and bank loans, trade credits and currency deposits. Insofar as assets and liabilities are denominated in different currencies, their values will fluctuate with changes in the exchange rate. The equity investment and foreign direct investment are affected by fluctuations in stock prices as well as by the exchange rate. Since valuation effects are important in measuring these stocks of assets and liabilities, the annual changes in the measured values of external assets and liabilities are not necessarily closely tied to the flow, which is current account[2]. For example,

---

[1] I am deeply indebted to Peter Clark, Catherine Mann, and John Williamson for their cogent criticisms of an earlier draft.
[2] See International Monetary Fund (2005), Box 3.2, p. 120, "Measuring a country's net external position".

a stock market boom/bubble abroad will raise the value of equity and FDI. So the ratio of external assets/external liabilities can remain unchanged or even rise when the US has been running current account deficits.

A more relevant variable to evaluate the development of the net external position, that minimizes the volatile valuation effects, is to focus upon the current account which is a flow variable. Figure 9.1 plots in *normalized form* during the period 1977:1–2004:2 the ratio of the US current account/GDP, equal to net foreign investment/GDP (NETFIGDP), and the price adjusted dollar exchange rate *vis à vis* the major currencies (REATWD) – the real exchange rate of the United States dollar. A rise is an appreciation of the dollar. Although the decline of the current

Table 9.1. Ratio of external assets/external liabilities

	United States	Europe	Asia-Pacific industrial	Emerging markets
1980	1.11	0.93	0.73	0.22
1985	0.98	0.97	1.05	0.21
1990	0.86	0.95	1.03	0.28
1995	0.88	0.95	1.17	0.30
2000	0.81	0.98	1.23	0.41
2003	0.73	0.98	1.17	0.43

Source: Derived from data in International Monetary Fund (2005), Chapter III, Table 3.1, p. 112.

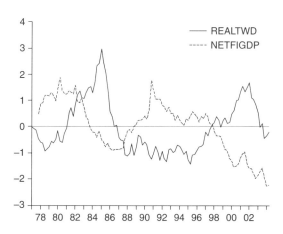

Figure 9.1. United States current account/GDP = net foreign investment/GDP = NETFIGDP, and the real value of the dollar against the major currencies = price adjusted major currencies dollar index = REALTWD. Normalized variable = (variable − mean)/ standard deviation. The mean NETFIGDP was − 1.8%, with a range of (1.1%, − 5.4%) and a standard deviation of 1.57%.

Source: Federal Reserve, Washington DC and Federal Reserve Bank of St. Louis, FRED data bank.

account/GDP has been very large – three standard deviations since the early 1990s – so far the real value of the US dollar does not appear to have suffered significant ill effects from these developments, despite widely expressed fears of a "hard landing" and other recurrent dire warnings of a catastrophe. Questions discussed in the literature are:

- What is a *sustainable* ratio of external debt?[3] What are the consequences of an "excessive" or "unsustainable" debt?
- How should sustainability be achieved? By how much does the dollar need to decline in order to achieve a *sustainable* current account position for the US and the rest of world?

In the first section, we survey and evaluate the literature. In the subsequent sections of this chapter, we apply our analyses of an external debt based upon stochastic optimal control/dynamic programming[4] (SOC/DP) to provide alternative estimates of an optimal debt ratio and optimal current account deficit and to explain the consequences of an "unsustainable" debt.

9.1. A survey and evaluation of the literature

In this section, we first survey the literature and then evaluate its ability to answer the questions in bullets. The existing literature focuses upon the crucial issues, but lacks a consistent theoretical framework. In the later sections of this chapter, we explain how our SOC/DP analysis of an optimum debt ratio contributes to answering the first set of questions in bullets. The SOC/DP approach provides a framework whereby one can derive the optimal debt ratio, based upon both objective variables and upon preferences. The deviation of the actual debt ratio from the derived optimum increases the vulnerability of the economy to external shocks. Alternatively, the contributions of the existing literature can be viewed within the framework of SOC/DP analysis based upon intertemporal optimization.

9.1.1. *A Survey*

The writings of Catherine Mann (1999), Michael Mussa (2004) and John Williamson (2004a, b) can be considered the state of the art on the subject

---

[3] We measure the variables, other than the exchange rate, growth rate and interest rate, as fractions of GDP.   [4] The SOC/DP analysis is developed in Chapter 3.

of the questions in bullets.[5] Michael Mussa, formerly Director of Research of the International Monetary Fund, considered the question: Are the US external deficit and the associated buildup of US net foreign liabilities really important problems that require urgent attention? He contrasts two positions. Richard Cooper is much less apprehensive than is Mussa. Cooper (2005) argues that the US economy accounts for over a quarter of the world economy in output, it provides higher real returns to capital than do Europe or Japan and returns that are more reliable than those offered by emerging markets. The growth of US liabilities is unlikely to pose a serious problem as long as strong growth in the US economy continues to imply rapid increases in total US wealth, and social (public plus private) saving continues to exceed investment in the creditor countries.

Mussa does not share Cooper's insouciance. Mussa's concern is based upon the well-known dynamic equation (9.1a) for the ratio of the external debt/GDP, denoted by $h_t = L_t/y_t$, where L_t is the external debt and y_t is the GDP. The trade balance/GDP is B, the interest rate is r, the growth rate of GDP is g, and $A_t = r_t h_t - B_t$ is the current account deficit/GDP. Asset revaluation effects are ignored, for the reasons discussed in the introduction.

The change in the debt ratio dh_t/dt is equal to A_t, the current account deficit/GDP less the product $g_t h_t$ of the growth rate g_t and the ratio of external debt/GDP. The current account deficit is equal to the net income payments abroad rh_t less the B_t ratio of the trade balance/GDP. If the current account deficit/GDP is constant at A, and the growth rate is constant at $g > 0$, debt ratio converges to h_e in equation (9.1b).

$$dh_t/dt = A_t - gh_t \qquad (9.1a)$$

$$h_e = A/g. \qquad (9.1b)$$

The scenarios are based upon equation (9.1b). If $A = 5\%$ and $g = 5\%$ per year then $h_e = 100\%$. If $A = 2\%$, $h_e = 40\%$. Mussa argues that there probably is a practical upper limit for US net external liabilities h_e at something less than 100% GDP, and consequently current account deficits of 5% or more are not indefinitely sustainable. For the US, which is particularly attractive to foreign investors, current account deficits up to 2% GDP or slightly more, and net foreign liability ratios as high as 40–50% of GDP, are probably sustainable without undue economic strain or risk of crisis.

He argues that bringing the A down from 5% to 2% requires a 30% depreciation in the real effective exchange rate. In addition there must be

---

[5] See Bergsten and Williamson (2004) for a survey of the many articles on the subject.

macroeconomic adjustments. In the US, domestic demand must grow more slowly than domestic output to make room for an expansion in US net exports. There must be a corresponding improvement in the US national saving/investment balance. For the US the most important policy adjustment necessary to contribute to a successful policy is a gradual and cumulatively substantial reduction in the government deficit.

No one claims that the debt ratio can rise indefinitely. Mussa cannot justify his quantitative estimates and his disagreement with Cooper, because he develops no theoretically valid objective measure of sustainability. As Cooper stresses there are good reasons why the US is a particularly attractive place for foreigners to invest significant fractions of their wealth. These attractions may be an important part of the explanation of why, with a net debtor position of 25% GDP, the US still is able to secure inward foreign investment.

As the net debtor position rises ever higher, will the US have to offer more attractive terms to continue to attract large additional inflows of foreign investment, and what will be their effects upon the US economy? Mussa states that no one knows, or can estimate with great confidence, the outer limits of US net foreign liabilities that would be tolerable both to US residents as net debtors to the rest of the world and to the rest of the world residents as holders of claims on assets located in the US. However, no country of significance has ever run up a net external liability position approaching 100% of GDP. While there is no absolute proof that there is an impenetrable upper bound on US external liabilities/GDP of 100%, it is prudent to conclude that this boundary should not be tested. He wrote that his guess is that for the US, a net external liability ratio 40% GDP and probably up to 50% is not a problem, but sustainability becomes highly questionable for ratios rising to 100% of GDP.

Fred Bergsten and John Williamson organized several conferences where the authors addressed the central issues concerning sustainability. There was unanimous agreement that further depreciation of the $US was needed to achieve a *sustainable* relationship among national currencies and current account positions. Authors disagreed on the magnitude of the further decline needed in the dollar. These differences mainly reflected the varying views on the sustainable level of the current account deficit, which ranged between 2 and 4% GDP. There are also significant differences concerning estimates of "equilibrium" exchange rates, the distribution of the further dollar depreciation among counterpart currencies, and how to promote the further needed adjustment among the key currencies.

Williamson asks how large a dollar decline is required for sustainability? The first step in deciding how much of a dollar decline is needed is to address the question: what does a decline need to achieve? The larger the improvement that is sought in the current account balance the larger is the needed decline in the dollar. Williamson asserts that a reasonable target would be to halve the current account deficit during the next three years. No rigorous justification for an objective of exactly this size is offered, but he argues that deficits of the present size result in an explosive growth in the ratio of foreign debt/GDP. Debt is the US net international investment position, which includes foreign direct investment and other equity type assets and liabilities.

Ellen Hughes-Cromwick, a discussant at the 2004 conference, asks how long a deficit of the present size might be sustainable, and what reason there is for thinking that deficits of this size are unsustainable. She states that it may not be possible to give a satisfactory answer to these questions. One cannot place any definite limit on the duration of deficits of the current size, but it does suggest that the higher the debt/GDP ratio climbs, the more likely is a forced, abrupt landing. The usual fear is that a forced end to the debt buildup caused by a refusal of the rest of the world to finance increases in US indebtedness would lead to a "disorderly" decline in the value of the dollar. The market would push up long-term interest rates, which would spill over to the rest of the world.

Catherine Mann's book, which represents the state of the art, contains a comprehensive and perceptive discussion of the issues. The mathematical analysis based upon SOC/DP provides theoretical and quantitative precision for her insights. She poses the problem as follows. Whenever a country's current account deficit grows large, questions arise as to how large it can get, how long it can persist, and what forces might either stabilize it or cause it to shrink. The history of financial crises in Latin America and Asia shows that too much external borrowing and/or accumulated international obligations can precipitate financial crises and subsequently economic disasters. But what is it that precipitates the crisis? Is it the size of the deficit or the accumulated obligations? Do their particular characteristics – such as maturity or currency or their use such as consumption or real estate ventures – contribute to the economic forces that precipitate a crisis?

To answer the question as to whether the US current account deficit and net international investment position are sustainable one must define "sustainable" from two related perspectives: that of the net borrower (US) and that of the net investor (rest of the world). Experiences of different debtor countries with large current account deficits and net international obligations can help uncover empirical evidence of what constitutes sustainability. But will these be applicable to the US, or do different rules apply to the US because of the international role of the US dollar? The US is different from the rest of the world because of the depth and breadth of its financial markets and because it both borrows and lends principally in its own currency.

First, Mann looks at the borrower's constraint. A negative net international investment position (NIIP) cannot increase without bounds, since ultimately net investment payments on the negative investment position would use all the resources of the economy, leaving nothing for domestic consumption. For the domestic economy, the importance of the stock of foreign claims is measured as NIIP/GDP. Two factors enter: the growth rate of the economy affects the denominator and the interest rate on debt obligations in the NIIP affects the numerator. She states that the higher the share of equity obligations (which have a contractual service requirement less strict than bank debt), the longer a country can run current account deficits, since the investment service likely is lower. In addition, the higher the share of obligations in the domestic currency, the less vulnerable the country is to exchange rate volatility. It follows that a country that borrows in its own currency, at low interest rates, and with a high share of equity can continue along a trajectory of spending and saving for longer than could a country that borrows in currencies other than its own, at high interest rates, and using fixed maturity debt.

Second, she considers the portfolio constraints of the investors. How much lenders are willing to lend to residents of a country is a function of the risk–return profile of the borrower's assets relative to other assets as well as the investor's attitude toward risk and desire to diversify investments. The growth of the investor's home economy, the size of the global portfolio, and the size of alternative investments are important determinants of how much of a country's assets the foreign investor wants. If the variability of the rate of return on a foreign investment increases – because of variability either in interest rates or exchange rates – investment in that foreign asset generally declines.

Mann states that at some point, investors will want to be repaid their principal, not just have their debt serviced. The present discounted value of the future years of trade surpluses must equal the outstanding net investment position. When investors realize that the NIIP position is now too large it means that the current account deficits of the debtor are now too large. When investors anticipate that this situation might occur sometime in the future, they will not lend at current terms. The borrower's interest rate rises as it tries to attract lenders, or its currency depreciates as existing lenders try to sell their investments, or capital inflows cease. Once these forces are in motion, the current account deficit and the NIIP become unsustainable.

It is important to know how high the debt ratio $h_t = (L_t/Y_t)$ of the US will go. Empirical researchers start with equation (9.2), which is equation (9.1) where the current account deficit A_t is equal to the transfer payments on the debt $r_t h_t$ less the trade balance B_t. The debt and trade balance are measured as fractions of GDP, and the transfer payments include interest and dividends.

$$dh_t/dt = (r_t - g_t)h_t - B_t. \tag{9.2}$$

From an initial debt ratio of $h(0)$, solve a discrete time version of equation (9.2) for the debt/GDP ratio at some later date $T > 0$, denoted $h_T = (L/Y)_T$. This is equation (9.3). The trade balance/GDP at time s is B_s and α is 1 plus the interest rate r less the growth rate g. It is generally assumed that α is constant.

The summation of the trade balances is from time $s = 0$ to $s = T - 1$.

$$h_T = h(0)\alpha^T - \Sigma\, B_s\alpha^{(T-s-1)}, \quad T - 1 > s > 0. \qquad \alpha = 1 + r - g. \tag{9.3}$$

The US has been running trade deficits/GDP for some time, $B_s < 0$. The trade balance is saving less investment equal to GDP less absorption. The apprehensions are that if the interest rate exceeds the growth rate, $\alpha > 1$, and trade deficits continue, the debt ratio will diverge. Then both the borrower's and the lender's constraints will be violated.

The literature concerning the sustainability of the US deficits and debt can be summarized as follows. The analytic framework is equations (9.1)–(9.3). Economists ask: what will be the path of the debt ratio? At some arbitrary date $T > 0$, will the debt be repaid, will the ratio h_T equal zero?

This question cannot be answered objectively, because no one can know the future course of trade balances, equal to saving less investment or GDP less absorption, interest rates and growth rates. There are too many imponderables, such as US government budget deficits and growth, developments in the euro area, China, and the rest of Asia.

Empirical researchers are forced to make recourse to simulation or alternative scenarios, based upon equation (9.3). The trade balance B_s at time s is assumed to depend upon a vector Z_s of variables such as the US and foreign GDP, the nominal exchange rate, and a relative price index. Thus $B_s = B(Z_s)$ is the hypothesized trade balance in equation (9.3).

Arbitrary projections are made for the exchange rate, income, and price variables. On the basis of these possible scenarios, alternative projections of the external debt ratio/equation (9.3) and current account deficit A_t in equation (9.1a) are obtained.

Mann writes that from a simulation of the "bad case", by 2010 the current account/GDP ratio is beyond any empirical trigger suggested by the experiences of industrial countries. The external debt/GDP ratio grows, although net investment payments amount to 2% of GDP. Will investors be willing to add the increase in net US liabilities into their portfolios? The difficulty is that "...it is impossible to know whether investors' preferences for US assets will coincide with increased availability of US assets[6]. All told, this calculation for the investor constraint alongside the borrower constraint supports the notion that the US current account is sustainable for at least two or three years, or even longer as judged by the investors' constraint" (page 162).

9.1.2. An evaluation of the literature

Mussa concludes that no one knows, or can estimate with great confidence, the outer limits of US net foreign liabilities that would be tolerable both to US residents as net debtors to the rest of the world and to the rest of the world residents as holders of claims on assets located in the US. Mann advances the discussion of sustainability by focusing upon the *constraints* of both debtor and creditor. A negative net international investment position (NIIP) – which is the debt ratio h_t – cannot increase without bounds, since ultimately net investment payments on the negative investment position would use all the resources of the economy, leaving nothing for domestic consumption.

Her analysis can be formalized in a way that will set the stage for intertemporal optimization below. Consumption during a period, of length dt is equation (9.4). It is equal to the gross domestic product Y_t, less investment I_t, less the income transfers on the debt $r_t L_t$, plus new borrowing, dL_t. The US is the debtor country so L_t is positive.

$$C_t \, dt = (Y_t - I_t - r_t L_t) \, dt + dL_t > C_{\min} > 0. \tag{9.4}$$

A constraint is that consumption – or its utility – must exceed a minimum tolerable level $C_{\min}$. This means that a negative IIP cannot be so high that,

---

[6] The partial equilibrium CAPM and ICAPM models of the equilibrium return are of no use in answering these questions.

in the event of bad shocks to GDP and the interest rate, consumption must fall to an intolerable level. This would be one aspect of sustainability.

Net external borrowing, dL_t, can add to the resources available for consumption, particularly when negative shocks occur to the GDP and interest rates. However, one must impose the "no free lunch" constraint. This is the same as the "no bankruptcy" constraint. This constraint is that net worth, X_t, equal to capital K_t less external debt L_t, must always be positive. For example, if a country continues to borrow resources to finance social consumption, the debt L_t rises without a greater growth in capital. The accumulation of interest decreases net worth steadily, which leads to bankruptcy. The "no bankruptcy" or "no free lunch" constraint, that net worth X_t is always positive, means that the country cannot continue to borrow to finance the growing interest payments. Moreover if it is clear that the country is heading towards bankruptcy, there will be a capital flight $dL_t < 0$. Then consumption will be driven down to an intolerable level.

Equations (9.2) and (9.3) have limited use in evaluating the existing debt and current account deficit because the future growth rates, interest rates, and trade balances are not predictable. For example, in equation (9.3), suppose that the recent trade balances have been negative $B_s < 0$, $s < T$, because productive investment has increased relative to social saving. The investment increases capital and future GDP, so from a later date T on, the greater productive capacity of the economy permits saving to exceed investment. This means that $B_v > 0$, $v > T$. *The emphasis must be upon the trajectories of consumption over a long horizon, not upon extrapolation of the existing trade balance, growth rate, and interest rate.*

The US has both foreign assets and liabilities to foreigners, as shown in Table 9.1. If the net liabilities are denominated in foreign currency, a depreciation of the exchange rate increases interest transfers and adversely affects consumption in equation (9.4). If the US liabilities are denominated in US dollars, it would seem at first glance that there is no reason to consider the exchange rate risk in calculating the optimal US external debt. This is not correct. There is an exchange risk to at least one of the countries. To calculate the optimal debt, or an upper bound on the debt that will make the economy vulnerable to shocks, one must explicitly consider the exchange rate risk.

If the liabilities are denominated in US dollars, the foreign country bears the exchange rate risk. The optimum creditor position – negative debt ratio – for the foreign country must take into account the exchange risk. The market rates of interest will adjust until the quantity of debt supplied by the debtor is equal to that desired by the creditor. This means that the portfolio preferences of the creditor must be taken into account. In this manner, exchange rate risk must be taken into account in deriving the optimal debt, no matter which country seems to bear the exchange rate risk. The evaluation of the literature can be summarized as follows.

- Very little is learned by extrapolating the existing current account deficit, interest rate, and growth rates, to arrive at a hypothetical steady state debt ratio. Future growth rates, interest rates, and endogenous trade balances are unpredictable.
- From equation (9.1b) or (9.3) there is no objective way to evaluate what debt ratio are or are not sources of concern.
- Instead, the emphasis must be upon trajectories of consumption in a stochastic environment.
- The exchange rate risk must be taken into account explicitly, because the portfolio preferences of the creditor will be an important factor in determining the interest rate at which the debtor can borrow in the latter's currency.

9.2. The rationale of stochastic optimal control (SOC) and dynamic programming (DP)

The rationale of stochastic optimal control and dynamic programming, which we use to derive the optimal and sustainable external debt and current account deficits, is motivated by the evaluation of the literature summarized in bullets above. An informal discussion precedes the more precise analysis below. On the basis of our analysis that leads to explicit equations, we use data from the Federal Reserve System to obtain quantitative estimates of the optimal ratios, under alternative assumptions. The vulnerability of the system to unpredictable external shocks is a continuous function of the difference between the derived optimal debt ratio and the actual debt ratio. The SOC/DP analysis is our answer to the first point in bullets in the introduction. At the end of the chapter, we draw upon the NATREX model to answer the second point in bullets in the introduction.

The stochastic optimal control/dynamic programming SOC/DP approach[7] *can be outlined.* There are several parts to the solution for the optimal debt and current account. The first is the *criterion or optimization function.* The

---

[7] The books by Øksendal (1995) and Fleming and Rishel (1975) are basic references for the stochastic optimal control analysis.

second is the *model and the stochastic processes* on the key variables. Third, a *stochastic differential equation* is derived from the economic model. The resulting *solution* for the optimal debt and current account will vary according to the criterion function and the stochastic process. In each solution, some variables will be measurable and objective and some others will be preference or subjective variables. We use available data to derive estimates of the optimal quantities and sustainability. Our contribution is to provide an operational method of analysis and to show the sensitivity of the results to alternative specifications. Thereby, the reader can determine to what extent the results are changed when one selects different parameter estimates or preference variables.

Several *optimization criteria* can be used to derive the optimal debt/net worth ratio f_t and then the implied current account deficit/GDP. The first criterion is that the debt ratio f_t and consumption ratio c_t are selected to maximize the expectation of the discounted value of the utility of consumption over an infinite horizon. The utility function, the implied measure of risk aversion, and the discount rate must be specified. By specifying a utility function that is either logarithmic or with a risk aversion greater than unity, low consumption is heavily penalized. These preference variables are arbitrary and subjective.

The second criterion does not involve preferences. Let the *ratio $c > 0$* of consumption/net worth be constant at an arbitrary level. There is a dynamic process on net worth, which is described by a stochastic differential equation. The optimization criterion is to select a debt ratio f_t that maximizes the expected instantaneous growth rate of consumption and net worth. Both expected return and risk are involved in this optimization. *No subjective variables such as risk aversion or discount rate are involved. Thereby objectively measurable values for optimal debt ratio and current account deficit/GDP are derived.*

Since the expected utility of consumption is the crucial variable, equation (9.4) indicates that the level of GDP and the interest rate will play very important roles in determining the optimal debt ratio at any time. The stochastic aspect of GDP arises because the productivity of capital has an important stochastic element. The interest rate also has a stochastic element for several reasons. First, the US interest rate is stochastic. Second, the exchange rate is also stochastic. So if the debt is denominated in foreign currency the US debtor bears an exchange rate risk. The effective interest rate includes the exchange rate depreciation. If the debt is denominated in dollars, the foreign creditor faces a real interest rate risk in terms of his domestic currency. This risk will be taken into account in his portfolio selection, the amount of US debt that is optimal for the foreign country to have. The market rate of interest at which the US can borrow must take into account the exchange rate risk.

There are two approaches that we can take. The first assumes that the debt is denominated in US dollars. We then derive the optimal debt for the US, which has no exchange rate risk, and the optimal debt for the foreign country which bears the exchange rate risk. The next step is to use a market clearing equation that the optimal debt supplied by the US is equal to the optimal US debt that the foreign country is willing to hold. Thereby, there is a simultaneous solution for the optimal debt and interest rate. The second approach simplifies the problem, but does not distort the results. Assume that the US debt is denominated in foreign currency. Then the US bears the exchange rate risk as well as the interest rate risk. The optimal debt ratio for the US takes into account both risks, and the foreigners are willing to absorb the resulting US debt. The mathematical analysis uses the second approach.

The crucial stochastic variable is the *net return*, equal to the return on capital b_t less r_t, equal to the sum of the interest rate i_t on debt plus the rate of depreciation n_t of the currency. The uncertainty concerning the net return $(b_t - r_t)$ is almost always viewed in terms of the historical variance of the net return. This measure of uncertainty has its limitations. In the period prior to the South-East Asian crisis 1997–8, the interest rates and exchange rates were relatively constant. The same was true in the period prior to the Argentine crisis in 2001. The peso was pegged to the US dollar and the interest rates reflected the fixed exchange rate. There was almost no variation in $r = i + n$, where n is the depreciation of the local currency. In retrospect, the historical variance of $(i + n)$ did not reflect risk[8]. Several approaches can be taken to estimate risk. Instead of using simply the historical variances, a range of variances can be used based upon economic theory. Thus if the economist believes that the fundamentals are leading to instability, he can be "forward looking" and use higher values of the variances than are obtained from historical data. This range implies a range for the optimal debt and current account deficits. We shall use this more general approach below.

Another approach is to consider a deterministic game against Nature[9]. This is an intriguing approach. Since coefficient estimates in that

---

[8] Two excellent articles on the South-East Asian crisis and the Argentine crisis are by Williamson (2004) and Mussa (2002), respectively.

[9] An alternative approach to optimization is a deterministic differential game. There are no stochastic variables or distribution functions. However this approach can be given a stochastic

model are difficult to justify, we shall concentrate upon the stochastic approaches.

The state/dynamic variable in the growth process and the analysis of an optimal debt and current account deficit is net worth X_t, equal to "effective" capital K_t less external debt $N_t L_t$, where L_t is the debt in foreign currency and N_t is the exchange rate \$US/foreign currency. For the reason discussed above, we work with the case where the debtor bears the exchange rate risk. A rise in N_t is a depreciation of the \$US/appreciation of the foreign currency. All variables are real. Net worth is constrained to be positive to avoid the "free lunch" problem discussed above.

$$X_t = K_t - N_t L_t > 0. \tag{9.5}$$

From the SOC/DP analysis in the logarithmic case, optimal consumption C_t is a fraction $c_t > 0$ of net worth, and the external debt $N_t L_t$ is a fraction f_t of net worth. A debtor country has a positive f and a creditor country has a negative f ratio. Focus upon the US as the debtor country. When bad shocks reduce net worth, both consumption and the external debt must be reduced to maintain the optimal proportions. Consumption, debt, and net worth grow at the same rate. To the extent that the debt ratio exceeds the derived optimal, the expected growth rate declines and its variance rises. Since consumption is proportional to net worth, the expected growth of consumption declines and its variability rises. The probability of a decline in consumption increases – the economy is more vulnerable to external shocks – as the debt ratio exceeds the derived optimal. *In this manner, the SOC/DP analysis gives precision to the concept of sustainability in the manner suggested by Mann.*

In the next section, a stochastic differential equation for net worth is derived from which the optimal ratios are derived. The underlying economic assumptions are stressed at each point. The mathematical derivations are contained in Chapter 3 based upon Fleming and Stein (2004), Stein (2004), Fleming (2001, 2004) – and are not repeated here. Graphic

---

metaphor. The optimization is a game against Nature, which is the stronger player. The country follows a very conservative strategy. *In effect, the country selects a debt ratio that maximizes the minimum "expected utility" of consumption.* Nature knows the debt chosen f and the state of the economy, the net worth X. Nature generates bad shocks, but the cost to Nature is a quadratic function of the shock. Knowing the debt ratio chosen and the state of the economy, Nature produces a bad shock that minimizes the utility to the country plus the cost to Nature. Thereby one derives a measure of minimum "expected" utility of consumption. The country in turn selects a debt ratio that maximizes the minimum "expected" utility of consumption. Instead of stochastic distribution functions, the differential game involves a cost function to Nature. By varying the parameter concerning the effect of a "bad" shock alternative optimal debt ratios are obtained.

analysis is used as much as possible to emphasize the economic implications and conclusions. The corresponding empirical data are introduced quite early. In later sections, we use these data in deriving the optimal debt/GDP and current account/GDP ratios. These conclusions and implications are then compared to the survey of the literature in section 9.1 above.

9.3. A stochastic optimal control model of international finance and debt

The crucial variables, dynamics, and inter-temporal aspects of the model are implicit in the literature cited above. The state variable is the net worth equation (9.5), equal to the "effective" capital K less the external debt NL. The liability is denominated in the currency of the creditor, so that the foreign liability is converted into domestic currency by the exchange rate $N = \$US/$foreign currency. A rise in N is a depreciation of the dollar and the value of the external debt rises. Equation (9.6) is the change in net worth.

The production function, equation (9.7a), relates the gross domestic product Y to "effective capital" K, where the productivity of effective capital is β_t. Effective capital K is the product of a physical quantity measure Q and total factor productivity P, equation (9.7b). Therefore the production function is $Y_t = \beta_t(P_t Q_t)$, equation (9.7) – which is an A-K production function with "effective" capital.

The change in effective capital dK in equation (9.8) has two components. The first is investment $Idt = PdQ$, the change in the physical quantity dQ times P, the current level of factor productivity. The second component is the growth of total factor productivity dP/P times K, the existing capital.

The change in the debt $d(NL)$, equation (9.9), has two components. The first component is the current account deficit $N\,dL$. The second component is $L\,dN$, the change in the value of liabilities due to changes in the exchange rate, the asset revaluation effects. The current account deficit is equation (9.10). It is equal to consumption C plus investment I plus interest plus dividend payments on the debt iNL less the gross domestic product Y, evaluated at the current exchange rate. Alternatively it is equal to: (i) the interest plus dividend transfers iNL less the trade balance, or (ii) absorption less the gross national product.

$$dX_t = dK_t - d(NL)_t \tag{9.6}$$

$$Y_t \, dt = \beta_t K_t \tag{9.7a}$$

$$K_t = P_t Q_t \tag{9.7b}$$

$$Y_t \, dt = \beta_t \, P_t Q_t \tag{9.7}$$

$$dK_t = I_t \, dt + K_t \, (dP/P)_t, \; I_t \, dt = P_t dQ_t \tag{9.8}$$

$$d(NL)_t = N_t \, dL_t + L_t \, dN_t \tag{9.9}$$

$$N_t \, dL_t = (C + I + iNL - Y)_t \, dt. \tag{9.10}$$

Substitute (9.7)–(9.10) into (9.6) and derive the change in net worth stochastic differential equation (9.11). *Four stochastic variables* are considered. The first is the rate of technical progress dP/P, the second is the productivity of effective capital β. The third variable is the rate of interest i on the debt denominated in foreign currency, and the fourth variable is the rate of depreciation dN/N of the \$US relative to the foreign currency. When dN is positive (negative) the dollar is depreciating (appreciating). The third and fourth stochastic variables affect the income transfers on the debt. Equation (9.11) is a *stochastic differential equation* because the terms in parentheses are stochastic.

$$dX_t = K_t \, (dP_t/P_t + \beta_t \, dt) - C_t \, dt - (i_t \, dt + dN_t/N_t) \, N_t L_t. \tag{9.11}$$

The stochastic processes can be reduced to two variables in view of the form of equation (9.11). The first stochastic process is equation (9.12). Call variable b_t, equal to the sum of the rate of technical progress dP_t/P_t, and the productivity of effective capital β_t, the *return1*. It is decomposed into two parts. The first part is a *deterministic* mean $b \, dt$, with no time subscript. The second part is stochastic[10] with a mean of zero and a variance of $\sigma_b{}^2 \, dt$.

$$b_t \, dt = dP_t/P_t + \beta_t \, dt = b \, dt + \sigma_b \, dw_b. \quad return1 \tag{9.12}$$

The second stochastic process is equation (9.13) concerning the sum of the interest rate and rate of depreciation of the dollar. Call variable $r_t \, dt = dN_t/N_t + i_t \, dt$ the *effective interest rate*. The first part $r \, dt$ without a time subscript is deterministic. It is the *mean* interest rate plus depreciation rate. The stochastic part[11] has a mean of zero and a variance of $\sigma_r{}^2 \, dt$.

$$r_t \, dt = dN_t/N_t + i_t \, dt = r_t \, dt = r \, dt + \sigma_r \, dw_r.$$
$$\textit{effective interest rate} \tag{9.13}$$

---

[10] Variable w_b is Brownian motion. A variable has Brownian motions if it has stationary independent increments, normally distributed with a zero mean and positive variance.
[11] Variable w_r is Brownian motion.

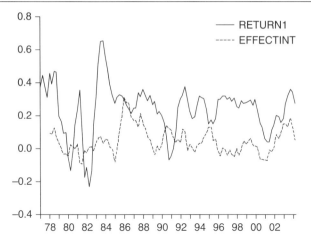

Figure 9.2. *Return1* = b = productivity of capital plus rate of technical progress and *effec*tive interest rate = r = real long-term interest rate plus real depreciation of the US dollar.

Table 9.2. Descriptive statistics of return $b_t\, dt = dP_t/P_t + \beta_t\, dt$ and effective interest rate, $r_t\, dt = dN_t/N_t + i_t\, dt$, 106 observations, 1977:1–2004:2.

	Return1 b_t	Effective interest r_t
Mean	0.23	0.04
Median	0.26	0.03
Max, min	0.63, – 0.23	0.311, – 0.09
Standard deviation	0.155	0.08
Coefficient variation s/m	0.664	1.739
Jarque–Bera Probability	0.006	0.000
Correlation $\rho = 0.216$		

These two variables are graphed in Figure 9.2[12] as *return1* and *effectint*. Table 9.2 summarizes the basic statistics, which will be used in deriving the optimal debt ratio and current account. There is considerable variability to these two variables. The coefficient of variation, standard deviation/mean, is 0.664 for the return $b_t dt = dP_t/P_t + \beta_t\, dt$ and s/m = 1.739 for the effective interest rate $r_t\, dt = dN_t/N_t + i_t\, dt$. The correlation $\rho = 0.216$ between the variables is small.

The model described by equations (9.6)–(9.13) is referred to as the prototype model, whose mathematical solution is in Fleming and Stein (2004). The main characteristics are that the two stochastic processes are

---

[12] See the appendix for a description and source of the data.

Brownian motion with drift. An alternative stochastic process for the *return 1*, called the Ornstein–Uhlenbeck equation is discussed below.

From the definition of net worth, equation (9.5), effective capital is $K_t = X_t + (NL)_t$. Define the ratio of the external debt/net worth $(NL/X)_t = f_t$. Then effective capital/net worth is $K_t/X_t = (1 + f_t)$. Define $c = C_t/X_t$, the ratio of consumption/net worth. Then stochastic differential equation (9.11) is expressed as equation (9.14), which is the basic equation of the model. The first set of terms in square brackets is deterministic, called the *drift*, and the second set is stochastic, called the *diffusion*.

$$dX_t = X_t\{[(b - c) + f_t(b - r)]\ dt + [(1 + f_t)\ \sigma_b\ dw_b - f_t\sigma_r\ dw_r]\}. \quad (9.14)$$

Insofar as optimal consumption is a fraction of net worth $c = C_t/X_t$, the time path of consumption will be tied to that of net worth. Using SOC/DP we solve for the *optimum debt ratio* $f^* = L_t/X_t$.

The *constraints* that optimal consumption will always be positive and that there is no free lunch will be satisfied for the following reasons. First, optimal consumption is a proportion c of net worth. If net worth goes towards zero, so must consumption and the debt. Second, the utility function with risk aversion equal to or greater than unity very severely penalizes low consumption. Third, net worth can never be negative – there can never be a free lunch – because in equation (9.14), as net worth X_t goes to zero, so will be dX_t which is its change. *For these three reasons the constraints $(C_t, X_t) > 0$ will be satisfied in the optimization.*

9.4. Mathematical solution for optimal debt ratio, consumption ratio, and current account deficit/GDP, and implications for vulnerability

The general approach to stochastic optimization is to select a consumption ratio c_t and a debt ratio f_t that maximize the expected[13] discounted value of the utility of consumption over an infinite horizon, equation (9.15). The discount rate is $\delta > 0$. The stochastic variables are the return b_t and effective interest rate r_t. There are many reasonable choices for the utility function. A popular function[14] is (9.15a), where risk aversion is $(1 - \gamma) > 0$, and $\gamma \neq 0$. Another reasonable function is the logarithmic

---

[13] The stochastic variables are dw_b and dw_r. Hence we write that the expectations are over b_t and r_t.

[14] Equations (9.15a) and (9.15b) are the only utility functions that permit analytical solutions. Otherwise, only numerical solutions using a computer are possible. Using (9.16), these problems are avoided.

function (9.15b), which is equivalent to (9.15a) when risk aversion is unity $\gamma = 0$. Dynamic programming is required to solve (9.15) using (9.14).

$$\max_{c,f} E_{b,r} \left[\int U(c_t X_t) e^{-\delta t} dt \right] \tag{9.15}$$

$$U(cX_t) = (1/\gamma)(c_t X_t)^{\gamma} \qquad \gamma \neq 0 \tag{9.15a}$$

$$U(cX_t) = \ln (c_t X_t). \tag{9.15b}$$

Another approach is to select an arbitrary ratio $c > 0$ of consumption/net worth that is less than b, the productivity of capital. Then select a debt ratio $f = L_t/X_t$ to maximize the expected growth rate of net worth and consumption over some arbitrary horizon $(0,T)$, equation (9.16). It turns out that the optimal debt ratio f_t derived from (9.16) is the same as the one derived from using the logarithmic utility function (9.15b) in the DP model[15].

$$\max_f (1/T)E_{b,r} [\ln X_T/X| \ b > c = C_t/X_t]$$
$$= (1/T)E_{b,r} [\ln C_T/C] \quad X = X(0). \tag{9.16}$$

Equation (9.17) is the solution of (9.14),(9.15),(9.15a) – or (9.14),(9.15), (9.15b) – for f^* the optimal debt/net worth[16]. Empirical estimates will be given for each of these terms in the empirical section below.

$$f^* = L^*_t/X_t = (b - r)/(1 - \gamma) \ \sigma^2 + f(0). \tag{9.17}$$

$\sigma^2 = \text{var } (b_t - r_t)$, $f(0) = \lambda(\rho\theta - 1)$, $\lambda = \text{var } (b_t)/\text{var } (b_t - r_t)$, $\rho = \text{correlation } (b,r)$, $\theta = \sigma_r/\sigma_b$. Equation (9.17) is graphed as Figure 9.3. There is a linear relation between the optimal ratio f^* of debt/net worth and $(b - r)/\sigma^2$, the *mean* of the return less effective interest rate per unit of risk. Variables (b_t, r_t) are graphed in Figure 9.2, and the relevant descriptive statistics are in Table 9.1.

9.4.1. *Economic implication of the stochastic optimal control solution*

The analysis above concerns the *optimal* solution for the debt and does not describe the *actual* debt or how it occurred. Insofar as the debt is not

---

[15] In the case of equation (9.16) dynamic programming is not necessary to find the optimal debt ratio. All that is required is to solve (9.14) for ln X_t, using the Ito differential rule, and then use calculus to determine the debt ratio from (9.16). The choice of a consumption/net worth ratio less than the productivity of capital ($c < b$) is necessary if optimal expected growth is to be positive. A great advantage of using (9.16) is that unambiguous and objective empirical estimates are obtained for the optimal debt ratio and current account/GDP. If (9.15a) is used, then an arbitrary number must be used for risk aversion. Not only cannot this number be justified, but also there is no reason why the debtor and creditor countries should have the same risk aversion.

[16] See Chapter 3 and Fleming and Stein (2004) for the derivation and details.

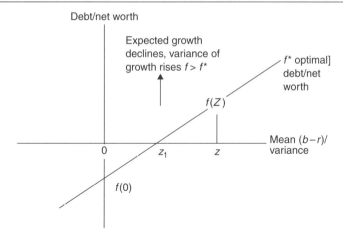

Debt/net worth

Expected growth
declines, variance of
growth rises $f > f^*$

f^* optimal]
debt/net
worth

$f(Z)$

Mean $(b-r)$/
variance

0 z_1 z

$f(0)$

Figure 9.3. Optimal debt/net worth f^* is a linear function of the risk adjusted *mean* net return $(b-r)$/variance of the net return. The slope is $1/(1-\gamma) = 1$/risk aversion. In the logarithmic case the slope is unity. Intercept $f(0)$ is the debt/net worth ratio where there is minimum risk. The country should be a debtor $f > 0$ only if the risk adjusted mean net return exceeds z_1. As the debt ratio f rises above the optimal line $f^*(\gamma = 0)$, the expected growth of consumption declines, and the variance of growth rises. The economy becomes more vulnerable to shocks coming from b_t and r_t.

optimal, the behavioral relations that produced it were not optimal. For example in the NATREX model described in Chapter 4, in the stable case the debt ratio converges to an equilibrium value based upon the ratio of social consumption/GDP and productivity in the country relative to its trading partners. However, there was no presumption that the derived equilibrium value was optimal in the sense of equation (9.15). We return to this issue later in this chapter.

The following implications of equation (9.17) for the optimal debt are very important. Empirical content is given to these propositions in the subsequent sections.

- The HARA utility function (9.15a) implies that the optimal debt is a *proportion* of net worth, $f = L_t/X_t$, and that the optimal consumption is a proportion c of net worth $C_t/X_t = c$. As the net worth changes according to (9.14), the optimal debt must change to preserve the constant ratio f. There is never a problem of a "free lunch", since net worth cannot be zero or negative.

- Given the stochastic processes described in (9.12) and (9.13), the optimal ratio of debt/net worth is a *constant* f^*, given by equation (9.17).

- The optimal debt ratio f^* is a linear function of the ratio of the *mean* net return $(b - r)$ divided by its variance σ^2 times $(1 - \gamma)$ risk aversion. In the logarithmic case, risk aversion is unity.

- The intercept term $f(0)$ is the optimal debt/net worth ratio, when the mean net return $(b - r)$ is zero. This is the minimum risk debt ratio. If the correlation ρ between the interest rate and the return on capital $\rho < \sigma_b/\sigma_r$ is less than the ratio of the standard deviation of the return on capital/standard deviation of the effective interest rate, then $f(0)$ is negative. Table 9.2 indicates that this is the case since $(\rho = 0.216) < (\sigma_b/\sigma_r = 0.155/0.08 = 1.94)$. Hence, unless the risk adjusted net mean return is greater than z_1 in Figure 9.3, the country should be a creditor.

- If the utility function is logarithmic – risk aversion is unity/$\gamma = 0$ – the optimal ratio c^* of consumption/net worth is equal to δ, the discount rate in equation (9.15). The expected discounted value of logarithmic utility is maximal.

- In the logarithmic case, where $\gamma = 0$, the expected growth rate of net worth and consumption is maximal. The optimal debt ratio is (9.17) evaluated at $\gamma = 0$. Call this optimal debt ratio $f^*(\gamma = 0)$.

- As the debt ratio rises above the optimal $f^*(\gamma = 0)$ in equation (9.17) or the line in Figure 9.3, then the expected growth of consumption declines, and its variance rises. This means that the probability is increased that bad shocks to the return and to the effective interest rate reduce consumption.

- *As the debt ratio rises above the optimal level, the economy is more vulnerable to shocks.*

9.5. Empirical estimates of optimal debt/GDP and current account deficit/GDP

9.5.1. *Comparison with literature*

The literature discussed in section 9.1 ended up with equation (9.1b). Given a current account deficit/GDP of A and growth rate of g, then the steady state debt/GDP ratio is $h_e = A/g$. There was no framework of analysis to evaluate whether the derived debt ratio should or should not be a cause for alarm.

The SOC/DP analysis developed here provides a framework for analysis. The implications of this analysis are the points in bullets and Figure 9.3 above. First, the optimal debt/net worth ratio f^* in equation (9.17) contains objectively measurable variables, the net mean return/variance, minimum risk debt ratio $f(0)$, and a preference variable risk aversion $(1 - \gamma) > 0$. Thereby, the appropriate optimum debt ratio depends upon what are the appropriate components.

There is no reason to believe that the creditor countries are automatically willing to hold any amount of debt that the US wishes to issue. First, the risk aversion variable for the US may not be the same as that for the creditors. If the US has a low risk aversion, then the slope of the debt ratio line in Figure 9.3 is large. For a given risk adjusted net mean return – point on the abscissa – a high debt ratio is optimal. Second, the risk depends on the denomination of the debt. If it is denominated in the currency of the debtor, then there is no exchange rate risk for the debtor. However, the creditor must bear the risk. Since risk times risk aversion $\sigma^2(1 - \gamma)$ varies between the creditor and debtor countries, the optimal debt/net worth ratio will have to satisfy a market balance condition for countries 1 and 2. Each country's optimal debt ratio f^* is given by an equation like (9.17). The optimal debt for country 2 is the negative of the optimal debt for country 1. The market balance equation is:

$$\text{(Optimal debt/net worth)}_1 \text{(net worth)}_1$$
$$+ \text{(Optimal debt/net worth)}_2 \text{(net worth)}_2 = 0$$

$$f_1^* X_1 + f_2^* X_2 = 0.$$

In this manner, differences in risk and risk aversion are explicitly taken into account.

We prefer to take a simpler approach. Assume that the creditors are willing to hold the debt supplied by the US, if the exchange rate risk is taken into account in calculating the optimal debt ratio in (9.17). This is done in equation (9.13) above by adding the exchange rate depreciation to the interest rate. Thus the debtor acts as if the debt is denominated in foreign currency. Then the creditor is willing to hold the debt supplied. Under these conditions, the optimal debt ratio for the US is equation (9.17).

The *conclusion* is that equation (9.17) provides a framework to analyze optimal debt. This is described in Figure 9.3. Vulnerability to external shocks is a continuous function of deviation of the actual debt ratio f_t from the optimal ratio f^*. The exact measure of the optimal ratio depends upon both the objectively measured variables, described by the point on the abscissa $(b - r)/\sigma^2$, and intercept $f(0)$ in Figure 9.3, and upon the subjective measure of risk aversion – which is the reciprocal of the slope of the line. In this manner, our SOC/DP analysis provides more structure to the approach in the literature summarized in equation (9.1b).

9.5.2. *Measurement of variables*

Net worth X is an important concept for the mathematical analysis. Empirically, it is desirable that we express the optimal debt and current account deficit as fractions of GDP rather than of net worth. The ratio of the optimal external debt/GDP, denoted h^*, is the product of the optimal debt/net worth f^* and the ratio X/Y of net worth to GDP, equation (9.18).

$$h^* = N_t L_t^*/Y_t = f^* (X_t/Y_t) = (f^*/1 + f^*)(1/\beta) \qquad \beta = Y/K. \qquad (9.18)$$

We have derived the optimal f^* debt/net worth in equation (9.17). The parameter β is the ratio of GDP/effective capital, equation (9.7). Hence we can translate all of the SOC/DP analysis above to the ratio h^* of debt/GDP. The data and measurement of the relevant variables are discussed in the appendix.

It is difficult to measure net debt, since it includes debt and equity on foreign assets in the US less US assets held abroad.[17] Much more reliable estimates are available for the current account. The "steady state" current account deficit/GDP discussed in the literature is A in equation (9.16). Insofar as the optimal debt/GDP ratio is h^*, the optimal steady state current account deficit/GDP denoted A^* in equation (9.16) is equation (9.19), where g is the growth rate of GDP.

$$A^* = gh^*. \qquad (9.19)$$

Based upon the derived optimal quantities in (9.17)–(9.19), in the next section we derive alternative estimates of the optimal debt/GDP and current account deficit/GDP. Insofar as the actual ratios exceed the optimal, then the economy is ever more vulnerable to external shocks.

9.5.3. *Empirical estimates of optimal ratios*

The crucial *objective* variable in equation (9.17) and figure 9.3 is the *net return per unit of risk* $(b_t - r_t)/\sigma^2$, where the components and descriptive statistics are seen in Figures 9.2, 9.4, 9.7 and Table 2. The return b_t is equal to the productivity of capital β_t plus the rate of technical progress dP_t/P, and the effective interest rate r_t is equal to the real long-term rate of interest i_t plus the depreciation of the US dollar dN_t/N_t. Thus we have

---

[17] See International Monetary Fund, (2005), Box 3.2 and Mussa (2004), pp. 119–21.

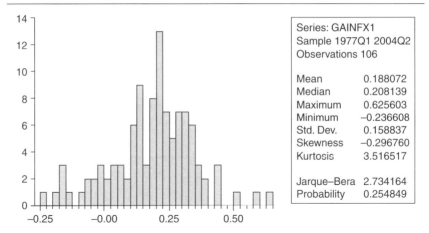

Figure 9.4. Distribution of $(b - r) = $ GAINFX1 = return1 − effective interest rate.

empirical measures of points on the abscissa in Figure 9.3. The intercept $f(0)$ is also objectively measured.

Figure 9.4 graphs the frequency distribution and important statistics of the net return $(b_t - r_t)$, labeled GAINFX1 to remind us that the depreciation of the US dollar is taken into account by both creditor and debtor. These statistics are used directly in the estimation of equations (9.17)–(9.19). Note that the distribution may very well be normal. In addition, the net return is highly variable: the coefficient of variation, equal to the standard deviation/mean is $0.158/0.188 = 0.845$. In our estimates of the optimal debt and current account deficit, we shall take this large variability into account.

Equations (9.17)–(9.19) provide a *framework for the derivation of optimal quantities* under alternative assumptions concerning objective variables and preferences. We take two approaches in deriving the optimal quantities. First, table 9.3 contains the basic results for alternative measures of risk aversion and parameter estimates. The statistics in Figure 9.4 are used in equation (9.17) and (9.18). This table shows how the results, concerning the optimal debt ratio and current account deficit/GDP, change for different values of risk aversion, and for alternative estimates of the mean net return.

Second, the **prototype model** is described by equations (9.6)–(9.13). However, an examination of Figure 9.2 and Table 9.2 suggests that an alternative model should also be considered. The stochastic process on the **return1** graphed in Figure 9.2 may be "ergodic mean reversion (EMR)", described by equation (9.12a) rather than the Brownian motion (BM) with drift equation (9.12). A unit root test suggests that this may be the case for

Table 9.3 Empirical estimates of optimal debt/net worth f^*, optimal debt/GDP h^*, and current account deficit/GDP, $A^* = gh^*$, under alternative assumptions in the prototype model.

Risk adjusted net return /risk = $(b-r)/(1-\gamma)\sigma^2$ risk aversion = $(1-\gamma) > 0$	Optimal debt/ net worth f^* from (9.17) (col. 2)	Optimal debt/ GDP h^* from (9.18) (col. 3)	Optimal current account deficit/GDP from (9.19), using growth rate $g = 0.03$ per annum (col. 4)
Risk aversion = 1 (row 1)	6.6	4.1	0.124
Risk aversion $(1-\gamma) - 3$ (row 2)	1.65	2.96	0.09
Lower confidence estimate $(b-r)_1/\sigma^2 = [(b-r-\sigma)]/\sigma^2$ risk aversion = 1 (row 3)	0.347	1.226	0.037

See Figure 9.4 and Table 9.2 for the underlying data. Also see appendix A for details. Using estimates in Table 9.2, the vertical intercept $f(0) = -0.9$ in Figure 9.3/equation (9.17).

return1. The effective interest rate may be the Brownian motion with drift, as described by equation (9.13).

$$db_t = \alpha \, (b - b_t)dt + \sigma_b dw_b. \qquad (9.12a)$$

This stochastic differential equation is an *Ornstein–Uhlenbeck* process. In (9.12a)/the EMR case, the return b_t is normally disturbed and converges to a distribution with a mean b and a variance of $(1/2\alpha) \sigma_b^2$.

Insofar as the stochastic processes are (9.12a) for the return and (9.13) for the effective interest rate **effectint**, the solution for the optimum debt ratio is no longer equation (9.17). The model (9.6)–(9.10), (9.12a) and (9.13) is reffered to as the *BM-EMR* model. This is a more complicated system than the prototype model. The mathematical details of the solution are similar to models analyzed in Stein (2005), Fleming and Pang (2004) and Fleming (2003) and are not discussed here.

The optimum ratio of debt/net worth is f^*_t described by equation (9.17a). There are several important characteristics of equation (9.17a).

$$f^*_t = (b_t - r)/(1 - \gamma)\sigma_r^2 + \rho W_t, \qquad (9.17a)$$

when σ_r^2 is the variance of the effective interest rate in equation (9.13), ρ is the correlation of returnl and the effective interest rate, and W is the complicated second-order differential equation.

First, the optimum debt ratio is not a constant, but varies with the *current value* of the return on investment b_t less the *mean* effective interest rate r.

Second, the appropriate variance in this case is just the variance of the effective interest rate.

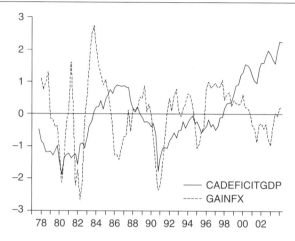

Figure 9.5. Current account deficit/GDP = CADEFICITGDP and net return $(b_t - r_t) =$ GAINFX. Normalized variables (variable – mean)/standard deviation.

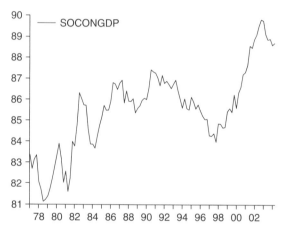

Figure 9.6. Social consumption/GDP = private plus government consumption/ GDP = SOCGDP, per cent.

Third, when the correlation ρ is zero, the optimal debt/net worth ratio should follow the movements in $(b_t - r)$.

Fourth, one can use Figure 9.3 to describe the optimum debt ratio f^*_t by measuring $(b_t - r)/\sigma_r^2$ on the abscissa.

Based upon (9.17a) and Figure 9.5 we analyze movements in normalized variables (variable – mean)/standard deviation. This approach has several advantages. (i) It is relevant for either equation (9.17a)/BM-EMR model or equation (9.17) in the prototype model when the means are changing

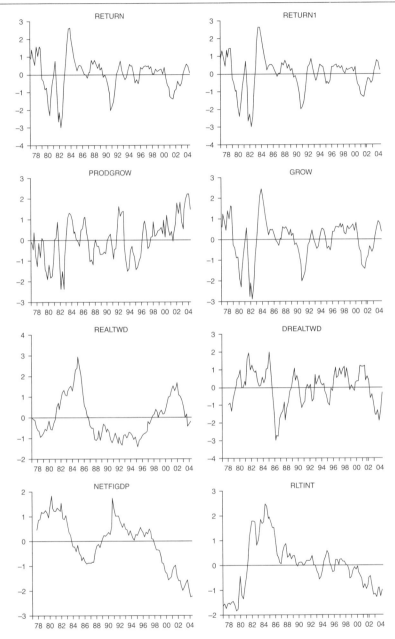

Figure 9.7. Basic variables: RETURN $= \beta$, PRODGROW $= dP/P$, RETURN1 $=$ PRODGROW $+$ RETURN $= b$, REALTWD $=$ real trade weighted value of the US dollar $=$ reciprocal of N, DREALTWD $=$ change in REALTWD, RLTINT $= i =$ real long term interest rate of 10 year Treasuries, NETFIGDP $=$ current account/GDP.

slowly. (ii) We avoid making specific assumptions about risk aversion. (iii) The focus is upon trends in deriving early warning signals of an excessive debt.

Table 9.3 shows the sensitivity of the results to alternative measures of risk aversion and parameter estimates. In rows 1 and 2 we show that the optimal quantities depend upon the risk aversion. *Row 1* in Table 9.3 assumes that risk aversion is unity. This is the logarithmic case where $\gamma = 0$. Row 1/column 2 contains the optimal debt/net worth ratio from equation (9.17), $f^* = (b\quad r)/\sigma^2 - 0.9 = 0.188/(0.158)^2 - 0.9 = 6.6$. Row 1/column 3 contains the ratio h^* of the optimal debt/GDP. Row 1/column 3 is gh^*, the ratio of the optimal current account deficit/GDP conditional upon the mean growth rate of 0.03 per annum.

Row 2 assumes that $\gamma = -2$ or risk aversion $1 - \gamma = 3$. Then the optimal debt/net worth in column 2 is 1.65, the optimal debt/GDP in column 3 is 2.96 and the optimal current account deficit/GDP in column 3 is 0.09.

A comparison of rows 1 and 2 shows how differences in risk aversion change the optimal quantities of the debt ratio and current account deficit/GDP.

The optimal quantities depend crucially upon the objective parameters used. In rows 1 and 2 we used $(b - r)/\sigma^2$, the historic mean divided by the historic variance, which is the point on the abscissa in Figure 9.3. The variance σ^2 is the historical variability of the net return, see the box in Figure 9.4. As seen in Figures 9.2 and 9.4, the variations in the return and the real interest rate including the exchange rate variation are significant. There are trends in the components of the productivity of capital, rate of technical progress, real long-term interest rate and exchange rate. See the graphs in Figure 9.7 and Appendix A.

Historical means and variances must not be taken as immutable and relevant for the future. The interest rate plus the depreciation of the US dollar has been extremely variable. The standard deviation of $r = i + n$ is twice the mean. With the fluctuations in the exchange rate \$US/euro and yen/\$US, foreigners who hold dollar denominated assets must be sensitive to exchange rate variations in estimating r, the effective interest rate. The productivity growth and the stock market return have also been highly variable.

Equations (9.17)–(9.19) provide a framework for the derivation of optimal quantities under alternative assumptions. The future is unpredictable and one can be "forward looking" in a very conservative way. If we take a very conservative approach by adjusting for the variability of each parameter, return b, and real interest rate r, in the numerator of (9.17), we obtain very different results. Instead of just taking point estimates, suppose that we use a lower confidence estimate of the mean net return.

In table 3/row 3, we take the distribution of $(b - r)$ into account by forming *arbitrary conservative* estimates. Assume that risk aversion is unity, as in row 1. Instead of using the mean net return over the entire sample period of 0.188, we reduce the mean return $b - r$ by one standard deviation $\sigma = 0.158$. Using the lower confidence limit, a new mean net return $(b - r)_1 = [(b - r) - \sigma]$ is obtained. Thereby $(b - r)_1/\sigma^2 = (0.188 - 0.158)/(0.158)^2 = (0.030)/(0.158)^2$ is used in equation (9.17). The optimal current account deficit/GDP becomes 3.7% pa. Insofar as the debt ratio and current account deficit/GDP exceed the optimal quantities, the vulnerability of the economy to shocks to (b, r) increases. Looking across the rows based upon different assumptions, the optimal current account deficit/GDP can vary considerably.

The differences between Table 9.3 and the literature summarized in equation (9.1b) are that: (a) the optimal quantities are derived theoretically from an inter-temporal optimization; and (b) the framework shows just how the results vary depending upon both preferences concerning risk aversion and objective parameters.

There is another and very flexible way, by focusing upon trends, to see that the actual ratios have been deviating from the optimal ratios without assuming any specific value for risk aversion. This approach is consistent with equation (9.17a) based upon the BM-EMR model. Assume that the risk aversion and intercept $f(0)$ are relatively constant. Then any trend in the optimal current account deficit/GDP should follow the trend in the risk adjusted net return $(b - r)/\sigma^2$. Examine whether the *normalized*[18] current account deficit/GDP has been deviating from *normalized* time varying risk adjusted net return. By using normalized variables, we do not have to worry about estimates of risk aversion. Figure 9.5 graphs GAINFX, the *normalized* net return $[(b_t - r_t) - \text{mean}]/\sigma_{b-r}$ and the *normalized* CADEFICITGDP = current account deficit/GDP = $(A_t - \text{mean})/\sigma_A$.

The implication of Figure 9.5 is that the debt ratio and current account deficit/GDP have been deviating significantly from optimality. Although the GAINFX has declined since 1996, the current account deficit/GDP has increased by more than two standard deviations. In terms of Figure 9.3, whereas z_t, the risk adjusted net return, has been declining, the debt ratio f

---

[18] Variable X is normalized as X′ by calculating X′ = (X − mean)/standard deviation. Thus X′ is measured in units of standard deviations. It is a simple way to see variations in orders of magnitude.

Table 9.4 Growth of productivity, per cent per annum

Country	1995–2002	2004	2005 (project)
US	1.9% pa	3.3	3.6
Japan	1.3	2.4	0.8
Germany	1.0	0.7	0.8

Source: Federal Reserve Bank of St. Louis, International Economic Trends, July 2005.

has been rising. This suggests that the debt ratio has been moving above the optimal line US, and the US economy is becoming more vulnerable to external shocks to the return on capital and effective interest rate, which includes the depreciation of the currency. These conclusions are not sensitive to either delicate econometric estimates or arbitrary measures of the risk aversion.

9.5.4. *Conclusions*

Should the current account deficits and external debt be sources of concern? Who is correct Cooper or Mussa? Cooper's optimism is supported in the following way. Relatively high optimal current account deficits/GDP in Table 9.3, rows 1 and 2, are derived, because the risk adjusted net return $(b - r)/\sigma^2$ is high relative to that prevailing in the creditor countries. The growth of productivity is a major component of b in the risk adjusted rate of return. The return on capital is measured as the growth rate/investment ratio. Compare the growth rates of productivity in the US debtor with that in Japan, a major creditor[19] and Germany over the periods 1995–2002, 2004 and a projection for 2005 (Table 9.4). The US is special as a debtor, not because the debt is denominated in US dollars[20], but because the risk adjusted net return is high. *Based upon point estimates, rows 1 and 2 of Table 9.3 tend to support Cooper's optimistic views.*

Mussa's pessimism, that there are reasons for concern, can be derived from Table 9.3, row 3 and from *Figure 9.5.* Table 9.3, row 3 uses lower confidence values for the net return and implies that the actual current account deficits/GDP are excessive. Moreover, Figure 9.5 implies that the debt ratio and current account ratio are deviating significantly from optimality. Although the net return GAINFX has declined since 1996, the

---

[19] See Table 9.1 for the net asset positions of countries.
[20] We took the exchange rate risk for the creditor into account in deriving the risk adjusted net return. See the discussion in the text above.

current account deficit/GDP has increased by more than two standard deviations.

My conclusion is that the current situation is not a cause for alarm, but looking at trends, the US economy is ever more vulnerable to shocks to the return and effective interest rate.

9.6. Sustainability of the debt and the depreciation of the real exchange rate

Questions discussed in the literature are: How should "sustainability" be achieved? By how much does the dollar need to decline in order to achieve a *sustainable* current account position for the US and the rest of world? What policies should be used to bring the current account and debt ratio closer to the optimal value?

Underlying these questions is the view that the evolution of the actual debt is quite different from the evolution of the optimal debt based upon the SOC/DP analysis of intertemporal optimization. In particular, the assumption is that whereas the private sector may try to make optimal decisions for the utility of consumption the government policy decisions are based upon short-run political considerations.

The first conclusion is that the exchange rate must depreciate steadily until an "equilibrium" debt/GDP ratio is achieved. The reasons are based upon the NATREX model of the *equilibrium* exchange rate developed in Chapter 4.[21]

The *equilibrium* real exchange rate, N_t, where a rise is a depreciation of the US dollar, equilibrates the current account deficit A_t to investment less saving $I_t - S_t$, when there is both external and internal balance. All variables, except the exchange rate and interest rate, are measured as fractions of the GDP. Saving is the sum of private saving and government saving, which is the negative of the government budget deficit. The equilibrium real exchange rate equates the sum of the current account balance and the non-speculative capital inflow to zero, equation (9.20). Speculative capital flows, based upon anticipations, are excluded from the concept of *equilibrium*, because they are noise. They produce large variations in the actual exchange rate, but do not affect the equilibrium value.

The current account deficit A_t is equal to the net income transfers on the "debt" rh_t less the trade balance B_t. The trade balance is positively related

---

[21] The reader should go back to Chapter 4, or at least to the summary in the overview Chapter 1, for the details. I am changing the notation from that used in Chapter 4.

to the exchange rate N_t, where a rise in N, which is a depreciation of the dollar, increases the trade balance[22], and to other variables denoted Z_t. The argument so far is summarized in equations (9.20) and (9.21a)/(9.21b). The implication is that the equilibrium exchange rate will change insofar as the debt ratio h_t changes.

$$I_t - S_t = A_t \rightarrow N_t \tag{9.20}$$

$$A_t = rh_t - B(N_t, Z_t) = \text{current account deficit/GDP}, \quad B' > 0 \tag{9.21a}$$

$$B(N_t, Z_t) = rh_t - A_t. \tag{9.21b}$$

The change in the debt/GDP ratio is equation (9.22). The current account deficit is $A = I - S$ and g is the growth rate of the GDP. This is the discrete time version of equation (9.1a) above. The solution of (9.22) for the debt ratio at any time is equation (9.23), where $0 \le s \le t - 1$.

$$h_t - h_{t-1} = A_{t-1} - gh_{t-1} \tag{9.22a}$$

$$h_t = h(0)(1 - g)^t + \Sigma A_s (1 - g)^{t-1-s}. \tag{9.23}$$

The equilibrium exchange rate at any time must generate a trade balance sufficiently great to pay the interest on the debt less the capital inflow, which is investment less saving. Equation (9.24) is derived from equations (9.21b) and (9.23), where we use the mean growth rate $g = 0.031$ per annum.

$$B(N_t, Z_t) = r\,[h(0)(0.97)^t + \Sigma A_s(0.97)^{t-1-s}] - A_t, \quad t - 1 > s > 0. \tag{9.24}$$

The path of the equilibrium real exchange rate N_t can be seen from equation (9.24). The *current* capital inflow $A_t = I_t - S_t$ *appreciates* the exchange rate. However, the *past* capital inflows, the discounted sum of the A_s terms, raise the debt and associated debt payments, and *depreciate* the exchange rate.

The debt ratio has risen because social consumption/GDP has risen. Social consumption is the sum of private consumption and government consumption[23]. Figure 9.6 shows the significant upward trend. This means that $I_t - S_t$ in equation (9.20) has been rising.

In the NATREX model, a decline in social saving has both medium and long-run effects. There is a dynamic process to the equilibrium exchange rate. A rise in investment less social saving appreciates the real exchange rate in the medium run, and increases the current account deficit A_t. This

---

[22] The other factors affecting the trade balance are subsumed under the Z_t term in $B(N_t, Z_t)$. These factors are discussed in the NATREX model.

[23] Government investment is included in government consumption.

is seen in the last term in (9.24). The debt ratio h_t rises as seen in (9.22). These are medium-run effects.

In the longer run, there are two effects[24]. First, the cumulative current account deficits raise the debt, which tends to depreciate the currency. This is seen in the terms in brackets in equation (9.24). Second, is a stability condition in the NATREX model. A necessary condition for the debt ratio to stabilize is that the rise in the debt should reduce social consumption/raise social saving. That is, the rise in the debt should reduce absorption less the GDP. In the case of intertemporal optimization, consumption is a proportion of net worth. With a logarithmic utility function the ratio of optimal consumption/net worth is the discount rate. As the debt rises, net worth declines and consumption is reduced. When optimal policies are followed, the debt ratio cannot explode. In the optimal case, current account deficits are given by equation (9.19).

Actual saving and investment decisions may not be optimal. Moreover, the ratio of social consumption/GDP may not be a fixed proportion of net worth. That is, as the external debt rises the government may not reduce the high employment deficit by any significant amount. It may even lower taxes and encourage private consumption. As long as social saving is less than investment, there will be a current account deficit. The term in brackets in (9.24) will continue to rise steadily. Several conclusions, marked by bullets, emerge from the above equations.

- The equilibrium exchange rate will only stabilize if the debt ratio in (9.23) stabilizes. If the debt ratio does not stabilize, then the equilibrium exchange rate will change steadily. *A once and for all depreciation is inadequate.*[25]
- The level at which the debt ratio stabilizes depends upon what happens to investment less saving $(I - S)_t = A_t$, as seen in equation (9.23). Investment less saving is equal to absorption less GDP equal to the current account deficit, equation (9.20).
- The greater is the deviation of the "equilibrium" debt ratio denoted h_e from the optimal h^* in section 9.4 above, the less sustainable is the exchange rate.

A policy question is how should social saving less investment be increased to stabilize the debt and bring it closer to the optimal ratio f^* above, or to change the trend of the current account deficits? There is a

[24] The trajectories of the real exchange rate and the external debt under different policies are graphed in Chapter 6/Figure 6.3.
[25] This is described in Chapter 1, Box 1.1, based upon Chapter 4, Figure 4.3.

difference between policies that raise social saving and those that adversely affect the return on investment. For example, policies that lower the return on capital reduce the optimal debt ratio, whereas policies that raise social saving do not affect the optimal debt ratio.

- Insofar as the debt ratio exceeds the optimal ratio, it is desirable that social policy induces an increase in the social saving ratio, without adversely affecting the productivity of capital and raising its variance.

The contribution of this chapter has been to develop a framework of analysis, based upon intertemporal optimization under uncertainty, whereby one can evaluate the difference between the actual external debt and the optimal. The quantitative answer depends upon assumptions of both risk aversion and estimates of measurable parameters. The measure of vulnerability to external shocks is probabilistic, and is a continuous function of the excess debt – actual less optimal debt.

Appendix A. Basic data

All of the empirical data are obtained from the Federal Reserve Bank of St. Louis, Economic Data FRED II data bank < http://research.stlouisfed.org/fred2 >, with the exception of the real trade weighted value of the US dollar, which comes from the Federal Reserve in Washington. All growth rates refer to the change from the same quarter, one year earlier, using logarithms.

Four basic parameters are used in the estimation of the optimal debt and current account. The return to capital β in equation (A1) is estimated as follows. The change in the GDP is (A2). Investment is (A3). Divide dY in (A2) by investment I from (A3) and obtain (A4).

$$Y_t = \beta K_t = \beta(PQ)_t \tag{A1}$$

$$dY = \beta \; PdQ + Q \; d(P\beta) + PQ \; d\beta \tag{A2}$$

$$I = P \; dQ \tag{A3}$$

$$dY/I = \beta + [Q \; d(P\beta)/P \; dQ + d\beta/(I/K)]. \tag{A4}$$

Assume that on average each of the two terms in brackets, $d(P\beta)/dQ$ and $d\beta/(I/K)$ is zero. Then (A5) is obtained. The estimate of the productivity of capital β is the ratio of the growth rate of GDP divided by the ratio of investment/GDP.

We have data on real GDP from which we establish the growth rate from the corresponding quarter a year earlier. Divide this growth rate by the gross private investment/GDP, and obtain the variable $\beta = $ RETURN.

$$dY/I = (dY/Y)/(I/Y) = \beta_t = \text{(growth rate/investment ratio)=RETURN.} \tag{A5}$$

The stochastic process is:

$$\beta_t \, dt = \beta \, dt + \sigma_b dw_b. \tag{A6}$$

This variable has a mean of $\beta = 0.21$ and standard deviation 0.148.

The second variable concerns the growth in productivity (A7). The mean or drift is the first term and the diffusion is the second term.

$$dP_t/P_t = \mu \, dt + \sigma_p \, dw_p. \tag{A7}$$

Output/manhour in the business sector OPHBS measures productivity P_t. We estimate $dP/P = $ PRODGROW as the growth of output/manhour in the business sector.

The estimate of b_t in equation (9.12)/(A8) comes from (A6), (A7).

$$b_t \, dt = dP_t/P + \beta_t \, dt = (\mu + \beta) \, dt + (\sigma_p \, dw_p + \sigma_b \, dw_b) = b \, dt + \sigma_b \, dw_b. \tag{A8}$$

We use the estimates of $b_t = $ PRODGROW + RETURN = RETURN1 in our equations. This is graphed in Figure 9.2 and descriptive statistics are in Table 9.2.

The next two variables are in equation (9.13)/(A9) concerning r_t the effective interest rate. It is the sum of the change in the exchange rate dN/N, where a rise in N is a depreciation of the US dollar and i the real long-term interest rate.

$$r_t \, dt = dN_t/N_t + i_t \, dt. \tag{A9}$$

The real trade weighted value of the US dollar REALTWD, where a rise is an appreciation of the US dollar, is graphed in Figure 9.1. Use the negative of the percent change in REALTWD as (dN/N), the depreciation of the US dollar. The change in the exchange rate is (A10), where n is the drift and the second term is the diffusion. A positive (negative) value is a depreciation (appreciation).

$$dN/N = n \, dt + \sigma_n \, dw_n. \tag{A10}$$

To derive the real long-term interest rate, use the Treasury 10 year constant maturity rate GS10 less the inflation of the GDP implicit deflator. The resulting $i_t = $ RLTINT.

$$i_t \, dt = i \, dt + \sigma_i \, dw_i. \tag{A11}$$

Therefore the effective real interest rate is equation (9.13)/(A12). It is graphed in Figure 9.2; descriptive statistics are in Table 9.2.

$$r_t \, dt = (n + i) \, dt + (\sigma_n \, dw_n + \sigma_i \, dw_i) = r \, dt + \sigma_r \, dw_r. \tag{A12}$$

The components of the basic variables, EFFECTINT = RLTINT – DREALTWD, are graphed in Figure 9.7. All variables in Figure 9.7 have been normalized, (variable – mean)/standard deviation, to give a visual measure of the variability. Figures 9.2 and 9.4 graph the return1 = b_1 and effective interest rate $r = (i + n)$.

The crucial variable $(b - r) = $ GAINFX = RETURN1–EFFECTINT, whose distribution and basic statistics are in Figure 9.4.

Net foreign investment/GDP is the ratio of NETFI, which is the current account, divided by the GDP. It is labeled NETFIGDP. Social consumption/GDP

(SOCONGDP) is the sum of private consumption and government (consumption plus investment).

References

Bergsten, C. Fred and John Williamson (ed) Dollar Adjustment: How Far? Against What? (2004)? Institute for International Economics, Washington, DC.

Cooper, Richard (2005), The Sustainability of the US External Deficit, CESifo Forum, Spring.

Federal Reserve Bank of St. Louis, Economic Data-FRED II data bank < http:// research.stlouisfed.org/fred2 >.

—— (2001) "Stochastic Control Models of Optimal Investment and Consumption", Apportiones Matematicas, Modelos Estocasticos II, Sociedad Matematica, Mexico.

Fleming, Wendell H. (2004) "Some Optimal Investment, Production and Consumption Models", American Mathematical Society, Contemporary Mathematics, 351.

Fleming, Wendell H. and Raymond Rishel (1975) Deterministic and Stochastic Optimal Control, Springer-Verlag.

Fleming, Wendell H. and Jerome L. Stein (2004) "Stochastic Optimal Control, International Finance and Debt", Journal of Banking and Finance, 28(5) May, 979–96.

Fleming, Wendell H. and Tao Pang (2004) An Application of Stochastic Control Theory to Financial Economics, SIAM Journal of Control and Optimization, 43(2) 502–31.

Fleming, Wendell H. (2003) Some Optimal Investment, Production and Consumption Models, American Mathematical Society, Contemporary Mathematics 351 Mathematics of Finance 115–24.

International Monetary Fund (2005), World Economic Outlook, Globalization and External Balances, April, Washington, DC.

Mann, Catherine (1999) Is the US Trade Deficit Sustainable? Institute for International Economics, Washington, DC.

Mussa, Michael (2002) Argentina and the Fund: From Triumph to Tragedy, Institute for International Economics, Washington, DC.

—— (2004) "Exchange Rate Adjustments Needed to Reduce Global Payments Imbalances", in Bergsten, C. Fred and John Williamson, op cit.

Øksendal, Bernt (1995), Stochastic Differential Equations, Springer.

Stein, Jerome L. (2004) "Stochastic Optimal Control Modeling of Debt Crises", American Mathematical Society, Contemporary Mathematics, 351.

Stein, Jerome L. (2005) Optimal Debt and Endogenous Growth Models in International Finance, Australian Economic Papers, 44, December.

Williamson, John (2004a), The Years of Emerging Market Crises, Journal of Economic Literature XLII(3), September.

—— (2004b). Overview: Designing a Dollar Policy in Bergsten, C. Fred and John Williamson (ed), Dollar Adjustment: How Far? Against What? (2004)? Institute for International Economics, Washington, DC.

INDEX

Index